T0243634

"*Hospital and Haven* describes well the lives of a physician and teacher who gave their all to provide care to a community they loved. The scope of medicine involves trauma, malnutrition, infectious disease, emotional illness, poverty, substance abuse, and chronic disease. Situations described in the book ring familiar to medical issues we currently address in the world: tuberculosis, access to care, affordable care, quality care, scope of practice, staffing, leadership, and burnout."

—**Jean Tsigonis**, MD, MPH

"*Hospital and Haven* is the story of the hardships Clara May Heintz Burke and medical missionary Dr. Grafton (Hap) Burke faced and the amazing work they did saving lives, raising orphans, and trying to ensure that the rules of law were upheld. The impact of their work is measured in lives saved and lives nurtured to maturity, a legacy reflected in those who still recall their gratitude to the Burkes."

— **William Schneider**, professor emeritus of library science, Elmer E. Rasmuson Library at the University of Alaska Fairbanks

"Grafton and Clara Burke are treasures in Alaska history. Their dedication and perseverance to meet critical needs of Alaska's Indigenous population were nothing short of heroic. Mary Ehrlander and Hild Peters provide an entertaining glimpse into the Burkes' thirty years of service while also introducing us to colorful characters waging their own battles to survive the challenges of the rugged Arctic environment."

— **Bill Gordon**, a lifelong Alaskan who has served at the highest levels in business and government and son of Alaska's Flying Bishop, William Gordon

"The Burkes made such a lasting impression on my home community of Fort Yukon and, three generations later, on my own life. *Hospital and Haven* is an enjoyable reading of their familiar story and their impact."

— **Grete Bergman**, Fairbanks and Fort Yukon, great-granddaughter of the Reverend William Loola

"Ehrlander and Peters's book is a well-researched and refreshing read as we live amid discord based on politics, economics, religion, ethnicity, and social beliefs. Dr. Grafton and Clara Burke chose to live with the Gwich'in people in Alaska for over twenty-five years in the early 1900s. The people stole the couple's hearts. Hap and Clara desired to teach the English language, medicine, and 'American' and Christian beliefs. This became a two-way street. The Burkes were inspired by and learned from the Native people they respected and loved."

—**Nancy Cook Hanson**, retired director of Catholic Schools of Fairbanks

"This masterwork of Alaska missionary biography is broadly imagined, meticulously researched, and engagingly written. Dr. Grafton Burke and his wife, Clara, emerge from its pages as multidimensional, flesh-and-blood missionaries who worked assiduously for three decades—with good humor and prodigious energy—to improve the health and well-being of the Gwich'in people of Fort Yukon and the surrounding region. Scholars Mary Ehrlander and Hild Peters are uniquely qualified to write authoritatively about the Burkes and the lifesaving work they performed under the auspices of the Episcopal church and with the aid of many people in the Fort Yukon community."

—**Janine Dorsey**, historian

Hospital

and Haven

The Life and Work of
Grafton and Clara Burke
in Northern Alaska

MARY F. EHRLANDER
with HILD M. PETERS

University of Nebraska Press *Lincoln*

The University of Nebraska Press is part of a land-grant institution
with campuses and programs on the past, present, and future
homelands of the Pawnee, Ponca, Otoe-Missouria, Omaha, Dakota,
Lakota, Kaw, Cheyenne, and Arapaho Peoples, as well as those
of the relocated Ho-Chunk, Sac and Fox, and Iowa Peoples.

Library of Congress Cataloging-in-Publication Data
Names: Ehrlander, Mary F., author. | Peters, Hild M., author.
Title: Hospital and haven: the life and work of Grafton and Clara
Burke in northern Alaska / Mary F. Ehrlander with Hild M. Peters.
Other titles: Life and work of Grafton and
Clara Burke in northern Alaska
Description: Lincoln: University of Nebraska Press, [2023] |
Includes bibliographical references and index.
Identifiers: LCCN 2022061328
ISBN 9781496236180 (hardback)
ISBN 9781496237392 (epub)
ISBN 9781496237408 (pdf)
Subjects: LCSH: Burke, Grafton. | Burke, Clara May, 1884–1962. |
Missionaries—Alaska—Fort Yukon—Biography. | Missions, Medical—
Alaska—Fort Yukon—History—20th century. | Gwich'in Indians—
Missions—Alaska—Fort Yukon—History—20th century. |
Episcopal Church—Missions—Alaska—Fort Yukon—History—
20th century. | Fort Yukon—Biography. | BISAC: BIOGRAPHY
& AUTOBIOGRAPHY / Historical | HISTORY / United States /
State & Local / West (AK, CA, CO, HI, ID, MT, NV, UT, WY)
Classification: LCC F914.Y8 E57 2023 | DDC
266/.3798—dc23/eng/20230103
LC record available at https://lccn.loc.gov/2022061328

Designed and set in Fanwood by L. Welch.

For my family: My parents, Con and Helen Frank, who provided me with a loving and secure childhood in Alaska; my siblings and their spouses, Randy and Georgianne, Andrea, and Steve and Linda, who continue to support and encourage my writing endeavors; my husband, Lars, whose unwavering love and patience have allowed me to complete this project; and to our children and their spouses, Susanne and Catrin, Staffan and Maud, Wyatt and Lana, and Marcus and Fehlya, and their children—Ayman, Emma, Liam, Elliott, Nadine, Marie, Alissa, Lynden, and Euell—who sustain us and brighten our lives daily

—Mary Ehrlander

For Guy, Caleb, and Ethan

—Hild Peters

"... of more value than 10,000 sermons ..."
—Peter Trimble Rowe to John Wood,
  July 25, 1925

As the catastrophic influenza epidemic of 1925 began to ebb, Bishop Peter Trimble Rowe wrote Episcopal Mission Headquarters in New York that the work at St. Stephen's Mission at Fort Yukon was "of more value than 10,000 sermons—making Christianity, the Gospel visible, a church of deeds not noisy words."

CONTENTS

List of Illustrations   xi

Acknowledgments   xiii

Prologue   1

1. Early Life and Arrival
   in Alaska, 1907–8   21

2. Fort Yukon, Courtship,
   and Marriage, 1908–10   40

3. Settling into Married Life at
   Fort Yukon, 1910–12   64

4. Hap's Term as Commissioner,
   1912–14   84

5. Opening St. Stephen's Hospital
   and Closing a Chapter, 1916–21   106

6. Deepening Resolve amid Increased
   Responsibilities and Challenges,
   1921–25   135

7. St. Stephen's Mission Work
   Expands as Support Declines
   Nationally, 1926–30   163

8. Struggling Yet Expanding during
   the Depression Years, 1930–35   190

9. The End of an Era, 1936–38   215

   Epilogue   231

   Glossary   241

   Notes   243

   Bibliography   315

   Index   333

ILLUSTRATIONS

Photographs

1. St. John's-in-the-Wilderness, Allakaket   30
2. Hap at Sewanee   33
3. Fish wheel on the Yukon River   43
4. Weekly bath at the mission, St. John's-in-the-Wilderness   53
5. Mother with brilliantly beaded baby strap   70
6. Hap with Hudson Stuck Burke, June 1911   80
7. Rev. William Loola with his Bible class   83
8. Fort Yukon, 1911   91
9. "The Fort Yukon Bunch," including T. A. (Harry) Horton and James Carroll   101
10. St. Stephen's Hospital, circa 1920   112
11. Bishop Rowe with Fort Yukon women   119
12. Hudson Stuck   133
13. John Fredson   141
14. Grafton and Clara Burke with Grafton and Hudson   147
15. Grafton at radio, circa 1924   150

16. Fire at St. Stephen's Mission Home,
     September 1924   153
17. Old Fred, John Fredson's father   154
18. David Wallis with daughters
     Ethel and Nina   158
19. Patient being brought into Hudson
     Stuck Memorial Hospital   170
20. Ma Stanford baking bread at St.
     Stephen's Mission Home, 1934   187
21. Presentation of altar hangings   195
22. St. Stephen's Mission Home
     and School, 1934   200
23. Hap showing film to about
     forty children   208
24. Hap and Clara Burke, Fort Yukon   220
25. Jean Fredson with Billy Burke
     and Virginia Louise   225
26. Michael and Hudson Burke with
     Rev. David Salmon, 1999   237
27. Clara with Grafton Burke Jr.,
     late 1940s   238

Maps

 1. Indigenous peoples and languages
     of Alaska   4
 2. Map of Alaska, with Episcopal
     mission sites   68

ACKNOWLEDGMENTS

Many people have contributed to our ability to complete this book—to research and compose the story of Grafton and Clara Burke's remarkable three-decade experience at Fort Yukon.

We thank Grete Bergman, great-granddaughter of Rev. William Loola, for sharing her insight on the influence of the Burkes and St. Stephen's Mission based on her upbringing in the Gwich'in community of Fort Yukon. Grete helped us understand how implicit messages in the Burkes' and the mission's teachings may have contributed to negative self-perceptions among the children they fostered and within the Gwich'in community. Hap and Clara, the hospital, and the mission home defended Alaska Natives, their lifeways, and languages against the people and forces that harmed them physically, culturally, and spiritually. Yet by introducing new belief systems and encouraging new practices, the Burkes and St. Stephen's also reinforced some of the negative stereotyping that pervaded Alaska society. Grete's willingness to share her memories and reflections, many of which have been painful, helped us to recognize the multilayered effects of the Burkes' and the Episcopal Church's presence in Alaska.

We thank Guy Peters, Koyukon knowledge bearer from Tanana, for his guidance regarding Dena' lifeways and values and Interior Alaska ecology and for sharing his recollections of his family's experience with the Episcopal Church's Native Deanery program initiated by Bishop William Gordon in the 1960s.

We thank Ouida Peters, RN (no relation to Hild and Guy Peters) for her careful reading of the manuscript with an eye toward the medical conditions that Hap encountered and the treatments he applied. Her questions and insight helped us clarify several incidents and methods of treatment.

We thank Hap and Clara's grandchildren, Geoffrey Burke, Debbie Burke, and Hudson Burke, and Hudson's children, Diane Burke and Michael Burke, for sharing their memories, family stories, and photographs. Long visits and phone conversations have enhanced our understanding of Burke family dynamics and the legacy that Hap and Clara left within their progeny.

We thank Rebecca Miles, granddaughter of Archdeacon Frederick B. Drane, and her husband, Jeff, for their transcription of Drane's journals and their clarifications and reflections on his experience in Alaska. We also thank journalist Diana Campbell, a granddaughter of John Fredson, for sharing family memories and her recollections of a 1999 interview she did of Hudson Stuck Burke.

We thank UAF professor Lawrence Duffy and the Arctic Division of the American Association for the Advancement of Science for their generous support of costs associated with this publication, including map production and securing high-definition images.

Finally, we wish to express our appreciation to the competent and patient archives personnel within the Alaska and Polar Regions Collections and Archives at the University of Alaska Fairbanks: Rosemarie Speranza, Della Hall, Becky Butler, Fawn Carter, and Rachel Cohen; and at the Archives of the Episcopal Church in Austin: Chris Paton, Mark Duffy, Amy Evenson, and David Hales. Personnel at both institutions have been extraordinarily helpful and accommodating during our in-person visits and when we have made electronic requests.

Prologue

Clara Heintz and Grafton Burke arrived in Alaska early in the twentieth century, when it remained a remote territory to most Americans. Although the Klondike gold rush had brought the Alaska-Yukon gold field into the world's consciousness and lured tens of thousands of gold seekers and entrepreneurs to the region, the vast majority of Americans developed their impressions of the region secondhand, from the vivid accounts of such authors as Jack London, Rex Beach, and Robert Service. Yet for millennia before the arrival of Euro-Americans, this land was known intimately by an array of Indigenous peoples for whom the vast wildernesses were their ancestral homes. As newcomers entered their lands and traversed their waters in the two centuries before Clara and Grafton's arrival, these peoples, long undisturbed by non-Indigenous intruders, experienced degrees of social disruption and trauma that were multigenerational in their impact. Russian fur traders and, later, Euro-American whalers, soldiers, and gold seekers exploited Alaska's resources and showed little regard for the rights or welfare of the Native peoples themselves. They introduced commodities and lifeways that often wrought havoc in Native communities and inadvertently—though no less destructively—spread diseases that were previously unknown or, in the case of tuberculosis, rare among Alaska Natives.

Russian Orthodox clergy and Euro-American missionaries typically arrived with three aims: spreading Christianity; guiding Alaska Natives' adjustment to the new order, including teaching new languages; and addressing health and social problems generated by contact with outsiders. Clara Heintz and Grafton ("Happy" or "Hap") Burke arrived in Alaska with these same intentions. Over the next three decades, Clara would focus her energies on children's welfare, and Hap would direct his attention primarily to the medical needs of the peoples of the vast northern Interior.

Between 1890 and 1900, Alaska's Indigenous population grew by 17 percent, from 23,500 to 27,000, while the white population grew by 700 percent, from 4,200 to 30,500, owing largely to the influx of gold seekers.[1] Meanwhile, the U.S. government did little to protect the Native peoples from the effects of these waves of migrants: depletion of subsistence resources, epidemics, and disruption of traditional lifeways through alcohol abuse and sexual exploitation. In the wake of a measles, influenza, and pneumonia epidemic in 1900 that for lack of medical care killed shockingly large numbers of Natives, decimating whole villages and leaving many children orphaned, Governor John Brady declared that "disease and death that ought to be averted by medical skill are doing their terrible work among them as never before."[2]

The greatest cause of death, however, year in and year out, was tuberculosis.[3] Early in the nineteenth century, the *M. tuberculosis* strain of the disease, which was prevalent in North America and Europe at the time, reentered Alaska, with devastating effects on Alaska Natives. Dr. Robert Fortuine, foremost expert in the history of tuberculosis in Alaska, believes that *M. tuberculosis* was a more virulent strain of the disease, to which Alaska Natives had less natural immunity than European Americans. Changing environmental and social factors, including the concentrating of Native people in permanent, poorly ventilated dwellings, also contributed to their vulnerability. Moreover, periodic epidemics of smallpox, measles, influenza, and diphtheria, among other infectious diseases, left survivors vulnerable to tuberculosis. Psychological and cultural stress amid rapid sociocultural change may also have contributed to the highly disproportionate deaths to tuberculosis among Alaska Natives.[4]

Although missionaries, Alaska's governors, and Bureau of Education personnel repeatedly bemoaned the negative impacts that newcomers in the territory brought to bear on the Native people, most non-Natives accepted no responsibility for the deteriorating conditions and high death rates among the region's Native communities. In fact, many presumed that Alaska's Native peoples would inevitably die out.[5]

Various bands of Asiatic groups, ancestors of Alaska's Indigenous peoples, had crossed Beringia millennia before and now lived in distinct regions of the territory, their cultures and lifeways reflecting their local environments. The Iñupiat inhabited the coastal regions of the far north and northwest, subsisting primarily on large marine mammals. Their relatives the Yupiit lived on the western and southwestern coasts and river deltas, their lifeways centering on fish and marine mammals. The Unangax̂ of the Aleutian Islands and Sugpiat, or Alutiit, of the Alaska Peninsula, Kodiak Island, Kenai Peninsula, and southcentral Alaska subsisted mainly on marine animals and plants, as well as birds and bird eggs.[6] The Tlingits, Haidas, and Tsimshians of Alaska's panhandle, which stretches southward along Canada's west coast, enjoyed the most plentiful renewable resources, including many marine and land animals. The many Dena' (formerly Athabascan) peoples who lived along the river systems of Alaska's vast Interior moved about seasonally in search of food, subsisting on fish, land mammals, and birds.[7] Hap and Clara Burke lived their entire married life among the Dena' of Alaska's northern Interior.

Clara's first Alaska home lay in remote northwest Alaska. The Episcopal mission St. John's-in-the-Wilderness opened with the arrival of Clara and Deaconess Clara Carter at Allakaket in summer 1907. The site lay at the Arctic Circle, on the left bank of the Koyukuk River, opposite the mouth of the Alatna River. St. John's-in-the-Wilderness was unique among Episcopal missions. It served both Yoonegge hʉt'aane Dena' ("people of the Koyukuk River") and Kuuvaŋmiut Iñupiat ("people of the Kobuk River") and thus required dual interpreters for the spoken portions of religious services and in school.[8] Common church services, Sunday football games, and school classes brought these historical enemies together and helped dispel distrust between them. The remote location offered ideal conditions for easing the peoples' exposure to Western norms while avoiding the negative influences of Western culture. The sparse population here relied on fish, especially salmon, as its staple food, along with land mammals, birds, and berries. Food was rarely plentiful in the region, and famine sometimes followed low fish runs.

Hap's first and only home base, Fort Yukon, also lay just north of the Arctic Circle, in northeastern Alaska at the Yukon River's northernmost

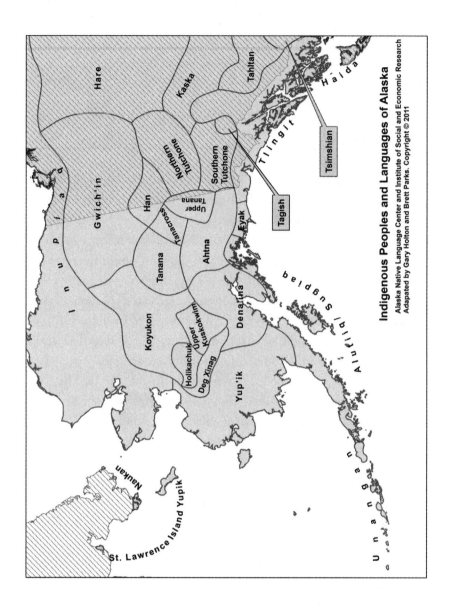

Map 1. Indigenous peoples and languages of Alaska. Michael E. Krauss, Gary Holton, Jim Kerr, Colin West, and Clemencia Merrill. 2011. Fairbanks and Anchorage: Alaska Native Language Center and Institute of Social and Economic Research. https://www.uaf.edu/anla/collections/map/.

point. The mighty Yukon flowed from its source in the Yukon Territory, Canada, northwestward to Fort Yukon, Alaska, and southwestward to the Bering Sea. Hap arrived in Alaska in 1908, and Clara joined him at Fort Yukon after their August 1910 wedding. The site lay at the center of the Yukon Flats, a triangular lowland region of about thirty thousand square miles dominated by myriad ever-changing channels of the Yukon River. The Yukon Flats was the homeland of the Gwichyaa Gwich'in.[9] Several Gwich'in groups and other Dena' of Alaska and western Canada, including the Han, Tanana, and Koyukon, lived in bands of a few families and moved in seasonal rounds to harvest food.[10] Salmon constituted the day-to-day staple food of the Gwich'in. They harvested large quantities in their fish wheels and cut, dried, and smoked it to feed themselves and their dogs through the winter.[11] Although fish fed the people year-round, they identified most closely with the caribou that migrated yearly through Gwich'in territory to their breeding grounds on the north slope of the Brooks Range. The Gwich'in also harvested various other land mammals for food and fur; in spring and early summer, they hunted many migratory birds.[12] Yet the boreal forest of the Interior provided the least abundant subsistence foods of any region in Alaska, with caribou, moose, and other subsistence resources varying significantly from year to year. Feast or famine typified life in the Interior, and the people often suffered from malnutrition.

Although the Gwich'in were well adapted to the frigid Arctic winters, the season posed significant hazards to life and limb. Every winter, the mercury dropped to −50°, −60°, and −70° Fahrenheit and lingered there, sometimes for weeks. Severe cases of frostbite led to amputations and sometimes death; Hap himself nearly froze to death in the winter before he and Clara were married.[13] In these subzero temperatures, survival, especially during travel, relied on an intimate understanding of the needs and capacities of both humans and dogs. Packing enough food, warm clothing, and bedding was imperative, as was constantly monitoring trail conditions.

The Russian Era of Alaska history began with Vitus Bering's 1741 arrival at Kayak Island in the Gulf of Alaska. Russian fur traders mined Alaska's waters and essentially enslaved the Native peoples of the southern coastal areas, especially the Unangax̂ and Sugpiak of southwestern and southcentral Alaska in the decades that followed. They managed to exert less control over the Tlingits of southeastern Alaska. In 1799 Emperor Paul I granted the Russian American Company (RAC) a monopoly on the fur trade. For two-thirds of the nineteenth century, the RAC and the Russian Orthodox Church, which the RAC encouraged to evangelize in Russian America, extended their influence in Alaska and down the Pacific Coast. Russia's Alaska footprint, however, remained largely confined to the western and southern coastal areas and to the lower Yukon River and inland areas of southwest and southcentral Alaska.[14] The Orthodox Church established a lasting presence in a limited region of Alaska: the southwest, including the Aleutian Islands, and south central and southeast Alaska. In the twenty-first century, linguists credit Father Ioann Veniaminov with contributing to the survival of the Unangan language, owing to his work in documenting it and translating religious texts into the language, with the assistance of a bilingual Unangan man, Ivan Pan'lov.[15]

In 1847 Alexander Murray of the Hudson's Bay Company (HBC) erected a trading post at Fort Yukon, well within Alaska's eastern boundary, the 141st parallel. The site lay more than a thousand miles up the Yukon River from the Bering Sea and thus well beyond the RAC's area of interest. Rivers formed the corridors and the lifeblood of the northern Interior, and major tributaries entered the Yukon near the site of the HBC fort: the Porcupine River from the northeast about five miles downstream and the Chandalar from the northwest about twenty miles farther downstream.[16] Several lesser tributaries entered the Yukon River in the general vicinity, making the site a strategic point. Dena' were not settled but moved about the vast Yukon Flats region in seasonal rounds. The Gwichyaa Gwich'in had been reduced substantially in numbers in the previous decades through warfare, and within a few years of Fort Yukon's establishment, illness and famine would further reduce Gwich'in and other Dena' populations in the Yukon Flats area.[17] As steamboats began to ply the Yukon, Dena' groups and whites congregated from time to time at Fort Yukon to trade goods.

The Church of England, or Anglican Church, expanded westward from its mission field in northwest Canada to build a mission at Fort Yukon in 1862.[18] The archdeacon Robert McDonald, who was Ojibwe and married to a Gwich'in woman, made Fort Yukon his headquarters for several years. During that time, assisted by the young Gwich'in man William Loola, he translated the Bible, the prayer book, and the hymnal into the Gwich'in language.[19] After the United States purchased Alaska from Russia in 1867, surveyors discovered that the HBC post lay on U.S. territory. The Alaska Commercial Company purchased the post, and the HBC moved to Rampart House, inside the Canadian border.[20]

In the decades that followed Alaska's purchase, national policies and non-Native migrants extended their reach into the homelands of far more Alaska Native peoples than the Russians had impacted. The nation's interest in exploiting the region's resources, its aim to bring the territory into the national fold, and numerous gold discoveries led to rapid socioeconomic, cultural, and political changes in much of the territory. Christian missionaries played varying roles in exacerbating and mitigating the effects of these changes on the lives and lifeways of Alaska Natives.

Anglican missionaries continued their work along the Yukon River following Alaska's purchase.[21] Archdeacon Thomas Canham noted that on his three visits to Fort Yukon in the 1880s, he typically found between one individual and several small groups of Dena', along with a few prospectors, camped there and interested in trading. Natives especially prized tea and tobacco and traded fish or furs for these commodities. Cash never changed hands.[22]

Meanwhile, American missionary societies, including Presbyterian, Swedish Evangelical Covenant of America, Moravian, Methodist, Baptist, and Friends (Quaker), entered limited regions of Alaska to spread Christianity among the Native peoples. In 1884, nearly two decades after the purchase, Congress passed the Organic Act, establishing a rudimentary civil government in Alaska, and allocated $15,000 for education, meant largely for Alaska Native children. The next year, the government appointed the Presbyterian missionary Sheldon Jackson as general education agent.[23] The government's education aims for Alaska Natives focused on assimilation.[24]

Between 1887 and 1895 the federal government contracted with mission societies to educate children near their Alaska mission stations, a pragmatic solution to the challenges posed by a vast territory with many small remote Native villages. This interim became known as the contract era in Alaska's education policy. Section 8 of the Organic Act allowed each mission station 640 acres of land.[25] The government-approved curriculum prohibited religious instruction during the school day. Government policy designated English as the language of instruction, although many missions conducted religious services in Indigenous languages.[26]

Jackson encouraged Protestant denominations active in Alaska and others that had not yet entered the field to assist with Native education and to provide other services to Alaska Natives. In the 1880s he met in New York with representatives of Protestant mission societies in Alaska to divide responsibility for the various regions of the territory and to avoid harmful competition. This comity agreement, as it was known, acknowledged the Anglican Church's historical presence along the Yukon and its tributaries and therefore accorded Alaska's northern Interior region to the Anglican Church's daughter institution, the Protestant Episcopal Church of America.[27] The Episcopal Church established its first Alaskan mission at Anvik on the lower Yukon in 1887 and its second at Point Hope, on Alaska's northwest coast, in 1890.[28] In 1896 the church sent a bishop, Rev. Peter Trimble Rowe, to oversee its mission work in Alaska.[29]

Beginning in 1896, concerns about government funding of public education through church organizations led the national government to end the contract system in Alaska.[30] Several missions maintained boarding schools, but they gradually transferred responsibility for the day schools to the government.[31] In 1905 Congress passed the Nelson Act, establishing a dual school system in Alaska—one for "white children and children of mixed blood who lead a civilized life" and the other for Native children. The territorial governor oversaw non-Native education, while the U.S. Bureau of Education retained responsibility for Native education.[32]

In 1899, three years after Bishop Rowe arrived, the Episcopal Church posted its first missionary at Fort Yukon, Rev. Leonides Wooden, and the site became known as St. Stephen's Mission.[33] The Episcopal Church assumed responsibility for the spiritual, social, and physical well-being of Alaska Natives along more than one thousand miles of the Yukon River, from Eagle just inside the Alaska border to Holy Cross in western Alaska; and along the Yukon's two longest tributaries, the Tanana and the Koyukuk Rivers. Contact with travelers and migrants had increased in communities on the middle and upper Yukon River as steamboat traffic grew following Alaska's purchase and especially after the gold strike near Circle City in 1893. Referring to Circle City's heyday from 1893 to 1896, territorial judge James Wickersham, who served from 1900 to 1907, wrote that despite the prohibition against liquor, "it was freely and openly sold over every bar, in every dance hall, and in every saloon."[34] The Klondike gold rush of 1898 brought "iniquity in like a flood," as Episcopal archdeacon Hudson Stuck, Grafton Burke's mentor and father figure, later put it. The negative impacts of economic and social interaction with non-Natives continued thereafter. During the winters of 1898, 1899, and 1900, steamboats that plied the Yukon River transporting people and goods in and out of the Yukon-Alaska gold field overwintered at Fort Yukon, leading to severe social disruption.[35]

Hudson Stuck arrived in Alaska in September 1904, after Bishop Rowe appointed him archdeacon of the Yukon (River), including its tributaries and drainage systems. Initially, he was based in Fairbanks, a gold mining town at the heart of Alaska's Interior founded just two years before. In 1904 Fairbanks consisted primarily of saloons, dancehalls, stores made of corrugated metal, and hastily constructed frame houses. Immediately upon Stuck's arrival on September 1, he and another cleric set to work completing the hospital that Bishop Rowe had initiated but on which progress had stalled. Two weeks later, the facility admitted its first patient; by the end of the month, it exceeded its capacity. The hospital admitted patients from all walks of life and from all over the world—Canadians, Britons, Scandinavians, Russians, Germans, Italians, and others.[36]

Next, Stuck built a church, given that none lay within twenty thousand square miles. The first services were held in the modest log building on the Chena River in mid-October. Dismayed by the lack of venues for wholesome activities, Stuck designed the structure to include a reading room, where people could relax and read books and magazines. His own library of 1,500 books served as the nucleus of the library's holdings, and he planned to enlist women from Outside, as Alaskans called the continental United States, to send used current magazines and newspapers. Within days of its opening, the reading room filled day and night. As boxes of reading materials arrived, Stuck sent duplicates to remote mining camps.[37]

Stuck began traveling along the river systems of Interior Alaska by dogsled in winter and by riverboat in summer, visiting the growing number of Episcopal missions, Native settlements and fish camps, and mining camps. As he observed the variable conditions in which the Dena' lived, he became convinced that their well-being depended on maintaining their traditional lifeways and having minimal contact with non-Natives. He aimed to spread Christianity and to offer Western education to extend economic opportunities to Alaska Natives, but he strongly urged both parents and children to maintain the subsistence skills that would sustain them and their families.[38] By 1909 Stuck was deeply discouraged by the high death rates and deteriorating social conditions among the Dena'. He came to believe that their very survival depended on the efforts of the Episcopal Church, inadequate as those efforts were, in his view.[39] A year later, he declared the Episcopal Church's "one prime mission" to be "the saving alive God's Indians in Alaska."[40]

Stuck's humanitarian focus had taken root during his tenure as dean of St. Matthew's Cathedral in Dallas, where he served from 1894 to 1904.[41] At St. Matthew's, the British-born cleric achieved a stunning record of accomplishments that reflected his orientation toward uplifting the "human race." He often maintained, "I am sorry for life in which there is no usefulness to others."[42] So unrelenting and effective was he in his efforts that his biographer, David Dean, termed him "the social conscious of Dallas."[43] He spearheaded a campaign that led to the state's first labor law in 1903, which placed age and work-hour limits on child laborers and protected their right to elementary education.[44] Meanwhile, he and parish women established St. Matthew's Home for Aged Women for the destitute. In a much more ambitious endeavor, he and women parishioners founded St. Matthew's Home for Children, for youngsters whose parents had "fallen on hard times." Both the women's and children's homes served people of all faiths.[45]

Stuck's humanitarian theology and his charitable works reflected Progressive Era reforms that spanned the late nineteenth and early twentieth centuries and the concurrent Social Gospel movement within Christianity. Both movements emerged as the industrial revolution increased disparities in wealth, health, and well-being in America. The Progressive movement entailed myriad efforts to address social problems that laissez-faire economic policies had aggravated, including alcohol abuse, domestic violence, and squalid conditions in inner cities, as well as dangerous, unhealthy, and inequitable workplace conditions.[46]

The Social Gospel movement, led largely by Protestant denominations, called on Christians to promote social justice. The movement shifted American Protestantism from its emphasis on the individual conversion experience, personal piety, and doctrinal considerations to ethical concerns, or *applied* Christianity. Social consciousness required directing one's influence, resources, and energies to reducing structural inequalities and alleviating social problems through collective solutions such as universal public education and health care and economic aid to the underprivileged. Middle-class urban women accounted for most of the volunteerism toward these causes.[47]

The Social Gospel movement turned its attention to Native Americans as awareness grew of the misery and poverty on reservations. The catastrophic failure of the government's relocation and concentration policies that had confined most Native Americans to reservations had recently prompted a policy shift toward allotment and assimilation. The 1887 Dawes Act allotted parcels of reservation land to heads of families to encourage individualism and individual responsibility, even as it dispossessed tribes of large expanses of land for railroad expansion, industrial development, ranching, and non-Indigenous settlement. Other reforms included a national system of boarding schools that immersed Native American children in mainstream American norms and values through English education and training for industrial work. Well-meaning Christian adherents of the Indian reform movement, often termed Friends of Indians, enthusiastically endorsed these policies, convinced of their capacity to improve conditions among Native Americans. As historian Tom Holm noted, "Without much apparent thought, the Indian reform movement played into the hands of the railroads, land companies, farmers, and ranchers, as well as the timber, coal, petroleum, and steel industries."[48] Neither policymakers nor Friends of Indians anticipated the long-term trauma that would result from removing Native American children from their homes and "reeducating" them in ways that implicitly and explicitly denigrated their languages, cultures, and lifeways. To reduce costs, the government relied heavily on Catholic and Protestant missionaries to implement its policies. Friends of Indians and the missionaries devoted themselves to the cause with a fervor that the Jesuit historian Francis Paul Prucha termed "ethnocentrism of frightening intensity."[49]

While Prucha captured reformers' zeal, narrow-mindedness, and naivete, he overlooked the differences in perceptions and approaches among progressives and religious denominations in their work among Native Americans. This variability was especially pronounced in Alaska, where Christian missionization efforts began in the decade that followed Alaska's 1867 purchase, as the U.S. government responded slowly to the negative impacts on Alaska Natives of heavy in-migration of Euro-Americans. Some denominations, especially the Presbyterian Church, energetically endorsed the government's English-only policy. When it tasked one of its earliest missionaries, S. Hall Young, with translating the Bible and other religious texts into Tlinglit, he objected forcefully. Later, Young took credit for having influenced the Presbyterian Church to endorse the English-only effort:

> One strong stand, which so far as I know I was the first to take, was the determination to do no translating into the Tlingit language or any other of the native dialects of that region. When I learned the inadequacy of these languages to express Christian thought, and when I realized that the whites were coming; that schools would come; that the task of making an English-speaking race of these natives was much easier than the task of making a civilized and Christian language out of the Tlingit, Hyda and Tsimpshean [sic], I wrote to the mission Board that the duty to which they had assigned me of translating the Bible into Tlingit and of making a dictionary and grammar of that tongue was a useless and even harmful task; that we

should let the old tongues with their superstition and sin die—the sooner the better—and replace these languages with that of Christian civilization, and compel the natives in all our schools to talk English and *English only*. Thus we would soon have an intelligent people who would be qualified to be Christian citizens.[50]

The Presbyterian Board of Missions implemented Young's recommendation at its Alaskan missions, including the Sitka Training School, later named the Sheldon Jackson Institute.[51]

Other denominations, most notably Episcopal, Moravian, and Catholic missionaries, in the late nineteenth and early twentieth centuries exhibited appreciation for Alaska Native cultures and languages by documenting and learning to speak Native languages, providing native-language religious services, translating religious texts in collaboration with English-speaking Natives, resisting official English-only policies in schools, and encouraging Alaska Natives to maintain their traditional lifeways. The Episcopal Church emphasized education of Native children in academic subjects, traditional subsistence skills, industrial training, and health and sanitation at all its Alaskan missions, and it engaged numerous Natives in teaching. Industrial schools at Anvik and Nenana provided practical education to prepare students to support themselves and serve their people. These schools taught gardening, basketry, dogsled and snowshoe making, working with fish wheels, and carving for those who showed talent.[52] By 1911 the government posted teachers at Fort Yukon, Eagle, Circle, Stevens Village, Rampart, and Tanana in the Interior, usually hiring individuals whom Bishop Rowe recommended, to foster harmony between school and mission authorities.[53]

Hudson Stuck exemplified the Episcopal Church's orientation toward Alaska's Indigenous peoples and the church's work among them. His many years of interaction with Alaska Natives reinforced his esteem for the people and their cultures.[54] Stuck's protégé, Grafton Burke, exhibited a similar appreciation for Alaska Native peoples and cultures. Many times over the years he would say that he "had not converted the Native to his way of life so much as he had been converted to theirs."[55] Despite these "enlightened" attitudes and policies and their many positive effects, missionaries of all denominations played active roles in the colonization of Alaska, and their actions and attitudes as a whole had far-ranging and long-lasting impacts—some of them negative—many of which can be seen today.

While missionaries generally sought to mitigate the harmful effects of migration into Alaska Natives' homelands, they, too, introduced changes that implicitly and often explicitly suggested their superiority to the people's traditional worldviews and lifeways. Various Euro-American institutions and influences—schools in particular but also the people themselves, films, radio, and later television—conveyed messages of Euro-American cultural superiority. The very existence of a dual school system and the fact that the parents of mixed-race children sought to enroll their children in territorial schools, rather than Bureau of Education schools for Native children, reinforced notions of the superiority of Euro-American culture and English. It is difficult, if not impossible, to separate and assign relative blame to these various institutions and forces for the resultant harm to Alaska Natives.[56] Missionaries' tendency to claim the moral high ground as they mediated between old and new ways—even when they advocated for the former—implied that their judgment capacities were superior. Moreover, missionaries' arrival sometimes divided Native communities or tribes between those who adopted and those who rejected the new paradigm, in some cases prodding people to realign their identities with one group or the other, thereby causing confusion.

Many people did not fit neatly into either group, which made them outsiders within their own communities. The newcomers became authority figures, especially among adherents of the Christian faith, which subverted traditional leaders, including shamans, or medicine men. As the Christian belief system began to dominate, traditional beliefs, and in some cases traditional lifeways, became sources of shame. For instance, the new emphasis on sanitation and hygiene, coupled with the oft-used expression "cleanliness is next to godliness," implied the moral superiority of those who emulated the sanitation and hygiene habits practiced and advocated by missionaries and teachers.[57] Ironically, the presence of missions and schools contributed to the sanitation problems that they themselves sought to combat. The services that missions and schools provided, including medical, educational, and religious, encouraged Natives to settle nearby. Increased population density in those areas depleted subsistence resources, created sanitation hazards, and exacerbated health problems associated with poor ventilation.[58] Thus the missions and schools were in part responsible for creating the conditions under which sanitation and hygiene measures initially deteriorated.

Alaska Natives responded in a range of ways to missionaries' presence, the new worldview and spiritual message they brought, and the aid they provided. In most cases, missionaries arrived after the social fabric of Native communities had been disrupted by migrants and after epidemics had decimated local populations. Missionaries' ability to treat or prevent these new diseases, after shamans had been helpless to do so, enhanced their credibility and fostered trust.[59] The physician Robert Fortuine, who in the late twentieth century wrote a history of health and disease in early Alaska, noted, "In times of sickness and death the missionaries tried to be a help and comfort in any way they could. . . . During the epidemics the missionaries worked to the point of exhaustion to treat the victims, comfort the dying and their families, and bury the dead. Although it is doubtful that they thereby changed the course of the epidemic, such self-less behavior on their part often made a deep impression on the Natives."[60]

The anthropologist Ernest "Tiger" Burch noted that Indigenous Christians' capacity to break taboos with impunity contributed to high conversion rates among the Iñupiat at the dawn of the twentieth century.[61] Various anthropologists, historians, and other scholars have suggested that the benefits of association with missions explain Alaska Natives' high conversion rates. Many have argued that acceptance of the new religion was largely superficial.[62] Burch, on the other hand, described the syncretism between traditional Iñupiaq beliefs and Christianity, noting that in many ways, the two belief systems complemented one another. Furthermore, while Christianity in theory requires exclusivity, traditional Iñupiaq spirituality permits belief in additional religious paradigms, which eased the synthesis of Christian beliefs with traditional Iñupiaq beliefs.[63]

Several anthropologists have made similar observations about the concurrent Christian and traditional beliefs of the Dena'. Edward Hosley noted that from a Dena' perspective, shamanism did not directly conflict with Christianity, because they addressed separate domains.[64] James VanStone observed that Dena' were "perfectly capable of seeing the two systems, Christian and traditional, as complementary rather than conflicting."[65] Frederica de Laguna wrote of her experience among the Dena', "Despite the fact that probably all the Natives we met in 1935 would have believed themselves good Christians, I think that a considerable number of the old shamanistic beliefs and practices still held, especially since these were not felt to be in conflict with the new faith."[66] Hudson Stuck found the retention of traditional spiritual beliefs among Alaska Native Christians unremarkable, writing, "Every one familiar with the history of Christianity knows that [the retention of former belief systems] has characterized the progress of religion in all ages."[67]

Undeniably, Alaska Natives enjoyed advantages of association with missions. Yet much evidence suggests that many Alaska Natives embraced Christianity sincerely, bringing their babies to be baptized, seeking Christian marriages, and urging that a mission be built in or a pastor be assigned to their communities.[68] Many Alaska Natives held strong, active leadership roles in mission work and took initiative in spreading the word, and many among them were eventually ordained to the priesthood. To this day, the Episcopal Church remains strong in Interior Alaska.[69]

William Loola, who had collaborated with the Anglican archdeacon Robert McDonald to translate the Bible and other religious texts into Gwich'in, was ordained deacon in 1904. Reverend Loola, as he was known, led religious services and taught Bible study classes in the Fort Yukon region, having come to an understanding with his father, a shaman, that their belief systems could coexist.[70] David Wallis, a devout congregant at Fort Yukon, served the mission in various capacities, including leading church services in Gwich'in. Albert Tritt spearheaded the effort to build a church at Arctic Village and became a deacon there. Throughout most of his adult life, John Fredson engaged in and supported Episcopal Church work in both official and volunteer capacities at Fort Yukon and at Chandalar Village, or Venetie. In villages throughout the Interior and at Point Hope/Tikiġaq on the northwest coast, Native children and adults attended church services and Bible study sessions in large numbers, participated actively, and sang with gusto.

On the other hand, Velma Wallis, a granddaughter of David Wallis, related in her memoir, *Raising Ourselves*, the traumatic effects of new belief systems and lifeways that, together with waves of epidemics, contributed to multigenerational grief, shame, alcohol abuse, and family dysfunction among the Gwich'in. David Wallis's work with St. Stephen's Mission so dominated his time that his wife, Martha, took their boys trapping while David remained in Fort Yukon responding to church and hospital needs. Peter Trimble Wallis, Velma's father, may have resented his father's sense of duty that kept him from traditional pursuits with his family. In his teens Pete began using his earnings from trapping furs to buy bootlegged liquor and had many alcohol-related run-ins with the law. Alcohol abuse later marred the home life of Pete and Mae Wallis and their thirteen children.[71] Regardless of the benevolent intentions and positive developments surrounding Christian missions, their presence and efforts contributed to divisions within families and communities, with long-term and arguably multigenerational harmful consequences. Hap recognized that the church sometimes failed in "deed or word" and that the trust that intermediaries such as David Wallis fostered between the mission and the people enhanced the mission's capacity for good. William Loola, David Wallis, John Fredson, and many other Native congregants eased communication and understanding in both directions. Hap hoped to increase the number of Native clergy and medical personnel at St. Stephen's Mission.[72]

By fall 1908 Episcopal missions operated in the northern Interior at Anvik, Tanana, Rampart, Circle City, Fort Yukon, and Eagle on the Yukon River, Nenana on the Tanana River, Fairbanks on the Chena River, and Allakaket on the Koyukuk River. All these served Dena' peoples, while the mission at Allakaket served Kuuvaŋmiut Iñupiat as well. The Episcopal Church also operated missions with schools in the Iñupiaq community of Point Hope/Tikiġaq on the northwest coast and the Tlingit community at Ketchikan in southeast Alaska.[73] The schools at Anvik, Nenana, and Fort Yukon were orphanages and boarding schools.[74]

To the extent that the federal government honored its trust responsibility toward Alaska Native peoples, it did so primarily through the Bureau of Education. The U.S. commissioner of education Harlan Updegraff informed Bishop Rowe in 1908 that the Alaska School Service's purview would include "the general oversight of the natives of Alaska." He assured Rowe that he did not mean to "unduly" emphasize the bureau's authority but rather hoped to cooperate with the church in serving Alaska Natives.[75] Tensions nevertheless arose between the bureau and Episcopal mission personnel as their understandings of Natives' best interests diverged and as each chafed at perceived infringements by the other on its authority.[76]

Stuck and other Episcopal missionaries held strong views on Native education, especially their belief that Western education should not detract from Native language fluency or traditional Native life skills.[77] Stuck admired the "flexibility and picturesque expressiveness of an indigenous tongue."[78] From the Bureau of Education's perspective, however, St. Stephen's Mission's use of Gwich'in in school elevated church positions over national law.[79] Such tension reflected the paternalism of both toward Alaska Natives, an orientation whose effects were far from benign. It illustrated the belief on both their parts not only that they knew better than the other what was best for Alaska Natives but that they knew better than the people themselves.[80] Despite such disagreements, Episcopal authorities and Bureau of Education personnel largely saw eye to eye about their responsibilities toward Alaska Natives. Both sought to advance the interests of the people and to protect them from harms related to Western contact.

Teachers and missionaries acted as social workers, making house calls to check on the welfare of Native school children and their family members.[81] Both superintendent of schools George Boulter and Archdeacon Stuck urged their superiors to do more to mitigate the dire health conditions among Alaska Natives, especially the pervasiveness of tuberculosis. Boulter, Stuck, and Grafton Burke exasperated their superiors with the costs of their efforts on behalf of Alaska Natives, as they exceeded their budgets in responding to needs.[82] Stuck, Boulter, and the Burkes also lamented the impacts of alcohol abuse on Native individuals, families, and communities. They all railed against the illegal activities of whiskey peddlers, and they decried juries' refusal to convict such men.[83]

From Alaska's purchase in 1867 until 1898, Congress treated Alaska as it treated Indian Country in the continental United States, prohibiting the importation and sale of alcohol in the territory to protect Alaska Natives from its negative effects. Enforcement was uneven, however, and with the Klondike gold rush of 1898, Congress abandoned any pretense of restricting alcohol's entry into Alaska, permitting importation and sale while continuing to prohibit alcohol trade with Alaska Natives. In 1909, in response to pleas by Alaska's governors and other concerned citizens, Congress elevated the crime of selling or trading alcohol with Natives to a felony, aiming to improve enforcement. Alaskans continued to flout the law, however, and juries rarely convicted individuals accused of trading in alcohol with Alaska Natives, regardless of the strength of the evidence.[84]

In 1908 George Boulter had asked Governor Wilford Hogatt to appoint him as a special peace officer so that he could arrest whiskey peddlers. It took four years for Boulter's request to work its way through the government bureaucracy. Frustrated at Hogatt's inaction and at continuing disregard for the law, Boulter appealed to Governor Walter Clark, who in 1912 appointed him peace officer for the district he oversaw as superintendent of schools.[85] Grafton Burke also served a two-and-a-half-year term as commissioner at Fort Yukon, a position that allowed him to bring violators of the law to justice. Among non-Natives, however, Bureau of Education personnel and Alaskan missionaries were outliers in their views on the liquor trade with Alaska Natives.[86]

The negative impacts of Western influence were perhaps most evident at Tanana, whose proximity to the U.S. Army post Fort Gibbon near the confluence of the Tanana and Yukon Rivers exposed Tanana residents to alcohol abuse and exploitation. Stuck's despair with conditions at Tanana drove his decision to establish future missions in more remote locations, where he believed missionaries could slow the pace of change, inevitable though that change was.[87]

Clara began her missionary service in Alaska almost on a lark, aiming to spend one year in remote Allakaket before returning to family and friends in Los Angeles. Hap, having given much more thought to his future as a medical missionary, followed his mentor, Hudson Stuck, to Alaska, envisioning a long-term commitment. Both Hap and Clara discovered the needs to be overwhelming and the resources—human and fiscal—wholly inadequate. When he arrived in 1908, Hap was the only physician in more than eight hundred miles along the Yukon River from Dawson, Yukon Territory, to Fort Gibbon. Clara found her purpose in giving orphaned and needy children a loving home. Believing that God had called them to this service and finding their lives and work deeply gratifying, they lived among the Gwich'in people of Fort Yukon and, until Hap's death in 1938, dedicated their lives to their physical, spiritual, and mental health. During that time, as the Gwich'in people and the community of Fort Yukon embraced the couple and engaged in the mission and hospital work, St. Stephen's Mission and Hospital (later the Hudson Stuck Memorial Hospital) became community institutions that saved lives and enhanced well-being. Along with these profoundly and unequivocally positive impacts, Hap and Clara's presence, and that of the Episcopal Church, directly and indirectly contributed to the sea change in Native lifeways wrought by myriad outside influences whose impacts were complex and whose legacies have been felt by generations.

1   Early Life and Arrival in Alaska, 1907–8

When Clara May Heintz met the Episcopal deaconess Clara Carter in 1907 and offered to accompany her to a remote region of Alaska for mission work among Native people there, she could not have envisioned what lay ahead. In the coming year, Clara would fall in love with the Yoonegge hut'aane ("people of the Koyukuk River") Dena' and the Kuuvaŋmiut ("people of the Kobuk River") Iñupiat at Allakaket. She and Deaconess Carter transformed the newly built rustic mission house and church into cozy and welcoming institutions. The mission fostered improved relations between these former enemies, while the women's efforts improved health and well-being in the region significantly. The people, the work, and the setting so captivated Clara that she extended her one-year commitment to two years. That decision would lead to a loving marriage and a fulfilling, three-decade partnership in service to others that would entail far more action, drama, and peril than the life of travel and adventure she had yearned for as a child.

Nor could Dr. Grafton ("Hap") Burke have foreseen the gratifying life he would lead in the coming decades when he followed his mentor, the Episcopal cleric Hudson Stuck, to the northern Alaska mission field in 1908. Hap and Clara met soon after his arrival in Alaska, and they married two years later. For the twenty-eight years that followed, the couple made their home at Fort Yukon, a Gwichyaa, or Di'haii, Gwich'in Dena' community just north of the Arctic Circle, immersing themselves in community life and earning the love and respect of the Gwich'in people. Hap directed St. Stephen's Hospital, the only such facility that served Alaska Natives within more than five hundred miles along the Yukon River.[1] He saved countless lives—both Native and non-Native—and together, he and Clara improved quality of life in the region. Meanwhile, they raised two sons and cared for scores of orphans and foster children in their home, which served as an orphanage, boarding school, and community center. During that time Hap's religious duties expanded from those of a lay missionary, to the myriad responsibilities of an ordained deacon, to the rites officiated by an ordained priest. The Gwich'in people embraced and participated in the work of the hospital and mission, which lay at the center of community life in Fort Yukon. The couple's story is a testament to the profound, multigenerational effects of lives dedicated to the well-being of others and the deep gratification that such commitment can bring.

Clara May Heintz was born November 10, 1884, in Kansas.[2] Her father, Carl Martin Heintz, had immigrated from Denmark and traveled extensively before the family settled in the St. James Park area of Los Angeles and he became a U.S. citizen. He published the *Rural Californian*, a weekly agricultural newspaper that frequently printed articles by the renowned agricultural science pioneer Luther Burbank. Clara was the eldest of eight children—six girls and two boys. Her mother died after bearing six children. Her father remarried two years later, and the Heintz family grew with the births of another girl and boy. Clara's stepmother, Maude, devoted herself to the care of all eight children, and Clara maintained a loving relationship with her second mother throughout her life.[3]

The Heintz family enjoyed a comfortable, if unremarkable, lifestyle. Clara attended Miss Houts's private school in Los Angeles.[4] The family made yearly excursions to Mt. Wilson, northeast of Los Angeles, to escape the city's heat, but these outings failed to quench Clara's thirst for travel and adventure. To satisfy her wanderlust, a trait she attributed to her Viking heritage, Clara read adventure stories by Robert Louis Stevenson, Jack London, and others. She later claimed, "Had I been a boy, I would undoubtedly have run off to sea." In January 1907 Carl Heintz died following a brief illness, leaving the grief-stricken family reeling and Clara's dreams of seeing the world dashed.[5]

The future looked bleak in May 1907 when the prospect of travel and adventure Clara had imagined suddenly appeared. Deaconess Clara Carter, a missionary in Alaska, dropped by while visiting her brother, the Heintz family's next-door neighbor. As she and Heintz family members talked, she told them of her dilemma: she was soon to return to her missionary work, but the nurse she expected to accompany her had backed out, and Carter's brother refused to allow her to return to the Alaska wilderness alone. Impulsively, Clara, who had no medical training, offered to take the nurse's place. Her mother protested, but their family doctor's approval of the plan overcame her objections. Within a week, Clara and the deaconess were on board a northbound train to Seattle.[6]

Allakaket, their destination, lay just above the Arctic Circle in northwestern Alaska. The Episcopal archdeacon of the Yukon (River), Hudson Stuck, had selected the remote site where the Alatna River feeds into the Koyukuk River for the new mission named St. John's-in-the-Wilderness. Upon first entering the area in 1904, Stuck had met Dena' of the Koyukuk River who had never been exposed to Christianity and who had seen few non-Natives.[7] Here, Stuck thought, missionaries could bring Christianity, medical care, and Western education while shielding the people from negative influences of Western society and encouraging them to maintain their traditional lifeways. In more accessible regions of Alaska, especially along the great Yukon River, migrants had depleted Native people's subsistence resources, introduced alcohol—with devastating consequences—and brought deadly diseases. River traffic and, ironically, missions themselves had attracted the people to settle along the Yukon River, where these perils were much more prevalent.[8]

Although just two or three Native cabins lay near the Allakaket mission site, Stuck anticipated that once a mission was erected, Natives from nearby villages and encampments would settle there. The Episcopal Church offered doors and windows to any Native who built a log cabin near its missions.[9] Under current conditions, with tuberculosis and other respiratory diseases so prevalent, the roomier and better-ventilated homes provided healthier living conditions than the crowded semi-subterranean dwellings of the past, although the tents the people lived in as they migrated during their subsistence rounds delivered even better ventilation.

En route to Allakaket, the Episcopal bishop of Alaska, Peter Trimble Rowe, joined Clara and the deaconess in Seattle. The steamer took them through Alaska's fabled Inside Passage to Skagway, from where they continued by rail and then river to Allakaket. As they traveled, the bishop and Deaconess Carter introduced Clara to life in Alaska and to Episcopal mission work.[10]

After five weeks in transit, traveling nearly three thousand miles, the women arrived at their destination in July 1907.[11] Clara would serve primarily as a schoolteacher, with an annual salary of $500. The deaconess would provide medical care and religious instruction; as a trained nurse, she earned $600 a year.[12] Archdeacon Stuck had spent the winter of 1906–7 overseeing the new mission's construction.[13] An encampment of Dena' now lay near the mission site, while a small village of Iñupiat lay one to two miles downriver on the right bank of the Koyukuk River. Following the mission's establishment, as Stuck had anticipated, families began to settle nearby. As the only mission in Alaska that served two distinct ethnic and language groups, its worship services used two interpreters, one Kuuvaŋmiut (Iñupiaq) and one Yoonegge hʉt'aane (Dena'), while the congregation sang heartily and in unison in English.[14]

A modest church and mission house of unpeeled logs with moss and mud chinking awaited the two Claras upon their arrival, thanks to the work of Stuck, his Dena' trail guide, Arthur Wright, and several men he hired from the region.[15] Clara's first encounter with the formidable archdeacon left both unsettled. She found his nervous demeanor and clipped speech intimidating. Moreover, he bluntly questioned her suitability for her position. Upon learning that she had training neither in remote mission work nor in teaching and cooking, he reportedly declared, "Humph! Well, if you have any brains at all you should be able to learn to cook!" Turning to Deaconess Carter, he exclaimed, "I don't understand why you brought this inexperienced girl up here, Deaconess. This is no kindergarten, you know," and stomped off.[16]

The Native construction crew, on the other hand, greeted the women shyly and graciously, giving Clara the impression that they may have been the first white women the men had seen. The crew carried the women's bags to the mission house as the newcomers followed, with Iñupiaq and Dena' women and children crowding around them, peering up at their strange clothing and faces. Clara's pompadour hair style, long full skirt, and high buttoned boots surely looked out of place. A chubby-faced baby broke the ice, grinning and playing hide-and-seek from within the hood of her mother's summer parka. Soon the women and children were laughing and admiring the baby's antics. The people later returned with gifts of fish, meat, and beaded moccasins and belts. That first day, they chose a nickname for the five-foot-nine-inch Clara: Navasoo Ruck, which meant "big funny girl." The charming baby was later christened Miss Heintz in honor of Clara; although Clara suggested that her given name would be more suitable, the child's mother insisted on Miss Heintz, the name the people called Clara. Later, villagers referred to the child as Little Miss Heintz to distinguish her from Big Miss Heintz.[17]

Clara's impression of the archdeacon began to soften as he spoke of his vision for expanding the mission work to serve more Native people and when he fretted over her many mosquito bites.[18] She could not have known then that she and Stuck would develop a deeply affectionate relationship. In fact, Clara would be one of the few women Hudson Stuck ever truly loved. "She has more practical good sense than Hap & I put together," he wrote of her.[19]

The women began organizing the space in the mission house, which contained a large living and dining room, a small kitchen, and a bedroom for each of them. Other structures on the property included a small guest cabin, an outhouse, and a dog yard for the team of eight sled dogs the archdeacon had left the women for their winter travel needs. They partitioned off an area for a clinic at the entrance of the mission house and organized it with shelves for drugs, benches for waiting patients, and an examination table that doubled as a desk.[20] Natives and non-Natives, young and old, began to arrive at the mission seeking medical care, some of them very ill and beyond saving, often from tuberculosis. Many patients came from nearby settlements.[21]

Using materials on hand, the women decorated the mission home and responded to local needs. Clara fashioned warm clothing for four children from a heavy piano cover sent by well-meaning mission friends (church groups collected and sent used clothing and household goods, most of them useful, to missions throughout the world).[22] Beyond organizing the household, Clara tackled her primary initial responsibility—cooking—

beginning with learning to build a fire in the stove. She became, in her words, a "better than average cook and a good nursing assistant," at least partially perhaps "out of sheer pique over the Archdeacon's jibe at our first meeting."[23]

The two women prioritized establishing friendly relations and building trust with the local people. With Oola as their Iñupiaq interpreter and George as their Dena' interpreter, they made daily visits to the two budding villages—the nearby Dena' encampment and the Iñupiaq settlement across the river—focusing on sanitation and hygiene. The Iñupiat received the women more cordially than the Dena', although the shamans of both settlements eyed them suspiciously and resentfully, given that the missionaries challenged their roles and wisdom. The Dena' women and children brought gifts of berries and fish to the mission, but Clara found that the Dena' men, like the shamans, remained wary and reserved.[24]

On the first Sunday morning after their arrival, all families from the Iñupiaq encampment, about fifty people, filed into the rough church building that Clara and the children had adorned with spruce boughs and wildflowers. Even the shaman came, seemingly out of curiosity. Only a few Dena' attended. Following the people's traditions and expectations, the congregation sat in four sections. The Iñupiaq women and children sat on one side in the back, with the men in front of them; the Dena' women and children sat opposite their Iñupiaq counterparts, with three male youths in front of them. Deaconess Carter began with a simple hymn, "Onward Christian Soldiers," that Stuck had been teaching them. Although it was unclear how much they understood, Clara found the singing enthusiastic and on pitch.[25]

For several weeks, many more Iñupiat than Dena' attended Sunday services. A turning point came when the Dena' shaman's youngest son fell into a campfire and was severely burned. The deaconess tenderly and skillfully nursed the boy back to health, winning the shaman's deep gratitude. Appreciative community members made a moosehide mattress for the clinic's examining table, and from then on, Dena' attended church in large numbers.[26]

That summer and fall, Clara began developing an array of skills useful to living in the far north, where many months could pass without contact or supplies from Outside.[27] The women planted a vegetable garden and marveled at the rapid growth of their produce in the long daylight hours. They fished, and Clara became a capable hunter, learning to use a 12-gauge shotgun and a .22 rifle to harvest the plentiful rabbits and birds. They picked hundreds of quarts of blueberries, cranberries, and salmonberries and preserved them in the permafrost, the permanently frozen earth of much of northern Alaska.[28]

By fall a community began to develop as Iñupiat and Dena' built and improved cabins at their separate sites near the mission.[29] Although the mission's presence reduced the historical enmity between the two peoples, tensions during that first winter sometimes ran high as rumors spread of impending battles, and the Dena' and Iñupiat kept loaded rifles in their tents and cabins. In the mission house, a quart of ammonia placed at the head of each of their beds, ready to be splashed on intruders, allowed the women to sleep soundly.[30]

Clara opened a day school in mid-September with seventeen students.[31] The children arrived each morning eager to learn, bringing lunches of dried fish and sourdough cakes.[32] She took delight in her teaching duties, finding the children charming and quick learners. In late October she opened evening classes for adults.[33] That fall the superintendent of schools inspected and accredited Clara's classroom as a government school, which meant the government would pay her salary and provide books and supplies, saving the Episcopal Church the expense.[34]

In September, on the last boat of the season, a pipe organ arrived at the mission, courtesy of Archdeacon Stuck. Clara began training a boys' choir, selecting the six boys—four Iñupiat and two Dena'—with the strongest singing voices. She sewed vestments—surplices and cassocks—from sheets and a bolt of the deaconess's dress lining dyed black. School let out early on Friday afternoons, and the whole community came to witness and participate in the choir practices. Enthusiastic participation in daily practices brought results. By the following fall when the archdeacon visited, he was astonished to find the boys' choir singing in tune with near perfect English diction. He relished leading the boys in their daily rehearsals during this and subsequent visits, and he compared the choir favorably with the boys' and men's choirs he had led in Dallas. He and the women carefully instructed the choir and the other congregants on the meaning of the verses they sang.[35]

The first heavy frost came on October 5 that first year, and by October 11, the river had frozen. The people—including Clara, who had learned to icefish—now fished through the river ice, mainly for grayling and whitefish, which, frozen and stacked like cordwood in their cache, provided food through the winter for the women and dogs.[36] Clara's Arctic survival skillset expanded to include mushing dogs, traveling on snowshoes, and hunting small animals.[37]

As Christmas approached, the children wrote letters to the archdeacon describing their activities. The letters revealed much about lifeways at Allakaket and the mission's impact. Some of the children "worked" at the mission, earning various forms of compensation, such as warm clothing. Family life centered around subsistence activities. Tommy wrote of working hard for the mission and noted that Miss Heintz had made him "plenty" of clothes. He boasted of a new .22 shotgun and reported that he loved learning at school. Frank told of catching a rabbit and of his father's having felled two big bears and three little bears. Ten-year-old Susie had caught plenty of rabbits, and little Ola's mama had caught many fish. Jimmie proudly wrote of his work for the mission, of the small dogsled he had built and how Miss Heintz enjoyed riding on it.[38]

On Christmas Eve the school children hung stockings. The following morning they gleefully pulled treasures from them. Clara Carter described the day as "the very happiest Christmas in my life." About 125 Natives, fifty or so locals, and others from as far as 260 miles downriver at Koyukuk Station gathered at the mission. Perhaps fifty arrived from Arctic City, twelve miles downriver, and others traveled from the upriver mining communities of Coldfoot and Bettles.[39] After church services, everyone took part in the weekly football game on the river; according to Clara, moosehide balls filled with moose hair had been used since long before Europeans and Euro-Americans invented soccer and football. While the women were away from the mission home, miners from Bettles and Coldfoot arrived with a large cookstove to replace the mission's tiny portable Yukon stove. By the time the Claras returned, a delicious Christmas dinner of roast turkey, hash brown potatoes, cranberry sauce, and blueberry pie awaited them.[40]

In late February of their first year at Allakaket, Bishop Rowe arrived on his winter dogsled tour of Interior Alaska's missions. Iñupiat and Dena' rushed to the mission house from their traplines to greet the beloved bishop. He baptized seventeen congregants whom Deaconess Carter had prepared. Along with performing religious services and ceremonies, the bishop mediated intratribal disputes, at their request. As he pulled out of the mission to continue his journey, the missionaries and locals gave him a warm sendoff in the Alaskan tradition, running alongside his sled for a mile. By this time, Clara had decided she would stay on another year at the mission. The deaconess had devoted much time and energy to her training, and Clara had come to love the people. She took great pride in her steadily improving boys' choir.[41]

In early May, as the days grew longer and warmer, the snow began to melt. Everyone living along Alaska's northern rivers eagerly anticipated break-up, the release of the river ice caused by upstream water pressure during the spring thaw. At Allakaket, sometime in May, the ice heaved and cracked, reverberating like gunshots. Shouts rang out, and people ran to the riverbank to witness the spring ritual. Migratory birds joined in the cacophony, gulls shrieking, geese honking, and ducks squawking. Flooding was not a serious concern at Allakaket, because the Koyukuk's strong current kept the waters reasonably within its banks. There was always the chance, however, that a careening ice slab could take out a stand of trees.[42]

The arrival of the first steamboat marked another rite of spring. Shouts of "Steamboat!" went up at the first sign, usually the riotous barking of the dogs. Along Alaska's river systems, and even along the coast, from break-up to freeze-up, the arrival of steamboats generated shouts as everyone rushed to the water's edge. The vessel might be carrying much-anticipated letters, packages, food, or building supplies, as well as tourists interested in purchasing Native handwork. In spring 1908 the two Claras eagerly awaited the arrival of the first steamboat, with nearly all their

1. St. John's-in-the-Wilderness, Allakaket. Walter and Lillian Phillips Photograph Collection, #1985-72-139, APRCA, University of Alaska Fairbanks.

supplies depleted, including salt and sugar. That summer, friends from Los Angeles visited, expecting to take Clara home with them, but she disappointed them, remaining steadfast in her resolve to stay another year.[43]

In summer the construction of a playground at the mission site—a swing, seesaws, a jumping board, and a pole-vaulting bar—provided hours of daily entertainment for the children. A phonograph with the "sweetest tone" had also arrived, bringing the two women "untold pleasure," according to the deaconess. By now Natives living at Coldfoot and Arctic City spoke of moving to Allakaket.[44]

In fall 1908 Iñupiat built two more cabins in their settlement, and Dena' constructed two and enlarged and improved a third.[45] The mission community was growing as Stuck had anticipated. The fish run had been poor that summer, however, leaving the people without a good store of dried salmon for the winter. Subsisting in the northern boreal forest, where game and fur-bearing animals tended to be sparse, remained challenging for the people, and they looked toward winter with some foreboding.[46]

Grafton Rush Burke was born December 4, 1882, in Paris, Texas.[47] Sparse and conflicting accounts of his parents and family life make piecing together his childhood difficult. One account depicted his father, William Burke, as a well-known Tulane-educated Dallas physician who reportedly worked in various communities, including several Native American reservations, where he learned to speak the Native languages. In Dallas, where the Burke family had settled in 1894, Dr. Burke specialized in genitourinary and skin diseases, while reportedly doing postgraduate work in his fields of expertise on the East Coast.[48] Another account painted him as "a charming ne'er-do-well 'doctor' with little funds and no education."[49] A contemporary of Hap's described his father privately as someone "whose pills & potions were administered to cats and dogs."[50] Hap's mother's death in 1895 left the boy largely on his own.[51] In 1899 Dr. Burke married a strong-willed woman who reportedly took little interest in the adolescent boy and discouraged his father from devoting resources to him.[52]

Despite the loss of his mother and instability in his home, the lad became known for his cheerful disposition, which earned him the nickname Happy, or Hap.[53] In 1895 Hap joined the competitive boys' choir at St. Matthew's Cathedral in Dallas and came under the mentorship of its founding director, the British-born Hudson Stuck, dean of the cathedral.[54] In 1899 he entered St. Matthew's Grammar School, a preparatory school that Stuck also founded, and he took up residency at the rectory. During the four years that he lived with Stuck, the two developed a close, father-son-like relationship, and Stuck assumed responsibility for Hap's education.[55] Hudson Stuck would have more influence than any other person on the man Hap was to become and on his approach to life and to his medical and pastoral work.

After Hap graduated from St. Matthew's Grammar School in May 1903, Stuck helped him secure admission on scholarship to his alma mater, the Episcopal University of the South at Sewanee, Tennessee.[56] Stuck wrote his former professor Benjamin Wiggins, describing Hap as "true as steel, an influence for good in any environment . . . a devout Churchman and as earnest and consistent as I have ever known any man to be." Stuck presented his protégé as "indefatigable" and "never happier than when he

[was] doing something for somebody."[57] This portrait that Hudson Stuck drew of Hap at twenty-two held true throughout his life.

Hap planned eventually to enter Sewanee's medical school but began his studies in a bachelor of arts degree program, taking Greek, Latin, math, and English, among other subjects.[58] He immersed himself in campus life and flourished, making friends and endearing himself to faculty and administrators. By the time Hap entered his second year at Sewanee, Stuck was preparing to leave Dallas for missionary work in Alaska. The two envisioned Hap's joining him there as a medical missionary. With Stuck and Alaska bishop Peter Trimble Rowe's encouragement, Hap therefore shifted from the academic to the medical track, with an eye toward completing his medical training as soon as possible.[59]

Stuck lobbied Sewanee administrators for continuing scholarships for Hap while pledging to support his living expenses. During his first year in medical school, Hap volunteered among missions in the Tennessee mountains and spent his vacation there, assisting a physician caring for coal miners. In his final two years at Sewanee, he interned at the Gulf and Ship Island Hospital in Mississippi during breaks from school. There he served as superintendent of a Sunday school and organized and secured a charter for the Brotherhood of St. Andrew, an Episcopal prayer, Bible study, and community outreach organization.[60] As Sunday school superintendent, he reportedly "was honored & loved by all his pupils, and trusted & respected by the Rector."[61]

Meanwhile, Hap remained active in campus life, in particular competing annually in the school's contest for the prestigious Knight Medal in declamation. In 1906 he performed Kipling's "The Recessional," earning high marks as "one of the best declamations of the evening." That year's competition was reportedly one of the most successful and competitive Knight Medal contests in recent memory. In 1907 judges selected his speech on Kipling's "Young British Soldier" as one of four performances to move on to the finals.[62]

Hap graduated from medical school in October 1907. Although he was not first in his class, his peers chose the amiable young man with a reputation for masterful elocution to give the valedictory speech. Hudson Stuck, who had left Alaska in late August on furlough, arrived at Sewanee

2. Hap at Sewanee. Geoffrey Burke private collection.

in time for the week of festivities. His biographer wrote, "Never was a father prouder of a son than Stuck was of his ward Grafton Burke ('one boy that no one will ever regret befriending') when Hap, as valedictorian, received his medical degree." Hap, in turn, took delight in Stuck's participation in commencement exercises. Stuck reportedly gave a "splendid and eloquent" address. Throughout his visit, people sang Hap's praises, and Stuck commended his protégé, especially for his accomplishments in the liberal arts.[63]

Following his graduation, Hap served a six-month residency at New York's St. Luke's Hospital while also gaining experience at New York Hospital's House of Relief.[64] Among the courses Hap took during his residency was one in eye diseases, having learned that many Alaska

Natives suffered from disease-related blindness.[65] Meanwhile, Stuck continued his travels, raising funds and seeking recruits for the mission work in Alaska.[66]

In January 1908 Alaska's bishop Rowe asked the Episcopal Mission leadership in New York to approve hiring Hap as a medical missionary on the upper Yukon in Alaska. Rowe had struggled for years to find male missionaries, and he had begged the federal government to provide medical care for the peoples of the vast Yukon River drainage. Securing a *medical* missionary in the northern Interior would be a double blessing.[67] That same month, Hap applied to the Episcopal Church's Mission Society for the position of medical missionary on the Yukon River in Alaska. He wrote in his letter of application that he had "long [ago] decided upon volunteer work in Alaska."[68] One of his character references, a professor at Sewanee, wrote that he expected that Hap would "make a most useful man wherever he is for his unselfishness, kindness of heart, desire to do good, and cheerfulness."[69] In late January Hap received his appointment. He would assume the position in July 1908. As a single male medical missionary, he would receive $1,200 a year in salary, along with $500 for medical supplies for the dispensary and other expenses.[70]

That summer, Stuck met Hap in New York, and the two set out for Alaska. During his winter and spring travels, Stuck had raised funds for a power launch that would allow him to travel the rivers of Alaska's vast Interior, which he oversaw as archdeacon.[71] He had the thirty-two-foot gasoline-powered riverboat built in New York to his specifications; its sixteen-inch draft would allow it to move through shallow waters, and its sixteen-horsepower Speedway engine would permit travel between nine and a half and ten miles per hour.[72] Stuck named it the *Pelican* in recognition of Louisiana donors. Stuck, Burke, and the *Pelican* traveled by train across the country and by steamer to Skagway, where they boarded the White Pass and Yukon Railroad to Whitehorse, Yukon Territory. Arthur Wright, Stuck's Dena' trail guide, who had spent the year studying in California, joined them in Seattle; he would resume his position as Stuck's guide and interpreter.[73] At Whitehorse, Yukon Territory, a derrick lifted the *Pelican* and set it into the Yukon River. Stuck, Burke, and Wright boarded the launch and brought it down river, traveling in the first days between Eagle and Circle, perhaps the most picturesque landscape along the Yukon.[74]

On their journey, the men visited Native villages, mining camps, and Episcopal missions, with Stuck holding religious services and Hap treating injuries and ailments.[75] They traveled the Yukon to Tanana in the heart of the northern Interior, then up the Tanana River and back, and then continued southwestward down the Yukon River. The *Pelican*'s shallow draft allowed it to ascend much farther up tributaries than was possible for steamboats. In the coming years, Stuck and his crew would carry mail and reading materials sent by mission friends Outside, delivering them to remote locations throughout the Interior.[76]

Along with the work-related stops, Stuck occasionally paused to visit with friends. He called the Yukon "this most gossipy river" and likely thought himself above such "idle talk," but he appreciated keeping abreast of people's comings and goings and especially of any activities that would cause him concern.[77] One of his best non-Native friends in the region was Bill Yanert, a German immigrant whom he judged to be "the most intelligent man on the Yukon River" and who was well versed on northern and Arctic issues.[78] Yanert had taken part in expeditions that mapped large regions of Alaska's Interior during the Klondike gold rush. After retiring in 1903, he built a home at a place in the Yukon Flats he named Purgatory. There, together with his brother Herman, he lived a subsistence lifestyle, carving, writing poetry, and painting in his spare time.[79] The brothers operated a woodyard, where steamboats regularly stopped to replenish their fuel supply.[80]

On September 17, with freezing temperatures threatening to hinder their progress, Stuck, Burke, and Wright turned up the Koyukuk River, planning to carry needed supplies the 260 miles to Allakaket and St. John's-in-the-Wilderness. They aimed to leave the *Pelican* there for the winter and return to Fort Yukon by dogsled. In the weeks that followed, Hap experienced a harrowing initiation to winter travel in northern Alaska. The journey they envisioned as five days of relative comfort instead stretched into a several-week ordeal requiring grueling labor under life-threatening conditions and resulting in serious injuries.[81] The episode ended, however, more happily than Hap could have imagined.

Having traveled perhaps two hundred miles up the Koyukuk, the men awoke on September 23 to ice on the river. After several days of waiting in vain for the ice to melt, as it often did after the first freeze, the men pulled the four-ton launch out of the water with the help of a kindly prospector, unloaded and cached various supplies, and braced the boat for winter. For two weeks they waited for colder weather to produce safe travel conditions while helping their new friend complete his cabin. Then Stuck, Burke, and Wright began trudging toward Allakaket with a sledge they borrowed from the prospector loaded with 250 pounds of supplies.[82] One walked ahead to test the ice with an axe, one pulled the sledge with a harness over his shoulders and ice creepers on his feet, and the third pushed from behind.[83] Thin, unreliable, "rubbery" ice and overflow that welled up over the ice drenched their feet, legs, and supplies, threatening disaster. At times they had to carve a pathway among jagged ice chunks upended by the force of the yet unfrozen current. Hap fell during one such interval and injured his knee on sharp ice, which left him limping painfully for the rest of the journey. Meanwhile, rheumatism and a toothache plagued Arthur. After they had battled these conditions for four days, a Native couple welcomed them into their cabin to rest and allowed them to hang their wet clothes and bedding to dry.[84]

Two days later they proceeded with the help of William, a local Dena' man, and his dog, which greatly eased their labor in pulling the sled but did nothing to relieve the harrowing environmental conditions. At Arctic City, twelve miles short of Allakaket, the most arduous portion of the journey ended. Stuck retrieved the sled dogs he had boarded there, fully relieving the men of pulling the sled. They set out in the morning with confidence that they would reach the mission that afternoon. But slushy snow atop overflow forced them back to Arctic City. The following day Stuck and William again struck out for Allakaket on snowshoes. They arrived that afternoon. Hap and Arthur followed two days later with the dogs, sled, and supplies.[85]

Hap arrived at the mission with a severely injured knee, a frostbitten face, and a miserable cold. After two days under the women's care, his voice had improved and his face had healed, revealing a charming Texas drawl, self-deprecating humor, and handsome features— bright red mustache and all, as Clara later recalled. The men spent six weeks at the mission putting finishing touches on the building as Hap treated patients and recuperated himself and Stuck gave daily religious instruction to both Iñupiat and Dena'. Meanwhile, the two women made their visitors feel at home. Clara fed them well, her culinary skills having advanced so far that Hap showered her with praise, once declaring, "Turn Miss Heintz loose with a can-opener, and it's like eating at the Ritz!" To her delight, he even forced the archdeacon to concede that she was a great cook. Hap provided dinner-table entertainment with tales of the summer's mishaps: the *Pelican*'s frequent breakdowns and their harrowing journey up the Koyukuk. His storytelling, which would become legendary in later years, transformed the series of near tragedies into a comedy of errors.[86]

During their visit, Stuck baptized eighteen congregants after preparing them for two weeks and after they individually assured him that they understood the commitment they were making. He worked with the choir boys, helped settle marital and other disputes, and made a citizen's arrest of a combative man and sent him upriver to the mining camp Coldfoot.[87]

Although the archdeacon could be gruff with non-Native adults, he doted on children and charmed them with his antics and roughhousing, his love of teaching them in the classroom, and the candy he regularly doled out from his pockets. On this visit he seized on a set of playing cards with pictures of animals that Clara used as a teaching tool and delighted the children, especially the boys, by giving them animal nicknames. They reciprocated by calling him Elephunk.[88] He cavorted so energetically with the boys that the deaconess declared that they deemed him "the most wonderful man in the world."[89] Stuck himself described the boys as delightfully rough-and-tumble and bubbling with spirit. They would throw themselves from the riverbank headfirst into snow drifts and roll into balls and hurl themselves down the toboggan trail. "How they do love the snow!" he wrote. "How they roll in it, and bury themselves in it, and wallow in it, and come up with the blood flushing rich beneath their dark skins!"[90]

Meanwhile, as Clara accompanied Hap on his medical rounds, she noticed his gentleness and empathy for his patients. When a six-year-old boy who crawled, dragging a twisted leg behind him, caught Hap's eye, he examined the boy, recognized a congenitally contracted ligament, and, with the parents' permission, surgically repaired the boy's leg. He treated many other maladies, earning the gratitude of both the Iñupiaq and Dena' communities. A month after the visitors departed, the boy whose leg Hap had treated ran and played with the other children, a subtle limp the only indication of his previous impediment.[91]

Clara and Hap found so many common interests that they often passed the evenings in conversation, well after the deaconess had gone to bed and the archdeacon had retired to the guest house to write. Clara had warmed to Stuck by now, although she still found his brusque demeanor off-putting. During one of their conversations, Hap said of his mentor, "Oh I know the Deak gets snappish, and sometimes he's downright unbearable. You've got to know him to realize what a great chap he is." From that moment on, Clara took a kindlier view toward Stuck.[92]

During the final week of the men's stay, Tobuk, the Iñupiaq chief whose grandson's leg Hap had treated, invited Hap and Clara to a wedding ceremony, a sign of the respect Hap had earned among the people. In accordance with tradition, family members confessed known and unknown misdeeds, as did the couple, who then forgave one another. Much merriment accompanied these confessions, but the purpose was solemn. With the airing and forgiving of any failings, the couple and their families could look forward to a harmonious future. Clara later recalled that as she and Hap walked back to the mission that evening, he told her that he found the peace-making ritual in the ceremony "philosophically and psychologically sound."[93]

By the end of his stay, Clara had lost her heart to Hap. At one point during the visit, he told her that he had considered taking a vow of celibacy because he aimed to remain a medical missionary in Alaska for the rest of his life, and he could not imagine burdening a wife and family with such a lifestyle. Clara winced at his disclosure. Having learned of his unhappy childhood, she felt that he deserved a home and family.[94] Later, when his knee injury flared up again and Miss Carter insisted that he lie down on the cot, Clara asked him whether at times he regretted coming to Alaska. He looked her straight in the eyes and said, "No, I'm glad I came. Especially to Allakaket." He never again mentioned vows of celibacy. As the men's departure day neared, Clara took heart in his confession that he would miss her.[95]

As the men prepared to leave, Clara and the deaconess packed food for their journey, including homemade doughnuts and fruitcake, ideal trail food because they would not freeze solidly.[96] As they left the mission, traveling by way of Bettles and other mining camps toward Fort Yukon, where Hap would settle in as medical missionary, he repeatedly turned back to wave. When he blew a kiss, Clara secretly claimed it for herself. Sometime later, a pair of beautifully beaded moccasins arrived from Bettles with a letter containing the underlined words "Miss you very much." Clara immediately set to work on a moosehide hind sack for Hap's sled, which she planned to bead elaborately with his initials.[97]

2

Fort Yukon, Courtship, and Marriage, 1908–10

Stuck, Burke, and Wright arrived at Fort Yukon just before Christmas 1908. On the trail, Hap had marked his twenty-sixth birthday. Much feasting, revelry, and dancing surrounded Christmas at Fort Yukon. The community celebrated the New Year even more boisterously, following traditions the Scottish factors of the Hudson's Bay Company had established decades before, according to Stuck. Early in the morning, community members typically circulated from home to home shaking hands, and the women kissed one another. In 1908 the local men visited the mission to shake hands with Stuck and Burke and wish them a happy New Year. The local women did the same shortly thereafter. Much noise accompanied these morning rituals—hundreds of rounds of ammunition fired, shouting, and bell ringing, and of course, barking dogs joined in the clamor. Those cooking for the feasts slept little if at all. At daylight, villagers typically gathered at the chief's house and tossed him into the air, after which he made a speech.[1]

On Hap's first New Year at Fort Yukon, the people threw him into the air by his hands and feet to welcome him. Then the local boys came by the mission house with a blanket to collect offerings for the potluck. Hours of feasting ensued, followed by outdoor sports, mainly a game involving tossing a large moosehide ball with the hair on it and kicking the ball through a goal formed by two wooden stakes. Rifle shots signaled the evening feast, after which the people dressed in their finery and proceeded to the hall, where fiddlers provided the music for dancing.[2] According to John Fredson, who spent much of his childhood at the mission, the people danced "all kinds of dances—white people's dances, Han Gwich'in dances, and Eskimo dances. We dance all night, until morning comes. Some people sleep in the daytime. After New Year's Day, this goes on in this way for a week," he explained. "When all the money we made in the fall, and all the food, is gone, we leave Fort Yukon" to hunt and return to traplines.[3]

Soon after the New Year, Stuck and Wright left for their winter rounds of the Episcopal missions by dogsled, heading east toward Circle. Hap ran a mile with them, in the Alaska tradition, before turning back to Fort Yukon.[4] Stuck and Wright would return to Fort Yukon for a few days in early February before continuing westward on their winter circuit. On this departure, assistant superintendent of schools George Boulter traveled with them with his own dogsled. Perhaps inspired by the pleasant weather, Hap accompanied them with a third sled, traveling eighteen miles in four hours before he turned back.[5]

In one of his first initiatives, Hap enlisted David Wallis, a Gwich'in man of mixed ancestry, to teach him the local Dena' (Gwich'in) language—Dinjii Zhuh—a clear sign of Hap's commitment to Fort Yukon. An Anglican missionary couple had adopted Wallis and sent him to Canada to be educated. When he returned, his fluency in both Gwich'in and English made him a valued interpreter, considered one of the best, if not *the* best, in Alaska.[6] Wallis and his wife, Martha, had an arranged marriage, a common practice at the time. Her family had reportedly experienced starvation when she was a young child, and only she and her aunt had survived. She later converted to Christianity and became involved in Episcopal mission life at Fort Yukon.[7] David Wallis was a long-term, highly valued mission employee who filled multiple roles beyond interpreting. Over the years, Hap would rely on him increasingly, especially when Stuck was away and after his death.

Hap quickly earned the friendship of the Gwich'in people, who nicknamed him "Sutchah," or younger brother.[8] He developed deep attachments within the community, owing to his appreciation of the people and landscape and his engagement in his work. In spring 1909 he expressed his admiration for the "everlasting enterprising ability of the people, and their resourcefulness." He marveled at their ability to run fifteen to twenty miles a day. The role of the runner, in fact, was critical in carrying urgent messages from one village or camp to another. "Nothing daunts them, and they go on with their undertakings with such determination and resolute courage that a more admirable demonstration cannot be found anywhere," he wrote.[9]

Although Fort Yukon had not been a traditional Indigenous settlement, by about the mid-nineteenth century, when the Hudson's Bay Company established a post there, one large extended family of Di'hąįį or Neet'saii Gwich'in lived in the area, having migrated eastward owing to war and famine.[10] By 1908, according to Hudson Stuck, Fort Yukon was the largest Native settlement on the Yukon. Gwich'in who migrated in subsistence rounds throughout the region swelled the population during the Christmas–New Year's season and around the Fourth of July, when they gathered there to celebrate and to trade furs for ammunition, "grub," and other Western commodities. White trappers in the region, many of them married to Native women, did the same. Fort Yukon thus became the most important fur trading market in the northeast Interior, as well as the site to purchase some of the best beadwork along the Yukon.[11]

Salmon constituted the Gwich'in's day-to-day staple food. In the first years of the twentieth century, the fish wheel came into increased use for harvesting the year's supply of fish along the Alaska portion of the Yukon River and its tributaries.[12] Working day and night, they were highly efficient, provided that the fish were running. They required one or two men to build and position them, however, so people continued to use dip nets, poles with hooks, and weirs, depending on the circumstances.[13] In July each year, Dena' families scattered to their fish camps. For weeks they would harvest, cut, dry, and smoke as many salmon as possible. They tied the dried fish in bundles and stored it in fish caches, high above the reach of dogs and wild animals, to supply food throughout the winter for themselves and their dogs. The time spent in the open air restored the health and vitality of many an ailing person.[14] The fish camps lent a picturesque quality to the landscape along the rivers, which otherwise could stretch for many miles without noteworthy variation. Racks of dull red salmon multiplied as the season progressed, creating a mélange of color amid the white tents, the painted canoes and boats, and the women's bright silk handkerchiefs and colored cotton garments.[15]

Despite their heavy reliance on fish, the Gwich'in identified most strongly with caribou. Historically, they had tended to hunt the animals

3. Fish wheel on the Yukon River. Rivenburg, Lawyer and Cora Photograph Album, #1994-70-99, APRCA, University of Alaska Fairbanks.

using a surround or corral method for large hunts, but they also used bow and arrow and later, rifles. Caribou migrated yearly through Alaska's eastern Interior between the Yukon and Tanana Rivers, traveling through Gwich'in territory to their breeding grounds on the north slope of the Brooks Range. The Gwich'in also harvested moose, Dall sheep, black bears, hares, muskrats, and beavers for food, while using the furs of caribou, fox, and other animals for clothing. During the winter months, nearly all families in the region trapped fur-bearing animals, especially muskrat and beaver, after the cash economy developed. They would spend months out on their traplines, which could be as far as a hundred miles from the village and could cover one hundred miles. The trapper surveyed the line frequently by dogsled, collecting the animals caught. Thousands of rabbits inhabited the spruce and willow forests in the area, and willow grouse, spruce hens, and ptarmigans filled out the people's diets year-round. During the darkest time of the winter, Fort Yukon had only about two and a half hours of sunlight, but a rather lengthy dawn and twilight effectively extended the day. Moreover, on clear nights, the moon provided significant light. In springtime the people hunted various migratory birds, and in both spring and early summer, ducks supplied the staple food at Fort Yukon before the fish began to run. Animal populations fluctuated, however, and hunger and starvation threatened from time to time.[16] Prior to contact with non-Native settlers in the region, many commodities, including guns, ammunition, axes, knives, needles, beads, and tobacco, had entered the region, and Dena' had incorporated them into their lifeways.[17]

After four years based in Fairbanks, Stuck had chosen Fort Yukon as his home base and envisioned it as the center of the Episcopal Church's work in the northern Interior, owing to the community's strategic position within the Yukon Flats or Gwichyaa Zhee region. By 1908 the Episcopal Church operated missions in the Interior at Anvik, Tanana, Rampart, Circle City, Fort Yukon, Eagle, Fairbanks, Nenana, and Chena. Stuck may have avoided headquartering at Tanana, the traditional meeting place and major crossroads in the central northern Interior, owing to the strong influence of several band headmen, or chiefs, in the region and to what he considered the negative influence of Fort Gibbon. At Fort Yukon he foresaw a church, a hospital, and an industrial day school. He hoped the mission could have a positive influence on the region. Stuck lamented the fact that Fort Yukon had become a magnet for whiskey peddlers and drifters. With almost no law enforcement along the Yukon River in Alaska, law breakers had little to fear. Stuck looked wistfully toward the Yukon Territory, where Northwest Mounted Police patrolled the upper Yukon River with dog teams in winter and police boats in summer.[18]

At the mission and in the Native community, Hap worked to improve health and sanitary conditions. As the only physician within more than eight hundred miles along the Yukon River to treat Alaska Natives, he served Natives and non-Natives from a much broader region than the community of Fort Yukon (although most of his patients were Native). He toured the massive region by dogsled in winter to check on outlying individuals and treat ailments and injuries. Episcopal congregations in New York and North Carolina provided his medical and surgical supplies.[19]

During his first winter at Fort Yukon, Hap established the St. Stephen's Boys' Club to corral and focus the energies of adolescent boys, promote friendship, encourage their practice in speaking English (during the gatherings, they spoke a mixture of Gwich'in and English), and teach them basic rules of etiquette. Members included Lot and Johnny Fred (later Fredson)—president and vice president, respectively—and fifteen other boys. They met Friday nights to play games, conduct gymnasium drills, and sing and dance, accompanied by Hap on the harmonica. Singing was their favorite activity. They would memorize lively songs, although the lyrics often puzzled them. They also pored over photographs in magazines or from Hap's own collection for hours, peppering him with questions.[20] Hap later established a men's club that met once a week.[21] When the archdeacon was away, he led worship services for the non-Native residents of Fort Yukon. William Loola, who had been ordained deacon in 1904 but whom people referred to as Reverend Loola, led services, including Sunday school, in Gwich'in.[22] He traveled throughout the region to minister to the people.[23]

Loola, whose father was a powerful and respected shaman, had first met the Anglican archdeacon Robert McDonald when he was a young boy living in and around Fort Yukon. Several years later, Loola began working for the archdeacon, traveling with him along the Yukon River and its tributaries in both the Yukon and Alaska, visiting both Native and mining camps. The two developed a close relationship, and Loola came to love and deeply respect McDonald. For several years he and the archdeacon collaborated intensely in translating the Bible, the prayer book, and the hymnal into Gwich'in. Following McDonald's departure, Loola served the region as a catechist until Bishop Rowe ordained him as deacon in 1904.[24]

A corner of the old North American Transportation and Trading (NAT&T) Company building served as Hap's dispensary and "surgery." In that tiny dark corner, he dressed wounds, treated illnesses, and performed such surgeries as removing tumors and treating traumatic injuries. During the darkest time of the year, he generally scheduled surgeries between noon and two o'clock because daylight permitted better vision than oil lamps.[25] In his first year, on an average day, Hap saw ten patients at the dispensary and made five cabin visits. His first such visit left a memorable impression; he checked on an elderly Native woman with a fever, whom he found cozily wrapped in muskrat skins. His first white patient was an elderly U.S. mail carrier with necrosis of the scalp from a long-neglected abscess. Among the most frequent complaints of non-Natives Hap treated was "stomach trouble," which he attributed to "eating canned goods for months and months" while spending their days doing physically demanding work, such as woodchopping, carrying the mail by dogsled, and trapping. Poorly preserved foods contributed to digestive distress among both Natives and non-Natives. Hap regularly resorted to his stomach pump. Sometimes stomach trouble required surgery.[26]

Among both the Native and white populations, Hap stressed hygiene and sanitation measures. In the Gwich'in community, cramped, poorly ventilated permanent dwellings contributed to eye irritation and disease and respiratory illnesses. Such health risks had caused little concern among Dena' when they moved about frequently, slept in tents, and spent most of their time in the open air. After settling in Fort Yukon, accumulated human and animal waste outside dwellings became breeding grounds for disease. Throughout the winter, such waste and carcasses froze quickly, and fresh blankets of snow maintained a pristine appearance in the village. In spring, however, warm weather exposed the filth and invited disease. Poor health conditions tended to linger until early July, when families departed for their fish camps, where they lived in the open air.[27] Within the first months of his arrival in Fort Yukon, Hap surveyed conditions within both the white and Native communities, calling attention to health hazards. In spring, as the snow melted, he had a sign posted in the white area regarding the danger posed by animal carcasses, and he designated a dumping ground distanced from living areas and water sources. Among the Gwich'in, he, and later Clara, visited house to house.[28]

Less than half a century before, Western science had recognized germ theory and the role of germs in the spread of disease.[29] Medical professionals and other missionaries, who knew that contaminated water, fecal matter, and bodily fluids spread disease, now prioritized teaching hygiene and sanitation practices to Alaska Natives, whose lives and lifeways had been profoundly affected by the arrival of non-Native migrants into the region. Among Alaska Natives, both Burke and Stuck observed a distressing fatalism, perhaps owing to the extraordinarily high death rates in the previous decades from tuberculosis, epidemics of influenza, measles, pneumonia, and diphtheria, and other diseases brought in by migrants. For instance, in summer 1904, twenty-three children at Fort Yukon had died of diphtheria. Death rates from the disease were high all along the Yukon River; by 1906 the epidemic had spread to the more remote Chandalar mining district north of Fort Yukon.[30] Missionaries throughout Alaska made regular rounds in villages to encourage hygiene and sanitary practices. Whenever he was at his home base in Fort Yukon, Stuck preached from the church pulpit on sanitation and hygiene, with a dose of germ theory, and urged the people to follow Dr. Burke's guidance on the topic. Sanitation and hygiene concerns were not unique to Alaska. Stuck had much difficulty in leading such a campaign in Dallas just a few years earlier and had heard of such crusades elsewhere.[31]

Hap's experiences in late winter and spring 1909 illustrated how well he was acclimating to the life and work of a medical missionary in northern Alaska. In the weeks following the Christmas and New Year's celebrations, the Gwich'in gradually returned to their traplines or to hunting. At St. Stephen's, Hap, suffering from a worsening toothache, had been applying various remedies, including carbolic acid that blistered his mouth. Finally, in desperation, he tried to extract the tooth, only to shatter it. With no choice but to see a dentist, he set out in early March by dogsled for Fairbanks. On the first evening, after a twenty-mile run, he encountered a group of twelve Natives who were moose hunting. Upon greeting them in their tents, he found that they had their hymnals with them, and Old Moses was reading the Bible in Gwich'in. They asked for a service, so Hap huddled with them in one tent and gave a short sermon, after which they sang several hymns heartily.[32]

At Circle, Hap treated a Signal Corps youth who had burned his eyes with kerosene. Between Circle and Fairbanks, he stopped at four roadhouses, where he rendered medical aid. In Fairbanks a dentist extracted the remainder of Hap's painful tooth under anesthesia. The nurse reported to Stuck, who was in Fairbanks at the time, that upon coming out of the influence of the ether, Hap declared, "Paregorically speaking, from an antiphlogistine standpoint," a stark departure from his usual style of communication. Following the dental surgery, Hap saw a physician about his knee injury from the previous fall, which had flared up on the trek to Fairbanks. The doctor diagnosed a displaced ligament and ordered two weeks of rest and massage. Hospitalized with his leg in plaster of Paris but too energetic to lie in bed, Hap treated other patients, including one for acute alcoholism. He also led Lenten services and taught Sunday school at the adjacent St. Matthew's Church while the pastor was called away.[33]

On his return journey to Fort Yukon, medical crises at Circle City kept him four days in the former gold-rush town. Patients included "a very sick woman," an imprisoned individual, a clerk of the Northern Commercial (NC) Company, a woman in labor, a Native man whose hand injury required suturing, and a man with chronic venereal disease whom Hap brought back to Fort Yukon for further treatment. He and Hap stayed over at Half Way Roadhouse, forty miles from Fort Yukon, on Easter, and Hap held Easter services for a small appreciative group—a Gwich'in family, the innkeeper's family, and the patient who traveled with him. Hap and his patient reached Fort Yukon the following day.[34] Missionary teacher Florence Langdon and Reverend Loola had held Lenten and Easter services for the whites and Natives at Fort Yukon in the church decorated with pussy willows gathered by a Native congregant.[35]

Meanwhile, the people at Allakaket had been near starvation in late winter owing to a rare combination of circumstances—an abysmal fish run the prior summer followed by a fall and winter with scarce game in the area. Most of their dogs had died, and the people had no choice but to kill others. While at Tanana on his winter rounds, Stuck had learned of the crisis through a letter from Deaconess Carter, who estimated that one hundred people were in dire circumstances. Stuck and assistant superintendent of schools Boulter discussed the matter, agreed on the urgency of the need, and settled on a plan to appeal to both the Bureau of Education and Bishop Rowe for relief funds. Boulter wired Washington DC asking for $2,000 in aid, and Stuck wired the bishop, asking for backup.[36] The Bureau of Education approved aid for area residents, a rare occurrence. Stuck and Wright carried a fully loaded dogsled of relief supplies from Tanana to Allakaket on their regular spring visiting rounds.[37] Following the ancient Tanana-Allakaket trail north-northwestward saved them many miles and days of travel over the summer route that took them about 200 miles down the Yukon River from Tanana to the mouth of the Koyukuk River and then 260 miles up the Koyukuk to Allakaket.

The men spent five to six weeks, including Easter, at St. John's-in-the-Wilderness, waiting for spring break-up, when they could release the *Pelican* from her winter mooring and bring her down to the Yukon River for summer rounds. Stuck filled his days teaching English grammar lessons to the school children, holding daily hour-long choir practices, and giving Bible lessons with adults and children. On Sundays the Iñupiaq families came for church services in the morning and stayed all day. Natives from downriver at Arctic City and upriver at South Fork came as well. After the long morning church service—extended by the double translation of all Stuck's words—the people ate their lunches, which they had brought with them, and then played football on the frozen river for an hour. Following Sunday school they again played football for two or three hours. After evening services the football games continued well into the evening. Elders were among the most avid players. Even Clara participated enthusiastically.[38]

Back in Fort Yukon at St. Stephen's Mission after his trek to Fairbanks, Hap resumed the routine he had established: house calls, office hours, and meeting with the St. Stephen's Boys' Club on Friday evenings. On Sunday afternoons he held services for the children, and in the evenings he held church services for non-Natives, with between one and ten people attending, while William Loola led services for the Gwich'in.[39]

In his June annual report to Bishop Rowe, Hap reported 310 house calls among the Gwich'in, 112 patients seen at the dispensary, 83 treatments, and 121 surgical interventions in his first six months at St. Stephen's. He had treated thirty white patients. Forty-one children were enrolled in Sunday school. St. Stephen's Boys' Club members now numbered twenty-two, ages nine to sixteen.[40] Bishop Rowe wrote of Hap's valuable impact in his annual report for 1908–9: "It means very much to our work to have a medical missionary free to go up and down this great stretch of the Yukon, ministering to those in need, spiritually as well as physically."[41] Hap had won the affection, gratitude, and trust of Natives and non-Natives along the Yukon.

By summer 1909 Stuck sensed that Hap's arrival had sparked a turn-around at Fort Yukon. In an article in the Episcopal Church's *Spirit of Missions*, he wrote hopefully of the changes wrought by Hap's work and influence, as well as that of the missionary Florence Langdon and school-teacher Anne Cady. New buildings had replaced the "wretched cabins that for so long have done duty as mission buildings."[42] In the mission home, the two women cared for six children ranging in age from three to sixteen years, all orphans or "half-orphans" without others to care for them. Hap had much better clinic space in the new mission home than in the old NAT&T Company building. Miners and prospectors working in the region who came through Fort Yukon could enjoy a few hours in the mission's reading room that the women stocked with books and magazines sent in by mission friends from Outside. They gave the men bundles of the coveted magazines and newspapers with reports from the outside world to carry back to their remote work sites.[43] Miss Langdon's use of moral suasion had secured promises from the four white traders in the community to refrain from trading and selling alcohol to the Native population, in accordance with the law. Stuck noted that for the first time in years, the Christmas holidays had not been marred by alcohol abuse in the Native community.[44] The children reportedly loved coming to school. Even when temperatures in the unfinished log church that first served as a schoolhouse were below freezing on extremely cold days, they arrived hap-pily each morning. Reverend Loola, who was "past middle age" by now, attended the mission school in Fort Yukon, along with the children, per-haps to improve his English and to set a good example for the children.[45]

Despite these hopeful signs at Fort Yukon, serious problems continued to beset Alaska Natives, as newcomers pursued their interests unhin-dered by law enforcement. Bishop Rowe wrote an anguish-filled letter to Bishop Arthur Lloyd, president of the Episcopal Board of Missions, in June 1909 describing demoralized conditions among Alaska's Native peoples, especially in the Interior. Exploitation and alcohol abuse driven by non-Natives contributed to poverty and disease all along the Yukon. "This sad havoc proceeds apace and there seems to be no check to it any-where." At Circle City the teacher had "waged a splendid fight against the prevailing corruption, has even appealed to Washington, but what is this one woman against the many and especially when the commissioner and the Deputy Marshall are themselves offenders." At Rampart a Native woman had been sexually assaulted while her husband was away. "The story is the same everywhere," Rowe wrote. "The Government owes it to these people . . . to defend and protect them from the evils which white men ply among them." Yet placement of law enforcement officers in every community would not have solved the problems. Missionaries had brought many cases with "absolute proof in their hands," only to be met with "general dislike, hostility." No jury would convict "a white man of selling liquor or of immorality against an Indian," Rowe explained.[46] Throughout their years in Alaska, Archdeacon Stuck, Hap, and Clara challenged the frontier culture that promoted such attitudes and behaviors.[47]

In July 1909 Hap traveled to Nenana on the Tanana River to hold a clinic and assist in the work at St. Mark's Mission. Late that month Clara broke a tooth, forcing her to seek dental care in Fairbanks. Traveling on the steamer *Midhope*, she stopped in several communities en route, including Nenana. As she walked along the path toward St. Mark's Mission house on a Sunday morning, she heard children's voices singing and soon saw Miss Annie Farthing, the missionary she had heard so much about, through the window leading services. Suddenly, a man's voice startled her, calling out, "Miss Heintz!" and Hap and the entire congregation poured out of the church, midsong, to greet her. Hap and Clara had only an hour together before the ship's whistle blew signaling its departure, but they looked forward to a longer visit when she returned from Fairbanks to Allakaket.[48] A week later she and Hap found time for a lengthier visit, thanks to Miss Farthing. Sensing that they wanted to be alone, she sent the couple on an errand to purchase cooking oil at the town of Nenana, three miles away. Hap and Clara returned from the five-hour round-trip walk engaged to be married.[49] Stuck, who also was at Nenana at the time, wrote in his diary that night, "With much beating around the bush [Hap] managed to inform me that he and Miss Heintz were engaged to be married! He had proposed and been accepted this afternoon. I did not expect it so soon. She is an admirable girl . . . good as gold and with excellent taste & abilities. I am pleased that the boy has done so well."[50] On the last boat of the summer, a diamond engagement ring arrived at

Allakaket from Tiffany's in New York. The package also contained an ivory-inlaid gold cross for Clara Carter. Hap had purchased the gold for Clara's ring and for Deaconess Carter's cross at Chandalar on his return trek from Allakaket to Fort Yukon the previous winter. He had made his decision after their first meeting.[51]

Clara's acceptance of Hap's marriage proposal entailed a far more momentous decision than Hap's. In following his mentor to the far north, Hap had made a lifelong commitment to medical missionary work among Alaska Native peoples, and he now sought a life partner to share in that work. Clara, despite having recently extended her one year of service to two, fully envisioned returning to her family in California. In accepting Hap's proposal she was devoting her life to mission work in Alaska.

In fall 1909 the government provided a teaching assistant, Arthur Wright's sister Celia, for the day school, allowing Clara to organize afternoon activities for the children throughout the week. On Mondays they brought their soiled clothes to be laundered, on Tuesdays they ironed the clothing, and on Wednesdays they mended as needed. Thursday afternoons were devoted to Junior Auxiliary Day, with various activities to support the mission, and on Fridays, each child had a bath in a large metal tub.[52] The children's washing and bathing routine inspired the whole community to adopt such a regimen.[53]

At Fort Yukon a new government schoolhouse, including teacher's residence, opened in October 1909, a "first-class one in every way," as described by assistant superintendent Boulter, who oversaw the construction of this and two other schools that year. He had hired many local Natives on the construction crew, boosting the local economy.[54] A kerfuffle between Archdeacon Stuck and Boulter over a "huge hideous" twenty-inch by eight-foot sign on the schoolhouse reading "Government Public School, U.S. Bureau of Education" highlighted the tensions that sometimes arose between church and Bureau of Education personnel. Stuck appreciated the new school and supported its construction on mission property, but he chafed at the obtrusive statement of U.S. government authority on mission grounds. The U.S. flag flying outside the building "would inform the dullest passer-by" of the building's ownership and purpose, he wrote Boulter, noting that mission personnel avoided labeling

4. Weekly bath at the mission, St. John's-in-the-Wilderness. Walter and Lillian Phillips Photograph Collection, #1985-72-144, APRCA, University of Alaska Fairbanks.

buildings on mission property. He would accept a modestly sized sign over the door, but such "monstrosities," he wrote, "vexed my soul."[55] Although the two saw eye to eye on many issues, they differed on certain policies and practices, especially the government's English-only policy, and from time to time, each man's sense of responsibility toward Alaska Natives led to feelings of resentment that the other intruded on his domain. Yet they maintained civil relations with one another, sometimes traveling together by dogsled, for instance, and Stuck would ferry Boulter from one place to another on the *Pelican*.[56]

The national government assigned responsibility for Alaska Natives' welfare to the Bureau of Education. Thus, in addition to constructing and funding Native schools, the bureau dedicated some resources to Native health care. In 1909 it employed physicians in eight communities. Their duties included instructing school children and community members in sanitation and hygiene and traveling within surrounding areas to teach prevention and treat illness. The bureau provided teachers with basic medical kits and instructed them to treat minor illnesses and accidents at the schools and within their communities, but few had medical training. In 1909 the bureau operated seventy-eight schools in Alaska, including the new school at Fort Yukon, and employed eighty-nine teachers. The bureau allocated $200,000 for Alaska Native education that year, a woefully inadequate sum considering that this Department of Education funding accounted for the U.S. government's entire expenditures on Alaska Natives.[57]

The Christmas season brought Natives and non-Natives back into Fort Yukon from their traplines and hunting rounds. In the two weeks preceding Christmas, Dena' from the Porcupine and the Chandalar Rivers and from Birch Creek and Circle City swelled the Native population in Fort Yukon to over three hundred. The mission played a central role in community Christmas activities. Mission personnel made gifts and filled gift bags with candy for the ten children who lived in the mission home, as well as for every Native and non-Native person in Fort Yukon. After opening their stockings filled with toys on Christmas morning, the mission children played happily all day. The Native community gathered at 11:00 a.m. for church services in Gwich'in, with parts translated from English. At 6:00 p.m. the whole community gathered around the Christmas tree in the church. Mr. Davenport, the schoolteacher, played Santa Claus, distributing a gift and bag of candy to each person, after which the children sang Christmas carols.[58]

Stuck and Arthur Wright spent Christmas 1909 at Allakaket.[59] Staying from December 14 to January 3, they brightened the Christmas and New Year's season immensely. Cold weather had arrived early that year, and temperatures fluctuated wildly, with −60°F one day, +16° the next, and +28° with a blinding snowstorm the following day. Soon thereafter the mercury plummeted to −54° under clear skies and bright moonlight. Arriving while school was still in session allowed Stuck a favorite indulgence—visiting the classroom and assisting with teaching. Seeing the children thriving and learning that twenty-three babies had been born in the previous two years while only one had died, confirmed the value of the mission work.[60] Prior to the mission's establishment, about 50 percent of children in the region died in infancy, according to Stuck.[61]

Kobuk River Iñupiat and Koyukuk River Dena' traveled from far and near to attend Christmas services and activities—150 in all, Stuck estimated. They listened intently as the dual interpreters told the story of the nativity, over and over again, "morning and night, week day and Christmas Day and Sunday, during the whole season," he reported. One and all took delight in the potlatch, the Native dancing, and the colorful "fire-balloons" Stuck had ordered from Outside to be released into the air.[62] The children shouted with glee as they opened their stockings filled with treats, and young and old enjoyed the traditional football game on the river, although this year, the weather detracted from outdoor sport activities in general.[63]

The mission reportedly stood in high esteem with most of the non-Natives in the region, owing to Deaconess Carter's efforts on behalf of their health and well-being. She had traveled to Wright City, a mining camp, to assist a white woman in childbirth. There and at Nolan Creek, Stuck "heard her praises sung by everyone." Residents of mining camps Stuck visited en route from Fort Yukon to Allakaket had sent gifts for the mission, including a quarter of beef and a twenty-five-pound box of candy made by a former confectioner who owned a roadhouse in the mining district. Miners at the various camps between Fort Yukon and Allakaket reportedly appreciated Stuck's yearly visits as well. The whole adult populations of Coldfoot and Wright City attended worship services, and a large proportion of those at Nolan Creek did so. Stuck wrote that he had never been "more pleased with the interest displayed."[64]

Bishop Rowe frequently received requests to establish churches in the mining camps from white men who "understand what it means in any community to have the presence of the Christian Church," as he expressed it. Such men knew of the Episcopal Church's hospitals, reading rooms, and other works and hoped for such amenities in their camps and communities. Rowe anticipated that appeals would increase. With requests coming from Native communities as well, the Episcopal Mission Society could not keep up with demand. A primary impediment to expanding the mission work was the difficulty in recruiting men, ordained pastors. "Were it not for the women, God bless them, who are doing the work of men," the bishop wrote, "many of our Missions would be closed." He noted with some irony that "there seems to be no difficulty for men to come to Alaska and face all sorts of hardships to search for wealth, but the sign of such a spirit on the part of young men to search for souls seems lacking."[65]

In early February 1910 a toothache sent Hap to Fort Gibbon near Tanana for dental care, giving him an excuse to return by way of Allakaket. The journey provided harrowing lessons in the perils of winter travel. The archdeacon and Arthur had taken the strongest team of dogs on their winter rounds, which left Hap with his small sled and just four dogs, two shy of a solid team for such a long journey. The inexperienced fourteen-year-old Lot accompanied him as trail guide. Initially, they made good progress as they followed the mail route. Travel became difficult, however, when they had to diverge from the worn path. Lot snowshoed ahead to break trail and to urge the dogs to run faster, a common practice. He neglected, however, to look back to ensure that his travel partner and the dogs were keeping up. Meanwhile, Hap, who had been running behind the sled to ease the dogs' burden, grew tired and jumped on the runners to rest, which slowed the dogs' pace further. As the mercury dropped to $-50°$, Hap's feet became painfully cold, and the dogs grew increasingly tired. Eventually they stopped. Lot reached Stevens Village, confident that Hap was not far behind. When hours passed and he failed to arrive, two trappers set out with a dog team in search of him. They found Hap lying in his sled, half asleep. Had they waited any longer, he would have frozen to death.[66]

Hap remained two weeks at the trappers' cabin recuperating from the ordeal. When his frostbitten toes showed signs of gangrene, he removed parts of two of them, using a local anesthetic. The decision saved his feet. After he had healed enough to travel, the trappers loaned him two of their dogs to strengthen his team, ensuring a safer journey on to Fort Gibbon.[67] At Rampart, Hap and Lot crossed paths with the archdeacon and Arthur. Stuck was disappointed to learn that Hap intended to divert to Allakaket on his return journey from Fort Gibbon, knowing the need for his presence at Fort Yukon. Yet he wrote in his journal that night, "I cannot be hard on him under the circumstances," alluding to Hap's eagerness to see Clara.[68]

After completing his dental work, Hap struck out from Fort Gibbon toward St. John's-in-the-Wilderness. With six dogs, the journey went more smoothly than his earlier ordeal. Nevertheless, he stumbled into the mission house exhausted, half-frozen, and unrecognizable with his frost-laden fur-trimmed parka hood covering much of his face. The deaconess and Clara backed away from him warily, thinking the visitor must have been drinking. When he threw off his parka hood, they rushed to his aid with warm drinks and food and listened intently as he recounted his experiences on the trail.[69]

Revived by the food and warm drink, Hap took up the mail he had brought from Tanana, letters from Bishop Rowe and Mrs. Heintz. The bishop gave Hap and Clara his blessing and suggested a June wedding, at which he would officiate. Clara's mother, on the other hand, refused her permission for the marriage. Clara was too young, her mother insisted, and the decision clearly had been made hastily. Despite assurances from Bishop Rowe and Archdeacon Stuck of Hap's character, she could not support the notion of Clara's remaining in Alaska indefinitely. Furthermore, preparing for a proper wedding would require much more time. Clara should postpone any wedding plans, she declared, and return home at once. The letter left Clara deflated, but Hap refused to be discouraged. With the deaconess's assurance that the law did not require parental permission to marry, the couple made the most of the visit. Between Clara's teaching duties and Hap's house calls, they planned for the wedding and attended multiple celebrations hosted by community members in their honor. On his return trek to Fort Yukon, Hap checked on miners in the Coldfoot region, who gave him a "poke" with enough gold nuggets for Clara's wedding ring, a bracelet, and a necklace.[70]

Challenges on his return journey delayed Hap's arrival at Fort Yukon until mid-April. After he returned the two dogs he had borrowed, two of the remaining four came down with distemper, which left him stranded at Wright City for a week.[71] Hap learned invaluable Arctic survival lessons that winter. Having the optimal number of dogs and packing enough warm clothing, bedding, and food could mean the difference between life and death.

Following their chance meeting with Hap at Rampart, Stuck and Arthur Wright had continued on to St. Mark's at Nenana. Stuck loved to visit the mission schools, and students looked forward to his visits, knowing that he was always game for roughhousing and that his pockets would be full of candy. St. Mark's Mission and its boarding school exemplified the greatest potential Stuck envisioned for Episcopal mission work in Alaska. Under the loving guidance of Annie Farthing, whose engagement in the work "occupies her whole heart," as Stuck put it, Native children grew, learned, and thrived. The saintly missionary's devotion to the mission work, including her outreach into the community, earned her the abiding affection of the children, her colleagues, and residents of Nenana. Stuck had selected some of St. Mark's students himself—boys and girls such as Walter Harper, whom he encountered on his summer rounds, who showed great promise. With their parents' permission, Stuck delivered the children to the boarding school, where they received a good education that could lead to a bright future. St. Mark's also took in and educated orphans and children whose parents left them there temporarily when they were unable to care for them.[72]

During his February 1910 visit, Stuck wrote of the atmosphere Miss Farthing had created at the mission and its potential: "The whole enterprise is fraught with immense possibilities of good for the natives of Alaska." He noted the progress that Walter Harper had made in the few months he had attended the school. In fact, Stuck would hire Harper that summer as his riverboat pilot, winter trail guide, and interpreter, as Arthur Wright would be enrolling at Mount Hermon School for Boys in northwestern Massachusetts in the fall.[73] As Stuck and Wright left Nenana in the morning, nearly all the students accompanied them to the river. The older boys ran alongside the sled across the river and beyond until Stuck sent them back to avoid being late for school.[74]

Back at Fort Yukon, Stuck confirmed the rumors he had heard on the trail of abusive drinking and related problems in the community. In his and Burke's absence, the destructive behaviors that waxed and waned at Fort Yukon had escalated. "The white men here are for the most part antagonistic to the mission," Stuck wrote in May 1910. "They stand for the things that the mission fights—for the loose living that is dear to them, for the corruption of the native women."[75] Townspeople's resistance to the mission's efforts did not detract, however, from Stuck's affection for the Gwich'in community. "I grow more & more attached to Fort Yukon & its people—especially the children," he wrote in June 1910.

No businesses in Fort Yukon held liquor licenses. According to Superintendent Boulter, the main trading store illegally sold most of the liquor that Natives consumed. That June Boulter asked Alaska's director for the Bureau of Education, Tom Lopp, to urge Alaska's governor to appropriate funds to prosecute the store owner. "I feel certain that with sufficient funds these people could be brought to justice," he wrote.[76] Boulter had already raised the question of his being appointed a special peace officer so he could help enforce the liquor laws. He would press the issue again before finally being appointed in March 1912.[77] Meanwhile, with Stuck's encouragement, the Gwich'in men of the community formed a council to promote peace and well-being and to discourage alcohol consumption. Elected annually, council members mediated disputes, identified community improvement projects, and responded to special needs, such as cases of extreme poverty.[78]

In late May the first steamboat of the season arrived at Allakaket with a letter from Clara's mother, who had dropped her objections to the wedding following "strong intervention" from Bishop Rowe and Archdeacon Stuck. In fact, she sent a trunk and barrel of materials and supplies for the wedding and gifts for the couple's home. The contents ranged from satin fabric for Clara's wedding gown and artificial orange blossoms for her bouquet, to a wedding cake made of fruitcake that only had to be iced, to impractical negligees, to broken crystal engraved with the couple's initials. Clara decided that a lovely white dress of "lawn and lace" her mother sent would serve perfectly as her wedding gown. She would repurpose the satin fabric to drape the chapel altar and frontal. Many gifts from friends in Alaska and Outside arrived on the same boat. Based on her Alaska experience so far, Clara no doubt wondered how they would make use of the volumes of linens and bath towels, sterling silver, and a cut glass punch bowl in the modest quarters she and Hap would share at Fort Yukon.[79] In the coming years, however, they created a spacious and welcoming home in which they raised scores of children, including their own two boys, convened hundreds of community events, hosted travelers from far and wide, and held countless elegant dinner parties. They developed reputations as gracious hosts, with Clara being acknowledged as the best cook along the Yukon River.

As Clara prepared for the wedding that summer, Hap held a clinic at Nenana. Archdeacon Stuck, along with Bishop Rowe and Dr. Edgar Loomis, Hap's best friend from Texas who would serve as best man, were cruising the Yukon River aboard the *Pelican*, visiting missions, villages, and camps to hold services and provide medical care. Stuck, Walter Harper, and Johnny Fred had met Loomis at Eagle, just inside Alaska's border, on June 21.[80] To celebrate the solstice, Walter, Johnny, Loomis, and Stuck, along with Superintendent Boulter and George Burgess, the missionary teacher at Eagle, climbed Eagle Mountain at midnight in broad daylight. They came down at 1:30 "fatigued but happy," had lunch, and went to bed at 3:00 a.m.[81]

Such experiences for Walter and Johnny, who would follow in Walter's footsteps, and Arthur Wright, who preceded them in working for the archdeacon, illustrated the advantages and opportunities that opened to these bright Native adolescents. They attended St. Mark's Mission school at Nenana, and Stuck tutored and mentored them on the trail and river. He later sent them to school Outside to prepare them for leadership positions among their people. The position with the archdeacon brought the young men prestige and fostered self-confidence. Traveling throughout their homeland, they honed their subsistence skills while Stuck guided their immersion into Western culture and Episcopal mission work. Several of Stuck's protégés would have long careers in various roles within the Episcopal mission work and would become well-respected among Alaskans of all backgrounds.[82]

Bishop Rowe arrived at Eagle two or three days after Loomis, having traveled the same route from Skagway.[83] The bishop's summer visits stirred much excitement at Interior missions, villages, and fish and mining camps. People often waited for his arrival to hold weddings and to baptize their babies. With Dr. Loomis aboard, a medical flag flew below the mission flag to indicate the availability of medical care.[84] Traveling downriver from Eagle, they stopped at Circle and then Fort Yukon, where the bishop found conditions "very encouraging." During Sunday services he confirmed twenty-four Natives and gave communion to eighty-eight. He estimated that three hundred Natives were gathered at Fort Yukon for the Fourth of July celebrations.[85] An unsettling incident marred the visit, however. A man claiming to be the U.S. government's "chief explosive chemist" had "taken a fancy" to a five- or six-year-old Native girl at the mission and wanted to adopt her. When Bishop Rowe asked for the man's references, he became insolent, according to Stuck and Rowe, and when Rowe refused to turn the child over to him, he began making "malicious" accusations about the mission and the bishop. The man offered the girl's mother, a Native woman whose white partner had abandoned her, money for the girl, but she refused. Rowe noted that the Native community had come to "regard him as obnoxious."[86]

From Fort Yukon, Rowe, Stuck, and company traveled 225 miles up the Porcupine River to Rampart House just across the Canadian border. After returning to the mouth of the Porcupine, they continued down the Yukon River 320 miles to Tanana and turned up the Tanana River toward Fairbanks, the center of the Episcopal Church's work in the Interior.[87]

Their first stop on the Tanana River was St. Mark's at Nenana, where Rowe had arrived a few days earlier to prepare a class for confirmation. As the *Pelican* pulled in at 10:30 p.m. on July 16, Hap, the mission personnel and children, and many Native residents greeted the travelers excitedly. Many tents lined the riverbank, as people from the surrounding area had gathered in anticipation of Bishop Rowe's visit.[88] On Monday morning, with the Sunday services completed, the *Pelican* pulled out with Hap now on board. At Tanana, Walter Harper's home village at the confluence of the Tanana and the Yukon Rivers, he was confirmed at Mission of Our Savior.[89] The event marked a turning point in Harper's life. In the coming years, as Stuck's riverboat pilot, winter trail guide, and interpreter, he would develop a close father-son relationship with the archdeacon and would plan for a future as a medical missionary in his homeland.[90] From Tanana the *Pelican* continued down the Yukon about 200 miles to the mouth of the Koyukuk and turned upriver for the 260-mile journey to the wedding at St. John's-in-the Wilderness. Repeated engine troubles that summer, along with problems Rowe had to address at each of the missions, had slowed the *Pelican*'s progress, causing the bride-to-be anxiety.[91]

Since early June Clara had been preparing for the wedding, planting nasturtiums, poppies, forget-me-nots, asters, and other flowers, along with various vegetables, expecting them to be at peak season for the wedding and banquet. As June turned to July and July to August, with no word from Hap, she began to despair that he had changed his mind. By late July, the flowers she had so lovingly tended had bloomed and died, and night frost had taken all but the root vegetables. She and Deaconess Carter covered the potato patch with gunny sacking to encourage continued growth. By August 1 the birch leaves began to turn yellow and fall.[92]

Finally, early on the morning of August 5, the dogs howled and a shout went up: "Steamboat!" Clara jumped out of bed, dressed, and stood at the riverbank as the *Pelican* rounded the bend, "flags and pennants flying." Hap stood on deck waving his arms wildly, his bright blue eyes shining and teeth gleaming in the morning sun. He leapt from the boat and embraced Clara, as both exclaimed that they thought this moment would never come.[93]

That evening Bishop Rowe hosted all members of the Iñupiaq and Dena' communities at a potlatch. Guests showered the couple with rugs, mukluks, beaded items, and more—so many gifts that Hap and Clara wondered how they would transport them. The following day, on August 6, carrying a bouquet of white, waxy potato flowers highlighted with green carrot tops, Clara Heintz wed Grafton Burke, with both Bishop Rowe and Archdeacon Stuck officiating. All the residents of both villages attended, along with several men from nearby mining communities. Clara's choir boys sang the bridal hymn "The Voice that Breathed o'er Eden," accompanied by Deaconess Carter on the organ.

Later that day as they packed their belongings, Hap and Clara confessed their faults to one another, as the betrothed Iñupiaq couple had done. Clara admitted that she could be "frightfully stubborn," and Hap confessed that he sometimes had an "uncontrollable temper," a trait that would display itself in dramatic form some years later in a confrontation with a bootlegger. Three days later the steamer that would take them to Fort Yukon arrived.[94] For the next twenty-eight years, Hap and Clara would make the village just north of the Arctic Circle their home.

Dr. Edgar Loomis, Hap's best man, took charge of the Mission of Our Savior at Tanana for the coming year, to the bishop's great relief; twenty-six Natives had died of tuberculosis at Tanana in the past year.[95] The bishop transferred missionary Anne Cady from Fort Yukon to Allakaket to fill Clara's teaching role. Clara would take on Cady's duties at Fort Yukon.[96]

In the two years since St. John's-in-the-Wilderness had opened, a double community—thirty-three Dena' and forty Iñupiat—had grown up near the mission, a group on each side of the river. In the congregation as a whole, Deaconess Carter counted 109 Dena' and 62 Iñupiat. In summer 1910 the NC Company moved its trading post from Arctic Circle, or Moses's Village, to Allakaket, and all the Natives from that settlement were expected to migrate to Allakaket that fall. Others from the South Fork of the Koyukuk, about thirty miles upriver, were expected to settle at Allakaket as well. Clara Carter reported that all the Dena' had been baptized and that they "always [brought] their babies for baptism." Because some of the Iñupiat had been introduced to Christianity by the Moravians before the Episcopal mission was established, mission personnel "waited for them to come to us," Carter explained, "out of respect."[97] Carter would remain in her post at St. John's-in-the-Wilderness until 1913, when she left the Alaska mission field to assume the position of house mother at the Episcopal Church Training School and Deaconess House in Philadelphia. There she would train many women for nursing and other mission work in Alaska.[98]

3

Settling into Married Life
at Fort Yukon, 1910–12

The newlyweds received a warm welcome from Fort Yukon residents, who gifted them a supply of wild game for the winter. As William Loola and David Wallis greeted them, Wallis announced Clara's Gwich'in name, Sutrenjo, or Sutchah's Sutrenjo ("my younger brother's woman").[1] At the mission house, Johnny Fred, now fourteen, whom Clara had met when she first arrived in Alaska, awaited them. A large bathtub stood in the kitchen, with a gift tag from Mr. and Mrs. Will Rodman, who owned a trading post at Tanana and whose bathtub Clara had admired. Bishop Rowe gave them an iron cookstove.[2]

Going upstairs to the archdeacon and Hap's living quarters, Clara came upon an appalling scene, in retrospect the sort she might have expected of two bachelors with heavy demands on their time: cluttered desks, reading materials strewn about, clothing hanging on nails, outdated calendars on the wall, and collections of pipes, dirty ashtrays, and matches. Confident now in her homemaking skills, she began planning renovations. By the time Stuck returned from his summer rounds in October, Clara had transformed the upstairs area of the mission home. She had covered the walls with burlap painted a warm off-white, hung curtains, arranged his library on painted bookshelves, and cleaned the room's windows and his picture frames of dust and smoke film so they gleamed in the sunlight. His clothing now hung in closets. Her only mistake was to round up and boil the men's smelly pipes in soapy water. The well-seasoned pipe each carried in his pocket saved her from severe recriminations, but she learned never to touch their pipes again.[3]

Hap's salary increased from the $1,200 a year he earned as a single missionary to $1,500 when he and Clara married.[4] Clara, on the other hand, lost her $500 salary when she married, in accordance with church policy. The two worked side by side in the decades that followed, leading the mission work at Fort Yukon. Clara managed the household and raised scores of orphaned and foster children as she supported Hap in managing the hospital and treating many hundreds of patients each year. In all those years, she never received a salary from the Episcopal Mission Society for her work at St. Stephen's.[5]

In the coming years Hap and Clara experienced tremendous joys, including the happiness they enjoyed in their loving relationship and the births of their two sons. They found deep satisfaction in seeing the fruits of their labor and in the warm friendships they developed with community members and colleagues. Painful losses and calamities punctuated their experience as well, among them the 1920 death of Hudson Stuck, a fire that destroyed the mission home, devastating epidemics, and Hap's own health crises that culminated in his death in 1938. The weight of their responsibilities would have broken most people. Yet they persevered, approaching their work with energy and enthusiasm and the patients, children, and community they served with respect, love, and compassion.

Hap and Clara's ability to forge a successful marriage and complementary roles under such trying conditions—and to thrive while doing so—evokes even more wonder when considering their brief courtship and short "honeymoon cruise" from Allakaket to Fort Yukon. Their roles afforded them no time to adjust to married life in privacy. Nor did they have the luxury of anticipating the wonder of becoming parents through several months of pregnancy. Hap loved to tell people that "just three months after [we] were married we had fourteen children—all Indians!"[6] The delight he took in their startled responses did not diminish the magnitude of their responsibilities, of which fostering a houseful of children was only a part.

Several factors explain the couple's devotion to one another and to their life's work. First, they both believed that God had called them to the Alaska mission field. Witnessing daily the overwhelming needs within the community and region, they simply could not turn their backs on the people who trusted them and relied on them, no matter how burdensome their commitment felt at times. Second, they supported and strengthened one another in their separate but overlapping roles, and their personalities and character traits complemented one another. Efficient and organized, Clara oversaw the mission home that bustled with the activities of as many as thirty children at a time, always maintaining a cheerful and loving atmosphere. Fun-loving and energetic, though disorganized and forgetful, Hap attended to the pressing medical needs in the community and region, while also pastoring to the people. As they responded to the constant demands on their time and energy, their love and esteem for one another and their shared commitment gave them the courage to face each day's trials.

Third, during the first decade of their marriage, Hap's mentor and father figure, Hudson Stuck, guided Hap and Clara while providing physical, moral, and financial support for the mission work. A skilled writer and inspiring storyteller, Stuck regularly published articles informing mission friends of the work, the progress made, and the need for financial help. While on furlough Outside, he conducted speaking tours to raise funds for the Alaska missions and to recruit workers. At home in Fort Yukon, he performed much of the pastoral work at St. Stephen's. With Stuck's death in 1920, Hap and Clara lost not only a beloved father figure, friend, and mentor but his moral support, pastoring assistance, and financial backing. As they recovered from the loss, they took strength and inspiration from his vision.

In late fall 1910 Hap and Clara learned they were expecting a baby. The delighted archdeacon immediately presumed they would name the child for him. They assured him that they would if it was a boy. Stuck never doubted that he would have a namesake.[7] He and Walter Harper set out on their winter rounds in mid-November, leaving Hap and Clara to manage the medical and mission work without him. Hap ran ahead of them with his sled and three dogs to break trail, and David Wallis followed them. After helping Stuck and Harper ease their sleds down the steep bank of the Porcupine River, Burke and Wallis turned back.[8]

The landscape at Fort Yukon, which like Allakaket lay just north of the Arctic Circle, differed strikingly from Clara's first Alaska home. The many ever-changing channels of the Yukon River that flowed through the Yukon

Flats regularly broke off chunks of the riverbanks, threatening structures and often whole communities, especially during spring break-up. Fort Yukon, at the heart of the Yukon Flats, was relatively sparsely forested, which forced residents to travel by dogsled in winter to collect wood for heating. In summer they floated logs from upriver for construction and firewood and to sell for steamboat fuel.[9] During winter the Yukon flowed crystal clear beneath the ice and thus provided excellent drinking water. At break-up time, however, water from glaciers that fed the upper Yukon filled the channel with mud, silt, and debris. Thus, in summer, the river water was drinkable only after filtering or settling.[10]

Both Natives and non-Natives in the region tended to ignore their natural circadian rhythms in summer when the sun hardly set. Because the mosquitoes were less vicious when the sun lay low on the horizon, many people slept during the day and resumed typical daytime activities toward evening. Steamboats arrived at any time of the day or night, and like elsewhere along Alaska's river systems, the whistle halted activities, including sleep, and summoned people to the riverbank. They watched curiously or eagerly, depending on the circumstances, as crew members threw down the gangplank and the travelers disembarked, followed by the crew with the mail and cargo. During summers, hundreds of tourists poured off each steamer. Natives sold fur coats, hats, and beaded items, such as belts, leggings, moccasins, gloves, and cushions.[11] Around 1912, steamers began traveling downriver only as far as Fort Yukon, the river's northernmost point, to view the midnight sun. Locals called them "sunners."[12]

Virtually every family at Fort Yukon had a dog team. Dogs had become essential for winter travel and for hunting and trapping since their introduction in conjunction with the fur trade.[13] The hundreds of dogs quartered at Fort Yukon in the summer created a racket whenever a steamboat came within earshot. The dogs, often half-starved before the salmon run, would clamor for the scraps the steamers' cooks threw out during their stopovers. Dog yards at various fish camps along the Yukon boarded working dogs, including those of mail carriers. Fish wheels harvested the salmon the people dried to feed themselves and their dogs throughout the year. The dogs suffered during the summer months, tethered to stakes and mercilessly attacked by mosquitoes. The winter months, when they

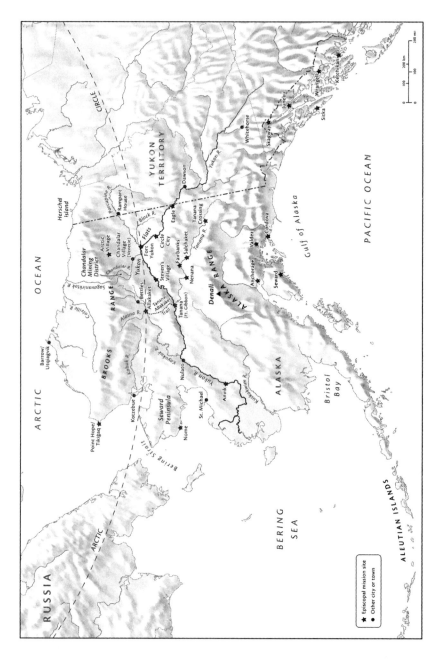

Map 2. Map of Alaska, with Episcopal mission sites starred. Erin Greb Cartography.

spent most of their days running, offered the animals far more pleasure, despite the hard work they performed.[14]

The Gwich'in and others in the Fort Yukon area enjoyed a relatively strong economy, with many fur-bearing animals such as fox, lynx, and muskrat supporting a robust trapping industry.[15] A beautiful lake lay five minutes' walk behind the village and beyond that many more, where hundreds and hundreds of muskrats lived. Families traveled up to sixty or even more miles away and remained months on their traplines to harvest other fur-bearing animals.[16] The women of the region were known for their exquisite beadwork.

The mission, and later St. Stephen's hospital, also provided employment opportunities, as did occasional construction projects, such as the new schoolhouse in 1909. The cash economy had negative impacts as well. For instance, it contributed to the alcohol abuse that waxed and waned in the community. In 1910 sales of liquor to Natives along the Yukon reportedly were rising, despite the federal law of 1909 making the offense a felony. With lax enforcement and juries unwilling to convict, the penalty did little to deter the alcohol trade.[17]

The day of Hap and Clara's arrival in Fort Yukon in August 1910, David Wallis informed them of a drinking spree within the Native village in the previous days. Men and women had consumed a large shipment of alcohol that they purchased from bootleggers with muskrat furs harvested the previous winter and spring. Selling their furs directly to bootleggers, who then resold the furs at market prices for double the profit, brought far less compensation than they would have commanded on the market, and the trappers now had nothing to show for their winter's work. Hap and Clara helped many incapacitated individuals back to their cabins and confiscated whatever liquor bottles they found. The following day a church full of contrite parishioners vowed never to drink liquor again.[18] Allakaket's remote location kept it isolated from the havoc wrought by alcohol abuse in villages along the Yukon River. At Fort Yukon Clara would witness and be drawn into a range of alcohol-related crises in the coming years. She and Hap saw the most crushing effects of alcohol abuse and related domestic violence in neglected and abused children. They

5. Mother with brilliantly beaded baby strap. Elizabeth Hayes Goddard—Alaska Diary, #1967-48-18, APRCA, University of Alaska Fairbanks.

took many such youngsters into their home over the years, nurtured and guided them, and prepared them for self-sufficiency as adults.

St. Stephen's Mission supported Dena' families of the vast northern Interior in various ways. Missionary Lizzie Wood had been stationed at St. Stephen's since 1905, fostering children in the mission house. In May 1909 six Native orphans and "half-orphans" ranging in age from three to sixteen lived with her.[19] Later, with funds donated by a mission friend, a suitable home for Wood and the children was built—the Cheney Memorial Hall. Shortly after Hap returned to Fort Yukon with Clara, however, Wood fell ill and went Outside for medical treatment.[20] Clara thus brought the children into the mission home to care for them.

The Burkes' devotion to children's welfare had far-ranging and multi-generational effects. Through donations sent by mission friends, Clara provided material assistance to many village children.[21] Within the mission home, the couple nurtured orphans and fostered children from destitute families, youngsters whose parents hunted and trapped, convalescent children, and hospital patients' children, caring for them as their own, in effect running a home-like boarding school.[22] Clara saw to the children's general care, bathing, mending, and feeding while Hap gave them fatherly attention. They gathered the children around the table each evening for supper and family prayers, in which the children participated enthusiastically.[23]

When Clara arrived in 1910, mission children included a girl, Jenny, whose father was an African American "stampeder," which subjected her to ridicule and shunning, and three Gwich'in boys—Johnny Fred, often called "Miss Wood's Johnny," because Lizzie Wood had raised him from a young age and doted on him; Lot, the president of St. Stephen's Boys' Club, who had become deeply devoted to Hap after leaving him behind on the trail; and George, whose elderly grandmother could no longer care for him. A few years later Clara and Hap were pleased to see Jenny marry an upstanding young Gwich'in man. Six-year-old Lottie was the next addition to the Burke family. She had nearly drowned when her drunken white father threw her headfirst into a water barrel, and her Native mother, who was ill with tuberculosis, had been unable to prevent the abuse or to rescue her. After Lottie recovered from the incident, Hap convinced her mother to allow her to remain where she would be well fed and cared for.[24] Margaret Enoch, a child who arrived from Circle after her parents died, never forgot the loving care the Burkes provided her; as many other parents did, she named one of her sons for Grafton.[25]

In their first years at St. Stephen's, Hap and Clara saved the life of William and Julia Loola's baby daughter, who was born with a severe cleft palate that would have kept her from nursing. William rushed to Hap and Clara in distress. They arrived and took charge of the situation, assuring the parents that Hap could surgically repair her nose and mouth in time. In the meantime, Hap devised a special contraption to allow her to drink milk. Hap and Clara monitored little Mary's welfare, and as she grew older, they encouraged her schooling. When she reached puberty, well after William died, they feared for Mary's safety, so they appealed to a Fairbanks judge, who granted them custody of her. Mary joined the mission family and blossomed in the Burkes' care. Later she began working at the hospital, wearing a gauze mask over her nose and mouth, which highlighted her beautiful dark eyes. She earned wages, thrived with the responsibility, and reportedly was beloved by the patients and other caregivers.[26]

Many of the youngsters Hap and Clara raised, especially in the early years, were mixed-race children whom people scorned after their white fathers abandoned them. Several were children of foreign fathers and Native mothers. The couple worked to dispel such prejudice against mixed race children. They fostered increasing numbers of youngsters as they raised their own two boys. Clara assigned chores to all but the youngest, and they vied for praise as they learned to "perform their tasks 'mission way.'" The children remained fluent in Gwich'in, and Hap and Clara made efforts to keep them immersed in Gwich'in lifeways, for instance by sending them to fish camp each summer with local families.[27]

The children experienced immediate and long-term benefits from their upbringing in the mission home. Nevertheless, living with non-Gwich'in parents, learning English, and acquiring mainstream American life skills and habits taught the children that the "mission way" was right or better and implicitly, if not explicitly, that other ways were wrong or inferior. By all appearances, the children thrived in the loving atmosphere Hap and Clara created, and they seemed to take pride in their new skills. Yet their upbringing at the mission set them apart and may have led them to question their identities. Especially when coupled with negative messaging from mainstream Euro-American society, the time they spent in the mission home may have undermined their sense of self-worth.[28] Many powerful forces converged to denigrate Alaska Native peoples, cultures, and lifeways at the time, among them the efforts of well-intentioned individuals and institutions like the Burkes and the Episcopal Church, despite the countless lives they saved and other positive impacts of their presence.

Hap and Clara strove to promote health and well-being throughout the community. They regularly made home-welfare checks in the Native village. If a teacher noticed an ill, neglected, or undernourished child and reported the concern, Clara would respond with clothing and other forms of support for the child and family.[29] As time permitted, she helped Hap in the infirmary. Johnny Fred assisted Hap so regularly that he came to be called Hap's "right-hand man," a description he prized. When he showed interest in going to medical school, Archdeacon Stuck told him he would do his best to win the church's support for his medical school tuition.[30]

Hap's medical practice grew as people learned of his presence at Fort Yukon and as he canvased outlying areas and held clinics at Tanana and Nenana. Among the most common complaints he treated in Alaska Natives were eye diseases. Many people suffered from "sore" eyes resulting from smoky, poorly ventilated dwellings. Later in the twentieth century, physicians and nurses recognized that much of the eye disease seen in Alaska stemmed from tuberculosis-related phlyctenular keratoconjunctivitis. The disease caused a painful eye condition that if left untreated led to corneal scarring and vision loss.[31] Trachoma, an infection that produced granulations on the eyelids that rubbed against the cornea, turning it opaque, was the most common cause of blindness.[32] Inadequate hygiene and traditional remedies, such as cutting the eyeball to cure snow blindness and treating inflamed eyes with spruce sap, exacerbated eye conditions.[33] For both Natives and non-Natives, Hap treated injuries ranging from gun shots to dog bites, broken limbs, burns, and frostbite that could lead to amputation. Without medical care, relatively minor injuries could lead to death.[34] Until St. Stephen's Hospital opened, Hap and Clara often had four or five patients bedded in the mission home.[35]

Tuberculosis and epidemics of influenza, measles, and smallpox took countless lives early in the twentieth century.[36] Only later did scholars and the public at large consider the multigenerational effects of the trauma and grief Alaska Natives experienced as loved ones and community leaders died year after year from these diseases.[37] School superintendent George Boulter estimated in summer 1911 that fully half the Native population in his district, which extended from Eagle at the Canadian border to Kokrines on the lower Yukon, had tuberculosis, the deadliest of the diseases. The disease manifested in various ways, most often in the lungs, but also in the spine, knees, and other joints, with crippling effects. Many had tubercular glands in the neck that discharged pus continuously.[38] Inhaling droplet nuclei or aerosolized droplets with live tuberculosis bacteria drove transmission, however, rather than touching pus or sputum. Inadequate ventilation in crowded cabins, having no place to remove ill family members, and social conditions such as poor nutrition that affected immunity contributed to the far higher rates of exposure, disease development, and death from tuberculosis among Alaska Natives. Hap and Clara encouraged the building of two-room cabins with windows to enhance ventilation and urged people to move into tents in the summer to benefit from the fresh air.[39]

Occasionally, in both summer and winter, Hap made runs to outlying areas to attend to acute illness, severe injuries, and reports of communal disease outbreaks. During Clara's first winter at Fort Yukon, she accompanied him on an emergency trek north to Chandalar Village in response to a rash of dysentery. David Wallis's wife, Martha, stayed at the mission home to care for the children. Johnny guided Hap and Clara to his home village. Layers of animal furs and clothing kept the travelers warm in the −30°F weather, even on the first night on the trail, when they slept in the open on spruce boughs. The second night they slept in the cabin of a Gwich'in family, grateful for the hospitality and the chance to dry out their clothing. At Chandalar Village Hap identified tainted caribou meat as the source of the dysentery. Luckily, no one died.[40] Hap regularly treated such food poisoning incidents.[41]

As the weeks and months passed, the vastness of the territory that St. Stephen's served and the scope and magnitude of the problems wrought by newcomers in the region dawned on Hap and Clara. Bishop Rowe's 1909–10 annual report graphically depicted conditions at Tanana, 320 miles downriver from Fort Yukon:

> The utter neglect of the Government in making provision for the protection and physical well-being of the natives will, unless something is done soon, leave the Bureau of Education without anything to do. In visiting one of our stations this year I was horrified to find that 50 percent of the people had died within the past year. This was due largely to the fact that these natives lived so near a White settlement that they were made the victims of the demoralizing influences of some few White people; that tuberculosis had become an epidemic among them, and that their food was scant because, with the presence of so many White people in the country, it had become more and more difficult for the natives to obtain their old supply of game.[42]

Nine liquor stores operated in the town of Tanana, which lay adjacent to Fort Gibbon and the Native village of Tanana. At least forty white men in the area reportedly made a living or partial living by illegally selling alcohol to Alaska Natives.[43] Rowe had hoped that Dr. Loomis's presence at the Tanana mission would improve conditions, but when Stuck and Harper arrived at Tanana just before Christmas 1910, they found Loomis deeply discouraged.[44] His work among the school children had produced heartening results, but his best efforts to improve health and welfare among adults had made little difference. Mission personnel were powerless to effect change, with alcohol so easily accessible, related social problems so deeply entrenched, and juries unwilling to convict bootleggers.[45]

Because Fort Yukon had no liquor stores, its alcohol problems tended to be more episodic. Bootleggers operated from trading posts and nearby roadhouses relatively discreetly. From time to time, during the winter holidays, when trappers were in town with cash in hand, for instance, a load of liquor might come down the mail trail from Circle. In summer, when trappers and prospectors were in town to sell their furs and buy supplies for the coming winter, a boatload of liquor could arrive from the Yukon Territory or Circle City. A terrifying experience during her first winter at Fort Yukon gave Clara a taste of the mayhem abusive drinking could generate.

In her telling of the story, Larry, a Canadian trapper who often visited the mission, had a history of abusive drinking, although she and Hap found him congenial. On one visit to Fort Yukon, however, he kept to himself. When Hap learned that he was locked in his cabin with a large supply of liquor, Hap tried unsuccessfully to coax him out. A few days later the man ran through the village screaming, clearly experiencing delirium tremens. Hap brought him to the mission home, made a bed for him in the dining room, and sedated him while treating him with nutritional supplements. Eventually, Larry came out of his stupor. He stayed at the mission through the Christmas season, helping wherever needed and showering the children with gifts.[46]

A week or two later, Hap made an emergency run to Circle where a miner had fallen into a shaft and broken an arm and a leg. By this time Clara felt perfectly comfortable with Larry in the house. But a few days after Hap left, Larry brought a load of wood into the kitchen where Clara was alone, the children being in school, and asked her for a drink. Seeing his glassy eyes and trembling hands, she told him he needed a cup of coffee and a solid meal, but he persisted. He told Clara he knew that Dr. Burke had alcohol in his locked drug room, and he demanded the key. She gave him a cup of coffee, and he sat down, appearing to submit. Believing the situation was under control, she opened the trapdoor to their underground cellar to retrieve a steak for him. As she held a candle to look for the meat, she heard the cellar door slam shut and the bolt snap. She stumbled up the stairs in the dark, the flame having died, and shouted and banged on the cellar door to no avail. She could hear Larry hacking his way through the door to Hap's supply of medicinal alcohol as she continued to pound on the door and shout. As her voice gave out and she grew cold, her mind raced with visions of being found frozen to death a few days later. Eventually, she heard soft, moccasined footsteps and began pounding on the trap door again, calling for help, but the footsteps retreated. Once again she was left in silence. Finally, she heard Johnny's familiar footsteps, and she called out to him for help. He ran to the cellar door and was horrified to find Sutrenjo in such a state. As Johnny rushed to heat coffee to warm her, the door burst open, and the trader Harry Horton ran in.[47]

As Clara lay in bed surrounded by hot water bottles and wrapped in blankets, she, Johnny, and Horton pieced together the story. When Johnny had stopped by Horton's store after school, a Native woman had run by, howling about an evil spirit in the mission house. Johnny, whom Hap had entrusted with looking after the pregnant Clara in his absence, bolted to the mission home, terrified for her safety and wracked with guilt that he had let Hap and Clara down. Horton followed soon thereafter, having noticed Larry lurking around suspiciously earlier in the day and suspecting a link between the two incidents. Reflecting over her trauma, Clara found herself marveling at the tenderness and concern "Hardboiled Horton" had shown her, since he had often chafed at the mission's policies. As for Larry, the white men of Fort Yukon banded together and ran him out of town. The Burkes never heard from him again.[48]

As Hap and Clara and other missionaries tried to shield Alaska Natives from the negative influences of Western culture and individuals, they met with resentment, indignation, accusations of exploitation themselves, and even threats of violence. Detractors spread rumors that missionaries exploited Natives by trading in furs and by selling them items from care packages sent by church woman's auxiliaries. The accusations referred to the practice of compensating both children and adults for chores or work done at missions with items of clothing and other valuables that mission friends sent them. In doing so, missionaries sought to discourage dependency while securing community help in providing mission services.[49] Stuck took personal criticism in stride. As his biographer wrote, "Most whites deplored his views on virtually every subject."[50] In fact, he took pride in his ability to ignore criticism.[51] He worried, however, that such rumors could detract from the mission work by making Alaska Natives suspicious of missionaries' intentions and by discouraging mission friends from continuing to support their efforts.

As Hap and Stuck tried to suppress illegal activities in the "road-houses" that served as saloons, resentment among the perpetrators of such exploitation grew. One night in April 1911, as Hap and Clara slept on the veranda of their upstairs bedroom to enjoy the fresh spring air, an explosion and the shattering of window glass awakened them. They and the children quickly gathered in the living room, where the picture window had shattered. Hap and Johnny surveilled the outer perimeter of the building and discovered that someone had used dynamite to send a warning to the meddlesome missionaries. They could identify multiple possible suspects, but many community members expressed concern and sympathy. The next morning several appeared at the mission house, tools in hand, to repair the damage.[52]

Missionaries' attempts to protect Native girls and young women from exploitation also caused much resentment. Mission personnel and government teachers tried to discourage relationships between schoolgirls and disreputable men. Many men, both white and Native, found female students attractive because they acquired cooking and housekeeping skills along with a general education. Superintendent Boulter stated the problem bluntly: "There are few perceptible good results to be seen from the education the native girls have received. The more care that is bestowed upon them by a teacher the more readily are they sought after and ruined by certain white men who have boasted that they are at or near a village 'waiting for the girls to grow up.'"[53] Hap and Clara rejoiced when girls they raised married solid young Native men.[54]

With break-up in spring 1911, thoughts turned to summer. Once the river was clear of ice, Stuck and Harper began their summer rounds, heading upriver in the *Pelican*. Gwich'in families prepared to go to their fish camps, where they would harvest the coming year's supply of fish. Children loved nothing better than preparing for and spending time at fish camp. In fact, according to Clara, the worst punishment a misbehaving child could imagine was to be held back from the carefree playtime that fish camp provided. More importantly, however, children learned by watching, and later they apprenticed alongside their parents and Elders, developing essential life skills. The mission home was unusually quiet each summer when Hap and Clara sent the children to fish camp with various local families.[55]

In summer 1911, after most residents left for fish camp with the mission children, Hap and Clara envisioned several relaxing weeks before the baby's arrival in August. Although Clara planned to give birth at the hospital in Fairbanks, she went into labor early, and on June 11, she delivered a tiny but healthy boy in their bedroom, with Hap attending. Upon receiving a wire with the news at Circle, Stuck and Harper turned the *Pelican* around and raced back to Fort Yukon, blasting the whistle all the way. The day after their arrival, the men took the baby to the chapel, where the archdeacon baptized Hudson Stuck Burke. Stuck took great pleasure in asking Clara each day how Hudson Stuck was doing. Soon a silver baby cup arrived from Tiffany's, engraved with the words "From Hudson to Hudson."[56] Clara and Hap's Gwich'in friends brought gifts of rabbit-skin blankets and tiny moccasins and mittens. When they learned his name, they dubbed him Ginkhii Tsal—Little Reverend.[57]

Six years later, Hap and Clara would have a second son. Becoming parents did not radically change their lives, given that Clara worked in the home and was already raising a brood of children. After their second child arrived, however, they gave increasing thought to the boys' education and eventually concluded that they would make the difficult choice that missionaries in foreign countries typically made: they would send their sons to boarding schools in their "home country." In her memoir, published in 1961, Clara noted this sacrifice on their part, a seemingly inescapable privation associated with their calling. The boys likely suffered far more than their parents, however, in being sent away at the ages of eleven and thirteen. Hap and Clara's responsibilities at Fort Yukon completely consumed them. The boys, on the other hand, were transplanted to unfamiliar environments and deprived of their parents' daily companionship and guidance. Moreover, they missed the opportunity during their adolescence to experience their loving and nurturing household and to witness and learn from their parents' affectionate relationship.[58]

In late summer 1911, residents of the Yukon River drainage system faced the threat of a potentially catastrophic epidemic. Northeast of Fort Yukon, just across the Canadian border at Rampart House, a virulent form of smallpox spread rapidly. At one time, sixty-three people were infected. The disease created deep lesions and pitting, with much tissue destruction. Upon learning of the outbreak, Stuck wired Episcopal Mission headquarters in New York to rush vaccines to missions along the Yukon

6. Hap with Hudson Stuck Burke, June 1911. Hudson Burke private collection.

in Alaska. Hap vaccinated four hundred people himself. Supported by the Bureau of Education, he maintained a quarantine at the mouth of the Porcupine River. Meanwhile, Stuck, traveling with Harper on the *Pelican*, intercepted Dr. Loomis at Anvik as he was heading Outside after his year at Tanana. With Loomis onboard, they made their way up the Yukon River, stopping at fish camps to vaccinate people. Mission personnel along the Yukon's tributaries vaccinated Dena' people in their vicinities. That summer Episcopal missionaries vaccinated almost every Alaska Native in the Interior, nearly three thousand persons. Owing to the competency of the medical personnel at Rampart House and the rapid response by Episcopal missionaries with support from the Bureau of Education, only one death occurred at Rampart House, and the outbreak did not spread into Alaska.[59]

The views and goals of the Episcopal Church and the Bureau of Education aligned well on most topics related to Alaska Natives' welfare. They differed regarding the value they placed on Native languages, however, as illustrated by a squabble between Archdeacon Stuck and Superintendent Boulter in fall 1911. Most residents of Fort Yukon used some English by now in trading and selling furs and handcrafted goods.[60] Children spoke Gwich'in at home and in the Native community but were expected to speak English at school, in accordance with government policy.[61] In fall 1910 Stuck had arranged with the government teacher, Miss Nielsen, for after-school lessons for the older students with Reverend Loola in reading the Gwich'in Bible, which he had helped translate many years before. Stuck would pay for heating and lighting the schoolhouse during the lessons, at a cost far less than heating the cold church building for short time periods. After Christmas break Nielsen cancelled the arrangement, however, and in fall 1911 she continued to deny access to the schoolhouse afterhours. She reportedly claimed that allowing the children to speak Gwich'in after hours in the schoolhouse undermined her ability to enforce the English-only rule during school hours.[62]

Stuck appealed to Boulter, noting parents' eagerness for the lessons, but Boulter backed Nielsen, citing her complaint that the lengthy reading sessions caused some children to skip regular school.[63] Second, he said, Nielsen had reported that the children were speaking more Gwich'in during school hours. Third, the after-school session delayed Nielsen's cleaning and preparation for the following school day. Boulter urged Stuck to adopt a practical alternative: missionary Lizzie Wood had offered to host Loola and the children in her orphanage-home at any time. Boulter concluded, "Although I am heartily in sympathy with the mission work among the natives, yet I cannot entirely agree with your ideas concerning the advisability of teaching these natives the [Gwich'in] tongue—a Mackenzie River dialect that is more or less unintelligible to the Yukon Indians."[64] W. T. Lopp, chief of the Alaska Division of the Bureau of Education, endorsed Boulter's decision, given the availability of an alternative venue.[65]

Stuck continued to press the issue, and in summer 1912, Lopp adopted a more conciliatory position. A new schoolteacher, Miss Hannah Breece, would be arriving soon, he wrote Stuck, "and I believe you can count on her cooperation with your missionaries."[66] U.S. commissioner of education Philander Claxton followed up with his "hearty" support of the missionary work among Alaska Natives and of his eagerness to have government schools used "for any purpose which is for the good of the natives," without extra costs to the government or inconvenience to personnel.[67] Thus ended this confrontation. Boulter, however, continued to perceive Episcopal Church personnel as antagonistic toward the Bureau of Education, which he said made it difficult to work harmoniously with them.[68]

Meanwhile, the death in early winter 1911 of a young Gwich'in father at Fort Yukon brought home to Hap and Clara the tragic costs of alcohol abuse on individuals and families. Stephen Crow, a good provider for his wife and children, fell asleep in his trapping cabin while intoxicated. The fire burned out and he froze to death. After Hap verified the cause of death through an autopsy, several people informed him that Crow had purchased the liquor from a roadhouse keeper not far from Fort Yukon. According to Clara's telling of the incident, Hap confronted the innkeeper, who denied having traded liquor for marten furs, even though marten skins hung in the corner, clearly visible. Accusations, insults, and threats flew back and forth as two onlookers chimed in, supporting the innkeeper's story. The mail carrier arrived in time to break up the confrontation by telling Hap that he was needed back at the mission. He

7. Rev. William Loola with his Bible class. Walter and Lillian Phillips Photograph Collection, #1985-72-29, APRCA, University of Alaska Fairbanks.

and Clara brought Crow's widow, Lola, and their two children into the mission family.[69]

Hap gathered witness reports and sent them to the Fairbanks district attorney, but with no non-Native witnesses willing to testify and with juries considering the testimony of Natives unreliable, the government chose not to prosecute the case.[70] The episode left Hap and Clara deeply dispirited. The felony penalty for alcohol trade or sales to Alaska Natives carried no teeth, given Alaska's frontier alcohol culture and the shortage of law enforcement officers.

Crow's death, in fact, convinced Hap to accept the position of justice of the peace, or commissioner, at Fort Yukon. With the authority to arrest lawbreakers, gather evidence, and support prosecutions himself, he hoped he could suppress the flow of alcohol into the Native community. The two and a half years he served in the position were among the most stressful and discouraging of Hap and Clara's married life. According to Stuck, Hap was "perhaps, the most popular man in all the country around until he became justice of the peace." By 1914 he had become "the most unpopular."[71]

4   Hap's Term as Commissioner, 1912–14

Alaska's frontier culture in the early twentieth century magnified the negative impacts on Alaska Natives of large numbers of migrants in the region. Federal law prohibited the sale or trade of alcohol with Natives, as it did on reservations elsewhere in the United States. Nevertheless, alcohol found its way into Native villages, generally through non-Native traders. While there were no saloons in Fort Yukon, boatloads of liquor arrived from time to time from Circle City, where it was easily accessible owing to flagrant disregard of the law.[1] Whites at Fort Yukon tended to have a "free and easy" standard of morals and therefore traded in alcohol and engaged in sexual relations with Natives, conduct missionaries and Bureau of Education authorities deemed exploitative and ruinous.[2] Archdeacon Hudson Stuck described conditions graphically: since mining had declined in the region early in the century, white men had tended to congregate at Fort Yukon, where they resorted to "drunkenness and debauchery."[3]

The high rates of alcohol abuse among Alaska Natives early in the twentieth century, as well as the fatalism that Stuck and Burke observed, can be seen as coping or escape responses when viewed in the context of the continual trauma the people had experienced in recent decades. Alaska's northern Interior remained relatively isolated until the final decades of the nineteenth century, when outside influences entered the region by way of the Yukon River. By the turn of the twentieth century, migrants had inundated Alaska Natives' ancestral lands, depleting subsistence resources, disempowering the people politically, and displacing traditional beliefs and lifeways. Meanwhile, wave after wave of new diseases left survivors reeling spiritually and physically, often too weak to harvest food for the day or the coming season and without the stamina to resist the next epidemic.

To mitigate these threats to Alaska Native lives and well-being, Episcopal missionaries urged maintenance of traditional lifeways, with health-related adaptations and avoidance of alcohol and corruptive outside influences. In 1908 Episcopal bishop Peter Trimble Rowe identified the church's greatest challenge as protecting Native Christians whom "a class of white men who seem to be without conscience and without any instinct of morality" exploited. The law, as currently administered, "fails absolutely wherever the native is concerned," he declared. Only missionaries protested, he noted, which invited the "hostility of the 'evil sort,' the criticism of the seemingly decent kind and (did) not gain for him even the confidence of the Indians."[4] Contrary to Bishop Rowe's assertion, the church had a strong non-Native ally in its fight against alcohol-related exploitation of Alaska Natives. Assistant superintendent of schools George Boulter (who later became superintendent) complained repeatedly to authorities about the "whiskey evil" that harmed Alaska Natives.[5] These two entities, the Episcopal Church and the Bureau of Education, represented the most effective bulwark against alcohol-related social problems in Interior Alaska.

By the first decade of the twentieth century, liquor problems affected virtually every part of the territory. In 1907 Governor Wilford Hoggatt wrote, "The worst enemy of the native is the whisky peddler." He recommended making the offense of selling alcohol to Alaska Natives a felony and asked for funding for enforcement.[6] In February 1909 Congress complied, raising the crime to a felony and appropriating $6,000 for enforcement.[7] In 1915 Congress increased the allocation to $15,000, which remained altogether inadequate.[8]

The stronger penalty did little to stem the flow of alcohol in the northern Interior. Just six deputy marshals served communities along the more than 1,300 miles of the Yukon River in Alaska, and before Hap became commissioner in late 1911, Fort Yukon never had an officer of the law. Furthermore, deputy marshals tended to be political appointees and often failed to suppress the liquor traffic effectively. The position of commissioner, or justice of the peace, attracted few reputable individuals, because it paid no salary; these officials depended solely on fees, for instance for marriage licenses, which provided minimal income.[9]

Not only were officers of the law too few, poorly committed, and ineffective in arresting lawbreakers; social norms, too, hindered the enforcement of laws designed to protect Alaska Natives. Liquor interests weighed heavily on government and juries. White jury members generally refused to convict other whites for trading in alcohol with Natives, especially on the testimony of Natives.[10] For their part, Natives hesitated to testify against whites, fearing retribution.[11]

The Northern Commercial (NC) Company was the largest importer and wholesale liquor distributor in Alaska.[12] Boulter reported that such companies were "too wise to sell liquor directly to the Natives," but they knew the aims of the men who purchased alcohol to sell it at camps and villages downriver.[13] Stuck accused the NC Company of opposing laws designed to protect Natives.[14]

When Hap became commissioner in November 1911, death rates had outpaced birthrates at every Episcopal mission along the Yukon River in the past few years, owing largely to the lethal combination of liquor and disease. Like Rowe, Stuck felt that missionaries presented the most effective barrier between bootleggers and Alaska Native people, and like Boulter, he urged stronger measures to "suppress the 'low-down whites.'"[15] Fairbanks district attorney James Crossley, Stuck's good friend, zealously prosecuted bootleggers and others who exploited Alaska Natives. W. F. Thompson, the editor of the *Fairbanks Daily News Miner*, whose fondness for alcohol was well known, attacked the two for always believing the "proverbial untruthful" Alaska Native and for "working hardship upon innocent white men."[16]

Although Alaska Natives exercised many forms of agency in their interactions with non-Native individuals and institutions, the Western legal and political systems clearly disadvantaged them. Frontier attitudes and racial prejudices protected whites from the consequences of their harmful and illegal actions while effectively denying Native people legal recourse and political influence. Lawlessness negatively impacted Alaska Natives in numerous ways besides alcohol-related problems, especially in the violation of fish and game regulations and in gambling. Migrants who settled in Native villages along the Yukon and its tributaries trapped and traded for income, reducing Native subsistence resources.[17] Trappers' illegal use of strychnine allowed them to secure large numbers of furs.[18] Game wardens' territories were far too large to police effectively.[19] As for gambling, both Natives and non-Natives took part, but prosecuting the offense was difficult. Even those who complained of it to authorities hesitated to travel to Fairbanks to testify under oath.[20]

Upon their arrival at Fort Yukon, Hap and Clara, like Stuck, did their best to "lay down the law" regarding alcohol consumption and gambling. The Burkes' zealousness in battling the bootleggers and other efforts to protect Natives from exploitation generated resentment from most of the white residents of Fort Yukon who felt the Burkes exceeded their authority and meddled in private affairs. Their efforts also deepened divisions among Native residents of Fort Yukon. After repeated fruitless efforts to have a deputy marshal posted at Fort Yukon or a commissioner appointed, Stuck convinced a federal judge to appoint Burke commissioner. He hoped that if Burke proved effective in suppressing the liquor trade, his appointment could serve as a model for the assignment of other commissioners throughout Alaska's Interior.[21]

As commissioner, Hap responded to an array of legal matters, including assault with a dangerous weapon (a loaded gun), petty larceny, larceny, gambling, an insanity inquiry, assault with intent to rape, making and possessing intoxicating liquor, drunken and disorderly conduct, and interfering with the duties of a deputy health commissioner.[22] He adjudicated a relatively small number of cases during the nearly three years that he served, but throughout his three decades in Fort Yukon, he interacted with the legal system frequently, as a juror and to testify in sanity cases and cause-of-death inquiries. A drunken brawl at a roadhouse in which one reveler was killed and two others were injured led to his first murder case; once the injured men were well enough, Hap sent them off to Fairbanks for trial.[23] Alcohol-related incidents dominated his duties, and his new role would try Hap's wits and stamina as never before.

With Hannah Breece's arrival in summer 1912, the Gwich'in people of Fort Yukon gained an experienced and affectionate schoolteacher, the Bureau of Education and the Episcopal mission restored mutual trust, and the Burkes found a friend and ally. As she renovated the teacher's residence, Breece stayed at the mission house, doting on the children, who called her Aunt Hannah, and endearing herself to everyone there.[24] Breece wrote in her memoir that she understood her duties to include working "in harmony" with the missionaries, given the alignment between the government's and church's aims.[25] The fifty-three-year-old Breece had taught on Native American reservations in the Rocky Mountains, where she witnessed severe problems with alcohol, an experience that had made her an avowed prohibitionist. She had taught eight years in Alaska before arriving at Fort Yukon.[26]

In addition to teaching basic subjects, Breece provided manual training for the boys and leather and beadwork practice for the girls. Upon noticing that the girls took less interest than their mothers and grandmothers in such handwork, she organized a sewing club and offered prizes for the best handcrafts. Fort Yukon women made significant income by selling their handcrafts to tourists on the steamboats that plied the Yukon River each summer. Breece often visited the homes of Gwich'in families to chat and to admire their handwork, and she taught women who were interested how to bake bread. At the schoolhouse she organized after-hours entertainment programs for the children and their families.[27] She formed a student council that earned the respect of the other children because their decisions were final.[28] Breece made friends in the Native community and served unofficially as a government representative on the Gwich'in Council that primarily addressed alcohol problems.[29] Her outspoken support for Commissioner Burke's anti-alcohol crusade attracted bitter criticism from community members aligned with the liquor trade interests.[30]

In fact, early in her first winter at Fort Yukon, rumors circulated that education authorities planned to reinstate Miss Nielsen (now Mrs. Curtis) in her teaching position. Breece received a letter notifying her that her contract would end the following spring, with no explanation, which appeared to confirm the rumors.[31] The news infuriated Stuck and revived his sense of antagonism on the part of the government toward the Episcopal mission. His impassioned letter to the chief of the Alaska Division of the Bureau of Education W. T. (Tom) Lopp and Bureau of Education director Philander Claxton clearly illustrated his paternalistic feelings toward Alaska Native people and his determination not to have the church's role among the people undermined: "The whole matter of the relations between the missions and the government schools on the Yukon cannot rest where it is. . . . We are willing to share with the Government the care of the natives; we are not willing to be elbowed out of long-established posts by the setting up, under government auspices, of antagonistic agencies in the very midst of our native tribes."[32]

Claxton assured Stuck that the bureau had no intention of dismissing Breece and reinstating Curtis.[33] Lopp wrote Breece, expressing his dismay that she could have imagined his doing her "an injustice or [giving] you anything but a square deal." Her contract was being terminated, he explained, owing to fiscal uncertainties. The bureau intended to reappoint Breece "as long as you are willing to remain at Fort Yukon and your work and loyalty is satisfactory."[34] This correspondence eased immediate concerns, but factionalism in Fort Yukon continued to color Breece's experience in the community.

Hap's energetic efforts to check the "lawlessness" in Fort Yukon deeply divided the community, even alienating some current and former missionaries. Boulter described "a feeling akin to hatred" between missionary factions in Fort Yukon.[35] Lizzie Wood, who had returned to Fort Yukon after taking medical leave in fall 1910, became a bitter critic of Burke, Stuck, and the mission. In early 1913 she married Frank White, a trapper and carpenter half her age. The union soured her relationship with Stuck, who found the match between the cultivated fifty-year-old missionary and the "wholly illiterate," much younger man unsuitable. Having lost many female missionaries to marriage, Stuck tended to resent Alaska men's penchant for depriving him of valued personnel.[36] Moreover, he often disparaged the character of the white male population of Alaska generally, using Robert Service's term "low-down white" from the *Ballads of the Yukon* to describe the worst lot.[37] This perspective, coupled with his stridency, caused many, including those whose views largely aligned with his, such as George Boulter, to bristle at his "arrogance."

In late January 1913 Stuck and Harper left Fort Yukon on their winter rounds. In spring they would embark on a quest to climb Denali, North America's tallest mountain and the most prominent landmark in the Dena' homeland, whose peak had never been summited. Stuck, an amateur mountaineer, spearheaded the effort and raised the funding privately. He convinced the rugged outdoorsman Harry Karstens to co-lead the expedition. Harper and Robert Tatum, a divinity student working at the Tanana mission, filled out the ascent team, while Johnny Fred and Esaias George, both now students at St. Mark's Mission, provided support.

In mid-March Stuck, Harper, and Karstens set out by dogsled from St. Matthew's Episcopal Church in Fairbanks, heading toward Nenana, where they would join up with Tatum, Fred, and George. From there the six continued toward the base of the mountain with two sleds and fourteen dogs.[38] In mid-April, after they had established their base camp at four thousand feet, Esaias returned to Nenana with one sled and dog team. Johnny remained to man the basecamp until the ascent team returned from the summit.

Along with the expected challenges of glacier crevasses, blizzards, Arctic winter temperatures, and altitude sickness, the ascent team overcame obstacles they could not have foreseen, including a fire that destroyed much of their supplies and a jumble of ice boulders that covered a three-mile stretch of the Northeast Ridge.[39] For three weeks, Karstens and Harper labored over the ridge, chopping steps in the ice to form a pathway upward. On June 7 the team reached the summit, with Harper in the lead. His physical stamina, stoicism, subsistence skills, and congeniality had played critical roles in the expedition's success throughout the ordeal. On summit day, Harper alone was unaffected by altitude sickness. Therefore, Karstens, who had provided the tactical leadership throughout the expedition, put Harper in the lead position. The stunning feat brought all members of the expedition acclaim, especially Stuck, who was the only one with a national reputation.[40]

After completing abbreviated summer rounds on the *Pelican*, Stuck and Harper traveled to the East Coast, where Walter enrolled at Mount Hermon School in Massachusetts, aiming to prepare himself for mission work in Alaska. Stuck remained Outside on furlough and traveled on a speaking circuit to raise funds for the Alaska mission work. As he had hoped, media coverage of the achievement on Denali enhanced his ability to draw crowds to his talks.

8. Fort Yukon, 1911. Rivenburg, Lawyer and Cora Photograph Album, #1994-70-279, APRCA, University of Alaska Fairbanks.

Meanwhile, at Fort Yukon, white men's bitterness toward Stuck for his seemingly wholesale condemnation of them colored their impressions of his protégé, Grafton Burke.[41] Hap nevertheless remained resolute. When a gang of angry men appeared at the mission home and demanded that he resign his commission, he refused. They responded with vague threats, whereupon, according to Clara, Hap calmly replied, "Gentlemen, . . . I intend to spend the rest of my life at Fort Yukon."[42]

His prosecution of the white trader Harry Horton especially angered whites, who felt he singled Horton out. "Hardboiled" Horton had flouted various laws, including illegally cohabiting with a Native woman. Cohabitation—that is, adultery or fornication—was illegal in Alaska, regardless of race, although prosecutions were rare. Stuck described the backroom of Horton's store as a drinking, gambling, and prostitution den.[43] In earlier days Horton had carried the mail on the Circle-to-Fort Yukon route.[44] Hap had saved his gangrenous arm, but the threat he posed to the trader's profits and lifestyle apparently overshadowed any goodwill he had earned.[45]

Hap also brought charges against two white men for supplying Alaska Natives with liquor.[46] In July 1913 the Burkes and Hannah Breece traveled more than four hundred miles downriver to Ruby, where the district court was in session. They remained five weeks as the grand jury considered the evidence against the accused. The jurors indicted all three, and the judge scheduled trials in Fairbanks in December.[47]

With the Burkes and Breece away at Ruby, criticism of Fort Yukon's mission and teacher intensified, as allies of Mrs. Curtis pressed for her reinstatement as schoolteacher. Rumors questioning Breece's character and treatment of students spread within the Native community. At a Native Council meeting that Superintendent Boulter attended, Native individuals asked about the possibility of replacing Miss Breece with Mrs. Curtis.[48] Boulter flatly denied the request. In relating the incident to his superior, Tom Lopp, he said he was certain that white women and "the worst class of white men in the town" had planted the idea of Breece's being removed. "Mrs. Curtis," he wrote, "is still, to the best of my knowledge writing to influential people in the States and making many charges—most of which are quite false—against the mission people." Boulter acknowledged that Breece's outspokenness put her at the center of the current controversies in Fort Yukon. He had advised her to consider "exercising a little more diplomacy in certain matters" and trying to "take Fort Yukon matters less to heart."[49] This would not be easy for Breece. The following month, Lizzie Wood White spread a story about her having injured a boy's legs when she disciplined him, a complete fabrication, according to Boulter. "Such is the ill-feeling between these two women," he wrote Lopp.[50]

Given the widespread knowledge of illicit activities in Fort Yukon, Hap issued numerous subpoenas for the trials to be held in Fairbanks. The deputy marshal at Circle City spent weeks tracking down witnesses, many of whom were out on their traplines and resented having their work interrupted. Among these was James Carroll, a twenty-year-old trapper who had arrived in the Interior three years before. He later recalled that other subpoenaed trappers were "dumbfounded at seeing the Marshal" and unaware of having committed any crime. As the marshal handed them the documents, they claimed they "knew nothing, heard nothing, saw nothing," the standard response of whites called to testify against other whites.[51]

As the Fort Yukon cases moved toward trial, resentment against Hap grew so strong within the community that residents lodged an array of charges against him, ranging from outlandish to trivial. Bishop Rowe reported that the liquor interests in Fort Yukon offered the Native Council $500 if members would denounce Dr. Burke, but the council "indignantly rejected" the bribe.[52] Stuck later wrote that William Loola never wavered in his faithfulness to Hap or to the mission's work,[53] and nearly all the Gwich'in of Fort Yukon stood by him, although some found common cause with the bootleggers.[54]

In December 1913 scores of Fort Yukon residents, including fourteen of the twenty whites living there, set out at two o'clock in the morning for the 250-mile journey by dogsled to Fairbanks for the trials. Clara and two-year-old Hudson traveled in one sled, Hap drove another, and Hannah Breece, who would testify on behalf of the government, rode in a toboggan with no runners. Her Native driver, Ginnis, jogged alongside her dog team. Wrapped in multiple layers of furs, the women and child suffered little from the severe cold. The rough frozen surface of the Yukon River, however, which served as their trail for the first leg of the journey— the eighty-mile run to Circle—jostled them fiercely at times.[55] An early hard freeze that fall followed by heavy rain at the Yukon's headwaters had caused the surface ice to heave, break up, and refreeze in jumbled masses. Both the lead dog and Ginnis were responsible for warning Breece's dog team to avoid thin ice and airholes, and as the dogs became increasingly unruly, Ginnis's swearing at them grew louder and cruder. Eventually, Breece scolded Ginnis, asking him what his wife, Rachel, her good friend, would think of his language. "All right, Teacher," he said, and abruptly stopped swearing. Shortly thereafter, the dogs ran straight toward a large hole in the ice, as Ginnis's polite pleas failed to divert them. Breece shouted, "Swear, Ginnis! Oh, swear!" and he promptly resumed his preferred command style, averting disaster.[56] Overnight stays at warm roadhouses punctuated the trying three-day journey to Circle. From there they traveled six long days in bitterly cold weather toward Fairbanks, crossing through mountainous terrain with deep snow.[57]

Apart from the anxiety generated by the trial, Breece relished her six-week stay in Fairbanks, as friends she had known in Seward graciously hosted her.[58] Other witnesses likely enjoyed the interim in Fairbanks as well, given the government's per diem rate of $15.[59] Breece pronounced that Fairbanks residents fell into two distinct classes. "The majority were pleasure-mad," she said. Others were "quiet, educated people" who filled their days with intellectual pursuits, playing tennis, and going for sled rides. On second thought, she admitted that the same could be said of any other city of similar size in the States.[60]

The verdicts could have been predicted. The grand jury failed to return "true bills" on charges against W. D. Clark and Maria Oats of Fort Yukon for selling liquor to Natives.[61] Representing the defendants, as well as Horton, was Thomas McGowan, the attorney for NC Company, the largest seller of alcohol in the territory.[62] The next week, Horton's trial generated great public interest. Large crowds attended each day's proceedings.[63] The charge was cohabiting with a Native female, Johanna Stevens, for nearly a year.[64] Assistant U.S. district attorney L. R. Gillette called witnesses who testified that they had seen the defendant and the "girl" in "improper attitudes." The prosecution submitted a letter Horton had written to Stevens telling her he was lonely, urging her to be a good girl, saying he loved her, and sending her love and kisses.[65] Numerous Native residents of Fort Yukon testified for the government, causing the trial to extend for several days owing to the use of translators. Despite copious evidence and incriminating testimony, McGowan asked the judge for a directed verdict, saying that no testimony corroborated the charge of illegal cohabitation. Judge Fuller rejected the request.[66]

Horton then flatly denied the charges, saying he employed the young woman as a domestic servant over the last three years. He said she was rarely there after six or seven in the evening and only for specific reasons. Horton testified that he paid her $5 a week for housecleaning work and sometimes more for extra tasks. As for the letter, he claimed that he meant only friendship and that Natives understood "love" to mean friendship.[67]

The defense then focused on Burke's conduct and St. Stephen's Mission operations. McGowan claimed that the Burkes had unduly influenced Native witnesses and accused Clara and Hannah Breece of using head signals to coach Native witnesses in their responses to questions. Superintendent Boulter stated flatly that no such signaling occurred and reported that these accusations had no bearing on the case.[68]

Witnesses for the defense, claiming that Burke and others aimed to destroy Horton's business, attested to Horton's reputation for honesty and said they had never seen Stevens in his domicile except to work or when other Natives were there. One witness testified that he had tried to bring charges against Burke to the district attorney and had written a letter to the grand jury, to no avail. Judge Fuller declared this testimony irrelevant to the issue at hand and ordered it stricken from the record. The judge also struck testimony of a Native female after the defense objected that the district attorney's office had tried to intimidate her.[69] Despite ample evidence and many witnesses who supported the government's case, the jury acquitted Horton after deliberating just seven minutes. According to George Boulter, the defense had resorted to "many mean methods" in disparaging the character of various government witnesses. "Much perjury has been committed" during the trials, he wrote Lopp. In reflecting on Horton's exoneration, Boulter described a prevailing sentiment that missionaries were arrogant and self-righteous, when their own conduct was not always "above reproach."[70] The *Fairbanks Daily News Miner* pronounced that "the verdict seemed to be one of general satisfaction to the public at large," noting the "throngs" of spectators who had filled the courtroom each day.[71] Reportedly, much of the Fairbanks public viewed the prosecuting attorney, James Crossley, as "a carpet-bagger ignorant of western ways."[72]

The trial of Merle McCambridge, also accused of illegal cohabitation with a Native girl for nearly one year, began the following day. Both Hap and Clara testified that the defendant had come to their home and promised to marry his girlfriend if Hap would drop the charges. Boulter testified that in August 1911 in Tanana, McCambridge had been accused of seduction of a Native girl and that he had been released after promising to marry the girl, although he never had. Reed Heilig, the defense attorney, objected to the admission of this evidence as immaterial, but the judge overruled the objection, saying that its purpose was to inform of the "disposition of the defendant toward native women generally."[73]

McCambridge denied all charges, saying he never spent the night at the girl's house. Defense witnesses testified that McCambridge had merely brought water and provided assistance at her home, just as others had done. Again, within minutes, the jury returned with an acquittal.[74] "It seems the jury acquitted anyone the mission folks testified against," Boulter remarked.[75]

Following these trials, a grand jury heard the charges against Hap.[76] "The Fort Yukon people, together with Burke's many enemies now at Fairbanks," Boulter observed, "appear determined to hound him to the finish."[77] The grand jury's effort to have Hap's case go to trial failed, largely owing to District Attorney Crossley's forceful defense of Burke. Five men on the grand jury were currently under investigation by authorities,[78] which underscored Boulter's complaint from a few years earlier that it was "almost impossible to secure an honest jury."[79]

The trials cost the government over $20,000, including witness per diem fees, an enormous sum, yet they yielded no convictions. The expense fueled outrage among critics of Crossley's, Stuck's, and Burke's efforts to control such "harmless" behaviors. One newspaper editor in Fairbanks renewed his call for the church to pay court costs when prosecution efforts failed.[80]

During the trials, both Lizzie White and Mrs. Curtis (Miss Nielsen) lobbied Boulter to hire them as teachers at Fort Yukon, claiming that Breece "would hardly dare return" there after the trials ended. In reporting these events, Boulter assured his supervisor, Tom Lopp, that Breece would indeed return, although life there would be "unpleasant owing to the acute ill-feeling displayed toward her" by white women who identified with "the vicious element in town." Boulter described Mrs. Curtis's disposition as "venomous" and the women's complaints as trivial. He speculated that Curtis's "somewhat worthless" husband had lured her away from the principled residents of Fort Yukon toward the disreputable crowd.[81] Lizzie White's animosity toward Fort Yukon mission personnel and supporters was more lamentable. The former Miss Wood had served the Episcopal missions at Circle and Fort Yukon for many years and had joined Stuck and the Burkes in fighting alcohol abuse among the Gwich'in.[82] Perhaps a sense of betrayal at Stuck's disapproval of her marriage had led her to sympathize with opponents of mission and school authorities.[83] Stuck held out little hope for a happy marriage for Lizzie, but James Carroll claimed that the Whites remained a devoted couple until her death in 1920.[84]

Hap's "exoneration" on the charges of malfeasance did little to restore peace at Fort Yukon. A deputy marshal finally assigned there was a drunk who sold alcohol to Native residents. When Hap had him removed and replaced, the marshal flew into a rage, went on a drunken rampage, burst through the door of the mission home, and attacked Hap with a bear claw. Hap reportedly pummeled him senseless—and then treated the injuries as the patient looked on warily. The encounter earned Hap respect in some quarters, but tensions remained high.[85] Thomas Wonecoff, the second deputy marshal posted at Fort Yukon, had been a member of the grand jury that sought to indict Hap. James Carroll later described the marshal, who liked to be called Doc, in colorful terms, noting his penchant for drinking. "Dock [sic] sure liked his drinks. He used to wrap his thumb and forefinger around the top of his glass; these acted as sideboards. He could double the volume of his drink this way. Dock claimed he was the son of a minister, but nobody believed him."[86] Crossley described Wonecoff as "absolutely unreliable in every way." According to Crossley, he and others harassed the Burkes and Breece, owing to her solidarity with them and her testimony at trial.[87]

Meanwhile, Archdeacon Stuck had been defending the interests of the Gwich'in of Fort Yukon by other means. A trader and known whiskey peddler who claimed he had purchased a cabin within the Native village planned to build additional structures there. Stuck, who was aware of the legal precedents on Native title, urged his friend James Crossley to file suit to stop the encroachment on Native lands.[88] Crossley won *U.S. v. Cadzow*, in which the Alaska District Court upheld the right and obligation of the federal government to protect Alaska Natives' title to their land.[89] In February 1914 President Woodrow Wilson, at the urging of both Stuck and Rowe, issued an executive order reserving seventy-five acres, including the Native village of Fort Yukon, under the Department of Education's jurisdiction, for the exclusive use of area Native people. This was the fourth such reserve established in Alaska, and the federal government intended to establish others to protect Alaska Natives "from the intrusion and evil influences of unprincipled white men," according to Commissioner of Education Claxton.[90] Stuck's role in this effort attracted negative attention from the press and the public. *Fairbanks Daily News Miner* publisher W. F. Thompson accused him of "slandering" Alaskans as he raised funds for mission work and lobbied policymakers Outside.[91]

The Fort Yukon trader later established his post directly outside the reserve.[92] Fort Yukon residents who remained indignant over the perceived restriction on their economic freedom posed by the reserve, along with "powerful agencies which do not want the law enforced," as Stuck put it, pressured Wilson to remove Crossley and Judge Frederick Fuller, who presided over the Cadzow case. Both men eventually lost their positions, illustrating Alaska's dominant frontier political culture that favored the interests of non-Natives.[93]

In summer 1914 Stuck returned to Fort Yukon, having raised sufficient funds to begin construction on a long-overdue hospital at Fort Yukon, and a crew began the groundwork for the foundation. Johnny Fred, who had returned to St. Mark's in fall 1913 after the Denali expedition, joined Stuck on the *Pelican*, assisting him as Harper had.[94] Just after they departed Fort Yukon, a tragic accident occurred, reminding Hap and Clara that despite the inroads they had made in suppressing the liquor traffic, they had not won the war.

A Native runner arrived at St. Stephen's with news of a boat accident and serious injury. Billy Moore, Horton's business partner, an honest, sober, and well-respected man, had taken a paddle wheeler with a hired crew up the Porcupine River, heading toward Horton's trading post at Old Crow in the Yukon Territory. The crew saw the journey as an opportunity for drinking, and they brought a supply of liquor with them. When the boat ran aground on a sandbar, Billy climbed down with a crowbar to release the paddlewheel, firmly instructing the crew members not to start the engine. As he labored, one of the drunken crew members started the engine. The blades nearly severed his legs and left his body with gruesome injuries. Crew members rushed him in a rowboat downriver to Rampart House, where the trader tried to stop the bleeding. Then Billy was moved to a cabin within a five-mile portage of Fort Yukon, where he lay for three days, as the runner dashed to Fort Yukon to summon Hap.[95]

Upon Hap's arrival at the cabin, he dressed Moore's wounds as best as possible and had him transported to Fort Yukon. There, Clara and Lizzie White took turns assisting Hap in the kitchen as he treated Moore's injuries, with Johnny observing. Hap soon recognized that he would have to transfer Moore to the hospital at Ft. Gibbon. Moore lost both legs, but when Stuck stopped at Tanana to visit him, Moore was in good spirits. With Hap's assurance that he could have him fitted with artificial legs so he could resume his work as a trader, Moore looked forward to traveling Outside with the Burkes at summer's end. Moore pledged to do all he could in the fight against the liquor interests in Fort Yukon. He died shortly thereafter, however, of an abdominal hemorrhage. The incident and Billy's death shocked Fort Yukon residents, including the remorseful drunken crew members.[96] The experience helped heal relationships as well. The bitterness Lizzie White had felt toward mission personnel seems to have faded as she worked alongside Hap and Clara to save Billy's life. Stuck wrote that some of those within the white community who had stood with the liquor interests apologized to Hap.[97] According to Clara, the rest of the summer at Fort Yukon was the most sober in their experience.[98] Even Harry Horton eventually became an ally.

That summer, at Stuck's request, two men representing the Indian Rights Association (IRA) visited Alaska's Interior to evaluate living conditions among Alaska's Native peoples. Stuck hoped their report would stir action in Congress to protect Native rights and to respond to their medical needs. He also hoped it would influence mission friends of various denominations to support the construction and operation of hospitals and dispensaries in the region.[99] The IRA, a European-American group concerned with the well-being and acculturation of Native Americans, was influential in Indian policy from its founding in 1882 through the 1930s. Matthew Sniffen, an IRA board member, and Thomas Carrington, a physician, surveyed conditions among the Dena' peoples along the Yukon and Tanana rivers and produced a report on their findings for the IRA. They traveled as tourists, and no one except Stuck, the Burkes, and perhaps one or two other mission supporters at Fort Yukon knew of their purpose.[100]

Sniffen and Carrington learned much about public opinion on an array of matters, including attitudes toward the missionaries, relations between

Natives and non-Natives, and living conditions among the Native peoples. Their report, which Sniffen wrote based on the pair's observations and interpretations and that Carrington read and approved, offers outsider observations of public opinion near the close of Burke's tenure as commissioner.[101] While their sympathies lay with the Burkes and Stuck, given their common aims in advancing the interests of Native peoples, the report nevertheless provides a useful assessment of social dynamics amid the controversies. Along with their own observations and interpretation of opinions people expressed to them directly, the report includes information they learned after the fact.

The travelers described Fort Yukon as a "hostile camp" when they arrived in June, owing to the conflict over the liquor trade with Natives, the illegal cohabitation cases, and the Native land dispute.[102] Because they traveled ostensibly as tourists, they "mingled very freely with the whites at Fort Yukon," who spoke "very frankly" with them, Sniffen wrote. "A number of them have good traits, but the majority have a 'free and easy' standard of morals, and according to their code the Indian women are regarded as the legitimate game of the whites." These men reportedly reasoned that because Native women generally were sexually experienced, no harm could come from their having sexual relations with white men. Sniffen reported that they "bitterly resent Archdeacon Stuck's assertion that the white men at Fort Yukon are degenerates." The missionaries, on the other hand, viewed the "promiscuous mixing of Indians and whites" differently from sexual relations between Natives, because Native mores differed from those of whites. Missionaries understood that "in the case of the white man these relations bring whisky and disease."[103] About twelve white men in Fort Yukon reportedly were married to Native women, and through marriage, these women gained the legal rights of whites to purchase alcohol. Sniffen and Carrington surmised that some of the alcohol these Native women purchased found its way into Fort Yukon's Native community.[104]

As they traveled downriver that summer, the visitors heard "all sorts of extravagant and slanderous stories about Doctor Burke," which "investigation proved [to be] either grossly exaggerated or absolutely without foundation."[105] They had occasion to observe Hap as commissioner during

The Fort Yukon Bunch - Left to Right: Harry Horton, Trader, W.C. Curtis, John McNickel, Bill Mason, Unidentified Mountie, Rube Mason, Unidentified, Jim Carroll, Bill O'Brien. Seated, Pete Nelson, Joe Ward, Tommy The Mate.

9. "The Fort Yukon Bunch," including T. A. (Harry) Horton and James Carroll. Fabian Carey Collection, #1975-209-15, APRCA, University of Alaska Fairbanks.

the trial of a man accused of being insane. "Dr. Burke handled the case in a direct and business-like manner," Sniffen reported, demonstrating that he understood his duties, contrary to some of the gossip they had heard.[106]

Despite the resistance Hap faced in enforcing the law, the social climate in Fort Yukon had improved during his term. Sniffen described a "moral wave" sweeping Alaska that summer that extended far beyond the shock and grief at Fort Yukon surrounding Billy Moore's death. According to Sniffen, saloons closed on Sundays, open gambling no longer took place, and in some areas, laws against open illegal cohabitation were enforced. Typically, either marriage resulted or the man left the country; even Harry Horton had married the woman he had claimed was his housekeeper.[107] The tide seemed to be turning in both social and health conditions. In the past four years, since Clara had joined Hap at Fort Yukon, health and well-being in the community had advanced markedly. Infant mortality had dropped by 70 percent,[108] sanitation had improved, and drinking had diminished.[109]

In 1915 Stuck reported on the changes in conditions since Hap's arrival six years before. The vital statistics at Fort Yukon were "more encouraging than at any other point on the river" where they had data. In 1912 deaths exceeded births nineteen to eleven. In 1913 births outnumbered deaths twenty to fourteen. At all other points along the Yukon, deaths exceeded births, Stuck noted, while acknowledging that such figures varied from year to year. Living quarters and the standard of living had improved at Fort Yukon. A recent census documented forty-five cabins occupied by 211 persons, with about 200 more traveling to the village for Fourth of July and Christmas. The cabins contained fifty bedsteads, twenty sewing machines, nine phonographs, fifteen rifles, and seventy shotguns. Sixteen fish wheels had been in operation the previous summer. The community was currently experiencing a recession, however, because the war in Europe had decimated the demand for fur, the primary basis of Fort Yukon's economy, and almost no fur sales had taken place the previous winter.[110]

The strain of slanderous accusations and physical attacks on Hap eventually proved intolerable. Billy Moore's death was the last straw.[111] Hap resigned as commissioner in summer 1914. He and Clara looked forward to an overdue furlough, when he would conduct postgraduate surgical training in New York, one year at Cornell University's medical school, and a year at Bellevue Hospital in New York City.[112] The responsibilities of the mission and medical work at St. Stephen's had been onerous even before Hap had taken on the commissioner position.[113] Moreover, Stuck's absence from winter–spring 1913 through spring 1914 had left Hap to respond to the community's medical, spiritual, and legal needs and problems without direct support from his father figure. Sniffen described Hap as "on the verge of a nervous collapse" in summer 1914 and noted that he was "'going out' for his vacation none too soon."[114]

In his annual report of 1914–15, Bishop Rowe wrote with satisfaction, "The Church is familiar with the story of the heroic struggle made by Archdeacon Stuck and Dr. Burke for righteousness, against desperate foes—a struggle gloriously won." Fort Yukon had transformed from one of the villages with the most alcohol-related problems to one of the most peaceful. The Gwich'in Council, he said, had helped turn conditions around and promoted the Native community's unity and independence from negative influences.[115]

In retrospect, Hap's appointment as commissioner had put him in an unworkable position. In his role as justice of the peace, he had sown rancor within the community that compromised Episcopal mission goals and destroyed much of the goodwill he had earned with his sunny disposition and the competent, compassionate medical care he provided. Sniffen observed that virtually all who sympathized with the missionaries' efforts now viewed his appointment as commissioner as regrettable. Yet they seemed to believe that Burke had had no other choice, given the absence of law enforcement at Fort Yukon.[116]

By the time Hap and Clara returned to Fort Yukon in early summer 1916, many of their former critics welcomed them. In their absence Stuck had begun construction on the hospital with funds he, the Burkes, and Bishop Rowe had raised, and the community looked forward to the opening of its first hospital that fall. Misgivings about the couple who had filled in for the Burkes during their furlough likely contributed to a renewed appreciation of Hap and Clara. Community members reportedly perceived the interim doctor as incompetent and his wife as "shrewish."[117] In fact, he had been unscrupulous, among other things charging exorbitant fees for medical services rendered in outlying areas and retaining the payments himself.[118] Bishop Arthur Lloyd, president of the Episcopal Board of Missions, wrote Hap in September 1917 that he was hearing reports now, after the hoopla had died down and the results of his commissioner work were seen, that "you were a pretty decent sort," whereas "I used to hear that you ought to be hung!"[119] Some years later, James Carroll wrote, "That particular eager commissioner was retired of his commissionership and Fort Yukon has lived quietly and in peace ever since."[120] In fact, both Stuck and Burke continued their efforts to suppress the liquor trade with the Native people, but they did so less obtrusively within Fort Yukon. Stuck lobbied in Washington DC and through articles, lectures, and interviews with newspaper journalists for full prohibition in Alaska. His and others' actions led to a 1916 plebiscite in which Alaska voters overwhelmingly supported prohibition in the territory. Based on this advisory vote, Congress passed the Alaska Bone-Dry Law to enact prohibition in Alaska. The act took effect on January 1, 1918.[121]

Hap's tenure as U.S. commissioner illuminates Interior Alaska's complex sociocultural and political dynamics in the early 1900s as the non-Native population grew. Newcomers tended to be rough-around-the-edges individualists who contributed to the prevailing frontier atmosphere. They enjoyed their liquor, felt antipathy for almost any sort of regulation, and flouted the law as they pursued their economic interests and fulfilled their appetites for pleasure. Non-Native men tended to attract Native women easily. The men often abandoned the children born of these liaisons, moving on before their birth or deserting their families when they returned Outside or sought economic opportunities elsewhere in the territory.[122]

Christian missionaries arrived with intentions of bringing the message of Christianity to Alaska Natives, improving their health conditions, educating them in preparation for adapting to Euro-American culture and U.S. citizenship, and protecting them from the negative effects of exposure to mainstream American society. Some of their efforts, including improving sanitation and hygiene, providing medical care, and protecting hunting and fishing rights, clearly had positive effects. Missionaries exhibited a range of attitudes toward Native cultures and lifeways, some explicitly denigrating them and others, like the Burkes and Stuck, warmly embracing them and urging the people to maintain their traditional ways. Yet even those with the most respectful intentions acted paternalistically, exerting authority and imposing their Christian and Victorian values on the Native people, which challenged traditional beliefs and customs, creating divisions within families and communities.

Likewise, government agents—law enforcement and school authorities—arrived to serve and protect, but they, too, asserted themselves in ways that constrained Natives' personal and collective sovereignty. Moreover, lower-level law officers were often incompetent and/or alcohol abusers themselves and committed far more harm than good. The goals of missionaries and Bureau of Education agents generally coincided, but the two groups sometimes found themselves at odds, and each resented perceived infringement by the other on their authority.

Alaska Natives responded variously to the waves of migrants whose presence transformed their lives dramatically and to the religious and civic agents of change who sought their cooperation as they implemented their well-meant, though ethnocentric, goals. Some largely maintained their traditional lifestyles while selectively adopting beliefs and habits they found credible and useful. Some warmly embraced Christianity and actively engaged in mission work, transforming the missions into community institutions. Many eagerly sought schooling for their children, especially industrial training that would lead to employment. Many pursued economic opportunities that supported and complemented their subsistence lifestyles. Far too many succumbed to the deadly combination of disease and vices that newcomers brought.

After Hap and Clara returned from their well-earned furlough, they continued to dedicate their lives to the physical, social, and spiritual health and well-being of the Gwich'in people. Hap focused his efforts more narrowly on his pastoral duties and his medical work, which expanded tremendously with the opening of St. Stephen's Hospital in fall 1916. In typical fashion, he welcomed the challenge, eager to extend medical care to more people, to bring medical advancements to Alaska's northern Interior, and to expand his surgical skills.

5   Opening St. Stephen's Hospital and Closing a Chapter, 1916–21

With their return to Fort Yukon in June 1916, Hap and Clara refocused their efforts on their strengths, gathering children in need of care into their home and preparing to open St. Stephen's Hospital. Clara prioritized the children while transforming the mission home into a community center. She began a Sunday night supper club, inviting the local single white men—a colorful cast of characters—to dinner after Sunday evening church services. She made the events "gala affairs," using the silver, fine china, and linen they had received as wedding gifts and creating delectable meals. The soirees offered a stimulating alternative to drinking and gambling at the roadhouse, and they helped mend fences following Hap's contentious term as commissioner. Johnny Fred returned from school at St. Mark's Mission to assist Hap with the hospital work.[1]

Hap's first few years directing St. Stephen's Hospital would test his mental, emotional, and physical capacities. The heavy responsibilities, along with harrowing personal experiences and deaths of loved ones, would cause him to question his career and life choices. The exuberance and perennial cheerfulness that had earned him his nickname veiled a tender, vulnerable soul and a physical constitution less resilient than it appeared. Hap loved unconditionally and relied heavily on those closest to him—his wife and his father figure Hudson Stuck—for strength and moral support. In 1914, when they had been on furlough, Clara's mother had convinced the couple that she and little Hudson should remain in California while Hap began his medical studies in New York. "Can't stand this," Hap wired Clara two weeks after leaving for New York. "Take next train." Clara and Hudson left immediately to join him.[2] In the coming years, amid extended periods of joy in their life's work, Hap would experience episodes of frustration, anguish, self-doubt, and prostrating grief as financial and personnel challenges, health crises, and Stuck's death revealed how close to the limits of endurance he functioned.

By summer 1916, when Hap and Clara returned, the hospital's exterior was complete, but much work remained on the interior. The hospital, mission home, and government schoolhouse lay between the Native and non-Native sections of Fort Yukon.[3] The many windows of the long, two-story hospital structure let in the natural light. St. Stephen's would be North America's only hospital above the Arctic Circle and the only one within more than 800 miles along the Yukon.[4] Dawson, the capital of the Yukon Territory, which lay nearly 500 miles upstream, and Fort Gibbon, which lay 320 miles downstream near Tanana, had hospitals, but neither treated Alaska Natives. After decades of fruitless pleas to Congress from Alaska's governors and from Episcopal mission leadership for a hospital for Alaska Natives of the northern Interior, Bishop Rowe and Archdeacon Stuck had finally convinced the Episcopal Mission Society to fund the hospital. With Hap and Clara, they personally secured much of the $25,000 cost through speaking tours Outside.[5] When St. Matthew's Hospital in Fairbanks closed in 1915 after the Catholic St. Joseph's Hospital opened, equipment, instruments, and supplies from St. Matthew's were sent to Fort Yukon for use at St. Stephen's until Hap could purchase new equipment and supplies.[6] Bishop Rowe would eventually deem St. Stephen's hospital operations at Fort Yukon the Episcopal Church's most vital mission work in all Alaska.[7]

Yet from the hospital's inception, Stuck, Hap, Clara, and Rowe struggled mightily to obtain funds for operational costs and to secure and retain qualified personnel.[8] The church failed to budget sufficiently for fish, meat, and fresh vegetables to feed the patients and hospital personnel, for repairs to the building and equipment, and for utilities and incidentals. Woman's auxiliaries sent boxes of items, some of which could be used as in-kind payments to Fort Yukon residents who provided services for the hospital and mission.[9] In a March 1917 article in the Episcopal Church's *Spirit of Missions*, Stuck appealed for financial support for the hospital's operations, noting the high costs in the Arctic.[10] In the ensuing years, Rowe, Stuck, and the Burkes would regularly appeal to mission friends to finance both general and specific needs that exceeded St. Stephen's allocations.

In July 1916 Lester Bradner, an Episcopal pastor who worked within the church's department of education, visited Interior Alaska with his family, traveling down the Yukon River from Whitehorse. The family stayed a week at Fort Yukon, during which Bradner acquainted himself with the community and with mission operations. Upon their departure, he summarized his impressions of Hap and Clara: "Dr. Burke and his wife are a great team. He . . . jovial, hearty, full to overflowing of boyish fun and humor, undaunted in emergencies, but a little haphazard in work, more methodical in family prayers than in anything else, I noted, and interested alike in Indian and white man. Mrs. Burke . . . is frank and attractive, heavy in figure but animated in face and movement, steady, methodical, uncomplaining, an excellent cook and careful mother to her little five year old Hudson."[11] Visitors would describe the two remarkably similarly over the years, except that their wonder at Clara's management of a large household of happy, rambunctious children would grow. Bradner also noted William Loola's strong character and his respected standing in the community, as well as David Wallis's elevated stature, his value to the mission work, and his fine family.[12]

On August 6 Stuck, Walter Harper, and Rev. William Thomas arrived at Fort Yukon to a warm welcome from the Native people and a joyous reunion with Hap and Clara.[13] Stuck had met Walter at Mount Hermon School where he had been studying for three years, and the two headed home to Alaska, traveling by train to Seattle. In Chicago the twenty-seven-year-old Thomas joined them. The young cleric had heard Stuck lecture and seen his accompanying lantern slides on the Alaska mission work and had been inspired to enlist in the cause.[14]

Each day at Fort Yukon brought Thomas new experiences. He noted the "three hours backward" schedule based on the constant daylight and the brilliant colors of the evening sky as the sun descended toward the horizon. He found the Gwich'in people's evident faith moving, and he appreciated their spirited singing in their Native language in church. Thomas spent eight days assisting Hap in moving, unpacking, and arranging boxes of supplies and equipment in preparation for St. Stephen's

Hospital's opening. He and Hap would work late into the night at the hospital, go to bed at 2:00 a.m., and rise at 10:00 a.m. to begin the next workday. Occasionally, he took breaks to sit with patients.[15]

Thomas marveled at Clara's fine culinary skills and the overwhelming scope of her mission duties. His introduction to northern Interior Alaska cuisine included dinners based on an array of local fish and game: caribou steak soup, freshly caught king salmon, mallards, moose, and teal. Of the women's responsibilities at the mission, he observed, "The work here is very heavy on Mrs. Burke and Miss Kanton. These women missionaries are the most self sacrificing souls in the world."[16]

In mid-August Thomas traveled downriver to Nenana to begin his first official assignment as pastor at St. Mark's Mission. He immersed himself in the mission work, visiting the fish camps in the region and taking delight in the landscape and the warm reception he received from the Native people. He and Rev. Frederick Drane, superintendent of the Tanana Valley mission work, who was based at Chena, became good friends. Drane had arrived the previous summer fresh from seminary school and ordination to the priesthood and was about the same age as Thomas. The following year Thomas transferred to St. Thomas Mission at Tikiġaq/Point Hope on Alaska's northwest coast, and Drane moved his headquarters to Nenana.[17]

In summer 1916 much of Interior Alaska bustled with activity surrounding construction of the Alaska Railroad from Seward at tidewater in southcentral Alaska to Fairbanks. In March 1914, with the enthusiastic backing of James Wickersham, Alaska's delegate to Congress, Congress had passed, and President Woodrow Wilson had signed, the Alaska Railroad Bill.[18] The Alaska Engineering Commission that Wilson appointed to recommend the most favorable route had chosen the Seward-to-Fairbanks option that passed through the fertile Matanuska Valley, northward through Dena' territory to Fairbanks. The village of Nenana, where St. Mark's Mission had developed a model boarding school for Alaska Native children, lay a mile from the boomtown of Nenana, where the railroad crossed the Tanana River. Tents that housed migrant workers would give way to standard homes and businesses, including pool halls and a cinema; even the Roman Catholics and Presbyterians built churches there.[19] Most non-Natives in the Interior celebrated the opportunities for natural resource development and commercial agriculture that rail access to tidewater permitted.

Although few of those who celebrated the advent of the railroad considered its impacts on Alaska Natives, Wickersham had long demonstrated his interest in the Native people's well-being. In summer 1915, when he returned from Washington DC, he surveyed conditions in the Tanana Valley, where he met with Chief Alexander of Tolovana, an outspoken advocate for Native interests. He warned the Dena' chief of the changes to come, especially the threat to Native lands with the influx of land-hungry migrants, and he urged Alexander to have his people consider reservations or Native allotments. Alexander spread word of Wickersham's warning, and in early July 1915, fourteen Native representatives, including chiefs, other leaders, and an interpreter, met with Wickersham in Fairbanks. At the historic 1915 meeting of the Tanana Chiefs, these leaders, some through an interpreter, asked for Wickersham's frank opinions, and they stated their positions regarding the railroad and the threats to their lands.[20] They rejected the notion of reservations. Chief Alexander testified, "We are people who are always on the go, and I believe that if we are put in one place we would die off like rabbits."[21] Interpreter Paul Williams summarized the chiefs' concerns; they wanted industrial schools to train their people for employment opportunities, having been denied access to such work in the past. In short, they wanted "school, a doctor, and some labor."[22]

Meanwhile, work had already begun at Nenana, and Episcopal mission personnel foresaw the end of the isolation that had allowed St. Mark's to flourish. When the church built the mission in 1907, the idea of a railroad passing adjacent to the site had not arisen. By 1916 Rowe noted similarities between Nenana and Tanana, where bootlegged alcohol and other forms of exploitation disrupted traditional lifeways and led to domestic violence, disease, and high death rates. Visiting-priest Lester Bradner noted the "cloud" hanging over mission personnel in summer 1916, owing to the growth of the "white town" at Nenana. Rowe, Stuck, and other missionaries considered moving St. Mark's to a more remote site, but Native residents objected to leaving, according to Bradner, because the village lay at a traditional site.[23]

Late that summer, Johnny Fred entered Mount Hermon School in Massachusetts, with Stuck committing to pay his tuition. Stuck had recognized Johnny's potential when he first met the eight-year-old boy in 1904 at Fort Yukon, and Johnny's performance on the Denali expedition had deepened their bond. When Walter left for Mount Hermon in summer 1913, Johnny had assumed his position with Stuck on the *Pelican* and winter trail. As Stuck assisted Johnny in applying to Mount Hermon, he suggested that the young man adopt the last name Fredson, a more familiar sounding name from Stuck's perspective and a natural choice, from a Western perspective, for the son of Old Fred. Having assisted Hap for several years in the infirmary and this summer in preparing for the hospital's opening, Johnny envisioned going to medical school, a goal Stuck supported.[24]

That fall a new government schoolteacher, Winifred Dalziel, arrived at Fort Yukon. The petite, cheerful "dynamo," as Clara described her,[25] was "amiability and kindness itself," in the words of Hudson Stuck.[26] She became a valued friend, trusted ally, and tremendous support for Hap and Clara in both the mission home and hospital. A trained teacher with practical nursing experience, she regularly volunteered at the hospital.[27]

Just as the hospital was to open in early October, an enormous swath of earth in front of the mission home broke off and fell into the Yukon River, damming it and deflecting the current. Just six feet remained between the riverbank and the mission's front porch. Quick action—placing sandbags and brush to hold the bank as the water dropped—held it, safeguarding the home for the time being.[28] In the coming weeks, the main river channel changed course, leaving the channel in front of the mission no more than a slough, which froze solid by October 31. The mission home clearly would have to be moved before next year's break-up.[29]

Pride and excitement surrounded the opening of St. Stephen's Hospital that month. Its remote Arctic location, however, posed enormous challenges that neither Hap and Clara, nor Stuck, nor Rowe could have appreciated fully. As director of the hospital, Hap bore ultimate responsibility for operations, in addition to his medical work. When the hospital opened, the building had no electric lights, running water, heating system, or laundry and drying space. An acetylene-gas plant that burned 250

10. St. Stephen's Hospital, circa 1920. Alaskan Missions of the Episcopal Church.

gallons a week in midwinter provided the lighting. The most onerous task by far was hauling water to the mission home and hospital. Water had to be drawn from the river, which in winter required breaking a hole each day through thick ice, dipping out the water into a galvanized iron tank on a dogsled, hauling the tank to the hospital door, and transferring the contents to buckets to be distributed throughout the hospital and mission home. Several holding tanks in the hospital, mission home kitchen, and lighting plant had to be filled regularly. The furnaces, once installed, burned countless cords of wood through the winter, at a cost of $1,000 a year.[30]

Hospital operations required a full-time handyman or two, an expense mission headquarters had difficulty accepting. At times both Stuck and Burke paid for the help from their own meager salaries.[31] In fall 1917, at Stuck's urging, the board allotted $50 a month for Esaias George, the youngest member of the Denali expedition, as a "man-of-all-work."[32]

One of the hospital's first patients was Lizzie Wood White, who while helping her husband operate his sawmill had fallen against the circular saw, tearing the muscles of her neck and exposing major veins and arteries.

As she lay at the hospital in shock from loss of blood, Hap sutured and dressed her wounds, saving her life.[33] This experience likely removed any residual ill will on the Whites' part related to Hap's tumultuous term as commissioner. She supported the mission work and the mission family in various ways in the coming years.

The hospital's impact on health in the region proved itself immediately. An outbreak of pneumonia in November brought five patients to the hospital, where they recovered under the strict care regimen: sleeping in a cold ward with open windows and warmed by hot-water bottles regularly replaced by the nurses.[34] Hap believed that without hospitalization, these pneumonia patients would have succumbed to the disease that took many lives each year in Alaska. Open air and sunshine were now the preferred treatments for both pneumonia and tuberculosis.[35] Hap also successfully treated a young girl with tuberculosis that winter. Her recovery likely owed as much to her own immune system, good nutrition, rest, and perhaps the cheerful atmosphere in the hospital as to the fresh air and sunshine. Hap sent a plea to mission friends for warm clothing for hospitalized children and adults receiving their treatment in cold quarters.[36]

Even as the patient load at St. Stephen's grew, Hap ventured out from time to time to attend to injured or ill individuals or to rush to the aid of whole communities stricken with an epidemic.[37] On Thanksgiving evening 1916, a runner brought word of a woman one hundred miles away who had been in labor for three days without progress. Hap and Walter Harper set out by dogsled to aid the woman, sleeping outside en route. By the second morning, the mercury had dropped to −57°F. Sixty miles out, a messenger informed them that the baby had been stillborn. Deflated, the men turned back toward Fort Yukon. After another night on the trail, they arrived home, weary and frostbitten.[38]

Soon after the hospital opened, Hap put out a call for two additional nurses.[39] The hospital's sole nurse had been driven to exhaustion by the heavy workload, forcing both Clara and Winifred Dalziel to take evening and night shifts. Hap hesitated to entrust critically ill patients entirely to the "volunteers," so he made rounds at night.[40] "I have been going night and day," he reported, "with night nursing and heavy out-patient work, and I hardly know whether I am awake or asleep."[41]

The Episcopal Mission Society's perennial problem of finding sufficient qualified personnel for its Alaska missions, especially individuals with medical training, had worsened with the outbreak of war in Europe. Many of those inclined toward humanitarian work answered the call to "do their bit over there," as the expression went. By spring 1917, when America entered the war, the Mission Society intensified its recruitment efforts of medically trained individuals. Unsurprisingly, with placards posted throughout New York City seeking individuals with medical training for the war effort, the mission board failed to recruit nurses for its missions in Alaska, China, and Japan in 1918.[42] Further exacerbating the worker shortage, the Social Gospel movement that had inspired many Christians to dedicate years of their lives to less fortunate people, was in transition. Within Protestant churches, financial and personal support for mission work waned, while the movement gained ground in ecumenical and more secular circles and took on broader social justice goals.[43] Many Alaska mission workers resigned.[44] By 1920, with prospects for recruiting mission personnel remaining grim and financial support dwindling, a deeply dispirited Bishop Rowe wrote mission headquarters, "I never felt so discouraged in the work in Alaska as at this moment."[45]

Finding and maintaining temperamentally suited employees was equally challenging. Both mission home and hospital personnel sometimes lacked the ability to work harmoniously with colleagues and with patients of diverse ages and backgrounds. Isolation, darkness, and overwork exacerbated depression, anxiety, and other mental health problems. Over the years several nurses appeared to suffer from melancholia or paranoia, and several had difficulty working amiably with others. Hap set the tone in the hospital with his cheerful and kindly demeanor, and he urged staff to keep their annoyances and squabbles to themselves. Nevertheless, tensions flared among personnel from time to time, given human nature and the demands of the work. Spring break-up always raised people's spirits; as Clara recalled, "As soon as the ice went out and the sun shone warm and bright, conflicts vanished and the girls were arm in arm again, chatting and laughing as though they had never quarreled."[46]

Shortly after the pneumonia outbreak of November 1916, a whooping cough epidemic brought sixty-seven patients to the clinic and hospital, of whom two infants died. By all accounts, the disease was previously unknown in the region. Hap described the crisis: "From a cabin in which many slept and with out ventilation, we took kiddies barely skin and bones that were whooping and vomiting night and day, and gave them clean decent quarters, and nourishing food, . . . and watched for the complications. We have a little boy in the hospital now 5 years old, whom I found in a cabin where eleven were sleeping, and there were four cases of whooping cough in the same cabin."[47]

Despite the improved conditions at Fort Yukon in terms of alcohol abuse, such problems reappeared from time to time. An incident in December 1916 illustrated graphically how Hap and Clara were drawn into such "social" problems. A Fort Yukon resident had returned from Circle with the mailman and a sled of whiskey. A drunken row involving both Natives and whites ensued at Short's Roadhouse. A married couple had quarreled, and a bottle the woman threw at her husband missed its mark, hit another man in the forehead, and broke, leaving a deep gash and severing the facial artery. Hap and Clara learned of the brawl when "Black Jack" pounded on the mission home door at four o'clock in the morning, demanding that Hap stop the bleeding. The following evening the Gwich'in Council called three women before them and "laid down the law," effectively telling them they would be banished from Fort Yukon if such behavior recurred. Stuck visited Short and the combative couple, no doubt threatening to bring in the law. Alluding to the mission's battle with lawlessness a few years before, he wrote in his diary, "If this fight is to be begun again, we will wade in, much as we regret it."[48]

In January 1917 St. Stephen's had 20 in-patients and the clinic saw 193 out-patients. Each new patient received a thorough physical examination and had a medical record established.[49] The patient load continued to grow, and expenditures rose accordingly. By summer, a line of tents stood behind the hospital, filled with tuberculosis patients. Hap sent a plea to mission friends for additional ten-by-twelve-foot tents.[50]

Clara took delight in her work with children, whom she described as "a merry lot." One could coax a smile with a kind word or a piece of candy, she wrote, even from those with adult burdens. In Fort Yukon and gener-ally among Gwich'in and other Dena', children largely roamed and played as they pleased. They would wander home when their bellies signaled it was mealtime. The boys at Fort Yukon loved "playing dog team," nailing a few boards together for a sled, crafting a harness from bits of moose skin, and running with two to ten boys serving as the dog team. Among the young boys, Grafton Wallis, David's son and Hap's namesake, often drove the sled. "Like his father," Clara reported, Grafton "rules the vil-lage." In winter boys and girls enthusiastically played football. Above all, the children loved to play camping in spring, making a tent of available materials, building a fire, and hanging a bucket over it to brew tea. If the fish were running, they would fasten one to a stick over the fire to roast it.[51]

Young Hudson took part in all these activities, speaking Gwich'in with the children of the village, going to school with them, and becoming so tan that he sometimes was mistaken by tourists for being Native. Hud-son later recalled that his English and Gwich'in became so intertwined that his parents worried about his English-language development. In the coming years he accrued subsistence skills, learning to hunt, trap, and fish, to work with machinery, including boat engines, and to build boats.[52] At least once, David Wallis took Hudson and other children out on his trapline. Hudson later recalled that upon their return to Fort Yukon, furs in hand, a tourist pulled some coins out of his pocket and offered them in exchange for the skins. Mildly rebuking the man, Wallis responded, "My good man," in the distinctive English tone he had acquired from his adoptive father, an Anglican priest, "we will be taking folding money."[53]

Orphans and neglected children, typically those of mixed heritage, faced a much bleaker outlook. They often bore adult responsibilities and anxieties. Clara focused on such children, bringing them into the mission fold, offering them love and security, and teaching them life skills to pre-pare them for the future.[54] In spring 1917 Clara and Hap learned they were expecting a second child in September. Although she confessed that morning sickness made her "useless" for a couple of hours each day, Stuck reported that she continued her "ceaseless hard work."[55]

Each spring the tumultuous break-up of the Yukon River carved away at the riverbank in front of the mission site. With only six feet of earth now between the mission home and the river, Hap and Clara, along with Stuck and Harper, relocated to the upstairs area of the hospital before break-up in 1917, and mission personnel partially dismantled the home to save it from the brink of disaster. When the hospital's foundation was poured in 1914, it was 300 feet from the river; now the building had only 160 feet of protection. The men fortified the riverbank with sandbags, bulkheads extending into the river and rooted well back into the permafrost, and other materials to deflect the current. As Stuck wrote, it was "an expensive business to enter into a contest with the Yukon River." He estimated the cost of moving and rebuilding the mission home at $5,000. Mission headquarters later authorized the emergency work, but St. Stephen's would have to reimburse the expense through "specials," funds that Stuck, for the most part, raised for the Alaska mission work.[56] Later, the mission board, yielding to Stuck's persistence, approved the rebuilding of the mission home as well. Throughout his sixteen years as archdeacon, Stuck usually achieved his goals. His motto since his days at Sewanee had been the Latin *Haereo* ("I stick" or "I persevere"), which later featured prominently in the beautifully beaded hind sack that hung from the handles of his dogsled.[57]

In early July 1917 two nurses arrived at St. Stephen's, having trained at Deaconess Clara Carter's Church Training and Deaconess House in Philadelphia after nursing school. Vivacious, capable, and deeply dedicated to mission and hospital work, Frances Wells and Lulu (Beatrice) Nuneviller would become valued members of the mission family.[58] As Frances had trained with Deaconess Carter and exchanged letters with the "crazy nut of a medical missionary" Happy Burke, her enthusiasm for mission work in Alaska, where "God reigns supreme" in nature, had mushroomed.[59] As she and Beatrice traveled from the Canadian border to Fort Yukon in the *Pelican*, the Interior Alaskan landscape exceeded her expectations. She wrote family members, "No words of our language no matter how fantastically put together could possibly make you get more than a glimpse of Alaska's beauty and vastness." Frances embraced the mission work and the people, earning their affection in return. After two weeks on site, she wrote family members, "This work up here is wonderful—The most worthwhile I have ever done." The people's evident faith and loyalty to the mission deeply impressed her. She reported that nearly all the Native people of the area attended church, some traveling five to ten miles by river. In addition to the hospital work and regular home visits she made, Frances took on carpentry projects, earning the nickname "boss carpenter." She and Beatrice lived upstairs at the hospital, along with the Burkes, the archdeacon, and Harper.[60]

Bishop Rowe, the Episcopal mission's foreign secretary John Wood, and Rev. Benjamin Chambers, also of New York, had accompanied Frances and Beatrice from Seattle. Stuck had been urging his friend Wood to visit Interior Alaska and survey the mission work for several years. Since the previous fall's erosion crisis, Stuck had worried that the Mission Society would not fund necessary repair, prevention, and rebuilding work, and he felt certain that if Wood witnessed the valuable work done by St. Stephen's Mission and saw the environmental context firsthand, he would recognize the need for the expenditures.[61] Stuck's intuition proved correct. The efforts at St. Stephen's and on the length of the Yukon River and its tributaries made a profound impression on Wood—as did the scope and weight of Clara's responsibilities. Upon his return to New York, he advertised for a matron to assist her in running the mission home, but to no avail, given the war-related labor shortage.[62]

Interior Alaskans typically marked the Fourth of July with contests, feasts, and dancing. With three Episcopal dignitaries in town on July 4, 1917, festivities at Fort Yukon surpassed the usual fanfare. Between afternoon sporting events, residents conducted a flag-raising ceremony. School children filed in two by two to encircle the flagstaff, followed by the chiefs, the members of the Native Council, and finally all other community members. The children sang "America (My Country, 'Tis of Thee)" as the flag was raised, finding "The Star-Spangled Banner" too difficult to sing. After Wood gave a patriotic address, the festivities continued until the final event—a canoe race across the river and back at 1:00 a.m. Instead of fireworks, celebrants fired off hundreds of rounds of rifle shots, a tradition followed in every Native community. Wood and Chambers, fascinated by the midnight sun, perched atop St. Stephen's Hospital's gate posts at midnight to photograph the sun, which was visible just above the horizon.[63]

11. Bishop Rowe with Fort Yukon women. Geoffrey Burke private collection.

After the Fort Yukon visit, Wood and Chambers joined Stuck in the *Pelican* for the summer tour of Interior missions, villages, and fish camps, with Harper serving as pilot and chief engineer. At Nenana, the young Moses Cruikshank, a student at St. Mark's Mission, came aboard to help with the manual labor. He later recalled the experience as a thrilling opportunity to assist the archdeacon, especially in the company of so many church dignitaries.[64] In the coming years Cruikshank would follow in Walter's footsteps as Stuck's riverboat pilot and winter trail guide. The *Pelican*'s tour in summer 1917 stirred much excitement. People traveled long distances and camped at various mission sites and villages, awaiting the visits by church leadership, including Bishop Rowe, who traveled separately. Throughout the Interior, the clergy conducted worship services, baptisms, marriages, and burials. At St. John's-in-the-Wilderness, they learned that a Dena' woman and child had been severely burned in a tent fire. Upon determining that they needed immediate attention from a doctor, the men loaded the mother and child onto the *Pelican*'s deck and ran forty-three hours straight to the mouth of the Koyukuk and then twenty miles down the Yukon River to the hospital at Nulato.[65]

On September 11, 1917, Clara and Hap's second child arrived. The otherwise joyful event led to the greatest health crisis Clara faced in her three decades in Alaska. She became so ill, with a high fever, that both Hap and Stuck feared for her life. Stuck's October 1 letter to missionary Frederick Drane revealed their mental states: "Mrs. Burke's condition has become so alarming that we have decided to send her and Dr. Burke and one of the nurses to Dr. Smith at Nenana. An abdominal section will probably be necessary to save her life and Dr. Burke is in no condition to perform it—what with his worry + anxiety + sleeplessness. The last boat comes down tomorrow and they will go on it. When they will return and who will return is in the hands of God."[66] Stuck "never saw a boat depart with such heaviness of heart" as the one that carried Hap, Clara, Beatrice Nuneviller, and the baby.[67] As soon as they left, five-year-old Hudson, whom Hap and Clara had left in Stuck's care, developed a fever. Frances Wells diagnosed typhoid fever and supervised his care.

Almost immediately upon their departure, Clara's fever broke, and her condition began to improve. By the time they reached Nenana, Dr. Smith determined that she would not need surgery.[68] After several days, with Clara's condition steadily improving, she and Hap began their return journey, only to be delayed thirty-six hours when the boat ran aground on a sandbar.[69] As Stuck saw the revived Clara walk from the boat, he embraced her, exclaiming in a shaky voice, as she later recalled, "You don't know how glad I am to see you on your feet!" True to form, he promptly regained his composure, turned to Hap and quipped, "Was there anything wrong with her, Hap? Or did she just want a boat ride?"[70] Clara and Hap named the child Grafton Edgar, in honor of Hap's friend Edgar Loomis, and Stuck ordered a silver cup from Tiffany's for him.[71] Little Hudson was convalescing when his parents returned, and "still looked like death."[72]

As Hap later reflected on Clara's illness, he wrote to Wood:

I wonder sometime if it is not wrong for a man to get as "wrapped up" in a woman, and as dependent on one, as I am on Clara. When Clara was so low, there seemed nothing worth living for, and now as she returns steadily to her old self again, life goes so smoothly, and everything seems worth doing. You can imagine, therefore how profoundly grateful I am, and how I thank God that she is spared. She is a great wife, and the Archdeacon has often said: "Hap you need not think it is because of you Clara is loved, you have nothing to do with it."[73]

In its first year of operation, from October 1916 to October 1917, St. Stephen's Hospital had treated eighty-five in-patients, seventy-two of whom were Alaska Natives. Patients often required weeks or months of confinement for diseases such as tuberculosis and pneumonia and for serious injuries. During the same period, 887 out-patients had received care. Patients came from well over one thousand miles away, including across the Canadian border on the Arctic coast. The Board of Missions provided St. Stephen's Hospital with funds for one physician, two nurses, one orderly, and maintenance and supplies, for a total of $3,600—an altogether inadequate sum, with fuel alone costing $1,000; Stuck estimated that the hospital needed $2,000 a year for maintenance. The national Episcopal Woman's Auxiliary sent myriad supplies, such as bedding and bath towels, bathrobes, and night and day clothing for adult and child patients. St. Stephen's local woman's auxiliary supported the hospital through volunteer work, including doing the hospital's scrubbing, laundry, ironing, and mending. During winter 1916–17, when wood for the furnaces ran low, these women set out with dog teams and worked several days in the nearby forest chopping wood. When the ice went out on the Yukon River, Hap had the nine cords of wood they chopped rafted downriver to St. Stephen's.[74]

In late summer 1917 Stuck and Harper prepared for their long-planned winter circuit of the Arctic coast. Neither had visited the northwestern and northern perimeters of Alaska. Stuck looked forward to spending time among the Iñupiat, whom he admired. Planning to publish a book on the Episcopal Church's Alaska missions and refusing to write about the one mission he had not seen in person, he prioritized visiting the remote St. Thomas's Mission at Point Hope on the northwest coast. He and Walter looked forward to seeing Rev. William Thomas, who was now stationed there. In September their plans appeared to be dashed when Walter was diagnosed with typhoid fever about the same time as Hudson Burke.[75]

Salmonella typhi, the bacteria that caused typhoid fever, was known to spread by food or water contaminated with the fecal matter of an infected person. Crowded ship conditions promoted the spread of the disease. The source of Walter and little Hudson's infection was thought to be peaches that a riverboat pilot brought from Dawson.[76]

As Walter lay hospitalized with a high fever, Frances Wells devoted herself to his care, and the two fell in love. Neither Stuck nor the Burkes encouraged the romance. Stuck feared it would derail Walter's plans for medical school and returning to Alaska as a medical missionary, and the Burkes fretted they would lose a fine nurse if Frances followed him Outside for college. Walter's serious illness brought home to Stuck how deeply attached he was to "the boy." He agonized over Walter's condition and prayed fervently for his recovery.[77]

Whether it was Stuck's prayers, Frances's skilled care, or his own resilience, Walter recovered. Stuck was overjoyed when in early November, Hap pronounced Walter fit for travel. Their six-month, 2,500-mile trek by dogsled brought the seasoned outdoorsmen many new and memorable experiences. From Fort Yukon they traveled westward to Kotzebue on the Arctic coast, north to Tikiġaq/Point Hope, northeast to Utqiaġvik/Barrow, farther east to Herschel Island, just past the demarcation point, and then south again to Fort Yukon.

During their six weeks with William Thomas at Tikiġaq, the three men renewed their friendship as the visitors relieved Thomas of his teaching duties, with Stuck teaching the academic subjects and Walter teaching industrial arts. Stuck appreciated hearing the children speaking Iñupiaq in school and enjoyed the congregants' heartfelt singing in Iñupiaq in church. The men spent a memorable two weeks at Alaska's northernmost settlement, Utqiaġvik/Barrow, hosted by the renowned whaler and trader Charles Brower. During their visit, Walter built a new sled for high Arctic coastal conditions and Stuck enjoyed long walks and talks with Brower.

Throughout the journey, as they guarded one another's lives during the day and as Stuck tutored Harper in the evenings, the two grew closer than ever, as close as two people could be without blood ties, Stuck wrote. On most of their trek, Stuck hired local guides to shepherd them safely across the unfamiliar terrain. As novices in the region, he and Harper had trouble distinguishing land from sea ice, which could have had fatal consequences. After their stop at Herschel Island, when they turned south toward Fort Yukon and came into the familiar landscape of the boreal forest, they no longer needed a guide. On their own now, the two resumed their natural communication style, speaking of personal topics once again. To share his thoughts with Stuck, Harper handed him the journal he had been keeping. The diary revealed that Walter and Frances planned to marry and that Walter aimed to join the Army Air Corps to serve in the war cause. Stunned by the revelations and filled with anxiety about Walter's future, Stuck could not immediately congratulate him or support his plans. By summer, however, Stuck and the rest of Fort Yukon looked forward to the wedding.[78]

In early April a telegram reached St. Stephen's with the news that the renowned Icelandic-Canadian explorer Vilhjalmur Stefansson was ill with typhoid fever at Herschel Island. Stefansson's Canadian Arctic Expedition had been mapping the high Arctic for several years. In Herschel Island's infirmary since January, his condition had deteriorated, and now his life appeared to be in peril. A support team had set out with Stefansson toward St. Stephen's Hospital. With time of the essence, the telegram urged Hap to meet them at Rampart House at the Canadian border.[79] Hap headed north, accompanied by the trader Harry Anthony and a second dog team, expecting a ten-day journey. The rendezvous took place as planned. Hap examined Stefansson, whose condition had already improved in the fresh air, and encouraged him to eat whatever he desired. The two parties turned southwest toward Fort Yukon, and shortly thereafter, Stuck and Harper chanced upon them. It was a happy reunion.[80] Stuck and Stefansson launched into a lively conversation that left Stuck with a highly favorable impression of the explorer. As they traveled southward, the two men continued their discussion at every stop.[81]

Stefansson remained at Fort Yukon for three months, longer than necessary for his health's sake. Later writing of the experience, he described the overwhelming hospitality extended to him in the hospital, at the wireless station, and in "every private house."[82] The renowned Czech anthropologist Aleš Hrdlička, who was in the region that summer conducting population studies on Indigenous peoples, visited Fort Yukon during Stefansson's stay.[83] Stuck, Burke, and the two visitors engaged in many spirited exchanges on a range of topics. Harriet Bedell, the Episcopal missionary at Stevens Village, who participated in one of their extended dinner table conversations, reported that the men debated intensely. On one point they agreed—that Natives should not be exploited or encouraged to abandon their traditional lifeways, although Hap insisted on an exception for hygiene and sanitation measures.[84]

During his visit, Stefansson, whose criticism of missionaries was well known, assured Stuck that many of his negative comments had been overblown in the press. It was more difficult to explain away the "animus" in his book, Stuck noted, "thou he tries his best." Stefansson attended church services during his stay but declined to kneel during prayers, because "it would be hypocritical," he told Stuck.[85] A legend later spread of an exchange between Stefansson and Hap. Stefansson reportedly thanked him, saying, "Money cannot repay what you have done for me. You have saved my life. But I should like to make one criticism. You would accomplish more if you did not spend so much time in religious work and in prayer." Hap reportedly responded, "If it had not been for prayer, I should not be here, this hospital would not have been here, and you would be lying dead in the snow."[86]

Such occasional stopovers by researchers, explorers, and travelers from around the world, along with regular visits to Fort Yukon by Natives and non-Natives living in the region, gave the village a cosmopolitan quality. Hap loved to give hospital tours to steamboat passengers traveling on the Yukon River. Clara's wonderful meals provided the setting and sustenance for stimulating discussions that kept the mission family abreast of world affairs. The couple's hospitality was well known, their invitations to travelers ranging from a dinner and evening of conversation to a week or more as houseguests at the mission.

In spring 1918 another violent break-up swept away more earth in front of the mission complex, taking the front of the old mission house, including the upstairs veranda. Anticipating the flood, the Burkes evacuated the residents and most of the furnishings.[87] The flood collapsed concrete slabs from the hospital's façade but left the structure intact.[88]

Before long, the hospital, too, would have to be moved. The Native village regularly relocated.[89]

The new two-story mission home had nine rooms, including a suite for the archdeacon with a bedroom and adjoining study.[90] The large living room permitted community gatherings, and the dining room could seat sixteen people comfortably. Behind the kitchen, which had two stoves, lay the children's dining and playroom, under which was a large laundry and drying room heated by the building's two furnaces. Water tanks in the attic provided running water for the kitchen, laundry, and an indoor bathroom, reportedly the first in Fort Yukon.[91] The costs rose well beyond the $7,500 the mission board initially allocated for the new mission home.[92] Bringing water to the home and hospital cost far more than estimated.[93] Eventually, the mission board approved $10,000, which included furnishings for the home.[94]

In June 1918 the mission family suffered its first great loss of the year with the death of Rev. William Loola at the age of seventy-seven from a gastric ailment. Given his advanced age and poor condition, Hap declined to operate, offering only palliative care. Loola had fulfilled his duties as "minister-in-charge of the native congregation" throughout his illness. After he could no longer walk to church, friends carried him on a sled; when he was too weak to leave his home, parishioners came to his bedside for worship services. Loola relinquished his duties only after Stuck returned from his winter circuit of the Arctic coast in late April.[95]

Loola had earned the Burkes' and Stuck's respect and affection many years before, owing to his steadfast faith, the dignity he displayed, and his loyalty to the mission. The oldest and most influential member of the Native Council, Loola seldom spoke until all others had done so. Always soft-spoken and judicious, he invariably stood on the side of righteousness. When Hap faced bitter opposition during his term as commissioner, "Loola stood like a rock beside him, resisting all persuasions and inducements to desert," Stuck recalled, without compromising his stature within the community. The entire Native population, along with every white currently in town, attended his memorial service, including the three traders, who closed their businesses to attend. Native Council members carried the coffin shoulder high to the graveyard, followed by children walking in pairs and carrying wildflowers to cast on the grave, and finally the adults.[96] The mission board approved a widow's pension of $200 a year to Loola's widow, Julia, his second wife, with whom he had four children.[97] Hap and Clara worried about little six-year-old Mary's welfare after the death of her father, who had done his best to protect her against cruelty. Hap was confident that he could correct her cleft lip and palate one day.[98]

John Fredson, who had been a Bible study student of Loola's and was away at Mount Herman School, carved an oaken plaque memorializing him, to be hung in the church at Fort Yukon. Stuck had suggested the project, selected the oak slab, and shipped it to Mount Hermon. He knew Johnny had taken wood carving classes at St. Mark's Mission School and hoped the project would ease his grief and homesickness after Loola's death.[99] The plaque hangs in the church at Fort Yukon today.

With Loola gone, St. Stephen's relied more heavily on David Wallis, "one of the best if not the best interpreter in Alaska," according to Frederick Drane.[100] Only a month before Loola's death, Stuck had beseeched John Wood at mission headquarters to hire Wallis as a regular staff person at $300 a year, because the mission relied so heavily on him. At his current pay of $100, he often had to be away hunting to feed his family when Stuck and Hap needed him. "We use him all the time," Stuck wrote. "What Burke would do without him I do not know."[101] Rowe endorsed the salary increase, and the mission board approved it.[102]

In early September Walter Harper and Frances Wells were married in St. Stephen's Church, with Archdeacon Stuck officiating.[103] An informal reception followed at the hospital, with Clara's "famously good 'eats.'" Hap had pitched a tent on the Porcupine River for their wedding night. Their honeymoon consisted of a three-week hunting trip in Walter's favored hunting area. He aimed to bring home the winter's meat supply for the mission and hospital before he and Frances traveled Outside, where he would join the Army Air Corps and she would join the Red Cross. Seven weeks after their wedding, as the newlyweds traveled aboard the *Princess Sophia*, their plans for a bright future and Stuck's vision for his beloved protégé were shattered with the sinking of the passenger ship in Lynn Canal on October 25. Not one of the more than 350 persons aboard survived. The event remains Alaska's worst maritime disaster.[104]

Harper's death dealt a crushing blow to Stuck. The event was "the most terrible thing" he had ever experienced, he wrote.[105] He had seen in Walter the fulfillment of his life's work—resilient Dena' peoples thriving in their ancestral lands long after his own death. "I need not tell you how like a son he was to me," Stuck wrote to Frederick Drane, "how proud I was of him, how eagerly I looked forward to his usefulness as a medical missionary by the by. He was, I think, the strongest, the gentlest, the cleanest young man I have ever known. Of splendid stamina and tireless constitution, with the rifle, with the dogs, with an axe, with any sort of boat from a birch-bark canoe to a power launch, he had no superior in Alaska."[106] That winter, neuritis in Stuck's arm from his many years on the trail and depression following Walter's death left him unable to make his usual winter rounds by dogsled. Despite the extensive therapy Hap provided for him and Hap's assurances that the condition would pass, Stuck doubted whether he was "fit for long winter trips any more." Drane took the 1918–19 winter circuit for him.[107] In his and others' opinions, Stuck never recovered from Harper's death.[108] That winter Stuck began to write an account of their final winter circuit as "a memorial of my dear boy." He dedicated *A Winter Circuit of Our Arctic Coast*, published in 1920, to Walter.[109]

The Burkes and Stuck had moved into the new mission home just days before the tragedy. Immediately, the building showed its usefulness. The "great chamber" or long room offered space for community gatherings and proved beneficial to the mission work. On New Year's Eve, the Native men of Fort Yukon met there to elect new Native Council members. The next Saturday Hap and Clara hosted the nine new council members for dinner.[110] In December the Native congregation contributed $105 to the annual offering for general missions, more than ever before, which heartened Stuck. "We have our troubles," he wrote, "but I am much encouraged with the people and grow more and more attached to them, and, I like to believe, they to me."[111]

Meanwhile, Hap's caseload continued to expand. He treated a full range of injuries and ailments in patients for whom the journey to St. Stephen's was sometimes as much of an ordeal as the injury or disease itself. He found the work completely engrossing. "The medical [cases] are varied and keenly interesting; the surgical are of a fascinating variety," he would later write.[112]

In March 1919 a young girl suffering from "infantile paralysis," or poliomyelitis, appeared at St. Stephen's Mission Home. Her journey from the isolated Stevens Village, about 140 miles downriver, stunned even experienced Sourdoughs along the route, but she and her three guardians arrived unscathed. When little Ida had fallen ill and developed increasingly alarming symptoms, missionary Harriet Bedell enlisted two men to help her transport the girl to St. Stephen's Hospital. Both men balked, judging the scheme foolhardy in subzero temperatures with no broken trail, but Bedell insisted. The thermometer read −32°F when the four set out with two sleds, one loaded with provisions for the week-long trek and the other carrying the heavily bundled Ida. The party traveled over rough terrain, sleeping in makeshift camps the first two nights, but thereafter they found refuge in warm dwellings. With detours around obstructions and four steep riverbanks to be descended and ascended, the circuitous route far exceeded the 140-mile distance by river. Finally, on the seventh day, they reached St. Stephen's Mission, which "seemed to radiate warmth, help and companionship," Bedell later recalled. Archdeacon Stuck answered her knock at the door and carried the child to Hap. Clara whisked Bedell off with a promise of a warm bath, hot meal, and a comfortable bed. After three days' rest in the mission home, Bedell left Ida in Hap's care at the hospital, and she and her two male travel companions, who had chosen to stay with friends in the village, returned to Stevens Village. Hap judged Ida to have a fair chance of recovery.[113] In another dramatic case, in summer 1920, a girl who had been mauled by a dog arrived at the hospital from 250 miles up the Porcupine River. Despite her appalling facial wounds, Hap restored the child's face.[114]

During summer 1919, the U.S. Fish Commission permitted the opening of a salmon cannery at the mouth of the Yukon, despite protests from Bishop Rowe, Archdeacon Stuck, and many others concerned with the lives and livelihoods of people living along the Yukon River's drainage system.[115] As feared, a disastrous fishing season followed. St. Mark's Mission failed to harvest enough fish to feed the children and dogs through the summer and put up none for the coming winter. At Fort Yukon, more than one thousand miles from the Yukon's mouth, traders sold salmon for thirty-five cents a pound in early winter, seven times the normal price. On the Tanana and Koyukuk Rivers, owners had to kill their dogs to spare them from the prolonged suffering of starving to death. Stuck sprang into action, lobbying the national government and the American people to close the cannery. The December 1919 issue of *Spirit of Missions* published a full-page bold-print plea for donations to purchase $1,500 worth of substitute foods. Salmon runs were low all along the Pacific coast that year. Unrestricted fishing by trappers, seiners, and trollers close to the mouths of spawning streams in recent years exacerbated the shortage, threatening depletion of the resource and imperiling the commercial fishing industry and the lives and livelihoods of many peoples.[116]

Stuck's arm had improved by summer 1919, enabling him to tour the Interior in the *Pelican* accompanied by Bishop Rowe.[117] At the close of the season, he traveled Outside, where he spent nearly a year raising funds and recruiting personnel for the Alaska mission work, lobbying in Washington DC to shut down the Carlisle Packing Company's cannery at the mouth of the Yukon and finishing two books—*A Winter Circuit of Our Arctic Coast* and *The Alaskan Missions of the Episcopal Church*.[118] During winter of 1919–20, William Thomas transferred from Point Hope to Fort Yukon to perform Stuck's clerical duties, including traveling part of his winter circuit.[119] On the Chandalar-Koyukuk round, he surveyed conditions after the disastrous fishing season. Coldfoot, Bettles, and Southfork were doing well, because they had work, either mining or making snowshoes and trapping furs they could sell. Other settlements were destitute. The people of the twin settlements of Allakaket and Alatna, where game was never abundant, were "in dire straits" and depended on mission support.[120] "Of course no one has any dogs left to speak of," Thomas reported to Stuck. "Here's praying your splendid efforts against the Cannery are not in vain!"[121]

At St. Stephen's, patients arrived from far and wide that winter. A man who had been lost in the mountains and nearly starved was carried ten days by dogsled in −50° weather to the hospital. Some years back he had lost an arm to frostbite when gangrene set in, and he now arrived at St. Stephen's with both feet and his only hand severely frozen.[122] Some people, both Native and non-Native, resisted medical aid, and not all patients appreciated the care they received. Frederick Drane, who shared winter rounding duties with Thomas, met a cantankerous old-timer with badly frozen feet that winter. Drane urged the man to seek help at St. Stephen's, but the man resisted. "The fool said he knew as much about nursing frozen feet as Dr. Burke," Drane reported.[123] He encountered the man again at St. Stephen's Hospital, where he had finally gone when gangrene set in. "Well Dr. Burke saved part of his feet, but instead of being thankful for that he did not have a good word for anybody. He was the worst crab I ever saw," Drane wrote.[124] Hap was by now a skilled surgeon with extensive experience in operating on frozen limbs, diseased gastrointestinal systems, gunshot wounds, and myriad other injuries.

In spring 1920 the great influenza epidemic, often referred to as the Spanish flu, reached Interior communities. As the virus wrought havoc on the Seward Peninsula in winter 1918–19, killing large percentages of Iñupiat and leaving many children orphaned, the Burkes and Stuck had watched for signs of the disease at Fort Yukon. Based on reports in his medical journals, Hap anticipated that if the flu swept through Fort Yukon, at least fifty deaths could occur among the white population. "God only knows what the mortality would be amongst Indians," he wrote Stuck. "May He avert that calamity!"[125] In May 1920, as the epidemic spread through Native villages in Interior Alaska, Hap wired John Wood, asking for vaccines. Wood contacted the Mayo Foundation in Rochester, Minnesota, and secured a commitment to send, without charge, one thousand vaccines, which Burke could distribute to other mission sites as needed.[126] Dr. Edward Rosenow, at the Mayo Clinic, had developed these vaccines using, among other ingredients, the bacteria that cause pneumonia. The vaccines proved to be ineffective against influenza.[127] High percentages of the populations in Interior communities contracted the disease that summer and many died.[128] At Fort Yukon, Hap and Clara "waited with dread" for their first case, but they were spared that year.[129]

Back in Washington DC, Stuck convinced Alaska's delegate to Congress, George Grigsby, to introduce a bill to prohibit salmon fishing for canning or export on the Yukon River, its tributaries, and at its mouth.[130] Fifteen hundred residents of Interior Alaska signed a petition in support of closing the cannery. Missionaries, traders, trappers, prospectors, and others sent letters, and Interior newspapers regularly published articles and opinions opposing the cannery.[131] According to Frederick Drane, no one advocated more strongly for the Alaska Native position on the cannery than Stuck.[132] His "vigorous fight against the cannery had aroused the admiration of more than one 'sourdough,' who was formerly prejudiced against anyone 'who worn his collar buttoned on backwards.'" Stuck's efforts prompted fisheries experts to survey the scene. They recommended closing the cannery and prohibiting fishing on the Yukon River for export.[133]

In May Stuck testified before the House committee considering the bill, making the case for closing the cannery.[134] As Congress prepared to adjourn in summer 1920, however, he sounded defeated. The committee had not acted on the bill, and the cannery had resumed operations. In a poignant letter to supporters of the cause, Stuck admitted there was "no hope of relief for the people of the Yukon" that summer. Accepting partial blame for arousing "sharp antagonism" among some officials, he acknowledged that "wiser and more accustomed leadership" might have accomplished more. He promised to continue his efforts when the bill was reintroduced. Thanking supporters, he declared, "The menace of the present situation is the most serious that has ever overhung the people of the interior."[135]

Stuck arrived back in Fort Yukon on July 26, 1920, accompanied by a young Englishman, Michael Mason, whom he had met on the steamer from Seattle. Stuck had promised Mason that he could join Hap on his fall hunt for the winter meat supply. The warm welcome Stuck received from the Burkes and others at Fort Yukon assured him he "was indeed home."[136]

In September Hap and Mason went upriver to hunt, expecting to be gone two weeks. Soon after they left, Lizzie White fell ill with pneumonia and died, a Fort Yukon Native died, and the hospital filled with patients. Meanwhile, a cold that the archdeacon had caught developed into bronchitis, with excruciating shoulder pain. As his symptoms worsened, Clara wired Hap at Circle, urging him to come home at once. She, Winifred Dalziel, and the other schoolteacher took turns sitting with Stuck around the clock. Upon Hap's return, he found Stuck in a "state of collapse and [mental] apathy." He seemed despondent over Lizzie White's death and his inability to officiate at her memorial service. Shortly thereafter, Stuck became semicomatose, with a fever and severe coughing spells. At one point, Hap leaned in, stroked his forehead, and said, "Archdeacon, do you know Hap loves you and loves you?" Stuck responded, without opening his eyes, "I am glad, glad, Hap, you love me—I am poor on love." Understanding his time was near, Stuck asked to be buried in the Native cemetery. He died on October 11.[137] The following day, as a "silent stupefying sorrow" filled the mission home, Hap conducted a service in St. Stephen's Church with "every native and white here" in attendance. Frank White, Lizzie's husband, made Stuck's coffin and lined it with silk.[138]

Hap wrote John Woods two weeks later:

> In this isolated life of the north, the loss of one with whom you have been in almost constant companionship for over twenty-six years, is profoundly sorrowful. He was such a champion for this work—for the mission of the North—for righteousness. My medical work is due entirely to him; he was the very stimulous in every one of my cases. He visited systematically and regularly the sick in the hospital and the village, and the children swarmed around him for play and the sugared almonds he carried with him. . . . He presented me for confirmation; he educated me and married me to my wife, who loves him as I. What can I do for him?

Hap closed with a vow that the work "must live as never before."[139]

Stuck had been a "tower of strength and a source of inspiration" to mission staff throughout the Interior, according to Frederick Drane. "He more than any of us, was the champion of the native people of this country."[140] Drane and others believed that the "shock and bitter grief" of Walter Harper's death "was the chief cause of his final break-down, and his death."[141]

The poet Edwin Ranck wrote in a *New York Times* obituary that Stuck had "the face and the eyes of a dreamer, the education of a college professor, and the pluck and endurance of a highly bred racehorse."[142] On November 7 a memorial service at the Cathedral of St. John the Divine in New York attracted perhaps 1,800 people, many from other denomi-

HUDSON STUCK, D.D., F.R.G.S.
Archdeacon of the Yukon
Died October 10, 1920.

12. Hudson Stuck. *Spirit of Missions* 85 (1920): 688. Courtesy of the Archives of the Episcopal Church.

nations who knew Stuck through his Alaska work. Eulogies focused on the contrast between his background and the life he had chosen among the Native peoples of Alaska.[143]

Stuck had fought tirelessly for the well-being of Alaska Natives; for their right to maintain their traditional lifestyles, unimpeded by migrants to the region; to protect them from abuse by whites who exploited them for pleasure or gain; and for their right to live with dignity and to have their lives and cultures valued. Stuck's efforts incurred the wrath of many, yet he neither flinched nor retreated in the face of criticism. As he had once written his friend John Wood, "You know very well that like Lord Nelson I have a blind eye, and a positively unerring intuitive sense of the proper and fitting occasion to set the telescope to it."[144]

In early January, as Hap began to "emerge from gloom," he wrote Wood of the "pleasure and stimulus" that continuing the archdeacon's work afforded him.[145] After his mentor's death, Hap took on increased pastoral obligations, regularly conducting religious services and preparing young people for confirmation. Meanwhile, he performed his medical duties, spending most mornings in the hospital, which was filled to capacity.[146]

6   Deepening Resolve amid Increased Responsibilities and Challenges, 1921–25

In the years that followed Hudson Stuck's death, mutual trust and shared commitment to mission and community goals deepened the bonds between the Burkes and St. Stephen's Mission and Fort Yukon residents, both Native and white. Several crises tested the mission's and the Burkes' personal capacities: floods, having to relocate the hospital, a catastrophic fire, an influenza epidemic, and mounting fiscal woes. Local and national responses to the crises reflected growing recognition of Hap and Clara's efforts and of St. Stephen's positive impact on the region.

The Briton Michael Mason remained with Hap and Clara through spring 1921, then traveled in the Alaska-Canada Arctic and sub-Arctic through summer 1922. In *The Arctic Forests*, a book he later published on his experiences, Mason described "the American Mission at Fort Yukon" as the "most beneficial establishment in the country." Of Hap and Clara he wrote:

> They have a small hospital up there, and have probably saved more lives than they can count (including my own). Their door is always open, and they have a cheery welcome for any stranger, be he bishop or ex-convict. Their house is always full of about a dozen Indian children who have either lost their parents or are being kept to attend the little Indian school while their fathers are out on their hunting grounds. Unlike most Missions I have seen, there is a continual atmosphere of cheerfulness, and if the Doctor and his wife were to leave Fort Yukon, a light would go out of the place which would never be replaced. . . . If ever two people gave up their lives to ministering to the needs of others, it is Dr. and Mrs. Burke.[1]

Hap sensed a "spiritual awakening" within the Native community in winter 1920–21. He noted "the ease and directness with which [the people's] spiritual natures are reached" and the devotion they showed to the memories of Archdeacon McDonald, Reverend Loola, and Archdeacon Stuck.[2] Frederick Drane, who ran Stuck's circuit of the Episcopal missions that winter, stayed twelve days at St. Stephen's Mission in March.[3] He described how deeply St. Stephen's influence permeated Native society in Fort Yukon and the surrounding area. Since Loola's death, four Native lay readers conducted church services. Native teachers led Sunday school classes, and David Wallis conducted Bible classes in Gwich'in during the week. Fort Yukon residents attended services in higher percentages and sang more heartily than in any other community Drane visited. At least seventy-five people received Communion, some having traveled from as far as sixty miles away.[4]

Drane praised the "usefulness" of the work at St. Stephen's Hospital, which was filled to capacity. Hap was managing with the help of the deputy marshal, who had become "proficient," as he put it, "in administering anaesthesia."[5] Hap spent his mornings treating hospital patients. Mr. Chisolm, an "old man" of sixty-four, had been lost in a snowstorm at −40°F and had nearly frozen to death. Hap had amputated parts of his feet and fingers and the flexible part of his nose, yet he was "not at all downhearted," Drane reported, but rather "loud in his praise" of his treatment at the hospital.[6] A twelve-year-old boy from 120 miles upriver, ill with tuberculosis of the lymph nodes for years, had finally recovered at St. Stephen's and would soon return home.[7] An old man arrived from eighty miles away with advanced, inoperable stomach cancer, but with "repeated washings of the stomach" and other treatment, he could now eat, was gaining weight and strength, and hoped to return to his cabin soon.[8] In the afternoons, Hap operated a walk-in clinic with the aid of Deaconess Smith. In the mornings, she made home visits, charted conditions observed, and assisted as needed.

Clara cared for ten children in the mission home, in addition to her own two that winter.[9] Hudson and Grafton were well immersed in Gwich'in culture by now. Hudson later recalled having a strong sense of the power of the shamans and recounted an incident that left a deep impression on him. Once, a shaman visited Fort Yukon and set up his birchbark canoe on the beach as a shelter. He sat and slept under the canoe for three days, sometimes chanting, always keeping to himself. He left and returned shortly thereafter, followed by a run of salmon.[10] The story aligns well with Dena' beliefs about shamans' powers, which, as VanStone explained, derived from their abilities to interact with the spirit world. "Shamans brought game to the hunters, predicted the weather, and were able to foretell the future."[11]

In his travels that winter, Drane saw time and again the "stimulating force" of Archdeacon Stuck's rounds of more than a decade. "There was a power in his personality and in his outspoken championship for the cause of righteousness and justice, both among the whites and the Indians of the interior," he wrote.[12] Drane and his trail guide, the capable, "tireless," and even-tempered Moses Cruikshank, were warmly received wherever they traveled.[13]

On November 12, 1920, Stuck's birthday, white residents of Fort Yukon had pledged $1,600 to establish a memorial fund to honor him and to further his work. By December the fund had grown to $7,000, of which $3,000 had been pledged by Native individuals. Michael Mason donated $500 and helped raise additional funds locally. In response to the initiative, the Episcopal Board of Missions established the Hudson Stuck Memorial Fund, for the support of St. Stephen's Hospital, with a goal of at least $25,000.[14] In early 1922 Bishop Rowe renamed St. Stephen's Hospital the Hudson Stuck Memorial Hospital at the request of the Burkes and other Fort Yukon residents.[15] The entire Episcopal complex at Fort Yukon retained the name St. Stephen's Mission.

Other developments had improved the financial outlook at St. Stephen's and other Episcopal missions. In fall 1918 the mission board approved salary raises for male missionaries, increasing Hap's salary from $1,500 as a married physician to $1,800.[16] The board raised women missionaries' salaries in 1921.[17] In 1919 the church had launched the Nationwide Campaign, which increased its emphasis on benevolent giving, with marked results.[18]

The pay differential between single and married missionaries and the policy of not paying spouses posed an interesting dilemma in late 1920 in the context of William Thomas's return to Point Hope as missionary-teacher.[19] While en route in the company of Bishop Rowe and Ruth Ward, a nurse newly assigned to Point Hope, Thomas became so enamored of Ward that he proposed to her. She accepted, and Rowe married the couple the day after their arrival at the village.[20] In his appropriations schedule for 1921, Rowe included Thomas's salary as a married male missionary, along with Ruth Thomas's salary as a nurse.[21] The $600 budget line for Mrs. Thomas caught John Wood's attention at mission headquarters in New York.[22] Why had Rowe listed a separate salary for Mrs. Thomas, he asked Rowe, when Mrs. Chapman at Anvik and Mrs. Burke at Fort Yukon served those missions without pay?[23]

Eventually, because Rowe had made a commitment to the Thomases, Wood approved $50 a month for her from January through July 1921. He admonished Rowe, however:

> I am sure that, after this experience, you will do your best, in making arrangements with married couples or with those who may seem to be matrimonially inclined, to see that they understand that the man gets all the money, even if the woman does most of the work. Just as soon as we abandon the long established practice of paying a larger salary to a married man than we do to a single man and begin employing a man and his wife each with an individual salary, we are going to be in trouble. At least, so it seems to me.[24]

Wood's advice may have merely reflected his financial concerns rather than a vision of social mayhem should married female missionaries be paid as individuals for their work. The totality of his warning nevertheless illustrated the state of gender perceptions and expectations of female spouses of missionaries. It likely represented a mainstream American view of the concept of the male as the head of the household, with all that entailed.

In June 1921 Bishop Rowe ordained Hap as a deacon, which allowed him to perform some religious rites. Although his ordination reduced the problem of having no clergyman at Fort Yukon after the archdeacon's death, it increased Hap's responsibilities.[25] He and Clara postponed the furlough they had planned for summer 1921 because several missionaries planned to leave that year, some on furlough and some permanently. In a positive development, Wood sent two new nurses that summer.[26]

The perennial problem of insufficient hospital staffing, worsened by the Great War, had eased by early 1921.[27] On the other hand, incompetency and temperamental unfitness among hospital staff continued unabated. Moreover, the heavy workload and frontier conditions often led workers to resign before completing their three-year contracts. Hap found that nurses trained in the east "with orderlies at every call" tended to arrive ill prepared for the "practical duties" associated with remote hospital work. Some had "silly finicky ideas" about ideal, highly professionalized routines and felt that "to wash the toe of a man is a most immoral thing." He had offended one nurse's "sense of modesty" by asking her to sponge bathe a severely injured man who had been "packed, hauled and boated 142 miles."[28]

Regardless of their training, prospective nurses could hardly have envisioned the scope of their duties at Fort Yukon. The day nurse attended to all patients, made home visits, and worked one hour each afternoon in the out-patient clinic. The kitchen nurse, or matron, cooked all meals for the patients and did the cleaning. The night nurse attended to patient needs during the evening and night hours. This schedule held seven days a week, although sometimes the nurses, who slept upstairs at the hospital, rotated among the positions. Nurse Fannie Cleaver, who arrived in summer 1921, wrote cheerfully, "After we get settled we are planning to have two hours off each day and a half day a week. This will give us some time for recreation, for here we need it, and it is such a marvelous country in which to get it."[29]

A series of personnel problems disrupted the hospital routine in the early 1920s, compounding Hap's daily challenges. Deaconess Smith's arrival in September 1920 had demoralized the staff. She wrote friends Outside complaining of individuals and practices, which pulled Hap from his medical tasks to soothe ruffled feelings and to clarify matters for Rowe and Wood.[30] Another nurse, Nellie Landon, wrought much greater havoc, as her machinations extended into the community, where she gained supporters in the trader Harry Horton, whom Hap had prosecuted as commissioner, and Mr. Short, a roadhouse operator who flouted the alcohol laws.[31] Landon ensnared new hospital recruits in her web of conspiracy and negativity, and they continued to sow discord even after her departure.[32] Eventually, each personnel squabble would resolve, and peace would reign again for a time. Hap, who led by example with his perennially cheerful disposition, craved harmonious relations among the staff, loathed any kind of discord, and resented having to waste his valuable time on such nonsense.

In August 1921 Johnny Fredson returned to Fort Yukon after graduating from Mount Hermon School. He had excelled academically, despite the war—he had been conscripted and served in the U.S. Army from October to December 1918—and the loss of loved ones.[33] His final years at school had been marred by the deaths of Reverend Loola, Archdeacon Stuck, Walter Harper, and his friend Richard Bristol, who died in the war. Johnny's Gwich'in language skills had become rusty during his five-year absence. After returning to Fort Yukon, he wrote John Wood, "It's fun trying to talk my own language. I blunder and stammer, but I can make myself understood. I can understand other[s] allright." The children took a great interest in Johnny, "asking loads and loads of questions." His fluency quickly returned, as he interacted with Gwich'in children and adults.[34]

That fall, Hap, Johnny, and Robert Tatum, who had returned to Alaska after earning a bachelor's in theology at Sewanee, participated in the annual moose hunt for St. Stephen's Mission complex and returned with a raft full of meat.[35] Caribou hunting season followed. The game commission allowed the mission to take dozens of caribou, owing to the many people the mission and hospital fed.[36]

Through fall and winter, Johnny oversaw the construction of the Frances Wells Harper Solarium at the hospital. In February 1919 the Episcopal Mission Society had established the Frances Wells Harper Memorial Fund with $2,500 in seed money from the Wells family. The Woman's Auxiliary of Germantown, Pennsylvania, Frances's hometown, also contributed.[37] While working at St. Stephen's Hospital, Frances had shown an interest in constructing a solarium for the treatment of tuberculosis patients. Heliotherapy had been developed recently in Leysin, Switzerland, and had become accepted worldwide as the most effective treatment for tuberculosis and other lung diseases. In addition to the healing effects of the sun's rays, the solarium offered patients an uplifting environment in which to rest and receive care, without being tormented by mosquitos.[38]

13. John Fredson. John Fredson Collection, #1992-6-1, APRCA, University of Alaska Fairbanks.

The structure increased substantially the hospital's capacity year-round.[39] Johnny's work on the solarium reduced the cost significantly.[40]

Johnny supported and enhanced nearly every aspect of the work at St. Stephen's. He played the violin, accompanied by Winifred Dalziel on the organ, during church services, and he directed a children's choir. He also oversaw St. Stephen's Boys' Club. Daily he visited and interpreted for the sick, bringing them to the hospital when necessary. Having shadowed and assisted Hap for years, Johnny remained committed to becoming a physician. In the evenings, Hap tutored him in physiology and anatomy in preparation for medical school.[41]

In winter 1921–22 Clara and Hap fostered fourteen children from Fort Yukon and several other Interior villages. Often, they cared for children discharged from the hospital who were not yet strong enough to return to their remote homes. At the mission home, the Burkes hosted weekly dances for the children, Men's and Boys' Club meetings, sewing classes, Native Bible classes, choir practices, moving picture shows, and kindergarten Sunday school.[42] When the hospital was fully staffed, Clara devoted herself completely to the children. During staffing shortages and other crises, she filled in at the hospital as well.[43]

Meanwhile, fiscal concerns weighed heavily on Hap and Clara. By late 1921 Wood's correspondence with Bishop Rowe registered the mission board's and his own "feeling that the Fort Yukon Hospital has become a very expensive institution, considering the size of the community that it serves." The hospital now received $2,500 per year for operational costs, and Wood did his best to secure "specials" to cover additional expenses, but these were mounting. Wood asked Rowe to urge Hap at least to use the wireless less often.[44] He also asked whether the Native residents of Fort Yukon could volunteer their labor for hospital operations and maintenance and whether they could provide wood for heating the mission buildings.[45]

Rowe and Wood both felt that Hap could be more cost conscious. In his defense, Rowe pointed out that Hap worked for far less pay than any other physician would. Yes, operations at Fort Yukon were "fearfully expensive," but the work was "most creditable," Rowe stressed. "It is real mission work, hard, in a very hard, difficult place." He would urge Hap to reduce his use of the wireless, but he could not ask the Native people to secure wood for the mission and hospital. They were occupied at their fish camps harvesting the year's fish supply when the river was open and logs could be floated downriver.[46]

Hap later explained for Wood the complexities of securing the mission's and hospital's wood supply. In winter 1921–22 it would have been "utterly impossible" for the Native people to furnish the wood, because it had to be hauled three to five miles, and most of the people's dogs had been put down owing to recent poor fish runs. Rafting the wood in summer was risky, he explained. Sometimes, whole rafts of logs were lost on sand bars or in strong currents. Furthermore, rafted wood sometimes turned sour, and it tended to freeze with silt and sand in it, which damaged the saw. The Native people chopped and hauled all the wood for heating the church. They also did the maintenance work on the church. "To ask more," Hap wrote, "would, I feel, interfere with their livelihood, for they must look after their traps now, and in the Spring ratting takes them, while in the summer all are fishing."[47] The Mission Society authorized payment of the $1,800 invoice for 150 cords of wood that winter.[48]

Clara's work on behalf of the mission and hospital, with no direct compensation, did not arise in this context. While she and Hap may have been less "cost conscious" than mission headquarters wished, the mission board received far more than a normal work week in labor from each of them in return for Hap's meager salary. Their income, in fact, was so low that they were completely exempt from federal income taxes. St. Stephen's Mission complex's expenses *were* disproportionately high, owing to hospital operations, but other missions also overran their appropriations. These charges ultimately lay at Rowe's feet.[49] Yearly, the mission board allocated several thousand dollars to Rowe from "specials," an account holding irregular gifts from donors. Mission headquarters drew from Rowe's specials account to pay cost overruns by the Alaska missions. With costs rising, Rowe's specials account regularly ran deficits, which accumulated as debt for which he was held responsible.[50]

In 1920, at Stuck's request, the mission board had erased Bishop Rowe's debt of nearly $20,000, in recognition of the bishop's twenty-five years of service in Alaska. One-third of the debt pertained to St. Stephen's Mission. The gesture relieved Rowe's immediate anxiety, but the problem of rising costs persisted.[51] By fall 1921 the fuel bill for St. Stephen's Mission complex had risen to $2,000.[52]

A highlight of winter 1921–22 for Hap and Johnny was a February visit to Arctic Village, a Neets'aii Gwich'in community of about sixty that lay one hundred miles north of Fort Yukon in the foothills of the Brooks Range. A group led by Chiefs Christian and Esaias had traveled to Fort Yukon with two special errands. Many residents of Arctic Village were ill, and the people wanted Hap to pay them a visit to examine and treat them. Secondly, the men invited him to participate in the dedication of the new Bishop Peter Trimble Rowe Chapel.[53] Hap and Johnny prepared for a three-week journey, including a five-day stay in the village, carrying among their cargo medical supplies along with Bibles and prayer books, altar hangings, and school supplies. With temperatures as low as −40°F and a bitter north wind blowing snow crystals in their faces, they had to break trail and often struggled to find the route. On the tenth day, as they pulled into the village at sunset, residents swarmed to welcome them.[54]

Community leader Albert Tritt had been studying the Bible for years and teaching it to adults and children. Tritt's father had learned to read Gwich'in as he traveled with Archdeacon McDonald, and he later taught Albert to read. Since being instructed by Archdeacon Stuck and Hap in 1918, Tritt had been leading church services in the village.[55] Inspired by Tritt, Arctic Village residents had hauled construction materials north from Fort Yukon and built and furnished the church themselves. Johnny had lettered and gilded the sign by the door:

Bishop Rowe Chapel
Episcopal
Albert Edward Tritt, Layreader
Nutihsekh ako Ttia tsut tihsyah
(Let us go into the House of the Lord)[56]

Bishop Rowe officially designated Tritt a lay reader and sent vestments and a bell for the church. Hap led the dedication service and regular church services in Gwich'in. During their stay, he visited each home, checking on the elderly, examining those who were ill, and vaccinating children. In a show of appreciation for the visit and for Hap's many years of promoting health and welfare in the region, community members adopted him into the Neets'aii Gwich'in tribe. They gave him the name Chukla Ho, the name of their greatest chief, and presented him with a beaded medical bag and hind sack for his dogsled. Hap treasured both the honorary tribal membership and the title, as well as the gifts that had been made with such care. He displayed them over his desk at the hospital.[57]

Frederick Drane, upon his appointment as archdeacon of Interior Alaska, planned to move his headquarters from Nenana to Fort Yukon. Given its location at the center of the Episcopal Church's "largest and most promising field," he suggested that Bishop Rowe post an ordained priest there as well.[58] Hap objected to the idea, asking in a letter to Wood that the Native leadership in place, specifically David Wallis, the two chiefs, the Gwich'in Council, and a lay reader, be recognized for their contributions to the community's spiritual strength. Wallis, he noted, held weekly Bible classes and provided other religious instruction. He, the two chiefs, and another lay reader were "indispensable in the native services." Wallis's training, beginning with his adoptive father, the Anglican priest Mr. Wallis, Hap wrote, made him so useful that "an entire theological school" could not replace him. The universally respected Wallis served as an intermediary between the mission and the Native community, increasing trust and "acceptance of our Society's good intention, even when deed or word may seem to fail." The Native people, he wrote, should be serving their own people as nurses, doctors, and ministers increasingly.[59] In essence, Hap urged indigenizing the mission work.

He related to Wood a moving illustration of the value the community placed on Wallis's service. After Archdeacon Stuck's death, when Wallis's duties had increased, the Native Council and others contributed over $300 to supplement the stipend he received from the Mission Society. After the New Year, they did so again. A new clergyman would take years to learn the language, Hap pointed out, and would never lead the service as effectively as the Native lay readers did. If the church insisted on assigning an ordained clergyman to Fort Yukon, he could recommend three local Natives, and with time, Johnny Fredson and Moses Cruikshank would make ideal candidates for the priesthood.[60] For some time, nothing came of this discussion.

In spring 1922 break-up at Fort Yukon once again wrought havoc, tearing away masses of earth in front of the mission buildings. As water and ice surged and crashed through the village, many Native residents sat on their rooftops watching the drama unfold. Hap and Clara kept their eyes on the hospital. They had fortified the riverbank, and they had set up tents well back from the river and moved beds and patients to the upper floor of the hospital. The river took thirty more feet of the bank, leaving just fifty feet of land in front of the structure. Several feet of water filled the ground floor of the hospital. The structure held—for now. St. Stephen's Church, which had been built four hundred feet back from the river in 1907–8, had to be torn down and rebuilt farther back that summer.[61] By mid-July the church had been dismantled and moved by volunteers, who then completed the roof, installed the floor, and finished the chancel, at a cost of just over $200. The tower and finishing work would require skilled labor. Hap estimated the project could be completed at a total of $500.[62]

In August 1922 the newly ordained Rev. Robert Tatum left Alaska with Moses Cruikshank and Johnny Fredson, planning to enroll Moses at Mount Hermon School and Johnny at Sewanee, the University of the South.[63] On his application Moses had stated that he aimed to be a "Minister and an Industrial Instructor."[64] Tatum had assumed the role of guardian for Moses and took responsibility for his tuition.[65] In a letter to Mount Hermon, he had written of Cruikshank, "He is clean minded with splendid moral character. . . . I have a good deal of hope for his future."[66] Moses remained at the school for four years, with a term off for work to help pay his tuition. In 1926 he returned to Nenana, where he resumed working for the Episcopal missions on a variety of projects over the years.[67]

At Sewanee Tatum introduced Johnny to the young men who would be his roommates. Tatum, a well-known alumnus, having participated in the 1913 pioneer ascent of Denali with the university's most famous alumnus, Hudson Stuck, reminded the roommates of Johnny's role in the expedition. The three became such good friends that both roommates invited Johnny home during Christmas breaks.[68] In summer 1923, while he worked as a counselor at Camp Red Cloud in Pennsylvania, Johnny assisted the renowned scholar of Native American languages Edward Sapir in documenting the Gwich'in language. He related numerous stories, including personal memories and accounts of life in the Fort Yukon region, as well as legends he had heard. Sapir expressed his gratitude for the opportunity to work with such "an excellent informant."[69]

Hap and Clara departed Fort Yukon on furlough in late August 1922 with sons Hudson, now eleven years old, and Grafton, soon to be five. Finding a physician to assume Hap's medical responsibilities had been difficult. Eventually, Wood found Dr. Ernest Cook of Michigan to serve as locum tenens, and Cook's mother, Annie, later joined him. Hap and Clara placed several mission children in local homes before leaving, and Winifred Dalziel cared for the others in her teacher's quarters.[70]

Dr. Cook arrived shortly before Hap and Clara left, and Hap took an immediate liking to him.[71] Cook enjoyed the medical work at Fort Yukon,

14. Grafton and Clara Burke (*center*) with Grafton (*front center*) and Hudson (*to his right*). Geoffrey Burke private collection.

although he had to navigate amid frosty relations among the staff, owing to discord sown by the now dismissed nurse Nellie Landon.[72] Bishop Rowe assured Cook of his authority in Hap's absence, advised him against tolerating any subversive or disruptive behaviors, and told him to dismiss any troublemakers if necessary.[73] St. Stephen's was not alone in having personnel problems. Other missions endured such squabbling, incompetence, and high turnover among workers, owing to disenchantment with the work, isolation, and the harsh environment. Weddings, too, frequently led to resignations. Soon after their arrivals, female missionaries often received marriage proposals from the disproportionate number of single white men in Alaska.

The Burkes arrived in Seattle in mid-September and remained there a month, while Hap had extensive dental work done and Hudson underwent eye surgery.[74] From Seattle they traveled east by train. They enrolled Hudson at St. James, an Episcopal boarding school outside Hagerstown, Maryland, and then proceeded to New York.[75] Furloughs every few years bolstered Hap's and Clara's mental and physical health, allowing them respite from the isolation and heavy demands of their work at Fort Yukon. As he had done on their previous furlough, Hap honed his surgical skills at New York's Post Graduate Medical School and Hospital and at Cornell University Medical School. Both he and Clara took on speaking engagements to attract support for the mission work.[76] John Wood reported to Bishop Rowe that they were "winning many friends" during this furlough.[77] The two were "among the most popular and effective speakers we have had here" and had done "a lot of good to the cause."[78] Knowing the tremendous strain the hospital and mission work placed on them, Wood offered to extend their furlough for another year. Both Hap and Clara declined, stressing their eagerness to return to the people of Fort Yukon, the mission children, and the hospital, which according to Wood "occupies almost the place of a child in Burke's thinking."[79]

Hap had good reason to be preoccupied with the hospital's future that winter. Engineers at Fairbanks and Dawson had told him that moving the log structure was impossible, and experts in New York and at Princeton and Harvard had concurred.[80] In late spring, as Hap and Clara anxiously awaited news of break-up at Fort Yukon, fearing they would have no hospital to move, Bishop Rowe suggested they contact a Seattle engineer named Nicholson.[81]

Break-up in spring 1923 caused the worst damage in memory, taking ten more feet of riverbank in front of the hospital. Three feet of water filled the cellar. Had the woodpile not been fenced in, it would have floated away. Residents expected continued erosion that summer. Hap and Clara left New York in early June, eager to return home and hopeful of finding a contractor in Seattle.[82] There they met with Neil Nicholson, of the construction firm Bailey and Nicholson. As Clara described the encounter, "Nick" studied the hospital blueprints, asked a few questions, and pulled several small wooden blocks from his pocket to demonstrate his plan. He estimated that he could move the hospital for $10,000. Hap and Clara could hardly contain their joy. She later told him that she almost flung her arms around Nick and kissed him. "You should have done it!" Hap exclaimed. They remained keenly aware, however, of the risks involved.[83] The family arrived at Fort Yukon on August 1.[84] Nick arrived later that month with a partial crew and outfit to begin the Herculean project of moving Hudson Stuck Memorial Hospital.

Nicholson led the massive undertaking with a crew of two men from Seattle and many locals, Native and white. Using jacks, rollers, slings, thousands of feet of steel cable, wrecking bars, sledgehammers, saws, chisels, and a Fordson tractor for towing, they rolled the hospital five hundred yards back to the shore of a freshwater lake. They began the project in late August and completed it in five stages: first, jacking up the building and placing cribbing for a track and rollers; second, turning the building so the end would lead; third, pulling it on rollers to the new site with the tractor; fourth, turning the building to align it with the new foundation; and finally, setting it down. About seventy timbers supported the hospital as it rolled northward—with patients, equipment, and nursing staff in place throughout the move. Once the building stood on its new foundation, Nick caulked seams, connected the furnaces, and rebuilt the concrete chimneys. Finally, he used the tractor to move the solarium, without breaking any of its large glass panes. Natives reportedly observed the process with wonder and considerable skepticism. Nicholson completed the project as promised, holding the cost to $10,000.[85] Moreover, the hospital now had a hundred-thousand-gallon concrete reservoir, filled by an electric pump from the lake, and septic tanks that treated the hospital's sewage.[86] The lake came to be called Hospital Lake.[87]

Upon their return home, Hap and Clara resumed their myriad obligations. Clara brought the children back into the mission home, managed the large household, and when needed helped at the hospital. Hap installed new 110-volt batteries and generators in the lighting plant and an x-ray machine he had purchased while on furlough.[88] Friends gave the couple funds to purchase a radio, a welcome addition to the mission home that reduced winter's isolation. One winter's night when the aurora borealis was especially strong, Hap turned on the radio and heard a sermon broadcast from a cathedral in Sydney, Australia. Later that evening he and Clara danced to a symphony concert broadcast from New York.[89]

As soon as the hospital was relocated, a surge of patients arrived from various directions. Hap had to amputate the leg of a boy from 150 miles

o in Arctic Circle

15. Grafton at radio, circa 1924. Geoffrey Burke private collection.

north. Just before freeze-up a young man arrived from 125 miles up the Porcupine with a diseased gallbladder. Then a family of six arrived from 150 miles away, having carried the eldest child, a fifteen-year-old boy stricken with meningitis, on a stretcher. With tears in his eyes, the father begged Hap to save his son's life.[90] Without the hospital and Hap's expertise, likely none of these people would have survived.

Despite Hudson Stuck Memorial's modern facilities and competent personnel, many lives could not be saved. Too often tuberculosis defied the best-known treatments. Alaska's tuberculosis mortality rate was more than four times the national average. Alaska Natives' mortality rate exceeded the national average by nearly eight times, and among Native children it was far higher.[91] No one was exempt from the threat. In March 1923, while Hap and Clara were on furlough, David and Martha Wallis's beloved son Grafton died of the disease.[92] Archdeacon Frederick Drane developed chronic tuberculosis that required a long convalescence Outside and prohibited him and his family from returning to mission work in Alaska.[93]

In winter 1923–24 Clara found a solution to their longstanding concern about Hudson's education—she secured a scholarship to the Harvard School, a boarding school in Los Angeles, where he could visit Heintz family members on weekends and holidays.[94] Adjusting to school in Los Angeles would not be easy for Hudson. He reportedly thrived at Fort Yukon, where he had developed an array of subsistence and other practical skills and often helped with maintenance at the mission complex, for instance helping to carry the power plant's dual 110-volt batteries outside to replace the electrolyte. At school Hudson was lonely and homesick. Once, when the headmaster asked him why he always sat by an open window, he replied, "White people smell funny. They smell like death."[95]

In August 1924 nurse Emma Gunz, whom Hap valued for her strong work ethic and generous spirit, resigned to be married after four years' service.[96] To Hap's relief, he found a "most satisfactory" replacement for Gunz in Nellie Mulroney.[97] Mary Ryder, the new nurse who arrived that summer from Lancaster, Pennsylvania, also possessed the qualities Hap valued in staff members. She immediately recognized the scope of his responsibilities and the toll they took on him. "Dr. Burke is not yet forty, but looks quite old," she wrote the Lancaster newspaper (Hap's hair had turned white shortly after Stuck's death).[98] "Frontier life is very hard and the responsibility very great. He has to do everything—doctor, lawyer, minister, Indian chief!"[99] Hap did in fact continue to interact with the legal system, although his days as commissioner were long past. He regularly served as a juror or expert witness, and on occasion, he represented a defendant. Clara described herself as matronly by this time, having added forty-five pounds to what had been her ninety-five-pound frame since coming to Alaska seventeen years before. Her hair was "brushed with gray," which she explained as "a revenge which the Arctic sometimes takes on those who are not native to it."[100]

Ryder would remain just a year at Fort Yukon before resigning to marry a Canadian Mountie she met at Dawson on her journey to Alaska. Her sojourn at St. Stephen's would coincide with the most harrowing year in the Burkes' and the mission's existence, beginning with a mission home fire, followed by a severely cold winter, a record-breaking spring flood, and Fort Yukon's worst influenza epidemic. That winter Mary assisted in the amputation of the mailman's feet after he had frozen them on the trail. Yet she found and created much joy in her work and life at Fort Yukon, for instance with her elaborate preparations for Christmas to brighten the season for the children in the hospital.[101]

Creosote buildup in stovepipes, carelessness, and other circumstances caused fires that destroyed homes and buildings. In December 1920 the wash house behind St. Stephen's hospital caught fire and burned to the ground. Community members' quick work shoveling snow onto the walls of the hospital saved it from catching fire, averting an immeasurable calamity.[102] On New Year's Eve 1921 the mission home and two-story schoolhouse at Anvik burned to the ground after the roof caught fire where the stove pipe passed through it.[103]

At St. Stephen's, in September 1924, just as guests at the mission home were sitting down to a festive birthday dinner, young Grafton ran downstairs yelling, "Fire!" The flames, spreading with lightning speed, soon engulfed the house. Guests lifted Clara's china, crystal, and silver candlesticks with the linen tablecloth and carried them outside, while Hap and Nicholson rolled the heavy safe with the hospital records into the yard. Luckily, the mission children were all in the playroom behind the kitchen and could be shepherded out quickly. Native and white villagers rushed to the scene and saved the furniture on the main floor. Then the mission family, dinner guests, and others stood mesmerized, helpless to intervene, as flames shot skyward and the house burned to the ground. Presumably, the fire started in the wiring within the wall of Grafton's bedroom.[104]

The mission family slept in the schoolhouse that night. Early in the morning, with the last steamer of the season scheduled to arrive momentarily, Hap, with his "hair, eyebrows and lashes [singed], and scalp and forehead blistered and right hand wrapped in bulky dressings," hastily wrote John Wood a letter informing him of the fire. Next he wired Wood: "Mission dwelling with all supplies and perishable food and clothing for the winter burned last night. Total loss leaving family of fourteen homeless."[105] Two days later came Wood's reply: "Deepest sympathy. Will stand by you. . . . On receipt of details concerning loss and insurance will begin planning for new residence."[106] Hap's wire had arrived just as the

Within the image: *Destruction By Fire Of The Mission House Fort Yukon Alaska Sep. 23-1924. 9.00 P.M.*

16. Fire at St. Stephen's Mission Home, September 1924. Drane Photograph Collection, #91-046-281, APRCA, University of Alaska Fairbanks.

October issue of *Spirit of Missions* was going to press, allowing Wood to insert a notice of the disaster and a plea for assistance.[107]

Hap's letter described the scope of the loss in greater detail. Only the day before the fire he had stored all the perishable "winter grub" in the house, including $200 worth of fresh vegetables. In the basement, more than $1,000 in personal food and supplies and food for the mission children had been lost. Their "wonderful supply" of clothing sent by the Woman's Auxiliary was destroyed. Letters he and Clara had written had burned, as had "all receipts, drafts, blanks, and accounts." To Hap, the loss of the archdeacon's effects was incalculable. And how were they to care for the mission children? "I hardly know how to start in," Hap wrote. "Then too, it mortifies me to have to seek help. There has been so much consideration to the Hudson Stuck Hospital." Obviously reeling, he concluded, "Our solitary consolation is that no lives were lost, and that the building was insured."[108] The home had cost $16,000 to build and furnish in 1918. It was insured for $14,000.

As shaken as Hap and Clara were, the community's response to the fire heartened them. Natives and whites from "hundreds of miles around" swarmed to St. Stephen's with bedding, clothing, moccasins, parkas, rab-

17. Old Fred, John Fredson's father. Dr. Ernest A. Cook Photograph Collection, #2003-109-96, APRCA, University of Alaska Fairbanks.

bits, dried fish, and dried moose meat. Old Fred, Johnny's father, brought $5 and would not accept Hap's "no thank you" in response. Whites pledged $150 to a rebuilding fund.[109] The captain of the last steamship of the season turned over his food provisions to the mission. Winifred Dalziel invited the Burkes to move into the empty room in the teachers' quarters, which was available since the assistant teacher had resigned abruptly that fall, and she hired Clara as assistant teacher. Clara used her entire salary that year—$900—to support the children.[110]

Within a few days, local men and boys built a lean-to onto the residence for the girls' sleeping quarters, while the boys slept in the schoolhouse. Mission headquarters' prompt approval of immediate excavation work allowed a crew to dig half the new cellar under the eighteen-inch snow covering, gaining six weeks on the next building season.[111] By mid-October, less than a month after the fire, $16,454 had been donated to rebuild the mission home. Gifts ranged from $1 to $2,500, with one donor sending that sum twice.[112]

Just when the mission family had settled into their makeshift living arrangements two months after the fire, Clara's routine was thrown into turmoil when Nellie Mulroney married and resigned.[113] Clara now had to rush to the hospital after school to cook for the patients and staff and then dash back to the schoolhouse to cook for her "brood of fourteen children," as she described them. Luckily, within two weeks, Hap hired a woman from the region as hospital matron, allowing Clara to refocus on the children and her teaching duties.[114] In mid-January Hap learned that nurses Mary Ryder and Theresa Sands both would resign the following summer to be married. "Matrimonial business here getting dreadful alarming," he wired Wood.[115]

Amid staff turnover concerns and upheaval caused by the fire, David Wallis's faithfulness to St. Stephen's weighed heavily on Hap's conscience. Wallis performed services of far greater value than the $400 stipend the mission board now paid him, a sum too small to purchase even the bare necessities. One bitterly cold day in late January, Hap learned that Wallis, after attending to mission needs all day the previous day, had been out at night to collect wood to heat his home. Chagrined, Hap wrote Wood a detailed account of Wallis's constant service:

> He interprets daily at the clinic in the hospital, and there is hardly a case in which he is not indispensable. [His] familiarity with the records, the cases the history of the people of their complaints and afflictions, and his ability to render into their tongue our medical instruction and warnings at the hospital and to faithfully truthfully

and willingly interpret our religious teachings keep him in demand at all times night and day in church work, medical work, and mission work. [His] loyalty to us is profoundly touching. [His] advice on native affairs in a thousand and one ways is constantly sought. . . .

Often when I am not available for a burial, he is at the church to take it. You may say he is the devoted layman and the senior warden and the sexton. From the repairing of the gasoline lamps,—the heating and lighting of the church the procuring of wood and cutting of it, his interest and influence is felt. . . . Is it not possible to allow him at least as much as our dear old native deacon William Loola received?[116]

The board had paid Loola $600. Surely this injustice could be remedied, Hap wrote.[117] In 1926 the board increased Wallis's salary to $500.[118]

As the mission work consumed increasing amounts of Wallis's time, Martha took their surviving sons out on the land to work a trapline she had "inherited" from the man who had trapped there for many years and who turned it over to Martha when he grew too old for such work. The Wallis family called the area, which lay about twelve miles from Fort Yukon, "Neegoogwandaa." Nina, the Wallis's eldest child, stayed back in Fort Yukon to look after her father while Martha and the boys went out on the trapline.[119]

Spring break-up in 1925 was the most catastrophic in recorded history. Just after midnight the ice upriver from Fort Yukon gave way. Water from farther upriver rose over the high banks above the Yukon Flats, flooding hundreds of square miles and spreading into nearly every cabin at Fort Yukon. Native and white residents rushed to the hospital to help save food and other supplies from the basement. "There we all were in rubber boots," Hap later wrote, "nurses and all, splashing around in the rapidly rising, roaring flood, saving whatever we could. From the hospital we hurried to the warehouse on rafts and boats, but the damage had been done." Some fifty-four thousand gallons of water filled the hospital basement for a week, before a sergeant with the wireless station found a rotary pump that he and Hap connected to the Fordson's pulley so Hap could pump out the water. He ran the pump for fourteen hours before the water was removed.[120] "For weeks," Hap later recalled, "we were pumping cellars and recapturing walks, gates, fences and wood piles that had floated away, making repairs, and tidying up things generally."[121] Reflecting on this and other Alaska experiences, Hap wrote Wood, "I am glad I did not know what the future had for me, when I came out as a kid with Hudson Stuck."[122]

Johnny Fredson had returned to Fort Yukon in spring 1925 and immediately began clearing away debris at the site of the burned mission home. Recurring eye disease had forced him to pause his studies at Sewanee.[123] Nicholson built a new launch, the *Pelican II*, that spring, with a heavy-duty Speedway engine that permitted transport of machinery and building materials. On its maiden voyage, the *Pelican II* carried fuel and building materials to Fort Yukon for rebuilding the mission home. Bishop Rowe planned to reclaim it for his summer rounds, but when the sawmill at Fort Yukon broke down, Nick had to piece together parts from an old mill and use the *Pelican*'s engine to drive the reconstructed mill. Working with logs floated from upriver, men squared off the timbers on the ends and three sides to allow fitting and smooth interior walls. Finished lumber and doors were purchased Outside and shipped in.[124]

The rebuilding of the mission home was progressing well when influenza struck in July. Nearly every Native resident of Fort Yukon fell ill. Hap reported the crisis to Bishop Rowe, who was at Dawson, en route to the Interior with two nurses for the hospital. Rowe enlisted the Yukon Territory's Archdeacon Shirley and his wife, chartered a launch, and rushed to Fort Yukon.[125] Upon their arrival, every ward of the hospital was full. Cots lined the hallways, and tents erected to house the overflow were filled. Hap and Clara were hard at work, but nurses Mary Ryder and Theresa Sands, along with volunteers Winifred Dalziel and Rev. G. H. Moody, who was on temporary assignment at Fort Yukon, were ill. The two new nurses began tending to patients immediately, but within twenty-four hours, six people had died.[126]

Rowe described the village as looking dead. "In every cabin the parents and children are sick together—helpless to help each other." Clara cooked to feed the whole village. "She is a wonder—so cheerful and efficient," Rowe reported. Pulling a wagon through the village, Clara, the Shirleys, Johnny, and Reverend Moody (once he recovered) delivered soup, meat,

18. David Wallis with daughters Ethel (*left*) and Nina (*right*). Frederick B. Drane Collection, #91-046-56, APRCA, University of Alaska Fairbanks.

potatoes, and water to each home so all received at least one hot meal a day. Nicholson, who had suspended work on the mission home, assisted wherever needed.[127] Even the Fordson tractor was enlisted to carry patients to the hospital.[128] Every member of David Wallis's family fell ill, and Wallis himself was hospitalized with symptoms of pneumonia.[129] It may have been during this epidemic and its long aftermath that David and Martha's daughter Ethel died. They lost three children, son Grafton and daughters Minnie and Ethel to disease, leaving Nina, Peter, and Timothy surviving.[130] Johnny, whose father, Old Fred, was one of the first to die, "was a tower of strength," Hap later wrote. His "interpreting and daily rounds were invaluable."[131] Archdeacon Shirley and Pastor Moody buried the dead. Bishop Rowe held religious services in the hospital and out-of-doors, judging gathering in the church unsafe.[132]

Hap sent medical supplies to locations on both sides of the border, and patients arrived at the hospital from numerous sites, including Rampart House in Yukon Territory. John Wood contacted authorities in Washington DC, who notified Alaska's newly appointed governor, George Parks, of the crisis.[133] Telegrams to Fort Yukon from the Red Cross, the bureau of education, and the public health service asked for data and specific needs. Rowe estimated that three hundred people were ill. He requested medical and non-medical personnel and funding. On the evening of July 18, pioneering Alaska aviator Noel Wien arrived from Fairbanks in a Hisso Standard biplane—the first plane ever to fly into Fort Yukon—with a nurse and medical supplies from the Red Cross, which had allocated $2,000 to the cause. Nurse Dorothy Schleester, who examined every case, taking notes, established a second kitchen and organized a staff of cook and carriers, greatly relieving the food crisis. By July 21 the epidemic was under control, although many weeks of convalescence lay ahead.[134]

By July 25 Fort Yukon had recorded 318 cases. Fifteen people had died. The rapid response likely saved hundreds of lives during the three-week siege. After the crisis peaked Rowe wrote Wood, "Had it not been for our hospital and workers here, I fear the greater part of the population would have died." The work at St. Stephen's, he said, was "of more value than 10,000 sermons—making Christianity, the Gospel visible, a church of deeds not noisy words." Rowe acknowledged that meeting needs would be costly. "I hope the Church will sympathize and support us, as doing what they would have us do."[135]

While at Fort Yukon, Rowe pressed Wood about the long-term under-funding of St. Stephen's. Rowe confessed that he had not advocated strongly enough for the mission. "I shall try to do better," he wrote. No allocation covered St. Stephen's yearly $2,000 fuel bill.[136] The mission's appropriations *must* cover its operational costs, he insisted. Moreover, the epidemic had exhausted its reserves for the coming winter. These would have to be replaced. "Either that," Rowe declared, "or let us throw up hands and quit."[137] Wood published a plea for aid in the August issue of *Spirit of Missions*, estimating Rowe's influenza-related costs at $8,500, and mission friends from across the country responded, erasing Rowe's debt.[138] Nearly $5,000 in the Mission Society's Indian Relief Fund provided direct support for Alaska Natives as well.[139]

The timing of the influenza outbreak compounded its impact. The epidemic raged just as the Native people prepared for the annual fish harvest, keeping families from securing their staple food supply for themselves and their dogs through the fall and winter. St. Stephen's distributed food and other necessities for weeks as the community recovered. Bishop Rowe transferred nurse Lossie Cotchett from Nenana to Fort Yukon to assist during the recovery period.[140] People suffered well into the winter with complications of the flu, and more died.[141]

Hap and Clara's work and the mission's impact on the region during the epidemic moved Bishop Rowe deeply. He had praised their efforts previously and had generally indulged their "overspending," despite the frustration it caused him. Experiencing this crisis firsthand, however, gave him a new appreciation of the vital roles they, the mission home, and the hospital filled in the community and region. "It is freely admitted here by the white people, that had it not been for our mission, hospital, the loss of life in this epidemic would have been a slaughter," he wrote Wood.[142] Rowe marveled at Clara's devotion to orphaned and needy children. "She is a wonder," he wrote Wood. "How she has been able to do it, I don't know." Now with the new mission home near completion, she wanted to take in up to twenty-five children. "She sees that easily that number will be left to her care," Rowe told Wood. "It is a most worthy work." Did Wood think the church could support this work? he asked.[143]

Wood's sobering response to Rowe's query highlighted his challenging position as foreign and domestic secretary. Convincing the board to increase Fort Yukon's allocation by $2,500 per year, Wood's estimate of the cost of Clara's proposal, was "at present out of the question." Nor was attracting that sum each year in specials a permanent solution. Furthermore, how could he recruit replacements for Hap and Clara when they went on furlough with such a large brood of children? And who would replace them when they left the field permanently?[144]

Wood's response reflected harsh fiscal realities. Ominous signs had appeared in the early 1920s with donations to the church's mission work dropping dramatically. Deficits of several hundred thousand dollars forced the National Council to consider "radical retrenchment." It had instead chosen "wise economy" in moving forward, which nevertheless ruled out expansion.[145]

Meanwhile, the epidemic had suspended construction on the mission home and required various creative measures. The man hired to bring the logs, as well as his crew, had fallen ill, which delayed filling the contract. When the work resumed in August, the *Pelican*'s engine supplied the horsepower for the sawmill. On its first day of use, Emil Bergman of Rampart, the married father of five, fell over the running saw, severely lacerating his arm and sustaining a head injury. Hap saved the man's arm, but Bergman lost his thumb and remained hospitalized for months.[146] Despite the crises and setbacks, Nicholson and crew completed the house by late summer. Hap and Clara relished living in their spacious new home with its beautiful maple floors and other amenities—electric lights and a concrete foundation, water reservoir, and septic system that permitted running water.[147]

In early August the *Yukon* arrived full of passengers, including Canadian Mountie Claude Tidd, who was to marry nurse Mary Ryder. The bride remained in bed with the flu the day before the wedding and feared she would miss the event. She rallied, however, for the big day. Tourists aboard the steamer joined locals in attending the ceremony, a welcome counterpoint to the harrowing experiences of the previous months. An elaborate dinner party aboard the steamer followed the ceremony. Hap later recalled that Bishop Rowe, who married the couple, remarked that he had never seen "a prettier wedding or a more impressive ceremony . . . in the little church within the Arctic Circle!"[148] Three "prominent surgeons" among the visitors toured Hudson Stuck Memorial, Rowe reported, and "were enthusiastic in their admiration" of the hospital and the church's work at the remote location.[149]

By fall 1925 the new, larger mission home was "packed full of children"—orphans or "partial orphans" and children whose health required "the attention of the Church to give them their chance," as Hap put it. On busy days, he left home for the hospital at seven o'clock in the morning and returned at six o'clock for supper. In the evenings, house calls or hospital emergencies often kept him out.[150]

The cost of rebuilding the mission home, $25,000, far exceeded anyone's estimate. Insurance had paid $12,000, and specials had brought in another $8,000. The $5,000 shortfall and the handwringing that ensued illustrated once again, on the one hand, the high living costs in the far north, the great needs within the Alaska mission field, and the unpredictability of conditions and, on the other, the Episcopal Mission Society's inability to recognize these realities, budget accordingly, and secure adequate funds.[151] The final tally on the mission home caused A. H. Horton, the fiscal officer charged with paying the invoices, such alarm that he berated Hap for putting him "in a very bad position" and told him that he would have to "square yourself both with the Board of Missions and Bishop Rowe" for "expending more money than you knew was available."[152]

Hap defended himself against Horton's "most unjust" accusations, noting that he had never been informed of the sum on hand for construction and suggesting that most of the cost overrun resulted from Nicholson's ideas for the enhanced cement basement, reservoir, septic tank, piped water, and an "elaborate fireplace." Hap praised Nick's workmanship and assured Horton that he and Clara deeply appreciated their new home.[153]

The exchange typified the regular correspondence among Rowe, Wood, and Burke, with Horton usually remaining behind the scenes and Rowe and Wood commiserating about the "embarrassment" that Burke caused the three of them with his inattention to costs.[154] After experiencing the influenza crisis firsthand, Rowe appreciated more fully the medical exigencies that Hap and Clara witnessed daily, as well as their selflessness. By now he deemed the work done at Stuck Memorial Hospital and St. Stephen's Mission the church's most important and laudable work in Alaska. Yet his responsibilities included the entire Alaska mission field, and the mission board held him accountable for not exceeding its yearly allocations for Alaska.

Neither Wood nor the board ever fully grasped the cost of mission work in the Arctic. Because allocations never reflected the medical needs, high heating costs, and heavy freight charges, Wood repeatedly had to ask the board for increased funds for Alaska. And he frequently had to make appeals to "friends" to cover both ordinary expenses and calamitous events, all of which left him exhausted, "embarrassed," and exasperated with Hap. In less than three years, $41,000 had been expended in specials at Fort Yukon to move the hospital and rebuild the mission home and to respond to the influenza epidemic. Wood warned Rowe, "People are most kind and generous, but I live under the shadow of the possibility that some day they will rise up and say 'You are making unreasonable calls upon us.'"[155]

7

St. Stephen's Mission Work Expands as Support Declines Nationally, 1926–30

In the 1920s many Episcopal dioceses failed to meet their pledges for contributions, or quotas, to the national church, forcing the mission board to make horizontal cuts to the mission work. Within this context, the ever-increasing costs at Fort Yukon triggered anxiety in Bishop Rowe and alarm at mission headquarters. By late in the decade, the stock market crash and the impending Great Depression would signal much more serious fiscal woes to come. For the time being, as general giving declined, necessitating reduced allocations to mission fields worldwide, individual "mission friends" continued to donate generously when contacted personally by Wood or by specific bishops and missionaries such as Rowe and the Burkes.

By the second half of the decade, Hap and Clara had earned the respect and gratitude of the overwhelming majority at Fort Yukon, Native and non-Native. They took pleasure in hearing old timers and Natives refer to Hudson Stuck Memorial as "our hospital."[1] They found their work deeply gratifying, although the "steady stream of difficulties and annoyances" discouraged and drained them at times. Clara later wrote in her memoir that from her perspective, the years 1926 and 1927 were their happiest. Grafton remained at home and regularly shadowed his father in his work, and Hudson returned home for an extended visit after two years away at school in California. Hap and Clara saw the fruits of their labors in the children they fostered, who were flourishing. The Boys' and Girls' Clubs were active. Many who had grown up and started families of their own remained close to the mission family, visited frequently, and brought their children to participate in activities.[2] Perhaps the greatest challenge, Hap wrote John Wood in 1927, was "meeting, and living, and working daily and intimately, for year after year with souls so new, and different, and strange."[3] Recruiting and training new personnel and contending with those who challenged hospital procedures, and sometimes even Hap's integrity, consumed far too much of his time and mental energy. Yet each resolved controversy brought greater recognition in Alaska and at mission headquarters of the couple's devotion to their work and its positive impacts on community and regional health and well-being.

The year 1925 had marked the dawn of aviation in Alaska, a development that would bring myriad changes, reducing the isolation of remote outposts, easing transport of people and commodities, and changing the pace of life, all of which affected Hap and Clara's work. After bringing the Red Cross nurse and other support during the influenza epidemic, Alaska aviator Noel Wien made a total of twelve flights beyond the Arctic Circle in summer 1925—with several flights into Fort Yukon—inaugurating the Arctic aviation era.[4] In the years that followed, people increasingly flew in and out of Fort Yukon, especially in times of urgency. In 1925 Alaska's territorial legislature diverted $40,000 from its biennial roads allotment for the construction of runways, and by 1926 nineteen communities had new runways, including Fort Yukon, Rampart, and Circle Hot Springs.[5] In early August 1927, with no other means of travel, Bishop Rowe flew the seven hundred miles from Nome to Point Hope. The first flight into the northwest coastal village created much excitement.[6] In 1928 three of Alaska's four commercial airline companies, as well as an aviation school, operated from and in Fairbanks.[7] With the advent of air travel, Hap on occasion flew to the aid of a stricken community or an injured individual.[8]

Steamers, however, remained the overwhelmingly dominant mode of travel for people entering and leaving the northern Interior. Thousands of tourists visited Fort Yukon each summer. The "Yukon Circle Tour" of about thirty days took them by steamer from Seattle through the Inside Passage to Skagway, where they boarded the White Pass and Yukon Route railroad to Whitehorse. From there they traveled by steamer down the Yukon River to Dawson, across the border into Alaska, and on down to Circle, Fort Yukon, and as far as Tanana, where they turned up the Tanana River to Fairbanks. There they boarded the railroad to return south to tidewater. Traveling in the opposite direction became more popular in the late 1920s. During fiscal year 1928, twenty-five steamers carried about thirty-three thousand passengers to Alaska's ports. All steamers reportedly ran at or near capacity, and tourist traffic was increasing.[9] At Fort Yukon, Gwich'in found eager buyers for their furs and beaded items among the tourists.

One summer the teenage girls of the Northern Lights Club that Clara supervised earned a substantial sum by selling rag rugs. They had learned to weave the rugs from wool remnants found amid the clothing and other items that woman's auxiliaries sent to Alaska missions. Tourists showed great interest in the girls' handiwork. When Bishop Rowe visited and learned of the project, he donated a pair of his cast-off woolen underwear to the cause. The girls wove strips of the fabric into a snow background on a rug depicting a northern winter landscape with dogsled teams, caribou, bears, and mountain sheep. The rugs typically sold for $15 to $30, but as Clara recalled, the "Bishop Rowe rug" sold for $100. The girls bought a phonograph and set of records with their earnings, and the mission home reverberated with popular songs such as "Let Me Call You Sweetheart." They used their remaining funds to purchase a leg brace for one of the mission girls.[10]

The many tourists, including physicians, who visited the Hudson Stuck Memorial Hospital often expressed astonishment at finding a first-rate hospital above the Arctic Circle. When Bishop Rowe traveled on steamers, the crew usually asked him to speak on the mission work. He enjoyed hearing the tourists praise St. Stephen's Mission, feeling certain that the "real mission work" done there elevated tourists' general impressions of the church's efforts.[11]

Winter 1925–26 was destined to be grim, given people's inability to harvest salmon the previous summer while the influenza epidemic raged. To make matters worse, for the second year in a row, "ratting," as the Gwich'in called trapping muskrat, was almost pointless; there were none in the region. With many survivors of the flu not yet fully recovered, only the mild winter saved the people from catastrophe.[12] The children's health class, held at the hospital each Saturday for two years now, boosted health and wellness among the children. About sixty attended each Saturday, along with their mothers and baby siblings. Hospital staff tracked children's weight and looked for other signs of illness. Each Saturday the class focused on a different topic, but overall, the classes stressed hygiene, nutrition, playing out of doors, and getting enough sleep, with windows open as much as possible, to combat tuberculosis, the greatest threat to life among Alaska Natives.[13] Ventilation and removal of those infected with the disease were by far the most effective preventative measures.[14]

The Episcopal Board of Missions' failure to adequately fund St. Stephen's Mission complex caused Hap and Clara continual anxiety. The high cost of wood for heating seemed to baffle both John Wood and the Board of Missions—somewhat understandably, given the mission's location "in the middle of the Alaskan wilderness" where, from their perspective, firewood ought to have been free for the taking. Bishop Rowe understood local conditions and consistently defended the work at St. Stephen's, despite finding Hap's fiscal habits wanting at times. St. Stephen's mission and hospital work "may not be as conspicuous a work as the Cathedral of St. John the Divine," he wrote Wood in 1926, but it was equally great because St. Stephen's "cares for sick, orphans, widows, poor and unfortunate, as the (cathedral) does not—not in the same way."[15] In spring 1926, when Hap submitted his $2,000 wood fuel invoice and Wood replied that no funds remained, Hap immediately wired friends pleading for help. The response was heartening—sufficient donations to pay both the current and next year's fuel bill.[16] Clearly, however, a long-term solution was needed.[17]

That spring, strained resources led Bishop Rowe and Wood to advise Hap and Clara to "begin to dispose of" the twenty-two children in Clara's care. Finding someone to look after the youngsters during the couple's coming furlough would be impossible, as was paying for their upkeep another year.[18] In a postscript Wood asked whether Hap and Clara had considered leaving Alaska. In just a few years, he reminded Hap, he would find it "difficult to locate satisfactorily" Outside.[19] The postscript, coupled with the call to "dispose" of the children, suggested that Hap and Clara's vision for St. Stephen's Mission had grown so burdensome that Wood and the Board of Missions hoped they would give it up.

Hap responded emphatically to Wood: "Someone must take Claras [sic] place [and] mother these twenty children."[20] Three weeks later he wired Wood that he and Clara would forego their furlough that summer if it meant giving up the children.[21] The same day, he wrote Bishop Rowe, copying Wood, of his shock and distress at being told to "dispose" of the children. Perhaps they could find good homes for a few of them, he wrote, "but what in the world would happen to the rest of them, only the Lord knows." To cast out these children, many of whom were convalescing from the flu epidemic, would be a calamity that no one along the Yukon River, white or Native, could ever understand, he noted pointedly. "To Clara who is getting absolutely no remuneration, and is going night and day for these children cheerfully, it would be like tearing out her heart," he added. As for fostering the children in the long term, "why not do it?" he asked, when he and Clara could thereby save lives, with just $1,000 from the mission board, along with meat supplied by Fort Yukon residents. "Must I say 'let them die'?" Hap and Clara postponed their furlough. They could not "chance jeopardizing this work, in which our hearts have long since been place[d]," he told Rowe.[22]

In the meantime, Clara had chosen a less direct but ultimately effective appeal. Writing to Wood on Easter Sunday, she enclosed a $35 money order, "a thank offering from the children . . . in appreciation for their new home and all the church is doing for them." The youngsters had worked hard to earn the money, she explained. Of the total, they designated $25 as their Lent offering, $5 for reducing the Mission Society's deficit, and the final $5 for "the [mission] workers in famine stricken China," who, as seven-year-old Mable pointed out, would not be able to care for "all the children" if they themselves were sick. Clara told Wood of Mable's circumstances and of those of the other children who were in no condition to go home, if they *had* a home. She noted that she had donated her teacher's salary the previous year to the children's needs. Without those funds this year, she and Hap had struggled to manage. "I'm hoping someday this work of caring for the children at the mission will be recognized by the Board of Missions, for it is truly a great work."[23]

The letter hit its mark. "You certainly are loading coals of fire on my poor head," Wood responded. He asked Clara to write more of the children's individual stories so he could use them in a *Spirit of Missions* article to appeal for support for this tender cause. He told her to emphasize the mission home's role as a clearing house for the hospital, anticipating that the request would be more effective if framed as such.[24] Rowe weighed in, stressing the work's "merciful, tender and beneficent" nature and reminding Wood that "Clara has made no end of sacrifices."[25]

The title of Wood's *Spirit of Missions* article hooked readers with Hap's heartrending question, "Must I Say: 'Let Them Die'?" Personalizing the dilemma, Wood named the children and described their needs: Jimmie, who had lived with the Burkes for seven years, still required regular medical care and was not yet strong enough to go to St. Mark's mission school; Sally, John, Enoch, Mabel, David, and Margaret remained in such precarious health that they could not yet return to their cramped, remote cabins; three small children whose mother lay dying in the hospital with a fourth sibling had nowhere else to turn. Their father could help but could not care for the children while earning a living.[26] The stories of individual named children resonated with readers. The article eventually garnered nearly $7,000, which Wood placed in a specials account for the children's care.[27]

Break-up in spring 1926 again caused catastrophic flooding. Up and down the Yukon River, huge swaths of the riverbank were torn away. Only Eagle, which sat on a bluff, was spared. The old site of the hospital was torn away, but Hudson Stuck Memorial stood secure in its new setting, although four feet of water filled the building. Opening the doors and allowing the waters to flow in prevented structural damage. Patients had been removed from the flooded area in advance, allowing their care to continue without interruption. Upon receiving word of a woman in labor who needed help, Hap set out in a rowboat in search of her. As he rowed through the village, Clara recalled, people greeted him cheerfully from their roof tops. He found the expectant mother on her roof top and helped her into the rowboat. She named her baby, who was born in the rowboat outside the hospital, Moses. In summer 1926 the "skeets" (mosquitos) were especially thick, the lingering floodwaters having made perfect breeding grounds for them.[28]

The highlight of summer 1926 for Hap and Clara was Hudson's extended visit. Clara's mother, Maude Heintz, brought the fifteen-year-old home from California. During his two years away, he had grown so tall that he stood "almost eye to eye with his father."[29] In her memoir published thirty-five years later, Clara reflected on the distance that had developed between parents and child. He had become more his grand-mother's son than theirs, she recalled, showing affection for them but turning to his grandmother for advice. Grafton, at eight, was still theirs, "but in a few years he too would go out to school," she wrote. She and Hap discussed the price that missionaries in "foreign fields" paid in sending their children to school in their "home countries." They took comfort in sensing that Hudson was happy in California.[30]

Family members' recollections suggest that Hudson was not, however, entirely content with his life in California. His little brother was shadow-ing their father in his work, and Hudson regretted that he would have no such experience. On the other hand, Hudson had shown keen interest in his dad's ham radio and had learned how to use it, including learning Morse code. While attending the Harvard School, he honed his mechan-ical skills outside the classroom and earned pocket money while doing so. During the Prohibition years, he maintained the engines on boats that ran liquor and gamblers to ships anchored outside the three-mile limit to circumvent California's law against gambling.[31] The gambling ships were so popular that a whole fleet clustered outside Santa Monica and Long Beach in the late 1920s.[32] One can only speculate about what Hap, Clara, and Hudson's grandmother would have thought of his entrepreneurism.

From the age of about seven, Grafton had often shadowed his father at the hospital. He helped the nurses, carried messages, and on occasion "assisted" Hap in surgery. Dressed in a surgical gown made by the nurses, with his hands sterilized, he handed Hap instruments, which he knew by name. Spending so much time with his father, Grafton learned to read his moods. Once, when Bishop Rowe cracked open the door to ask if he could come in and observe, Grafton reportedly tiptoed to the door shaking his head. "Daddy's foot is wiggling," he whispered, referring to the telltale sign that Hap was deep in concentration and must not be disturbed.[33]

The boys' grandmother made quite an impression in Fort Yukon in her elegant clothing, silk stockings, and "chic little tailored hat" with a "fine mesh veil" to guard against mosquitos. Clara described her as "a 'good mixer'" with "flawless" social tact. She "soon had a string of admirers"

19. Patient being brought into Hudson Stuck Memorial Hospital. Geoffrey Burke private collection.

who competed to "show her around and take her fishing." Hap reportedly dubbed his mother-in-law the "Yukon Belle" because she won the hearts of both Natives and whites "with her irresistible enthusiasm." She helped wherever she could in the mission home, to the delight of the children, who called her "pretty Miz' Heintz," and she even lent a hand at the hospital.[34]

A visiting Englishwoman's equally vivid depiction of "Mama" suggests that some Fort Yukon residents, perhaps even her own son-in-law, were less susceptible to her charm than Clara imagined. After Clara Rogers Vyvyan and her friend Gwendolyn Smith enjoyed the first of several "supper parties" and "cheerful tea-parties" at the mission home, Vyvyan made note of "a pecking kind of woman from Los Angeles, in silk stockings, whose speech was sharp and quick like the movements of a bird, and who seemed to get on Dr. Burke's nerves."[35]

The English women stayed for a week at Fort Yukon near the end of their three-month journey to the northwest Arctic. Weary of Victorian constraints on single middle-aged women and enticed by Robert Service's *Spell of the Yukon*, the women set out in search of adventure in 1926 and found it. From Waterways near Fort McMurray on the Athabasca River in northern Canada, they traveled the Slave, Mackenzie, Rat, Bell, and Porcupine Rivers and finally a few miles of the Yukon River to Fort Yukon. Vyvyan later referred to the trek as "not only the most formidable enterprise, but also in a spiritual sense, the high peak of my life."[36]

Shortly after arriving in Fort Yukon, they met the Burkes. "We shall never forget their large comfortable living room nor the lavish kindness of that couple," Vyvyan wrote. After chatting only a few minutes, Hap and Clara invited the women to stay at the mission home. They chose instead to camp just outside the community and visit often.[37] The women found the fascinating dinner conversation during their first evening with the Burkes even more delightful than the scrumptious meal Clara prepared. Vyvyan described Hap's "fine, sensitive, overwrought-looking face" and Clara's gracious, "happy homemaker" demeanor, in contrast with the overbearing "pecking" woman, Mrs. Heintz. Between themselves, the women thereafter referred to Clara's mother as Mrs. Pecker, claiming not to recall her name. Other dinner guests included three members of the geological survey working on the Sheenjek River. The memorable evening culminated for the women in hot baths in the mission home's luxurious bathroom.[38]

The following day, Vyvyan and Smith spent a "cool and blissful after-noon" in the mission home having tea and visiting with the Burkes and neighbors. People regularly stopped by "that hospitable home" for a meal, to seek help, or to borrow one thing or another, Vyvyan wrote. The mission home became the "centre of [the women's] lives" during their stay, but they also strolled about the community, talking with people and "spen[t] hours listening to their yarns."[39] Among the most fascinating of the old-timers was Frank Foster, who had come into the country during the Klondike gold rush of 1898. A voracious reader like Vyvyan, he would visit Fort Yukon to restock his supplies and then return to "his cabin, his books and his solitude" on the upper Porcupine. Everyone seemed to have a fantastical, allegedly true, story of adventure in the far north. Tony, for instance, told of shooting the rapids "in some canyon" with Buffalo Jim and saving "from the jaws of death" three men clinging to rocks by their fingernails.[40]

One afternoon Hap walked with the visitors through the old Hudson Bay Company cemetery, recounting stories of the men buried there. In the Native cemetery they lingered at Hudson Stuck's grave, as Hap spoke of Stuck's work and adventures. Vyvyan later read and treasured his books.[41] As for Hap, "Dr. Burke was a missionary and medical doctor in one," she wrote, "and a friend to every soul in Fort Yukon."[42]

Vyvyan took delight in the trove of books and journals in the mission home. When Smith was outside sketching, Vyvyan sat in the mission house reading. From time to time, Mrs. Heintz looked in on her, "for she was not one of those who love to bury themselves in an occupation," preferring instead to flit about. Vyvyan noted her "sharp eye and mind and tongue."[43]

One afternoon, as the women prepared tea at their campsite on the riverbank, Mrs. Heintz wandered over in her "town clothes, silk stockings and all." They offered her a mug of tea, a scone, and a box to seat herself and asked about her life in Los Angeles. As the American darted from one topic to another, the Britons did their best to keep up with her. "In her company," Vyvyan wrote, "I always felt that we had very sluggish minds." Their cheerful indulgence of Mrs. Heintz's chatter paid off. When Clara invited the women to stay in the mission home on their final night in Fort Yukon, her mother insisted they take her spacious room with a double bed. The dinner party that evening swelled to include "various unexpected guests, two geological surveyors, a gold-prospector and a trapper, all full of reminiscences and stories." The bedroom suited the women perfectly, but they hardly slept, as the sun shone "relentlessly" and the dogs "howled all night."[44] The Burkes' and Mrs. Heintz's warm send-off the next day left the women feeling a bit melancholy. "I shall always think of those two," Vyvyan wrote, "standing like beacon-lights in the lonely northland, keeping alive and shining the true spirit of Christianity."[45]

Although Grafton often spent time with his father at the hospital, he found plenty of time to play with his friends, take part in adventures, and accumulate scrapes and bruises. One of his most memorable experiences involved an encounter between a grizzly bear and an African American prize fighter. As he later told the story, the tall, heavily built Peter had killed his opponent in a bare-knuckled prize fight in Seattle. Such outcomes were not unheard of, but given the racial prejudice of the time, Peter ran off, fearing he would be lynched. He eventually floated down the Yukon River to Fort Yukon, where Hap befriended him, gave him a place to stay, and hired him to do maintenance work. One day a grizzly bear was roaming about Fort Yukon and broke into the NC Company warehouse after hours. Grafton and his friends scrambled into the crawlspace beneath the building and listened as the bear rummaged through the food supplies, knocking over flour barrels and containers of molasses, the contents spilling between the floorboards to the boys' hiding place. When word spread of the angry bear in the warehouse, Peter raced to the scene with a rifle in hand. The boys heard two quick shots and then watched in horror as blood poured through the floor to the ground. Shortly thereafter, Hap arrived and found that the bear had mauled Peter before dying. Peter was rushed to the hospital, where he recovered. Just after his release, the marshal came with a warrant for his arrest. Grafton recalled his father weeping as the marshal led Peter away in chains to be put on trial for murder in Seattle. Word later reached Fort Yukon that he had been acquitted.[46]

In 1926 the territorial government began coordinating with the U.S. Bureau of Education to provide medical care to the estimated four thousand Alaska Natives and two thousand whites in Alaska's Interior who had little access to such services.[47] In the summer months, the *Martha Angeline*, a riverboat outfitted as a clinic with living quarters for a doctor and nurse, traveled the waterways of the Yukon River drainage system from the village of Tanana to the mouth of the Yukon River. In summer 1927 a doctor and two nurses treated 1,473 patients and provided dental care to several hundred, including 884 extractions, apparently the favored treatment for toothaches. The two nurses carried on with their work even after Dr. John Huston fell overboard and drowned in mid-July.[48]

During the winter months, the medical personnel from the *Martha Angeline* worked at the U.S. Bureau of Education's newly opened hospital at Tanana, now called the Old Fort Hospital. The U.S. Army had abandoned Fort Gibbon, including the hospital, three years earlier. The twenty-bed facility became the first government hospital in north central Alaska to serve both the civilian population and any military detachments in the region. Episcopal mission personnel from Rampart to Allakaket reportedly relied on the hospital's services, which took some pressure off Hudson Stuck Memorial Hospital.[49]

A meeting Hap called in early winter 1926–27 lent weight to Clara Vyvyan's sense of him as a friend to every soul in the community. Taking advantage of the boom economy in Fort Yukon based on the high prices that furs commanded in the late 1920s, Hap asked the community for help in bringing the Hudson Stuck Memorial Endowment to its goal of $25,000.[50] According to one witness, within about fifteen minutes, forty-three old-timers jointly donated and pledged $2,760 over three years. The principal currently stood at about $14,000.[51] Attendees elected three men to lead the effort: Harry Horton, whom Hap had battled during his days as commissioner, J. A. Donald, an NC Company employee, and Hap.[52] While the community's show of support heartened Hap and Clara, the day-to-day struggles to make ends meet continued.

In early winter 1926 a thorny dilemma arose regarding wages owed Emil Bergman in the aftermath of the sawmill accident. Bergman had remained hospitalized into 1926, as Hap operated several times to improve his use of his injured arm. Recognizing that he could never resume his former work, Hap secured him a position at the local post office, beginning in August 1926. In the meantime, with Bishop Rowe's approval, he had advanced Bergman $500 against the wages owed him.[53] Late that year Wood wired Hap that he and Rowe felt the church had no further obligation to Bergman.[54] Hap's sense of responsibility toward Bergman led to another unpleasant exchange with A. H. Horton, the purchasing agent, who accused Hap of being negligent with church funds in fulfilling the obligation he felt to Bergman.[55] The parties eventually reached an amicable settlement, and Bergman maintained a warm relationship with Hap and Clara and St. Stephen's Mission in the years to come. He suffered from the disabilities incurred in the sawmill accident for the rest of his life.[56] After Bergman's wife, Annette, died, he married William

Loola's daughter Nina in 1927. They had a daughter, Adeline, in 1928, and a son, Grafton, in 1930.[57]

As if the headache surrounding Bergman's compensation were not enough, at about the same time, a cabal of hospital personnel caused another kerfuffle. The nurse Adelaide Duke had begun to stir trouble soon after her arrival in summer 1926. Duke second-guessed Hap's diagnoses and treatments, as well as hospital practices, causing anxiety among both staff and patients.[58] She made common cause with the new handyman William McCurdy and his wife, the hospital matron, after Hap reported them to the marshal for abusive drinking in the mission cabin they occupied.[59] Duke's bizarre and spiteful behavior turned nearly all of Fort Yukon against her.[60] Besides the McCurdys, just two people appear to have joined Duke's campaign to discredit the Burkes and run them out of town. Their complaints were hardly credible.[61]

On the other hand, three well-regarded men wrote Bishop Rowe amid the controversy, attesting to Hap and Clara's positive influence in the region and their unfailing dedication to community health and well-being. Harry Horton, Hap's one-time nemesis, noted the recent local pledges to the hospital fund and the universal praise for the hospital from old-timers treated there. "I personally believe it would be impossible," he wrote, "to replace [the Burkes] after their years of experience here."[62] The NC Company employee J. A. Donald wrote Bishop Rowe to denounce Duke and defend Hap and Clara, whom he regularly witnessed devotedly carrying out their work. No one, he declared "who is unbiased can say otherwise."[63] The old-timer Frank Foster also defended Hap, assuring Bishop Rowe that Duke's claims were baseless and her suggested hospital practices ridiculous. Diminishing Hap's role in managing the hospital would be a "deep injustice," he said, and removing him would be "little short of a calamity."[64]

A settlement of $300 rid Hap and Fort Yukon of Duke,[65] and by May 1927, Hap had hired John Helenius of Fort Yukon to replace McCurdy and Mrs. Norwood of Fairbanks to replace Mrs. McCurdy as matron.[66] He rehired Theresa Sands Bohmer, who had worked at the hospital before marrying in 1925; he would come to regret this decision, but for now, peace was restored.[67] The latest personnel crisis had tried Rowe's patience with

Hap's management style.[68] By mid-June, however, Donald's letter praising the Burkes had softened Rowe's outlook. He forwarded it to Wood with a note: "It is fine—from a man who is responsible and of finest character."[69]

By the following summer, Rowe viewed even more tenderly any role Hap's shortcomings may have played in the misfortunes that beset St. Stephen's Mission complex. "I am a friend of 'hap' and 'Clara,' as you are," he wrote Wood. "Fine, splendid, as Hap is, he has limitations, as we all have. . . . While he has been the victim of circumstances, at the same time he has not been blameless. But that is no condemnation. I love him—admire him—stand by him, all the same."[70]

In fact, Rowe had called for increasing Hap's salary from $2,000 to $2,400 in his 1928 budget proposal. He also called for increased funding for St. Stephen's operating costs by $2,500. "The splendid work and object justify it," he wrote. "It is simply out of the question to try and carry it on as we have tried in the past."[71] The board declined to raise Hap's salary.[72] It raised hospital maintenance, however, by $1,000.[73]

In summer 1927 playground equipment arrived at St. Stephen's Mission, thanks once again to mission friends' generosity. The children had "never seen anything like it" and took "the keenest pleasure" in it, Hap reported. They rushed out to play before breakfast and remained there after supper until bedtime. The events that culminated in the delightful addition to the mission home tickled Hap and Clara as much as the playground pleased the children. The story began with word from John Wood that a Pennsylvania family had made a bequest to the mission home children. Wood in turn asked Hap what would be most useful, and Hap suggested a playground "with suitable equipment for convalescent children." Before it arrived, Hap arranged for the materials and the help he would need to install the equipment. Winifred Dalziel donated fencing, John Helenius would sink the posts, and Emil Bergman would assemble the structure. Then came news that jeopardized the whole project: the playground would need a concrete pad. As Hap pondered how he would pay for the concrete, sand, and gravel, the answer arrived with a steamer full of tourists when an ad hoc committee from the vessel presented him with more than $200. He recounted the remarkable incident to Wood: "You can imagine my embarrassment as well as joy, when the whole company of 40 or 50 flocked in the hospital and mid the clicking of cameras—both movies and others, the committee presented me the offering. The speeches were made by some doctor and a wealthy man of California, telling me to receive the money which they all wished was many times more, from the passengers and the officers of the steamer, and use it where I saw fit in carrying on this 'admirable work.'"[74] The captain and crew gleefully informed Hap that such a collection had never been taken on the ship. "I wish you could have witnessed it," he wrote Wood. "It would have cheered you. . . . Indeed it makes one very happy, as it shows in what high esteem the Church's work is held."[75]

In the more than fifteen years Clara and Hap had been fostering children at Fort Yukon, dozens had grown up, had married, and were now raising their own children. Many maintained close ties with the Burkes including Moses Cruikshank and Johnny Fredson. The demand for such boarding schools and orphanages had risen in the Interior, as successive epidemics and the steady death toll from tuberculosis left many children parentless or with single parents who could not care for their children while making a living. Increasingly, as well, both Native and white parents sought industrial training for their children. Archdeacon Drane reported that during his summer 1924 rounds, parents of eighteen youngsters from various communities had asked him to enroll their children in the Episcopal boarding schools at Nenana and Anvik. Such requests illustrated the difficult choices parents were making amid rapid socioeconomic change. Many wanted to secure for their children the education and training that would open doors for them later in life, even if that meant having to send their children away to school, an experience that could alienate the youth from their traditional way of life. Drane could place just three at Nenana and none at Anvik, owing to the recent dormitory fire there. With larger buildings, he believed these schools could nearly double enrollment.[76] By the mid-1920s three new buildings stood at Nenana: the chapel in memory of Annie Farthing, the dormitory in memory of Charles Betticher, and a new school that was completed at Nenana in 1927.[77] Moses Cruikshank, who had returned to Alaska in spring 1926 after three years at Mount Hermon School, had worked with Nicholson on these projects.[78]

In fall 1927 John Fredson reenrolled at Sewanee after a three-year break from his studies during which time he worked in various capacities, primarily for the church, to save money for tuition.[79] Given Fredson's age of thirty-two years and his chronic trachoma, Bishop Rowe and John Wood had discouraged him from pursuing the academic route to becoming an ordained medical missionary. Wood urged him to take the two-year course of study at the Episcopal DuBose Memorial Training School in Monteagle, Tennessee, with an eye toward ordination as deacon. John remained determined, however, to complete his education at Sewanee. An eye specialist in Memphis prescribed glasses and a one-year course of twice-weekly eye-drop treatments, which encouraged him to believe he could complete dual medical and theology degrees. As the first semester back at school progressed, however, he recognized the challenges to completing the dual degrees, and he changed course to the bachelor of science degree program.[80]

Hap, Clara, and Grafton left on furlough in late September 1927. Dr. Floyd O'Hara arrived together with a new nurse, Miss Burgess, in time for Hap to see him well settled before he left. David Wallis and Miss Burgess would lead Sunday school, and Wallis and Albert Tritt would hold church services. With no one to care for the children, Hap and Clara had distributed them individually and in groups to various homes. "I have never done anything harder in my life than get rid of those . . . children," he wrote Wood.[81] As difficult as it was to make these arrangements, the furlough was vital to Hap's and Clara's health and well-being. The recurrent nuisances, far more than the medical and child-care work, drained them, especially the constant training of new personnel, adjusting to their idiosyncrasies, and settling disputes.[82]

Hap, Clara, and ten-year-old Grafton spent the autumn months in Los Angeles, hosted by Clara's mother, with Hudson close by at Harvard School. Hap and Clara accepted numerous speaking engagements to generate financial support for the work at St. Stephen's.[83] While Outside, Hap loved to entertain friends and acquaintances with tales and terminology from Alaska; reportedly, he once asked the dignified doorman of a luxurious Los Angeles hotel if he could feed his sled dogs that night.[84] In January Hap, Clara, and Grafton departed for New York, where Grafton enrolled at Riverdale Country School in Riverdale-on-the-Hudson in the Bronx.[85] The progressive boys' school founded in 1907 emphasized outdoor education and character building. Frank Hackett, the school's founder, conducted a chapel service for the boys each morning, but the school was secular.[86]

This choice of school would lead to a lifelong friendship between the Burke and Hackett families. Frances Hackett, Frank's wife, an active member of Christ Church Riverdale, invited the Burkes home for dinner after their talk at the church, an act of hospitality she extended regularly to missionaries who spoke there. Frank Hackett's views on character education, his love of nature, and his belief in the benefits to children of time spent in the out-of-doors, as well as his forceful personality, may have reminded Hap of Hudson Stuck. After Grafton returned to Riverdale in 1930, he would spend his summers with the Hacketts and attend Camp Riverdale on Long Lake in the Adirondacks, which the Hacketts also founded.[87]

Hap undertook surgical training with the renowned orthopedic surgeon Frederick Houdlette Albee, a professor of orthopedic surgery at Cornell University Medical College and visiting orthopedic surgeon at New York's Post Graduate Hospital, who had pioneered bone grafting.[88] Dr. Albee's anesthetist, Adelaide Gavel, impressed Hap with her extensive surgical experience and expertise. She in turn reveled in Hap's tales of his work at Fort Yukon. Addie, Hap, and Clara became friends, and before long, the native Canadian resigned her position with Dr. Albee and accepted employment at Hudson Stuck Memorial Hospital. She was at work there when Hap and Clara returned in November 1928.[89]

During their furlough, Hap also developed a cordial relationship with a prominent Park Avenue physician whom he assisted several afternoons a week. This doctor offered Hap a well-paid position in his practice that would have supported a comfortable lifestyle in New York, where both boys could have lived at home while attending school. After some thought, Hap declined. According to Clara, the work at Fort Yukon was more compelling, much more vital than "catering to spoiled women with too much money." Reportedly, the doctor was so miffed at Hap's decision that he sent the Board of Missions an irate letter suggesting that Hap must be "out of his mind" to reject his offer.[90]

Rowe and Wood, on the other hand, were relieved to know that the Burkes would return to Fort Yukon. They both recognized how fortunate they were that a physician of Hap's caliber devoted himself year after year to such demanding work. Given the board's unwillingness to raise Hap's salary above that of Dr. Chapman, who had served forty years at Anvik, Wood advised Rowe to ask for a $500 increase in the hospital's appropriation, with the understanding that Hap could use the funds for "meeting personal necessities."[91]

In 1928 the American College of Surgeons, founded in 1913 and dedicated to the highest standards in surgery, inducted Hap into its organization. Dr. F. J. C. Fitzgerald, an "old friend" of Hap's, nominated him. Fitzgerald told John Wood that he thought Hap reflected "glory upon the institution." Vilhjalmur Stefansson wrote a letter supporting his induction.[92]

With the work and expenses growing at St. Stephen's as church income declined nationwide in the mid-1920s, Rowe and Wood considered closing and consolidating Alaska missions to economize.[93] In summer 1928 Rowe closed the mission at Stevens Village, where few people now lived. He moved the building and those associated with it, including eleven children, to Tanana.[94]

Hap and Clara departed New York with Grafton in early November 1928 to return to Fort Yukon.[95] They arrived home to a constellation of crises. Hap described the scene:

> We returned after a hard trip and in the darkest time of the year, and found a pretty kettle of fish. Misses Pratt and Gavel depressed and discouraged, the hospital full of patients . . . the hospital power plant almost a complete breakdown, a wall in one of the wards almost cracked [in two] from the floor settling . . . the hospital roof leaking badly, and both building[s] in urgent need of caulking, the fuel supply gone, and Mrs. Norwood, cook who is around 70 going on nervous energy and looking like death. . . . Dr. OHara who has done excellent work here had been gone nearly two months.[96]

Hap immediately tackled the most pressing problems, jacking up the hospital wall, repairing the power plant as best as he could, and securing fuel, which entailed finding an alternative source to Fred Bohmer, who had steadily increased his rates for wood in recent years. He also dismissed nurse Theresa Sands Bohmer, owing to her "wolfish appetite for gossip." According to Hap, these affronts to the Bohmers "nettle[d]" the pair "beyond tolerance." They took revenge by accusing him of negligence in treating Bohmer's arm, which he had injured eleven days prior to Hap and Clara's return. Thus, Hap became embroiled in yet another controversy and once again had to defend himself against groundless allegations.[97]

Amid his exasperation with the Bohmers, Hap took heart in Pratt's and Gavel's competence and professionalism.[98] At the moment, however, Gavel lay hospitalized with a diseased gallbladder, and Hap feared Pratt would collapse from working "night and day" in caring for Gavel and twenty other patients. His most faithful volunteers could no longer fill the gap. Winifred Dalziel now served as U.S. commissioner and assistant postmaster, in addition to schoolteacher. Still, she relieved Pratt for two hours each day after school. Clara was completely occupied with her "swarm of kiddies."[99] Exhausted from overwork and his nerves frayed, Hap wired mission head-quarters pleading for another nurse. To his relief, Margaret Foster, whom Wood had already vetted and who was prepared to leave immediately, arrived from Colorado with almost lightning speed. She flew the final leg of her journey from Fairbanks to Fort Yukon.[100] Bishop Rowe flew to the remote St. John's-in-the-Wilderness and back to Fairbanks that summer, both episodes illustrating the increasing use of air travel in the territory.[101]

The most critical case in late spring 1929 concerned Beatrice, a three-year-old who arrived at the hospital "more dead than alive" after she climbed into a dog pen and was mauled by the startled dogs. Hap described her condition: "Her skull was bare like a billiard ball," her scalp was chewed full of holes and matted with dirt, her ear hung from her head, and her face was lacerated. Hap operated for four hours, reconstructing her ear and scalp, but skin on top of her head sloughed off and would require grafts. Beattie Ky, as the children called her because she cried so much following her surgery, required almost constant vigilance, and she was but one of many hospital patients.[102]

By summer Addie Gavel had recovered, Margaret Foster had settled in, and tranquility reigned once again. A new pastor, Merritt Williams, arrived and quickly became a valued member of the mission family, immersing himself in the mission work and community life. "He seems to be all around just the man for [this] many sided work here," Hap wrote Wood. "I never realized till he came how much time and strength the [religious] services take."[103] Williams lived in the three-room rectory beside the mission home but took his meals with the Burkes and spent much of his days at their home.[104]

Bishop Rowe enjoyed a "very happy visit in Fort Yukon" that summer. During his five-day stay, "no complaints, troubles" arose, and mission and hospital personnel were all in good health. In yet another show of their regard for the hospital, the "white men of Fort Yukon," Rowe reported, donated $1,000 toward a hospital addition.[105] Stories abounded of prospectors and trappers who had reached St. Stephen's in the nick of time and recovered thanks to Hap's expertise and diligence. Recently, a ninety-six-year-old prospector had lain helpless for six months in his remote cabin with frostbitten feet until his nearest neighbor discovered him and summoned help. The marshal and six other men rushed to the site and built a boat from old sluice boxes to carry him down a creek to the Yukon and Hudson Stuck Memorial Hospital. There, under Hap's care, he slowly recovered.[106]

Beattie Ky became a favorite of the nurses, the other hospitalized children, and the townspeople, who visited her, bringing toys and listening to her chatter. During her months-long recuperation, Beattie required multiple skin grafts, which initially were allografts, or donor grafts, some from children. Beattie's body would have rejected these donor grafts before long, but Hap likely used them to stabilize her and allow her to begin her recovery process before he performed any necessary autografts, that is, grafts from her own body. Eleven-year-old Grafton volunteered for the skin harvesting procedure, which encouraged others to do so.[107] Grafton, who would become a physician himself, bore the six-inch scars on both arms proudly for the rest of his life.[108] A few days after Beattie Ky received a skin graft from Pastor Merritt Williams, she reportedly told him, "Your skin feels good on my head."[109] Beattie remained in the hospital as her wounds healed through the end of the year.[110] Clara last saw her in 1940 at the hospital, where she worked as an aide. Clara remembered her as a lovely girl with eyes that sparkled when she bubbled with the same infectious laughter that had endeared her to all of Fort Yukon many years before. Her hair looked natural and pretty, Clara recalled.[111]

In another dramatic case in summer 1929, a boy arrived at the hospital with severe burns from his abdomen to his knees, having fallen into a scalding kettle of dog food. He required intensive care—removal of skin, regular dressing replacements consuming yards of sheets, and multiple bedding changes each day. His condition gradually improved. A young man who spent the summer of 1929 working on steamers plying the Yukon River later wrote Bishop Rowe of his esteem for Episcopal mission work in the Interior, especially of Hudson Stuck Memorial Hospital. "I think that the Fort Yukon Hospital is one of the most outstanding of God's gifts to humanity. It makes me shudder to think of that poor little girl who had her scalp torn off or that Indian lad who was burned in that boiling cauldron of dog feed."[112]

So far, the Alaska mission field, including St. Stephen's, had escaped debilitating budget cuts as nationwide support for mission work declined.[113] At Fort Yukon, the need for a completely new power plant— one designed to supply electricity to the entire mission complex at an estimated cost of $6,500—might have posed an existential crisis, given the national church's financial position.[114] However, an appeal in *Spirit of Missions* moved "generous friends of Alaska," as John Wood termed them, to provide the funds.[115] By December 1929 the new "power house" was completed. Its diesel engine and storage battery supplied lighting to the mission home, church, rectory, and hospital; and power for the x-ray machine, the autoclave used for instrument sterilization, the diathermy treatment for muscle and joint problems, and the ray lamps. Hap could now perform surgeries as necessary, night or day, with optimal lighting.[116]

A partial solution to the perennial struggle to secure heating fuel also emerged that year. The crisis they had faced upon their return to Fort Yukon in November 1928 spurred Hap to investigate an alternative form of fuel. He negotiated a contract with the White Pass and Yukon Route railroad, which operated steamers on the Yukon, to transport coal from Nenana at $8 per ton, one fifth the standard rate.[117] Coal would heat the hospital much more efficiently than wood, affording substantial savings, and transitioning fully to coal would relieve the staff of stoking furnaces with wood through the night. The first load of coal arrived in summer 1929.[118] Hap never achieved his goal of full reliance on coal, however, owing to transportation costs.[119]

The bitterly cold winter of 1929–30 tested everyone's endurance at St. Stephen's. Buildings remained so frigid that water and cream froze solid as they stood on tables. Mission and hospital personnel wore extra layers of woolen clothing to keep warm, and the mission family took their meals by the fireplace. A local "wood famine" caused the crisis. Even if wood had been available, Hap had no means to pay for it, having exhausted the year's fuel allowance on the coal that was already consumed. To survive the winter, he borrowed wood from the wireless station, which kept a two years' supply on hand.[120]

As challenging as the winter's heating problems were at St. Stephen's Mission, they paled in comparison to the double misfortunes that befell St. Mark's Mission at Nenana. In late January the beautiful new Betticher Memorial Building burned to the ground. The fire reportedly started in the hot-air furnace in the basement and roared up through the stove pipe to the attic, where it spread, disabling the electric pump, which rendered useless the water tanks kept there for fire control. The fire department and virtually all the local men rushed to the scene, but without water pressure, they were powerless to fight the fire. The dormitory housed thirty-four Native children and five female mission personnel. No one was injured, the building was partially insured, and local establishments offered housing and school space, providing some solace for the mission staff and children.[121]

Just four months later, the house serving as the rectory for St. Mark's burned to the ground.[122] By late summer Neil Nicholson, who by now was considered almost a miracle worker, and crew had rebuilt the dormitory.[123] Donors provided the $6,000 needed to furnish the building, along with $1,300 to re-outfit Pastor McIntosh and his family who had lost everything in the rectory fire.[124] Fire insurance rates for Episcopal missions in Alaska increased 50 percent in 1930, owing to the frequency of fires. Mission headquarters urged Rowe to ensure that each mission had a qualified man to maintain the furnace properly.[125]

By summer 1930 the new hospital wing at Fort Yukon was open and filled with patients. The addition housed a fifteen-thousand-gallon concrete tank to fill the hospital's winter water needs. Donations covered the full cost of the "old-timers' ward" as locals called it. A mission friend in New York furnished the new wing.[126] The separate ward for white patients reflected one of the forms of racial segregation in Alaska. Various ironies surrounded racial prejudice, even as whites and Natives intermarried and mixed-race children were born. One "perversity" that mystified Clara was white patients' refusal to sleep in hospital beds that Natives had occupied. Regardless of the scrupulous practices the hospital employed in disinfecting hospital equipment and replacing bedding with freshly laundered sheets *for all patients*, even men who were married to Native women stubbornly maintained this position. Assigning Native nurses' aides and attendants to the "white ward" also raised such objections.[127] Racial segregation was by no means strict. Natives, whites, and people of mixed backgrounds attended the weekly dances, for instance, and interacted at various other events and venues. Nevertheless, these illustrations of racial segregation in the hospital reflected prejudices and slights that permeated life at Fort Yukon and elsewhere in Alaska, daily reminding Alaska Native people, adults and children, of their second-class status within their ancestral lands.

The hospital now was not only busier but, from Hap's perspective, happier than ever, owing to the competent and harmonious staff he had assembled. "Miss Gavel is a jewel," he wrote mission headquarters, "a whirlwind of a nurse in any direction, but particularly in surgery." He especially appreciated her interest in the mission and community work. She had transformed the clinic's longstanding weekly health class into a community event that drew as many as one hundred people. With the classes having outgrown the hospital and clinic's front hall, she transferred them, at the chief's invitation, to his large community cabin. The dwelling now resembled a public health center, with a blackboard, posters promoting health, and weight charts covering the walls. A bed allowed a nurse instructor to demonstrate how to care for the sick at home.[128]

The other two nurses and the cook were similarly energetic, collegial, and competent. Hap described Margaret Foster, who focused on village nursing, as "conscientious and hardworking." Maude Pratt, who now served primarily as anesthetist, was "indispensable . . . a dandy!" The cook, Mrs. Stanford, who had many years' experience in the north, was a "general stabilizer," cheerfully helping wherever needed and keeping the institution running smoothly.[129]

Merritt Williams's assumption of many of Hap's pastoral responsibilities, his interest in the community, and his compatibility with mission and hospital personnel boosted Hap's spirits immensely. Addie Gavel took responsibility for much of the Sunday school program, allowing Williams to focus on church services and travel to outlying villages. Hap hoped "to Heaven" Williams would never leave.[130]

In summer 1930 a Mrs. Habersham of Los Angeles, with the Episcopal Corporate Gift or Advance Work Program, visited the Fort Yukon and Nenana missions to assess their suitability for financial support. During her month-long stay, she marveled at Clara's cheerful and efficient management of the mission household. In an article she wrote for a church publication, she described how Clara, with eighteen children underfoot, orchestrated the daily meal preparation, twice weekly laundry, including hanging the clothing to dry, and Saturday baths for all the children in perfect harmony. "Her sweetness, her brightness, floods the house. I listened in vain for one impatient word all those four weeks." After serving the children their evening meal each day, she produced a meal "fit for a queen" for the adults. "She would come out of the kitchen, having just cooked the children's and our own dinner, and serve the meal as quietly and coolly as though she had just finished an interesting book," Habersham wrote.[131]

Habersham also remarked on the "apparent devotion" of the Native congregants to the church, having attended the crowded Sunday morning service and the afternoon evensong. She described a "very charming, homelike picture," with toddlers rolling up and down the aisles as Pastor Williams preached with David Wallis interpreting, and as the congregation sang heartily in Gwich'in. Congregants attended nightly classes for a week prior to the twice-yearly Communion. That summer Williams expected at least one hundred to receive Communion.[132]

Hap and Clara had finally achieved the harmonious atmosphere he sought at the hospital, and community-mission relations were strong. Hap

20. Ma Stanford baking bread at St. Stephen's Mission Home, 1934. Elizabeth Hayes Goddard—Alaska Diary, #1967-48-14, APRCA, University of Alaska Fairbanks.

was busier than ever, but financial woes, rather than the hospital work itself, wore him down. Unpredictable expenses caused the greatest anxiety. Costs of construction and repairs typically ran hundreds of dollars over estimates. Emergencies arose regularly and had to be addressed immediately, yet the requisition process could be cumbersome, and funds were not always forthcoming.[133] As Hap poured every ounce of his energy and wits into the work, with the exuberance and warmth that earned him his nickname, he hid from all but a few his constant and mounting anxiety that at any moment, a crisis could bring his and Clara's life's work to an abrupt halt.

In summer 1930 Winifred Dalziel took Grafton, soon to be thirteen, back to Riverdale Country School in New York when she went on furlough. That September, Dan Hackett, the nineteen-year-old son of Riverdale's founding headmaster, Dr. Frank Hackett, arrived at Fort Yukon. According to Clara, Dr. Hackett had sent Dan to "work off some steam" after he failed to apply himself at Williams College in Massachusetts. This narrative may have been partially true, but more immediately, according to a family member, Dr. Hackett wanted to separate Dan from a love interest whom he deemed unsuitable. The elder Hackett hoped that exposure to real-world medical needs and caregiving at Hudson Stuck Memorial Hospital, a setting far removed from Dan's privileged upbringing, would give him some perspective.[134] Frank Hackett, a disciplined, self-made man whose holistic education philosophy emphasized social responsibility, was a force in the lives of his five sons and made clear his high aims for them.[135] As Clara recalled, Dan had a "chip on his shoulder the size of a log" when he arrived. He chafed at his father's expectations that he set a good example for others and that he become a physician.[136] During Dan's first week at St. Stephen's, he immersed himself in outdoor life, going duck hunting, cutting fish at the mission's fish wheel, and using the Fordson tractor to help stockpile the winter's wood supply. Then he took the last steamer of the season upriver to hunt caribou to supply the mission and hospital with meat for the winter.[137] As he settled in, Dan's sojourn in Alaska proved to be the perfect antidote to his youthful rebelliousness.

John Fredson returned to Fort Yukon that fall after graduating from Sewanee with a bachelor of science degree. He found work at the NC Company handling the furs that trappers brought in, earning a salary of

$2,000. John lived with the Burkes once again and more than earned his keep by volunteering at the hospital, leading St. Stephen's Boys' Club and filling in elsewhere as needed. A skilled fiddler, he often provided the music at local dances.[138]

Operations at Fort Yukon now consumed one-fourth of the mission board's Alaska appropriations.[139] In the past two decades, the board's allocations to the Alaska mission field had increased from $35,000 to $93,000.[140] In the latter half of the 1920s, the church had reinforced and expanded mission operations at several Interior sites. "I am somewhat staggered by the amount of building and repairing we have been [able to do] the past few years," the bishop wrote in his 1929 report.[141] The scope of Hap and Clara's work had expanded steadily during that time.

Several factors had contributed to the remarkable expansion at St. Stephen's Mission. The Burkes' warmth and charisma, their compassion for those in need, and their energetic efforts to promote community well-being had won the affection and gratitude of all but the most hardened local observers. Their Outside speaking engagements and the compelling articles they wrote for *Spirit of Missions* cultivated many loyal admirers who supported their work financially. Hap's dedication to improving and expanding his surgical skills, as well as his regular purchase of equipment that permitted advanced diagnostic and therapeutic measures, steadily expanded and improved the quality of care that Hudson Stuck Memorial Hospital offered.

Meanwhile, Clara devoted herself increasingly to nurturing children whose health or family circumstances limited their chances of a bright future or threatened their lives directly. As epidemics ravaged the region, leaving many orphans, and as more children required convalescent care after hospital stays, Hap and Clara expanded the mission home's capacity. In his allocations schedule for 1929, Bishop Rowe listed "Mrs. Burke's Orphanage, Fort Yukon," among the Episcopal "'industrial schools,' where children reside, receive their food, clothing and education."[142] The bishop increasingly recognized that St. Stephen's exemplified the purest expression of the church's mission.

8

Struggling Yet Expanding during the Depression Years, 1930–35

In response to the Wall Street crash of 1929, charitable giving, including to churches, dropped substantially. Giving began to rise in 1933 but did not reach pre-crash rates until 1939. President Franklin Roosevelt's New Deal programs, which signaled the government's expanded role in social welfare, explained in part the drop in private charitable giving. New Deal programs had no discernible effect, however, on conditions in Fort Yukon, where medical and social needs grew in the 1930s, especially with low fur prices, game shortages, and no letup in the diseases that took disproportionate numbers of Alaska Native lives. In 1931 and 1932 the mortality rates from tuberculosis among Alaska Natives were 922 and 986 per 100,000 population, respectively, compared with 58.5 and 78.6, respectively, for white Alaskans—that is, nearly fifteen times higher over those two years.[1]

As allocations from the Episcopal Mission Society dwindled in tandem with diminished giving by church members during the Great Depression, Hap and Clara relied increasingly on direct appeals to individual mission friends and appeals to the church laity through the Mission Society's journal the *Spirit of Missions*. Sometimes they wrote articles themselves. More often, John Wood composed appeals drawing on Hap's compelling letters about their financial struggles. Such pleas resonated, likely because people could sympathize with individual orphaned, ailing, and hungry children, with young mothers and fathers dying of tuberculosis and with whole villages stricken by diseases unknown to them only decades before.

As the Depression wore on, Hap felt increasingly beleaguered and at times felt abandoned by the church. His and Clara's commitment to the hospital, the mission, and the people of the region never wavered. Moreover, the collegial environment Hap had finally achieved at the hospital made going to work a joy. His resentment grew, however, as he had to defend basic expenditures to the mission board and repeatedly had to beg mission friends for support. Funding cuts now threatened everything that Hudson Stuck, he, and Clara had built.

In late summer 1930 a "violent" streptococcal intestinal infection spread through the Native community at Fort Yukon. The two-month-long scourge filled the hospital, pushing staff beyond the limits of their endurance and setting in motion a veritable game of musical chairs. Suffering children filled the thirty-two regular hospital beds and eight additional cots, while many people lay ill in their homes. Illness leveled Addie Gavel for several days. Seeing that Maude Pratt was near exhaustion, Hap sent her downriver to rest. Until school started, he replaced her with the teacher who had arrived to fill in for the furloughed Winifred Dalziel. When the matron left, Clara hired someone to feed and care for the twenty-seven mission children while she cooked for forty-seven at the hospital. When John Helenius fell ill, Pastor Williams took over his hospital duties, stoking the furnace, hauling water, and performing a multitude of other tasks. By the time school opened, requiring the teacher to assume her school duties, Helenius had recovered, which allowed Williams to serve as night nurse until Pratt returned. Three children died of the ailment. Hap was relieved the number was no higher.[2]

Just as the siege lifted, a strep throat epidemic filled the hospital. Pratt lay bedridden for a week. By this time Dan Hackett had enough practice to take over her night shift. Illness sidelined nurse Margaret Foster and the matron, Mrs. Stanford, for intervals as well. Stanford's bronchitis threw the whole schedule into turmoil. Pratt took over kitchen duty, forcing Hap to assume her nursing work, which threw his surgery schedule "sky high," as he put it; he had to postpone five operations. Meanwhile, he was battling a sore throat for a month, with no improvement. With no time for rest, he kept up his usual frenzied pace at the hospital. Alarmed by Hap's "septic throat" and by conditions in general, Wood put out an emergency call for a missionary nurse. Clara Dickenson of Portland, Oregon, arrived remarkably quickly, flying in from Fairbanks, but the hospital remained understaffed.[3]

In mid-November, a month after Hap was most ill, the workload remained so intolerable that Merritt Williams fired off a desperate letter to mission headquarters: "Dr. Burke has been carrying an almost impossible burden. . . . The Church has no right to make such demands on human strength as have [sic] on the medical staff at this place. Nor has it the right to maintain an institution at a strategic point such as this which is unable to meet the needs. It is plainly immoral. . . . We must have two doctors and four nurses and we must have relief from needless financial worry."[4] Williams warned that if Burke continued at his current pace, he might have to be "ordered out before the winter is over."[5] The tone of the letter and the accusations raised eyebrows in New York. Wood nevertheless calmly responded that he was "sorry that bad times seem to have hit Fort Yukon too," noting the long lines outside employment offices in New York. He assured Williams that the church had no desire to "be unfair to Burke" or other mission personnel. As the end of the fiscal year approached, the national church had received $1 million less from the dioceses than the quotas they themselves had proposed. Moreover, their pledges had been $1 million less than the General Convention had requested. The church simply lacked the funds to do more, Wood explained.[6]

Williams thanked Wood for his courteous response and apologized for the tone of his letter, while stressing that he had been "gravely alarmed, and rightly so, about Dr. Burke's health" and the inhuman demands on the hospital staff. "It seemed to me quite clear that overwork and worry and the shortage of professional assistance were being paid for with the health of Dr. Burke and his helpers."[7] The hospital census and outpatient visits remained high in late January. Meanwhile, Hap had been pulled away to Fairbanks to testify before a grand jury in a manslaughter case.[8]

In addition to confronting the two epidemics in fall–winter 1930–31, Hap treated chronic illnesses and several trauma patients. In one case, an old-timer who had shot himself in the arm and hand had lain in his cabin for two weeks until friends stopped by. When an x-ray revealed his wrist and arm to be filled with shot, Hap feared he would have to amputate. He saved the arm, but nerve damage cost the patient the use of some of his fingers.[9]

Diathermy treatment with the new equipment donated by a Philadelphia friend allowed the elderly Sara Black River to walk again after suffering many years from a chronic knee condition. Hap had been skeptical that the heat treatment could improve such a severely scarred and crippled joint, but after just three sessions, she made a dramatic turnaround.[10]

The case of four-year-old Peter, like those of too many other children and adults, ended sadly. The bright and charming boy showed great potential for growing into a fine man. His tuberculosis, however, was so advanced by the time he arrived at the hospital that the nurses could provide only palliative care, and he died within just two weeks. Two-year-old Esias suffered tuberculosis and hydranencephaly; despite his grim prognosis, the nurses rendered him the same compassionate care they gave other patients.[11]

In his most complex surgery that winter, Hap corrected Mary Loola's double cleft lip and cleft palate. Throughout her life, Mary had suffered from the severe birth defect, although in recent years, she gained self-confidence as she worked at the hospital wearing a gauze mask over the lower part of her face.[12] Addie Gavel assisted, and Dan Hackett observed as Hap filled the gap in the roof of Mary's mouth and reshaped her nose and lip. Following later dental surgery, she emerged with a beautiful smile. Hap and Winifred Dalziel, who returned from her furlough in summer 1931, provided speech therapy. "Now she sits smiling at the table with all the other people, and is so supremely happy, that everyone remarks how changed she is," Hap reported.[13]

Hackett immersed himself in the hospital work, taking occasional night shifts, sitting vigil with patients during the day, entertaining the children with stories, making sick calls in the village, transporting patients to the hospital on the toboggan, and assisting the mission mechanic Al Rowe with plumbing and steam-fitting work. When not helping at the hospital, he expanded his subsistence skills. His first serious hunting trip had been a great success. He, Merritt Williams, and their guide, Esaias, had bagged thirty-four caribou. With the arrival of winter, he snowshoed with village youngsters to their traplines, learned to drive dogs, and built an outstanding dogsled team of his own. He and John Fredson became fast friends.[14]

In early February Hackett stepped into John Helenius's shoes as hospital orderly when a badly sprained back forced him to resign. Hackett hauled thousands of gallons of water with the help of dogs, split logs for kindling, threw cords of wood into the cellar, and served as "waterboy at many washings." He assisted with Addie Gavel's health classes and John Fredson's Boys' Club, both of which impressed him deeply. The health classes promised long-term positive effects on residents' health and well-being. The Boys' Club taught sportsmanship and encouraged healthy exercise, lessons Hackett was certain would serve the boys well into adulthood. His admiration for the Burkes and the hospital staff grew as he observed their unwavering dedication to the people's physical and spiritual well-being. Hap, Merritt Williams, and the nurses constantly looked for signs of failing health or injuries within the community. When a nurse noticed something worrisome on her daily rounds in the village, Hap followed up with a house call. Often the nurses brought patients into the hospital themselves. In writing of his experience, Hackett described Hap's inspirational effect on the entire hospital staff. "I was most impressed . . . by the fitness of the name, Happy" he wrote. If the doctor could radiate happiness, despite the long hours he worked and the many travails he faced, then certainly the staff, including Hackett, could find joy in their work. He marveled as well at Clara's energy and devotion to her work. "She is cook, laundress, seamstress, and most of all Mother to the whole family, which includes the doctor, Mr. Williams, the children, and myself."[15]

In winter 1930–31 the Native Woman's Auxiliary of St. Stephen's Church, under Clara's general guidance, labored over a creation in honor of both Archdeacon Stuck and Bishop Rowe: a set of altar cloths for the Cathedral of St. John the Divine, the mother church of the New York Diocese. They scraped and prepared the caribou skin and beaded it in a brilliantly colored geometric design. The women, who were known throughout Interior Alaska for their exquisite beadwork, had made equally beautiful altar hangings for St. Stephen's Church in Fort Yukon. In February Grafton, who attended school not far from the cathedral, presented the gift, which bore the inscription "In grateful memory of the work for our people done by Bishop Rowe and Archdeacon Stuck, this hanging is made

21. Presentation by Grafton Burke of altar hangings made by St. Stephen's Woman's Auxiliary members for the Cathedral of St. John the Divine, New York. Those pictured include Grafton (*far right*), Bishop Manning (*opposite Grafton*), John Wood (*to Bishop Manning's left, in suit*), and Artley Parson (*to Grafton's right*). Geoffrey Burke private collection.

and given by the native women of Fort Yukon, Alaska."[16] Upon receipt of the altar hangings, New York City's Bishop William Manning, a classmate of Stuck's at Sewanee, gave an address at the cathedral praising their exquisite beauty, artistic merit, and craftsmanship and the many hours of work the women devoted to the gifts.[17] A decade before, in November 1920, the cathedral had held a memorial service for Archdeacon Stuck with nearly two thousand people in attendance.

Astonishingly, despite his own illness and the severe stress the hospital had endured, Hap reported finding winter 1930–31 especially gratifying. He wrote John Wood in March:

> You will be glad to know that in all the years, I have been here,
> I have not had as busy or as happy a winter, or has the post as a

whole turned out as much work. The cases run into thousands; the medical are varied and keenly interesting; the surgical are of a fascinating variety, and the operating room is a joy to so constantly and frequently bring the staff together for "keeping their hands in." . . . I am thankful to have lived through all these years in the work to see it grow, and turn out medical and surgical work that we take a keen delight in exhibiting.[18]

He estimated that the hospital's in-patient volume had increased more than 700 percent over the past ten years. The out-patient work had grown exponentially.[19] Considered in this light, it was no wonder that the mission board struggled to finance the work at St. Stephen's and that Hap perennially overspent his allocations.

The social work at St. Stephen's filled an equally vital role in the region, Hap pointed out. Eight children had joined the mission family over the winter, bringing the household to twenty-eight members.[20] One was the six-year-old child of a woman who lay dying in the hospital. She had arrived from four hundred miles to the north by dogsled, and with no local family able to care for the child, Clara had taken her in. Plans were underway for an addition to the mission home to provide a playroom for the children away from the stoves. The large room would double as a venue for church and community meetings and gatherings.[21]

In summer 1931 the government of the Yukon Territory in Canada began making greater use of Hudson Stuck Memorial Hospital in an effort to eradicate glandular tuberculosis, or scrofula. Hap operated on fifty-seven children with tubercular glands.[22] Surgery remained the preferred therapy for glandular tuberculosis until the 1950s, when a combination of antibiotics, including streptomycin, was discovered to be highly effective in treating *Mycobacterium tuberculosis*, or *M. tuberculosis*, in all forms.[23]

At Hap's invitation, Dr. Charles Dukes, a surgeon from Oakland, California, who visited Alaska that summer and stopped at Fort Yukon, toured the hospital along with another visiting physician. Hap took every opportunity to present the hospital to traveling doctors, not only to showcase the facility and the work being carried out there but to consult with them on cases and to keep abreast of medical developments Outside. Dukes later reported that Hap "pumped [the doctors] dry of all the information that [they] could give" during their seven-hour stopover. The existence of such a well-equipped and well-managed medical facility at the remote outpost astonished the physicians. The experience left such an impression on Dukes that he recommended that the American College of Surgeons' Hospital Standardization Committee recognize the hospital. The following winter, the organization rated Hudson Stuck Memorial Hospital a Grade A institution.[24]

In July of 1931 John Fredson and Jean Ribaloff, a nurse's aide at the hospital of Russian-Unangan ancestry, were married in St. Stephen's Church. Their paths had crossed many times in the mission and hospital work since John's return from Sewanee. Hap and Clara were delighted with the match.[25]

That fall Hap and Clara left Fort Yukon on furlough. Dr. A. L. Standfast would serve as locum tenens.[26] With no one to care for the children at the mission home, they closed the building for the winter, placing the children with the greatest needs in the hospital and the others in various individual and group settings.[27] As usual, Hap and Clara spent the winter in New York, where Hap did surgical training at the Post Graduate Hospital.[28]

While in New York, Clara wrote an article on the couple's quarter century of mission work in Alaska, highlighting how their lives and outlooks had changed since they arrived as naïve young adults. Fort Yukon, too, had changed dramatically since their arrival. Gwich'in people contributed to and benefited from every facet of the work at St. Stephen's. The mission complex now consisted of a thirty-five-bed hospital, a chapel, a rectory, a home for the orderly, a power plant, a large storehouse for both the mission home and hospital, and an icehouse. The mission home provided nurturing in a family setting for scores of children whose futures otherwise would have been bleak.[29] Understandably, Clara and Hap looked back with a sense of accomplishment on the expansion of the mission and hospital work, the lives saved, the health conditions improved, and the seemingly well-adjusted adults they had raised. The mutual trust between mission personnel and community members, and the people's engagement in the mission and hospital work, gratified them immensely. They saw signs of progress everywhere.

In summer 1932 "generous friends" sponsored a European tour for the whole Burke family in honor of their twenty-five years of missionary service in Alaska. Hudson had graduated from the Harvard School in Los Angeles the previous summer, while Grafton attended Riverdale in New York.[30] The Burkes' patrons may have been Frank and Frances Hackett, founders of the Riverdale Country School. Frank Hackett reportedly felt deeply indebted to Hap and Clara for the year they had hosted their son Dan. Frank Hackett believed Dan's experience in Fort Yukon had "saved" him; Dan now planned to attend medical school.[31] Alternatively, the aristocratic family of Michael Mason, who had visited the Burkes in 1920–21, may have sponsored the Burkes' tour. In England, Mason's mother, Lady Margaret Lindsay, hosted the Burkes on the luxurious Mason estate in Oxfordshire.[32] While in Vienna, Hap did specialized research on tuberculosis, which claimed so many Alaska Native lives each year. Clara later recalled that stirrings of Nazi activity in Vienna, Bern, and Hamburg created the only cloud over their summer.[33]

When Hap and Clara returned to Fort Yukon in late September 1932, they flew from Fairbanks on a float plane and landed on Hospital Lake. It was Clara's first flight. After overcoming her jitters, she opened her eyes to take in the panoramic view of Interior Alaska's spectacular landscape, a novel perspective for her. Tommy, the wire-haired terrier pup friends in Fairbanks had given them, would make a lively addition to the mission family. He reportedly held the huskies of Fort Yukon at bay with his ferocious yapping.[34]

Pastor Merritt Williams had left Fort Yukon earlier that summer. He and Lucy Cornell, a nurse who arrived in Fort Yukon the previous summer, were married on July 24 and departed on the *Yukon* the same day.[35] Now the "matrimonial game" had robbed St. Stephen's of both a nurse and a pastor who had been deeply engaged in the mission and community life, as well as the church work in the outlying communities. Finding a replacement would be all but impossible. The position remained open, largely for financial reasons.[36]

Construction on the addition to the mission home began that summer. It was sufficiently complete to hold its inaugural event on November 11, a celebration of both Hudson Stuck's birthday and Armistice Day. One hundred thirty community members, white and Native, attended the celebration, "and there was still room for dancing," Hap reported. Meetings now took place throughout the week in the "large assembly room," as Clara called it. These included the Hudson Stuck Bible Class twice a week, the Woman's Auxiliary, the Men's Club, St. Stephen's Boys' Club, and a mothers' meeting where the women brought their babies to be weighed and measured while a nurse instructed them in infant care. On Saturdays, health classes adapted to different age groups and genders took place much of the day. Large glass doors at one end of the room closed off a small area with an altar where English Sunday school classes and services for the mission family took place. When it was not otherwise occupied, the children made good use of their playroom. A girls' dormitory had been built atop the gathering room.[37]

Neil Nicholson had overseen the construction, taking minimal pay and using largely volunteer labor, which kept costs well below initial projections. Mission headquarters had encouraged *Spirit of Missions* readers to sponsor the addition in honor of Hap and Clara's twenty-fifth anniversary of service in Alaska, and contributions poured in.[38] That winter Clara took in several malnourished children whom she believed would not have survived without the mission's support. Poor fur harvests in winter 1932–33, coupled with low fur prices since 1929, had put many Gwich'in families under financial stress. Iñupiat suffered as well. Mushers coming from as far north as Herschel Island reported that the white fox harvest "amount[ed] to nothing."[39]

The children's Lenten offering in 1933 attested to the generous spirit that prevailed in the mission home and St. Stephen's church community, as well as the children's understanding of the church's mission work throughout the world. Despite the hard economic times, they toiled feverishly to earn and donate $113.15. "These kiddies here are strange little tikes," Hap wrote Wood in a note accompanying their gift. "I've never seen the like of it. They seem indomitable in their strife, gathering

22. St. Stephen's Mission Home and School, 1934. Elizabeth Hayes Goddard Diary—Alaska Diary, #1967-48-15, APRCA, University of Alaska Fairbanks.

Lenten money, with unbounded enthusiasm for the Church. It touches me deeply,—against their odds, their joyous spirit in giving."[40]

Soon after they returned from furlough, Hap began to lobby Bishop Rowe and mission headquarters for an addition to the hospital to relieve overcrowding and provide private quarters for the nurses, whose living space consisted of shared bedrooms, with no bathroom. Adding a second story to the main part of the hospital would allow individual bedrooms for the nurses, and a shared bathroom and sitting room. Removing the nurses from the main floor would relieve crowding in the operating room and open a single room for patients whose care regimen required privacy, isolation, or intensive care.[41] With no funds available through traditional channels, Hap proposed using part of a recent $20,000 bequest to the hospital, the "Hoffman Legacy," to pay for the addition. Nicholson built the addition and completed major repairs to the mission home's sewage system for less than $10,000. He also installed a new, more energy efficient heating plant. Nicholson's expertise in every phase of the construction saved the expense of hiring several skilled tradesmen. Moreover, he worked for just $100 a month while building and only room and board during the off-season.[42]

Cuts to the Alaska mission fields grew deeper with each year of the Great Depression. Bishop Rowe's allocation dropped by nearly 30 percent between 1929 and 1935, with another 11 percent cut projected for 1936.[43] Unrelenting pressure to make ends meet wore increasingly on the bishop.[44] "It seems that I have only hills to climb," he wrote Wood. "I am tired of my job. . . . I mean to 'carry on.' . . . Only forgive me when I am impatient, querulous, nasty." Rowe aimed his resentment regarding fiscal pressures at the Board of Missions, which he perceived as "hard-boiled" and inelastic.[45]

At Fort Yukon two young men who joined the mission family as lay workers for the year 1932–33 eased Hap's workload. Their active participation in community life earned them friends throughout the region, according to Clara. Wyatt Brown Jr. primarily assisted Hap at the hospital, although he participated in the fall hunt to bring in meat for the hospital and mission home.[46] George Whittlesey arrived as an emissary of Christ Church Cranbrook in Bloomfield Hills, Michigan, where Bishop Rowe had served as a missionary before being elected bishop of Alaska.[47] Both Brown and Whittlesey traveled by dogsled to outlying villages to provide religious services. Clara wrote at the time, "The most encouraging reports of their work come in. The natives have grown very fond of both of them."[48]

Early in 1933 Hap performed one of his most ingenious surgeries, restoring the sight of John Vendesquísí (Vanndeegwiishįį), a Neets'aii Gwich'in man of more than one hundred years. Using homemade surgical instruments and manicure scissors, Hap excised his cataracts. When his bandages came off a week after surgery, Old John reportedly danced with joy at being able to see Sutchah's face. The operation's success "created quite a stir" in the village, according to Hap.[49] Clara wrote that Sutchah's "miracle" brought around the last of those who feared the evil spirit would punish people who sought Hap's care. Eventually, Hap fitted Old John with eyeglasses that further improved his sight.[50]

In summer 1933 extended stays at Fort Yukon by a New York sculptor and a renowned ethnographer led to publications that provided vivid impressions of daily life and community dynamics in Fort Yukon. Lillian Harper, a New York sculptor who had created a baptismal font in honor of Archdeacon Stuck, traveled to Fort Yukon to see the font in place. She had created *The Angel of Fort Yukon*, as she called it, in Paris in 1930, following an earlier visit to the community. The sculpture had arrived in summer 1931. Reportedly, the font, which remains in the church today, had been used in more than fifty baptisms by the time of her visit.[51]

Harper stayed at the mission home and spent her days at the hospital and in the clinic. She took great interest in the patients, among them Old John Vendesquísí, who had injured himself in a fall while at fish camp after he had recovered from his eye surgery. She sculpted a bust of him as he sat in the solarium. Hap would stop by and encourage him to sing hymns and traditional songs in his native language. Harper reported that the tuberculosis ward was full throughout the summer. Twenty-two children lived at the mission home at the time. Harper described them as a happy group whom she never heard bickering and seldom heard crying. All but the youngest children had daily chores. The girls helped with housework and ironing their clothing. The boys chopped wood and ran errands.[52]

Bishop Rowe, who arrived together with Harper for an eight-day visit, took pleasure in seeing the mission and hospital's positive influence. The Hudson Stuck Club's seventy-five members cooperated in community improvement and support of the church. The Boys' Club worked on similar projects. The bishop confirmed forty-seven individuals during his visit, all of whom prepared for the rite through study with Hap and David Wallis.[53]

Although Rowe arrived at Fort Yukon by steamer, he traveled increasingly by air now, saving time, hard work, and expense. Owing to his age and the extensive travel demands of his work, the Mission Society appointed the suffragan bishop John Bentley to oversee the Interior missions in 1933. He remained based at Nenana and was building a home there, after living in St. Mark's dormitory for three years. Bentley would continue to travel by dogsled in winter to visit Interior missions so he could see people in out-of-the-way places.[54]

The ethnologist Robert McKennan, who had been doing ethnographic work in the Yukon and northeastern Alaska among the Chandalar, or Neets'aii, Gwich'in, arrived in Fort Yukon in mid-August 1933 to measure Gwich'in individuals and type their blood to test his theory on their insularity. Upon McKennan's arrival at Fort Yukon, Mr. Rodman, the manager of the NC Company, and his wife walked him over to St. Stephen's Mission, where Hap and Clara welcomed him with their usual exuberance. "I had heard a great deal about their kindness, but it exceeded all anticipations," he wrote in his journal. Within a few hours of his arrival, he had enjoyed "a meal of steak smothered in mushrooms together with real potatoes. . . . I have listened to the radio from the world outside, I have had a hot bath in a real bath tub, and I am now writing this by electric light as I lay in bed between real sheets. . . . I am not quite sure that I like all this luxury but I do appreciate the hospitality that prompts it."[55] He noted Lillian Harper's presence and described the Burke household: "The large house contains twenty-odd small boys and girls. They are everywhere, and each one has his duties to perform. A nice little twelve-year-old girl called Jemima makes my bed and cleans my room every morning. Mrs. Burke presides over this large establishment and keeps it running smoothly with the minimum of effort. At the same time she gently manages her husband who is of an entirely different type, impulsive, forgetful, and likable. The two make a fine pair together."[56]

McKennan hired John Fredson as his interpreter and soon regretted not having had his help with his earlier work.[57] Because John worked at the NC Company until six o'clock, McKennan scheduled interviews in the evenings. During the day he occupied himself otherwise, including visiting the clinic and observing Hap interacting with patients. The courage of two boys, aged four and six, astonished him. Each climbed onto a stool and allowed Hap to extract a tooth, with no medication and without making a sound. The day after his arrival, with Fredson's assistance, he interviewed Old John at the hospital for two hours, recording "quite a little stuff."[58] Hap allowed McKennan to use the hospital's facilities to type the blood of Neets'aii Gwich'in men. He found 100 percent uniformity in blood types among the men he tested, strengthening his theory of their historical isolation.[59]

One evening, McKennan and Fredson spent about two hours with Old Lucy and Old Maggie, who related many stories. "It seemed good to be in an Indian tent once more," he wrote. "Somehow or other I really do not feel quite at home getting ethnology in a modern hospital."[60] Together with John and Jean Fredson, McKennan attended the regular Friday night dance at the combination dance hall and movie theater. "The dance brought together all the varied elements of Fort Yukon, white, Indian, and mixed," he noted. "Fort Yukon affords a beautiful example of the melting pot in action."[61]

Hap took time from his medical and mission work that August to represent Chief Esaias Loola in a game violation case. As a child, Esaias had lived in the mission home and had taken the last name of Reverend Loola, whom he admired.[62] Chief Esaias and his wife, Katherine, were active members of St. Stephen's Church and were well respected for their civic mindedness.[63] Winifred Dalziel served as justice of the peace during the legal proceedings. The game warden had charged Chief Esaias with taking one marten over the legal limit. Loola did not speak, read, or write English, and he had not understood the form he had signed when he registered the furs. Together, he and his wife had taken less than the legal limit of marten. The jury acquitted Loola, finding no intent to defraud.[64] Although Hap participated in hearings and trials from time to time, he rarely represented a defendant. David Wallis did so on several occasions, likely when the defendants spoke limited or no English. Wallis also often interpreted during legal proceedings.

John and Jean Fredson's first child arrived on December 31, 1933, a boy they named William Burke Fredson in honor of Hap and Clara. Delighted at their latest namesake, they dubbed the bubbly little boy Billy Burke.[65] Clara later recalled that the child was so adorable that tourists would ask to adopt him. "It seemed so strange to them that the Indians would not give up their 'cute little papooses' to be brought up in luxury in the United States by white families. How little they knew of the deep love native parents have for their children," she wrote.[66]

In March 1934 Hap took part in a dramatic rescue, this time by air. Upon receiving a wire message of a severe dog mauling at Eagle, 340 miles up the Yukon River, he flew to the site and landed on a sandbar. The victim had severe bites on the face, neck, arms, body, and legs and was wrapped in bloody bandages. Hap gave the man a heavy dose of morphine, and a crew placed him on a stretcher in the plane. On takeoff, as they headed into the wind, the plane could not rise. They hurtled along at fifty to sixty miles an hour, Hap estimated, "bumping, and crunching and crashing" until the plane stopped at last, in a tilted position. He described the wreckage: "The fabric was torn here and there, one ski with struts was torn off, the propeller was curled like molasses candy, all the glass was broken, and one wing or part of it was smeared around the Yukon River like circus tents on exposition grounds." The patient was unscathed. That night, the mercury dropped to −70°F, and fog closed in. With no possibility of immediate rescue, Hap sutured the man's wounds until his thread ran out, and then he walked into the Native village and treated "some interesting cases." At the hospital in Fort Yukon, the man's wounds required more than one hundred skin grafts.[67]

This dramatic episode reached *Spirit of Missions* readers when Hap learned of another cut to the hospital's allocation in 1934. John Wood's article drew from Hap's heartrending response to the cut.[68] Just whom was he to turn away, he asked—the Native woman who needed a mastectomy, or the white woman who had traveled 150 miles to give birth to her first baby? Was it the man with puncture wounds covering his body after being mauled by dogs? What about six-year-old Joe, who had arrived from 300 miles away with tuberculosis of the lymph glands, or nine-year-old Silas, who came from 240 miles away undernourished and listless? Thanks to the von Pirquet test, Hap had detected tuberculosis early enough to heal him. "One might go on ad infinitum," he wrote.[69]

Despite the fiscal crisis, just a few months later, when suffragan bishop John Bentley and his wife, Elvira, visited Fort Yukon, Hap and Clara exhibited the same energy, enthusiasm for the mission and hospital work, and hospitality for which they were known. Thirty-six-year-old Elizabeth Hayes of Williamsburg, Virginia, the Bentleys' hometown, accompanied them. The journal Hayes kept of her travels on the *Pelican IV* with the

Bentleys provided no hint of the financial threat to St. Stephen's Mission, although Hayes may have been aware of Hap and Clara's concerns.[70] Her daily journal entries painted a vivid portrait of St. Stephen's Mission's place at the center of community life in Fort Yukon and of Hap and Clara's thorough integration into the community. As the *Pelican* tied up at the riverbank, dogs howled, and Native people greeted the bishop excitedly. With a "French beret" cocked on his head and pipe hanging from his mouth, Hap ran to welcome them. They had arrived just in time for Fourth of July festivities, he proclaimed delightedly. Taking their bags, Hap led the visitors to the mission home, where Clara "threw open the front door in a hearty greeting," Hayes wrote, adding that the word "hearty" captured the Burkes perfectly. "They are radiant people, full of zest." She and the Bentleys stayed in guest rooms at the mission home, which now housed thirty Native children.[71] During their week-long visit, the home bustled with the children's activities, along with numerous community events and dinners.

Roars of excitement beckoned the visitors to the field where races and other contests were underway. Townspeople cheered on contestants while young mothers walked about, their babies secured to their backs by distinctively beaded straps. The tug-of-war was the "chief event of the afternoon." Ten Native men, evenly divided, dug in their moccasined heels as they pulled the rope in opposite directions. From Hayes's perspective, Hap was everywhere, at the center of the action, "starting races, encouraging children to take part, helping in the tug-of-war—smiling, cheering, encouraging, joking—the leading spirit."[72]

That evening, Hayes and the Bentleys sat before the fire in the Burkes' living room as Clara prepared the children's supper, with help from several of the girls. The children ate at a long dining room table with Hap leading them in singing Grace. When not at the dinner table, they ran about the house, clearly feeling at home and appearing to view Clara as their mother, Hayes wrote. After she had served the children, Clara changed from her housedress into a simple black chiffon and called the guests to dinner. Silver candlesticks, a wedding gift that had survived the 1924 mission home fire, and fresh flowers adorned the large oval table where they dined. Clara created a delectable meal of canned chicken and other ingredients from the pantry.[73]

When the after-dinner conversation tapered off, the household ventured back to the field to watch the last inning of the baseball game. At eleven o'clock the dance began in the movie hall that had been cleared for the occasion. The event opened with Native boys and girls waltzing and dancing the one-step "with as much grace and smoothness as any of the white flappers on the Outside," Hayes wrote. When the fiddlers began the Red River Jig, Hap asked Old Maggie to dance. Hayes described the scene: "Facing each other but not touching, they circled around the room, feet flying in and out, stamping heel and then toe, until both were breathless. Dr. Burke would shout in time to the music and Old Maggie followed him seeming to float on her moccasined feet."[74] A man stepped in to relieve Hap, and soon a girl took Old Maggie's place. The jig continued until about twenty people had taken part. Next, Hap organized a square dance with a Native boy calling the figures, and he danced "as heartily and with as much gusto as he had led the games on the athletic field." They returned to the mission home at 12:30 to go to bed. Soon thereafter, the telephone rang, and Hap dashed out to the hospital.[75]

As Hayes shadowed Hap on his hospital rounds the next day, she found that he "showed as much enthusiasm for his work at the Hospital as he had over the games and dances." She had never seen, she wrote, "such an exuberant soul and one so completely self-forgetful. He had a word for each patient and their faces lighted with joy as he came through the wards."[76]

More than forty women, each with two or three children in tow, attended a meeting of the Woman's Auxiliary at the mission home that afternoon to hear Bishop Bentley. They listened attentively to the bishop, according to Hayes, with David Wallis translating. The women ooh-ed and ahh-ed with delight as he relayed greetings from the beloved Bishop Rowe. For the children's amusement, Hap set up a screen and showed a movie, *School Days*. By appearances, he appreciated the film as much as they did.[77]

One evening, Bill Yanert, the old-timer who lived downriver at Purgatory with his brother Herman, joined the Burkes and other guests for

23. Hap showing film to about forty children. Courtesy of the Archives of the Episcopal Church.

dinner. Archdeacon Stuck's visits at Purgatory with his old friends the Yanert brothers had been a highlight of his summer rounds on the *Pelican*. Hayes enjoyed the lively dinner table conversation with the well-groomed, distinguished looking Yanert.[78] After dinner, Albert Tritt arrived from Arctic Village about 250 miles up the East Fork of the Chandalar River from Fort Yukon to see Bishop Bentley. He sought the bishop's advice in convincing the government to build a school at Arctic Village. Community members had built a seventy-mile trail and a cabin, but the government had yet to respond. After midnight, Hap and Clara greeted the tourists on the steamer that arrived and offered them tours of the mission home and hospital. Clara warned Hayes not to be startled if someone opened her bedroom door.[79]

On Sunday a crowd including the Bentleys, the Fredsons, and Hayes joined Clara, Hap, and Hudson, who was visiting, for breakfast at the mission home. Hudson's mechanical interests had led to employment at Boeing and eventually would inspire him to learn to fly.[80] After the meal they all walked to St. Stephen's Church, where Hap delivered the service in Gwich'in, with Deacon Albert Tritt's assistance. Hap led the singing with a booming voice, making eye contact with those who held back until they joined in. "The building fairly rang with Indian harmony," Hayes reported. After the Sunday evening service in English, Clara invited the whole congregation to the mission home for a social hour. Visitors, including about twenty single men, mostly trappers, lingered until eleven o'clock in the evening.[81]

Monday was barber day at the hospital. Nurse Hanson cut the children's hair monthly, leaving them looking clean and neat. The solarium served as the children's ward at the hospital. Neil Nicholson, whom Hayes described as "a golden-hearted Old Timer, jovial, full of fun stories and loving children," arrived to begin work on enlarging the children's ward. The children adored "Mr. Nick," Hayes wrote. That day he brought a projector and films to amuse them, and they squealed with delight at Mickey Mouse's antics.[82] On their final day at Fort Yukon, the Bentleys and Hayes enjoyed a lunch of a "fat Yukon salmon and a sky high lemon pie," before departing on the *Pelican*. The Burkes waved farewell until their visitors turned a bend in the river.[83]

As the summer's activities and distractions waned, the days shortened, winter set in, and St. Stephen's economic woes could no longer be ignored. In November's *Spirit of Missions*, John Wood invoked Hap's name to personalize the dilemma Episcopal missions faced worldwide. "Dr. Grafton Burke at the Hudson Stuck Memorial Hospital, Fort Yukon, Alaska, voiced the pleas of every missionary, when he asked: 'Are we to turn away sick and suffering people? Shall we lie down supinely and let them die? Or shall we obey the Master's call, "Go preach, teach, heal."'" Wood described heroic work by Episcopal missionaries at various posts, declaring with a hint of reproach: "After three successive years of reduction and retreat the time for restoration and revival surely has come."[84]

Since 1932 the Episcopal Church had operated only one hospital in Alaska, Hudson Stuck Memorial.[85] As he absorbed cuts, Bishop Rowe concentrated his funds on Native communities, while increasingly asking majority white congregations to self-support.[86] He reminded Wood that self-support was out of the question at Fort Yukon, Anvik, and Nenana, which provided extensive social, educational, and medical services.[87]

Amid the darkness that winter, a letter from Rev. Artley Parson at mission headquarters that praised seventeen-year-old Grafton brightened Hap and Clara's mood. Hap's response to Parson brimmed with pleasure: "Your letter, you know, about the kid calling on you, was a treat, and created a stir in the household of Burke. How the mammy and daddy read and re-read your dandy touching letter. I don't think Clara would have taken $5 for it,-specially that stretch about Grafton being such a fine kid. You know,-it tickles the old folks. And we were so grateful to both you and Lena. That attention to one's young hopeful means a heap."[88]

With economic relief nowhere on the horizon, however, such moments of joy were fleeting. By early December, Hap saw the outlook for St. Stephen's as "dreadfully blue" and was "weary of talking in behalf of the cause; it's embarrassing," he wrote Wood.[89] Weeks later, he again wrote in despair, an excerpt of which Wood published: "It is profoundly distracting to throw everything one has of strength, training, sympathy into a problem such as this hospital presents, twenty-four hours a day, and then to find that the people of the Church at home, whom you have been representing in an outpost like this, are not supplying the money necessary to keep the work going. . . . Surely, surely, there are well-clad, well-housed, and well-fed, humans enough to feed and heal the less fortunate."[90]

Hap's "cry in the wilderness" resonated with Wood. In parts of New York City, he told Hap, one would hardly guess that a depression was underway. Human psychology nevertheless led even the well situated to feel insecure, and newspapers and radio fed such anxiety. Two years before, a prominent wealth manager, the Babson Financial Service, had advised its clients to reduce their giving, a message that received broad media attention. "We began to feel the worst of the depression very shortly [thereafter]."[91] While the American public may have grown weary of hearing of others' needs, people like Hap and Clara who worked the frontlines to alleviate suffering, who recognized how a single warm meal, warm bed, treatment, or operation could save a life, which in turn could sustain others, could not simply turn their heads.

In May, when Hap had to pay the fuel bill from the Hoffman Legacy, which he had hoped to place in the hospital endowment to help cover expenses on an ongoing basis, he railed again in frustration. For years he had cut costs to the minimum without complaint, but now he deeply resented the "grave anxiety" that simply heating the hospital caused him. "In countering the throttling suffocating circumstances of financial worry, I cannot,—must not, spend all my time fighting for breath. There is God's work to be done here by saving lives," he wrote Wood.[92]

Although they felt the decline in charitable giving, neither Wood nor Hap could have understood how the Depression affected the economic choices of the financially secure. Between 1928 and 1934, giving had dropped 35 percent nationwide, and wealthy donors had tended to shift their philanthropy from religious to secular causes.[93] Charitable giving to churches had plummeted just as New Deal programs began, dropping 30 percent between 1933 and 1939.[94]

Interestingly, the Episcopal diocese of Alaska regularly met its $1,500 quota—that is, its self-imposed commitment—for contributions to the national church, despite the depressed economy and reduced allocations from the Mission Society. Bishop Rowe asked congregants to make an extra effort, given the national crisis. In 1935 they responded with $3,350, more than double their quota.[95]

Break-up relieved the gloom of winter 1934–35, but shortly thereafter, a measles epidemic beset Fort Yukon, likely brought downriver from Old Crow in the Yukon Territory. In all, 350 people contracted the virus. The hospital, including tents pitched to accommodate overflow, housed the most critical cases. The vast majority lay bedridden at home.[96] The siege drained not only the hospital's medical supplies but the mission's emergency food supply, leaving Hap to fret about how he would replenish the reserves.[97]

When Bishop Rowe visited in late June, he was awestruck by Hudson Stuck Memorial's capacity to care for so many patients. "This Hospital is a wonderful place of mercy & help in this wilderness," he wrote Wood. "*It must be maintained even if we have to sacrifice everything else. It glorifies the work of the Church.*" Hap had hired four "helpers" to manage the crisis and now, he worried not only about how he would pay them, but about the next winter's fuel bill. "*He should not* be worried," Rowe insisted. "The Church is fortunate in having a missionary doctor on a paltry salary of $2000 or so who could earn $12,000 or so in private practice."[98] Rowe found the funds for the emergency hires and for a maintenance man at the hospital.[99]

Like the great influenza epidemic of a decade earlier, the timing of the measles epidemic during prime fishing season worsened its impact on the community. Families typically fished for at least a month during the summer to feed themselves and their dogs through the winter. With virtually the whole community sidelined by the measles, they would be ill prepared for winter.

Just when the worst of the epidemic had subsided, Hap and Clara's good friend Joe Matthews, the engineer on the *Yukon*, entered the hospital with double pneumonia. For six weeks the seventy-three-year-old fought for his life. Despite Hap's efforts to save him, he passed away in early September. During his final week, at Joe's request, Hap had sat vigil with him at night. After he died, Hap went home to his own bed for the first time in three weeks. The following day, September 9, he collapsed at home. Evacuated nearly five hundred miles upriver to Dawson, he was diagnosed with heart trouble brought on by overwork and sleep deprivation. Dr. Munn, who examined him, ordered complete rest. Knowing that he would find no respite at Fort Yukon, Hap and Clara traveled to Fairbanks, where he spent two weeks in St. Joseph's Hospital. Doctors there diagnosed a "breakdown" caused by overwork, sleep deprivation, and anxiety.[100]

Rather than finding rest in Fairbanks, however, Hap and Clara experienced a roller coaster of emotions, as bad and good news arrived from various directions. First came word from Fort Yukon that there was no fall migration of caribou. The mission complex typically consumed about 150 caribou a year, the majority of that supplied by the Native hunters of Fort Yukon and the rest by mission personnel and volunteers. The prospect of winter without caribou, after the disastrous fishing season and with dramatically reduced allocations from mission headquarters, left Hap and Clara reeling. The Native people relied more heavily on St. Stephen's for support during such hard times.[101] Bishop Rowe planned to request $6,000 in relief from the Bureau of Indian Affairs for the people of Fort Yukon.[102]

As Hap and Clara fretted over the caribou famine, a $500 donation to St. Stephen's briefly raised their spirits. Shortly thereafter, however, they learned that Bishop Rowe had eliminated the Fort Yukon fuel fund, which had been established to address the lack of a budget line for fuel at St. Stephen's Mission. The two struggled to imagine anything other than a grim future, and Clara wondered how Hap could withstand such prolonged stress.[103] Until then, Rowe had spared Fort Yukon heavy reductions.[104] Now in the proposed 1936 schedule, he had slashed $2,500 from St. Stephen's, anticipating that "specials" could be raised to pay for the fuel.[105]

After his release from St. Joseph's in early October, Hap and Clara traveled to Nenana, where he rested a week in the home of Bishop and Mrs. Bentley.[106] Buoyed by the many messages of concern and support that had poured in during his convalescence and by Wood's efforts to raise funds to pay the coming winter's fuel bill, they flew home to Fort Yukon in early November with "renewed energy and vigor," according to Clara.[107] There, the Arctic environment soon tested their resolve once again, however. For three weeks between Thanksgiving and Christmas, the temperature dropped as low as −73°F, and it never rose above −50°. Residents could gauge the temperature by the thickness of the frost build-up on doors, windows, and interior walls. The December issue of the *Spirit of Missions* published Clara's account of Hap's collapse, along with a direct appeal from Wood for contributions to the fuel fund. Once again, readers came through.[108]

By late 1935 St. Stephen's Mission had undergone tremendous growth, both in the work of Hudson Stuck Memorial Hospital that Hap managed and in Clara's orphanage and social work. The expansion had taken place despite incremental budget cuts, some of them potentially crippling, owing to the couple's unrelenting devotion to their work, to the highly capable hospital staff, and to the generosity of mission friends who answered the call when John Wood, Hap, or Clara sent a plea. The impact of their work could be seen throughout the region. In 1934 the hospital logged 39 births without a single neonatal death. The district recorded just 11 deaths, a remarkable figure given the hundreds of thousands of square miles St. Stephen's Mission served. Hospital patient days numbered 9,263, home visits numbered 3,169, and the clinic logged 2,083 visits. At St. Stephen's Church, 560 people were baptized in 1934, including 33 whites and 527 Natives. Communicants in St. Stephen's congregation numbered 258, and Sunday school had 153 children enrolled.[109]

As Hap approached his fifty-third birthday, signs began to appear that the all-consuming nature of the work was eroding his physical and emotional stamina. After exhibiting astonishing tenacity and resilience for more than two decades, he could no longer maintain the frenetic pace and boyish exuberance that had carried St. Stephen's Mission through crisis after crisis. Relentless financial worries now proved most debilitating.

9   The End of an Era, 1936–38

By the mid-1930s the non-Native population of the northern Interior had declined significantly. Only Fairbanks, as a hub for Interior Alaska aviation, the seat of the Fourth Judicial District, and the location of the University of Alaska, had a secure future as a permanent city; its population grew from 1,155 in 1920 to 5,692 in 1939.[1] All along the Yukon River, towns that had arisen or blossomed during the gold rush years had declined. Eagle, Circle, Tanana, Ruby, and St. Michael had lost most of their boomtown traits. Tanana remained a hub and gathering place for the middle Yukon region. Fort Yukon was the largest community along the Yukon River in Alaska and drew Natives and non-Natives from the northeastern Interior for trading and medical care. St. Stephen's Mission was the Episcopal Church's largest mission station and operated the only mission hospital in Alaska. Except at Fairbanks, the Episcopal Church work in Interior Alaska focused on the Native population.[2] The church had thirty-nine mission stations in Alaska.[3]

Residents and tourists increasingly used air travel to reach destinations throughout Interior and northern Alaska, although most still traveled by steamer along the Yukon and its tributaries. By the mid-1930s, however, gasoline and diesel had replaced wood as fuel for river travel.[4] In May 1938 a flight from Juneau to Fairbanks officially inaugurated airmail service in Alaska. Mail continued to travel from Seattle to Juneau by steamer and then was flown to Fairbanks, to be distributed to various sites in the Interior. The new service allowed mail to travel from New York to Fairbanks in five days.[5]

Despite these changes, day-to-day life at Fort Yukon and at St. Stephen's mission home and hospital remained much the same, although air travel improved access to emergency medical care. For instance, a plane carried to Hudson Stuck Memorial Hospital an Iñupiaq boy who had fallen and broken his hip on a chunk of ice. Hap set the fracture and placed the boy in a cast, giving him a chance at a full recovery. Most patients continued to arrive by traditional means, such as the sixteen-year-old girl with blood poisoning who arrived by dogsled a week after giving birth. Surgery at midnight saved her life.[6]

In late summer 1935 nurse Lucy Test joined the hospital staff.[7] Not long thereafter, twenty-four-year-old Hudson arrived to spend the winter volunteering at the hospital, having taken leave from his position at Boeing.[8] Oliver Beahrs, a University of California–Berkeley medical student, also spent the 1935–36 school year assisting Hap.[9] A romance soon developed between Hudson and the new nurse, which led to another staffing crisis at St. Stephen's.[10]

Clara reported that Hap felt "like his old self" again that winter. She nevertheless urged him to get more rest. In the aftermath of the measles epidemic, however, taking time off was not an option. In January hospital personnel transferred three young patients to the mission home to make room for critically ill children. All sixteen youngsters currently in the mission home were convalescing after in-patient care at the hospital.[11] One girl had stepped into an old fire pit where a porcupine had been skinned, and numerous quills had pierced her foot. Hap operated twice on the severely swollen foot, allowing her to walk again. After her release from the hospital, Clara cared for her until she could return to her home 350 miles away.[12]

Winter 1935–36 was bleak in terms of food supply. The late arrival of moose in the region following the previous summer's disastrous fishing season and the fall's failed caribou migration underscored how vulnerable Dena' people were to conditions outside their control.[13] Despite their precarious food supply, the children of St. Stephen's congregation gave generously during the Lenten season. With many families out hunting, the children who remained in the village earned and donated $206.68.[14] Artley Parson at mission headquarters in New York noted wistfully, "Would that our Church here had something of this generosity."[15]

Early in 1936, with offerings trickling in from the nation's dioceses, the National Council made a second cut to Alaska's allocation, bringing the total reduction for the year to $8,000. After having struggled to absorb the initial cut, Bishop Rowe was shocked by the news. Deeply disappointed in the failure of church members nationwide to support the mission work, Rowe refused to cut missionaries' salaries again, instead writing headquarters that he would forego his own salary and travel account funds. He would leave the question of his salary to his "friends who have stood by me for forty years," he wrote Mission Society treasurer Lewis Franklin.[16]

In spring 1936, as Hap rushed from one obligation to another, he fainted and was hospitalized for a week's observation. He continued to treat patients, however, during his confinement. The episode failed to discourage him from his decades-long pipe smoking habit, a practice he seems never to have questioned in terms of its health effects.[17] The rituals involved in pipe smoking, one of the few indulgences Hap allowed himself, may have permitted him to escape mentally to the cherished time he had shared with Hudson Stuck. In those days, his youthful energy and the inspiration he drew from his mentor more than compensated for the demands of the work.

During his hospitalization, Old Luke, a favorite of Hap's among Fort Yukon's Elders, entered the hospital with double pneumonia. Recently, Hap had repaired his broken leg; this time, however, medical care could not save him. As Hap offered his condolences to Old Luke's son, the younger man thanked Hap for mending his father's leg, for he would be able to walk well in heaven.[18] Often over the years, Stuck, Hap, and Clara had found Native people's seemingly fatalistic remarks troubling. In this case, given Old Luke's age, Hap may have taken solace in his son's jaunty response to his expression of sorrow.

Hap was back on his feet in May when influenza swept through the community. The scourge sickened 192 residents, Native and non-Native, including Clara and nurses Addie Gavel and Alice Hanson. Amid the flu epidemic, break-up occurred on May 10. Just after midnight an ice jam below Fort Yukon caused the river to flood the town, sending the people fleeing for safety, with children, bedding, and food in arms. In some places the water rose eight feet high. The flooding left the mission complex's one-hundred-foot-long woodpile strewn about the property, but the fence kept the logs from floating away. The waters destroyed the ninety-foot approach to the warehouse, leaving parts of it twisted and scattered throughout the town. By May 19 four people had died of the flu, and Hap anticipated more deaths. "You can understand the added misery, this flood was, coming on during the flue, and the people unable to rustle or wait on their sick," Hap told Parson. He signed his weary account of recent events incongruously with "Oodles of love from us both to you both, and Believe me, Faithfully Yours, Hap."[19]

Meanwhile, Hudson and Lucy Test were engaged to be married. Hap had informed Parson in April that Lucy was to be married soon, without identifying her fiancé, and that she would be resigning her position.[20] Parson tried to discourage the romance, reminding Lucy of her three-year contract, but the young couple would not be dissuaded.[21] They flew to Fairbanks in May and were married there. Clara later wrote of the romance and marriage in positive terms, saying she and Hap "couldn't have been happier with our son's choice."[22] Perhaps she had long forgotten the staffing crisis their marriage had caused. Alternatively, she may have understood the much greater appeal of a cloud-free love story in her memoir.

It may have been on this last return from Fort Yukon that Hudson took with him a ham radio set his father no longer used. Hap had taught Hudson Morse code when he was a child, and he had always enjoyed machinery. Trouble arose later when Jim Collier, a Seattle area debt collector, began pursuing Hudson; it seems that the bill for the radio had never been paid. In making repeated calls at the Burke home to collect on the debt, Collier sometimes brought his wife, Edna, with him. Lucy and Edna, both trained nurses, discovered much in common and became close friends. Before long, a warm and lasting friendship developed between the two couples. Whether Hudson ever paid for the radio remains a mystery.[23]

Lucy's sudden resignation caused panic at Hudson Stuck Memorial. "Matrimonial game staggering," Parson wired Hap upon learning of the marriage and resignation.[24] The "matrimonial game" had frustrated Hap for decades and Stuck before him. On the Alaskan frontier, where white men far outnumbered white women, female missionaries made attractive marriage partners. They often fielded proposals shortly after their arrival, which led to high turnover among nurses and other missionaries. In this case, the hospital crisis resolved quickly with the arrival of nurse Deborah Bacon in late May, soon after Lucy and Hudson left.[25]

As summer approached, mission headquarters struggled to recruit a physician to manage the hospital during Hap and Clara's forthcoming furlough.[26] Such leaves burdened the church substantially. They required payment of the furloughed employee's and family members' travel expenses, along with a stipend for living expenses, while also costing the church the salary and travel expenses of the locum tenens. The Burkes' furloughs created the dual challenges of locating people to fill both Hap's and Clara's multifaceted roles in a setting that most Americans would have deemed inhospitable.

By midsummer Dr. Robert Hume, the son and grandson of Congregationalist missionaries to India, was cleared for the position.[27] With Dr. and Mrs. Hume's arrival in September arranged, Hap and Clara departed Fort Yukon in July, leaving Addie Gavel in charge of the hospital. The Humes reportedly settled in quickly, and St. Stephen's appeared to be well positioned to carry out the hospital and mission work effectively. Three nurses, including Gavel and her cousin Olive Forbes, newly arrived, assisted Dr. Hume with patient care. Frances West looked after the children in the mission home.[28]

In fall 1936 a small caribou run once again left the Native people and St. Stephen's Mission short of meat for the winter.[29] Nevertheless, with the patient count at a manageable twenty, Gavel left on furlough, with the blessing of both Dr. Hume and Hap. In January 1937 she would enter a six-month program on the treatment of tuberculosis at the Trudeau Sanatorium on Saranac Lake in New York, the leading center for tuberculosis treatment in the United States. Hap envisioned substantial benefits to Stuck Memorial from her training. At the time, virtually no nurses were trained in treating patients with tuberculosis.[30]

In Seattle Hap and Clara visited Hudson and Lucy. Hudson was advancing in his career at Boeing and enjoyed painting, a talent he had developed as a child.[31] His work on airplanes led to some piloting experi-

24. Hap and Clara Burke, Fort Yukon. Hudson Burke private collection.

ence, although he likely was never licensed to fly. At work Hudson interacted with the founder of the fast-growing aviation company, William S. Boeing, himself. Once the two reportedly took up small planes together, Hudson flying a Ford trimotor.[32]

Bishop Rowe and Grafton joined Hap and Clara in San Francisco for a cruise through the Panama Canal and then north to New York. The canal route was no more expensive than alternate travel routes. Hap and Clara had not seen Grafton in four years. Having missed his graduation from Riverdale Country School in June, they looked forward with "keen pleasure" to celebrating his graduation with honors and earning a scholarship to Dartmouth College, where he planned to major in premedicine.[33]

The young man who greeted Hap and Clara at the airport differed strikingly from the boy they had envisioned as their eyes scanned the crowd. As they joyfully hugged one another, Clara again mused over the years of separation and the sacrifices they had made.[34] In her memoir she did not disclose whether she and Hap considered how the separation had affected Grafton, who was not quite fifteen years old the last time he saw his parents. As a child he had identified strongly with his father, shadowing him in the hospital and enjoying outdoor activities with him. Summers spent with the Hackett family and at Riverdale Camp could hardly have compensated for the loss of treasured time with his father.

The three-week voyage through the Panama Canal—and the longed-for time with Grafton—offered the rest, relaxation, and escape from worries at Fort Yukon that Hap needed. The tropical winds and stress-free days restored Hap's vigor and relieved the aging Bishop Rowe's achy joints.[35] They arrived in New York in early September refreshed.[36] The coming year would entail additional surgical training, much travel, and many speaking engagements, as well as the birth of a grandson, honors for Hap, and private, restorative interludes away from the public eye.

Soon after they arrived in New York, Dr. and Mrs. Robert Hume Sr. called on Hap and Clara in their rooms at the Gramercy Park Hotel. Dr. Hume, who was born in India of American missionary parents, had done mission work in India himself and now was professor of history of religions at New York's Union Theological Seminary. The couple invited Hap and Clara to their home for dinner with colleagues and friends from the seminary. They asked Hap and Clara to relate to the group conditions at St. Stephen's, where their son and daughter-in-law now served. That fall Hap and Clara gave numerous talks jointly and separately to raise awareness of and funds for the Alaska mission work. Clara enjoyed the speaking more than Hap, who by late October was already "'fed up' on this hopping" and longed "to settle down and learn something" at New York's Post Graduate Hospital.[37]

Bringing in specials funds was more important now than ever, though, as diocesan contributions to mission work continued to lag. Hap spent weeks on the speaking circuit in Pennsylvania in October and November,[38] and in January, he spoke in Baltimore.[39] In spring he and Clara gave a series of talks in Florida. A joint presentation in Jacksonville inspired the diocese of Florida's Woman's Auxiliary to donate more than $400 for an electric lamp in Hap's operating room.[40] During a two-week visit to New England in May, Clara spoke at several Boston venues on the medical work at Fort Yukon.[41]

In June Hap traveled to Tennessee, where the University of the South conferred on him an honorary doctor of science degree during summer commencement ceremonies.[42] Clara remained behind in New York during this visit, understanding that wives were "better checked at the gate" at such alumni rallies. To his delight the students inducted Hap into Sewanee's chapter of the Omicron Delta Kappa honor fraternity.[43]

Hap spent several weeks that summer on Long Lake in the Adirondacks helping Dan Hackett build a cabin on the family property near Camp Riverdale. Hackett was now attending medical school. The physical work in the out of doors, isolated from worldly concerns, likely did Hap a world of good.[44] Later that summer, he and Clara spent several weeks in Europe, including traveling to Scandinavia. Back in the United States, they attended the General Convention of the Episcopal Church in Cincinnati in early October, where Hap delivered an address before an audience of fifty-five Sewanee alumni at a reunion dinner.[45]

En route home to Alaska, financial concerns weighed heavily on Hap and Clara. "Somehow this seems to be the bluest return that I have ever had," he wrote Wood. "It seems, in a way, almost ludicrous that after all these years spent in the work, and so much accomplished, that I should feel dubious. At times I feel that I wish I were going either to Puerto Rico or to Tokyo."[46]

A several-day visit with Hudson, Lucy, and six-month-old Hudson Jr. in Seattle offered a bright spot amid the economic gloom. As they boarded the steamer and waved goodbye to the young family in mid-November, Hap's wallet bulged with snapshots of their grandson. That day Hap and Clara briefly discussed the idea of passing the torch. Hap reportedly had purchased land in Weston, Vermont, where he dreamed they would retire.[47]

Circumstances at Fort Yukon confirmed Hap's sense that their return to Fort Yukon was the "bluest" ever. Dr. Hume's performance had been "*disastrous*," in Bishop Rowe's assessment.[48] Locals reportedly told Rowe that Hume had shown contempt for both the hospital work and the church services. He left hospital equipment in disarray and departed with a debt of $1,500 that Hap would have to pay.[49] The Humes' correspondence indicates that they found the physical and social context trying and unstimulating. The weather had been bitterly cold, and Mrs. Hume was still recovering from surgery when they had left New York. Dr. Hume had hoped for career-enhancing experience at Fort Yukon but was disappointed to find that chronic illnesses such as tuberculosis dominated the medical work. "As you can understand," he wrote Wood, "the responsibility of administering a hospital for chronic disease does not furnish much stimulus or experience for a young physician."[50]

During Hap and Clara's absence, John Fredson had moved to Chandalar Village, his home village, with Jean and Billy Burke, to be its first schoolteacher.[51] In late 1936 John had become a candidate for holy orders, and Bishop Rowe requested a salary of $1,600 for him.[52] John Wood strongly supported the plan for Fredson's ordination in principle, but the church would not provide a salary sufficient to support a family. Ordained white male missionary salaries in Alaska began at $1,602 at the time, following a 10 percent cut in 1934. Native American clergy in South Dakota "[did] not begin to get such salaries as $1600," Wood told Rowe, acknowledging a salary differential between white and Native American clergy. The "Department" might support a salary of $1,200, he said.[53] The Fredsons' relocation to Chandalar Village led not only to the community's rapid growth but to improved education, health, and welfare, as John and Jean applied their education, skillsets, and experience to the betterment of the community. Their first impression upon arriving just before freeze-up in fall 1937, however, gave them serious doubts about their decision.

They found only two school-aged children in the village, as most families were away hunting. Moreover, John discovered that he would have to build the schoolhouse himself. Word of the Fredsons' arrival spread quickly, and by late October, eighty-nine people had settled in the village. Before long, John enrolled twenty-four students. As schoolteachers and agents of the Office of Indian Affairs, John and Jean were responsible for education, health care, and the broader political and economic well-being of the community. Reportedly, community spirit soared with the new schoolhouse, and people eagerly cooperated in whatever programs and projects John and Jean proposed or organized. John taught evening and summer classes to adults in English and basic literacy, and he and Jean conducted health clinics and encouraged the building of new homes with good ventilation.[54] On New Year's Day Jean gave birth to their second child, Virginia Louise. That spring, under John and Jean's guidance, villagers planted vegetable gardens and were astonished at the abundant results. As fish and game in the region dwindled with each year, potatoes, cabbage, and other vegetables provided the people with essential nutrition. In 1938 a post office opened, and Jean became post mistress.[55]

In summer 1938 John assisted Chief Johnnie Frank and the Chandalar people in writing a constitution and bylaws to gain federal recognition as a tribe under the Indian Reorganization Act of 1934, which Congress extended to Alaska in 1936. The first tribal council chose to change the community's name from Chandalar Village to Venetie, meaning "plenty game trail," to distinguish the settlement from the Chandalar River Village. To improve economic conditions, John spearheaded the establishment of a cooperative store and trading post. Local trappers garnered much higher prices for their furs by selling directly to Seattle buyers. Buying provisions wholesale and having them sent straight to Venetie cut shipping costs and the prices of the commodities themselves. John negotiated with the Office of Indian Affairs to use government relief supplies

25. Jean Fredson with Billy Burke and Virginia Louise. Alaska State Library, Butler/Dale Photo Collection, 1939. P306-0797.

to compensate people for work done for the school, such as sawing wood, hauling water, and construction labor. These measures allowed villagers to pay off their debt to the NC Company and to improve their food and economic security substantially.[56]

At Fort Yukon, moods lifted in early 1938, as the hours of sunlight increased and spring approached, along with a much anticipated visit by Bishop Rowe. The bishop planned to fly into several Interior villages in mid-April 1938 to provide Easter Communion services. After landing on skis at Fort Yukon, he and Hap flew to Arctic Village, where they held services and Hap examined ailing residents.[57] At Chandalar Village/Venetie, excitement built in the morning as residents heard on the radio that Bishop Rowe and Dr. Burke were on their way. The sky was clear, and residents looked toward the south for the incoming plane. As the visitors landed, the whole village, including the Fredsons and Chief Esaias, welcomed them. After greetings and church services where both Rowe and Burke spoke, they set off again, reportedly leaving the people a bit dazed at their sudden appearance and departure.[58] Rowe and Hap also flew to Beaver, where the bishop baptized fourteen children. Rowe visited Wiseman, Allakaket, Brant Creek, Tanana, and Fairbanks, as well. He stayed at Fort Yukon over Passion Sunday, Palm Sunday, and Easter. Throughout his visit the bishop held numerous well-attended services, including four separate events confirming a total of fifty-nine people. Among those confirmed were Addie Gavel, who had been a member of the Baptist Church when she met Hap and Clara, and Neil Nicholson, whom Bishop Rowe baptized and confirmed.[59]

More than three hundred people attended the two Easter services. "The spirit of Fort Yukon touched me as another Pentecost," Rowe wrote Wood. "To look in the hospital and see how the many patients, men, women, children, old prospectors, are cared for is an inspiration. Truly it is a work of love, mercy and healing, carried on in the name of the Merciful and Healing Saviour, [and it] filled me with joy. Dr. and Mrs. Burke are just wonders in the work they are doing and the Church has a multitude of reasons to thank God for them."[60]

Two months later, on June 29, 1938, Bishop Rowe ordained Hap to the Episcopal priesthood. As deacon since 1921, he had led church services and overseen the church work at the mission and in the region, when no resident priest was stationed at Fort Yukon. Now he could administer Holy Communion to individuals in the hospital, as well as to others in the community and region. Bishop Rowe, along with pastors Warren Fenn of Anchorage, C. P. Shelton and his wife of Fairbanks, and A. C. McCullum of Dawson took part in the ceremony.[61]

Clara described the excitement within the region as the momentous event approached: "Johnny Fredson and his family came down from Chandalar Village to attend the rite. Fort Yukon overflowed with visitors from upriver and down. Indians and Eskimos in their best spring regalia, white traders, trappers and miners, scrubbed and shaved and decked in their Sunday best, all came to see Sutchah Burke receive holy orders." Hours before the 9:00 a.m. start of the ceremony, people began pouring in, filling St. Stephen's pews, aisles, and the back of the church. Others crowded outside, peering through the windows and doors.[62] Bishop Rowe said of the crowd gathered. "It seemed as if the whole population was there. In a sense it was. I was reminded of the Pentecost 'they were all with one accord in one place.'"[63] Wildflowers adorned the altar and filled dozens of vases throughout the church. Clara and David Wallis had trained the choir that sang, accompanied by the organ, as Hap received the stole and Bible. Bishop Rowe, assisted by the three visiting clergymen, performed the rite, with David Wallis and John Fredson serving as acolytes.[64]

An outdoor public reception followed the ceremony. The village chiefs and Elders gave speeches, expressing their gratitude for Sutchah's many years of faithful devotion to the people of the region. David Wallis spoke of Hap's arrival as a "boy" thirty years before and how he had grown into a man "with the wisdom of Solomon," which sparked a burst of laughter from Hap that infected the crowd, as well, although they applauded Wallis's sentiments enthusiastically. Fredson presented Hap with a silver bowl engraved with the message: "Just a symbol of appreciation to Dr. and Mrs. Burke for thirty years of loyal service, from the people of Fort Yukon—1938."[65]

Feasting and dancing continued throughout the afternoon until those who had traveled to Fort Yukon began to depart in their canoes at about six o'clock, and Hap and Clara retired with their houseguests to the mission home for tea and a quiet visit. The more intimate atmosphere inspired retrospection, but not solemnity. Hap remained in high spirits, and he and Bishop Rowe regaled the others with stories of their most bizarre experiences over the years.[66]

That morning, unbeknown to Hap, a potentially catastrophic wire had arrived from mission headquarters: St. Stephen's allocation for the year was depleted, and Wood directed Hap to make no additional drafts on mission funds. Luckily, Clara had intercepted the message and kept it from Hap until the evening. Rowe later castigated Wood and the National Council for their insensitivity. "The telegram was not like the kindly sympathetic John Wood," he wrote.

I could say more but I am doing my best to restrain my feelings. You warn Dr. Burke, in your telegram, not to make any more drafts, that funds for his work are exhausted. Do you appreciate what such a warning means, if it were acted upon? It would mean the summarily [sic] closing of this hospital and mission. It would mean discharging the matron, cook, "man-of-all-outdoors work" etc, the staff, in a word, of the Hospital, and throwing out the sick in the Hospital etc. . . . . [T]hat is what would happen if your telegram should be acted upon.

Rowe reminded Wood that Hap made drafts on mission funds based on the National Council's appointment of personnel. Furthermore, the council had borrowed "again and again" to meet *its* obligations. Should a mission not be permitted to do so? St. Stephen's was "a healing mission as well as an Evangelical one," he continued. "It commends the mission of our Church far and wide." Tourists from all over the country, including physicians, have toured the hospital, and they "have a respect for the Episcopal Church they never had before," he noted. "For the *National Council* to fail to appreciate duly this work is due to their ignorance of it and their indifference. . . . In conclusion I must say that this work shall not be closed, that Dr. Burke will make drafts upon the strength of appropriations and if the National Council is not prepared or willing to care properly for it, then you can lay the responsibility on me and I shall appeal to my friends in the Church."[67]

In his report on Hap's ordination, Rowe noted that St. Stephen's had not had a resident priest for several years. In fact, for reasons of economy, no priest had been posted at Fort Yukon since Merritt Williams married and departed in 1932. With Hap's ordination, the church gained a priest who could perform all religious rites, including the Holy Sacraments, saving the cost of a separate resident priest. Rowe wrote presciently of the arrangement: "In caring for the sick in the Hospital, a (strenuous) work for one man, the additional work of a priest is laid upon him and I fear his task will be too great."[68] Hap's clerical duties, in fact, grew immediately. Congregants filled St. Stephen's Church each of the following Sundays, as those within traveling distance wanted to receive Communion from

Father Sutchah. He performed an unusually large number of baptisms that summer, as well, Clara reported.[69]

Before long, it dawned on the two that Hap's ordination had increased his workload significantly. Moreover, no hope of an assistant for either his medical or clerical duties lay on the horizon. As he and Clara mulled over their dilemma, Hap, in a burst of exuberance so like him, announced a solution—health classes! They would expand the reach of their health classes from Fort Yukon to the entire region that Hudson Stuck Memorial Hospital served. This would greatly improve health and well-being and thereby reduce the hospital's patient load. Their lack of resources to carry out such an ambitious program did little to dampen his spirits.[70]

Only days later, excruciating abdominal pain abruptly halted Hap's work and any such plans. When the pain continued without relief, Hap and Clara, along with Addie Gavel, flew to Fairbanks, where doctors at St. Joseph's Hospital thought he might be suffering from "spastic colitis" brought on by anxiety and exhaustion. They considered his condition "serious" and advised his transfer to Seattle for specialized care. Gavel accompanied Hap Outside, while Clara remained behind to consult with mission headquarters about finding someone to manage the hospital and mission home. Doctors at St. Joseph's promised to fly to Fort Yukon if a serious case arose at Stuck Memorial. Now Clara worried not only about St. Stephen's strained finances and Hap's health crisis but about how Hap's medical expenses would be paid. She considered borrowing against Hap's life insurance, but Wood strongly advised against doing so.[71] He promised that mission headquarters would pay Hap's travel and at least 80 percent of his medical expenses and that it would extend "every possible consideration." He assured her that "friends" surely would be happy to pay any outstanding bills.[72]

At Virginia Mason Hospital, Hap's condition perplexed the doctors. Bishop Rowe reported after seeing Hap, "They say 'it is not a typical case.'"[73] After failing to detect the source of Hap's pain, doctors diagnosed a "complete nervous collapse" and transferred him to Freidlander Sanitarium for convalescence.[74] There his condition deteriorated, causing Bishop Rowe to send for Clara. She arrived in Seattle on September 19. The following day, Hap was readmitted to Virginia Mason, where physicians diagnosed advanced pancreatic cancer.[75] Shortly thereafter he slipped into a coma. On Sunday morning, September 25, he passed away, with Clara at his side.[76]

At the time of his death, Hap was the senior Episcopal missionary in Alaska under Bishop Rowe.[77] Although the official cause of death was pancreatic cancer, the church and Clara attributed the deterioration of Hap's health to overwork and anxiety. A *Spirit of Missions* obituary noted, "Like many medical missionaries, Dr. Burke had the exhausting burden of the business management of his hospital, which in Alaska means acute problems of fuel and sometimes of food. . . . Worst of all were the reduced appropriations of recent years, causing anxiety which brought on a previous collapse and serious illness only a few years ago."[78]

A memorial service took place in Seattle's Church of the Epiphany, with long-term friends serving as pallbearers. Many Alaskans and former Alaskans attended. In accordance with Hap's wishes, Clara had his cremains flown to Fort Yukon, to be interred alongside Hudson Stuck in the Native cemetery.[79] Bishop Rowe, "dazed" and grief stricken, pledged to continue the work at Fort Yukon, "in memory of Archdeacon Stuck and Dr. Burke" and owing to its "great, merciful" mission. "As long as I live," he vowed, "this will be my purpose."[80]

Bishop Bentley and Rev. C. P. Shelton from St. Matthew's Church in Fairbanks flew to Fort Yukon to hold a memorial service on October 17. All the stores and both schools closed for the service, and the whole community, white and Native, including teachers, schoolchildren, and mission children attended. Neil Nicholson served as funeral director and carried the ashes. Chief Esaias Loola, David Wallis, Esau William, and "Peter" acted as honorary pallbearers. Wallis led parts of the service in Gwich'in, and Reverend Shelton delivered the eulogy and led the remainder of the service. From the church, attendees proceeded to the grave site, which had been prepared with spruce bows.[81]

Epilogue

Bishop Rowe enlisted personnel to carry on the work at St. Stephen's Mission after Hap's death. Senior nurse Addie Gavel managed Hudson Stuck Memorial Hospital, assisted by three other nurses, until a physician arrived in spring 1939. Gavel's cousin, nurse Olive Forbes, took charge of the children in the mission home. Rowe transferred Rev. C. P. Shelton and his wife from St. Matthew's Church in Fairbanks to oversee St. Stephen's Church. David Wallis and Albert Tritt led Gwich'in services and classes.[1]

Clara worked for Episcopal Church-related organizations for the rest of her life. The National Council awarded her an annual pension of $800, the maximum granted to a woman missionary of sixty years or older, although she was in her midfifties.[2] Initially, Clara served as Bishop Rowe's "field secretary" traveling the church's speaker circuit to raise support for the Alaska mission work.[3] By March 1939 she reportedly had raised sufficient funds to pay off St. Stephen's Mission's debt from 1938 and a substantial sum for 1939.[4]

In summer 1940 Bishop Rowe sent Clara and his secretary, Mabel Bergham, on a tour of the Alaska missions. At Fort Yukon community members young and old, Native and non-Native, welcomed Clara, and John and Jean Fredson came from Venetie for the occasion. Clara and community members gathered at the gravesite of Stuck and Hap, where David Wallis spoke of Sutchah's devotion to the community and how he would be remembered and loved.[5]

Throughout the 1940s tuberculosis deaths among Alaska Natives remained distressingly high. At Fort Yukon, weariness and grim resignation reigned as people shopped for caskets and burial clothes for loved ones.[6] In 1940, without consulting Bishop Rowe, the National Council had proposed transferring responsibility for Hudson Stuck Memorial Hospital to the federal government. Rowe objected strenuously. He recommended "the closing of every Mission in Alaska rather than that of Fort Yukon."[7] The council listened.

In June 1942 Bishop Rowe passed away at the age of eighty-five, having served as bishop of Alaska for forty-six years. He was buried at St. Peter's-by-the-Sea, in Sitka. In 1943 John Bentley, who had served as suffragan bishop under Rowe, was elected bishop of Alaska.[8]

David Wallis passed away the same month as Bishop Rowe.[9] Wallis had served St. Stephen's Mission for more years and in more capacities than any other Gwich'in congregant. His role as a liaison between St. Stephen's Mission and the community of Fort Yukon had built trust and eased relations between St. Stephen's Mission and the people and between Native and non-Native residents of the region.[10]

The community of Venetie flourished under John Fredson's leadership in the early 1940s, although tuberculosis raged there, too. After helping organize the community as a federally recognized tribe, John initiated the complex process of establishing a reservation under the Indian Reorganization Act to protect Gwich'in hunting and fishing grounds. The reservation covered 2,200 square miles of land and included the communities of Venetie, Arctic Village, Christian Village, and Robert's Fish Camp (Kachick); residents of Fort Yukon had opted out. In May 1943 the Department of the Interior officially proclaimed the Venetie Reservation.[11]

John credited the Episcopal Church for his contributions to the community and region. "Had it not been for missionary work in Alaska," he wrote his former teacher Laura Parmalee Adams, "I probably would not be able to do this work for my own people, for it was the Church who found me and gave me an education."[12] John passed away in 1945. Nearly four decades later, in 1982, the new high school at Venetie was named the John Fredson High School.[13]

In the early 1950s a survey of health conditions in Alaska, commonly known as the *Parran Report*, found strikingly different economic and health conditions between Alaska Natives and non-Natives. "The indigenous peoples of Native Alaska are the victims of sickness, crippling conditions and premature death to a degree exceeded in very few parts of the world," wrote Dr. Thomas Parran, the lead author on *Alaska's Health: A Survey Report*. Alaska Natives' tuberculosis mortality rate was nearly thirty times greater than the national rate. The mortality rate for Native children fourteen years of age and younger was one hundred times that of their age group nationwide.[14] Hap and Clara would have noted with irony Dr. Parran's statement that the American people and government would not stand for such conditions *if they only realized*. "If other Americans could see for themselves the large numbers of the tuberculous, the crippled, the blind, the deaf, the malnourished and the desperately ill among a relatively small population, private generosity would dispatch shiploads of food and clothing for Alaska alongside the cargoes setting out for Korea; doctors and nurses would be mobilized and equipped with the urgency of the great hospital units in wartime; the Alaskan missions would not need to beg for support."[15]

The seeming indifference of many Americans to the medical needs of Alaska Natives, needs that Hap and Clara witnessed daily, had driven him to despair in the 1930s. The *Parran Report* did lead to numerous improvements in health care delivery in Alaska.[16] By 1952 three drugs—streptomycin, para-aminosalicylic acid, and isoniazid—offered effective treatment of tuberculosis, finally bringing hope for an end to the deadly disease.[17] In 1957 the Episcopal Church transferred responsibility for medical care in the Fort Yukon region to the federal government.[18]

For over forty years, as epidemics periodically ravaged Alaska Native communities and tuberculosis took countless lives year in and year out, the Hudson Stuck Memorial Hospital had stood as a beacon, providing skilled and compassionate medical care to all those in need, regardless of race or religion and at no charge. Not until the Great Society programs and Native American rights movement of the 1960s and the Alaska Native Claims Settlement Act of 1971 did the U.S. government substantially assume its trust responsibilities toward Alaska Native peoples and respond to the glaring health and economic disparities between Alaska Natives and non-Natives.

The decades that followed Hap and Clara's sojourn at Fort Yukon brought tremendous socioeconomic and cultural changes to rural Alaska.

World War II and Cold War–era defense and infrastructure projects provided employment opportunities and reduced remoteness. Public education expanded to most villages. The Native land claims movement and concurrent nationwide civil rights and anti-poverty programs fostered the rise of a generation of Alaska Native leaders whose influence transformed local and state politics.

Meanwhile, Bishop William Gordon was leading a transformation in the Episcopal Church's approach to its mission work in Alaska. Recognizing that truly effective ministry could only emerge locally, the energetic young bishop began a campaign to train and ordain Native clergy and to transfer responsibility for the church's work to the laity within each village.[19] Rev. David Salmon of Chalkyitsik, the first ordained Dena' priest, and Rev. Walter Hannum at St. Stephen's Church in Fort Yukon played lead roles in the training of Native clergy through the establishment of the Yukon Valley Training Center at Fort Yukon.[20]

Each year, Gordon flew several individuals and their families to the non-denominational Cook Christian Training School in Tempe, Arizona, for academic, cultural, and theological studies in preparation for church leadership roles.[21] The initiative aligned well with Hudson Stuck's and Grafton Burke's vision for the Episcopal Church's ministry in Alaska. Moreover, it was timely. In 1973 the General Convention abolished missionary districts within the United States, making Alaska a diocese. Alaska's new status entailed shared leadership between the bishop and clergy, as well as far more local responsibility and an expectation of self-support.[22]

Hardy and Helen Peters of Tanana both participated in the Native Deanery program, attending the Cook Christian Training School with seven of their children from 1968 to 1971. Their son Guy recalls that being recruited carried lifelong benefits for those selected and their family members. On the other hand, the Native ministry program created tensions within Native communities as the Native rights movement and land claims movement also called for leadership. Individuals had to choose which cause and identity to embrace and prioritize. As Guy put it, "You had to choose your fight." Hardy Peters pursued a leadership role in the Native land claims movement. Helen Peters chose "to stick by and stick up for the church," her son explained. She was ordained to the diaconate in 1974 and to the priesthood in 2004.[23]

During World War II Clara served as secretary of the General Council of Associations of the Seamen's Church Institute of New York, an Episcopal Church–affiliated organization. She received Denmark's King Christian X Medal of Liberation for her efforts on behalf of Danish merchant seamen. The British Crown also honored her, naming her a Dame of the British Empire. After the war, Clara relocated to Los Angeles, where she worked with the Seamen's Church Institute. In 1961 the Native people of Fort Yukon sponsored Clara's travel to the community for the centennial celebration of the Episcopal Church's work in Alaska. Three Dena' priests, James Simon, Isaac Tritt (the son of Albert Tritt), and David Salmon, who had been a schoolmate of Hudson Burke at Fort Yukon, participated in the services. Clara passed away in October 1962.[24]

Hudson and Lucy continued to make their home in west Seattle. In 1941 they had a second son, Herbert, and much later, they adopted a daughter, Lisa. Hudson's pursuits reflected the resourcefulness he developed as a child in Fort Yukon, which spawned perseverance and craftsmanship in adulthood. He enjoyed a long career as inspector of quality control at Boeing. "He knew his stuff," recalled his son Hudson Jr. Hudson built the family's dream house on a hill on Beach Drive in west Seattle. While living there, he took an avid interest in boat building. As Hudson Jr. described it, "He would bring home a piece of butcher paper, loft all the parts, make the ribs, and then build the boats in the backyard." Over the years he built two or three cabin cruisers and a tugboat.[25]

Above all, Hudson Jr. attributes his father's "constitution" to his grandfather, Hap. Dr. Grafton Burke's persistence manifested in the management and growth of Hudson Stuck Memorial Hospital in the face of staggering challenges and in the medical care he provided the people of a vast, underserved region. In Hap and Clara's son Hudson, this "constitution" displayed itself in a career at Boeing, where his colleagues valued his expertise and productivity, and in his home and boat-building pursuits. Simply put, "He knew how to make things happen."[26]

The most striking outgrowth of Hudson's upbringing and the values Hap and Clara imparted may have been the many children he and Lucy fostered, including Lisa. Because Lisa had Down Syndrome, Hudson ensured that she would have lifelong Medicaid benefits before they adopted her. Lucy became an ardent advocate for Lisa's education before schools provided special education services. She focused so intensely on Lisa's schooling, in fact, that Lisa graduated from a standard public high school. Hudson Jr. and his wife, Judy, carried on the family tradition, fostering twenty-nine children in the interim between the birth of their third child and the arrival of their twins ten years later.[27]

In 1999, when Hudson Sr. was eighty-eight years old, he visited Fort Yukon with Hudson Jr. and his son Michael. Hudson had not returned to his birthplace since he and Lucy left in 1936.[28] The community welcomed the trio enthusiastically. Elders remembered Hudson, having attended school with him or having lived in the mission home. David Salmon spent an afternoon reminiscing with him about their childhood friendship and talking about the changes that had come about in recent decades.[29] At the age of twenty-nine, Salmon had been elected chief of Chalkyitsik. Twenty years later, in 1962, he was ordained to the Episcopal priesthood. Two decades later, at the age of seventy, he built the first church in Chalkyitsik, sawing and hauling the ninety logs himself. In 2002 the University of Alaska Fairbanks awarded him an honorary doctorate of laws. As an Elder, Salmon continued to share with Dena' youth the subsistence skills he had learned as a child and practiced throughout his life.[30]

As the three generations of Burke men strolled through Fort Yukon, individuals they encountered, old buildings, and other landmarks evoked memories of Hudson's youthful escapades. At the cemetery he viewed for the first time his father's grave marker beside that of Hudson Stuck, beneath the seven-foot Celtic cross erected to honor the archdeacon. A few years after the visit, in 2004, Hudson Sr. passed away. Nearly two decades later, Hudson Jr. remained grateful for the "long-overdue" visit that he had arranged for his father, his son, and himself.[31]

Grafton graduated from Dartmouth College and earned a medical degree at Long Island College of Medicine in 1945.[32] While in medical

26. Michael and Hudson Burke with Rev. David Salmon, 1999. Hudson Burke private collection.

school, he married Millie Kotek, and they had a son, Grafton Jr.[33] Eventually, the couple had four children, a daughter and two more sons.

Grafton resembled his father, Hap, in several ways, including his charisma and ease with conversation. He reportedly had a wonderful bedside manner. Family members often heard how "everybody loved Grafton." Unlike Hap, he made a comfortable living. For many years he practiced medicine from his office at Sixty-Seventh and Park Avenue, an upscale part of Manhattan, and the family lived in Manhattan. When the children were young, they moved into a large Dutch colonial house in Westchester County.[34] Clara visited the family from time to time. Geoffrey, the youngest child, remembers that his grandmother would sit at the table and do crafts with him. "She was good at children's activities because she raised all those children," he recalled.[35]

27. Clara with Grafton Burke Jr., late 1940s. Geoffrey Burke private collection.

Like Hap, Grafton was forgetful and disorganized. He managed the family's finances poorly and ran late for appointments, which may explain why he hesitated to bill his patients. When Geoffrey once asked his father what, if anything, he disliked about being a physician, Grafton replied that he found "capitalizing on people's misfortune" distasteful, an orientation that likely owed to his upbringing; his parents had never charged for their services. Grafton's carelessness with money negatively affected his family life; he and Millie separated when Geoffrey was nine, Grafton defaulted on the mortgage, and the bank foreclosed on the family home.[36]

The demands of his medical practice and the breakdown of his marriage limited the time that Grafton spent with his children. Nevertheless, Geoffrey Burke cherishes memories of nature walks and camping trips with his father when he learned to hunt and fish as Grafton had done in Alaska. Geoffrey senses that his father identified deeply with the lifeways in and around Fort Yukon, where he developed a love of the out-of-doors that he passed on to his son.[37]

The all-consuming nature of Hap and Clara's life's work would have defeated almost anyone else, especially given the financial burdens they faced. They not only persevered but thrived in their roles for several reasons. First, their Christian faith and conviction that God had called them to this work grounded them. Second, they drew inspiration and guidance from Archdeacon Hudson Stuck, in life and after his death. Third, their complementary personalities and assets strengthened them, as their love and respect for one another affirmed and uplifted them. Fourth, they daily witnessed critical unmet medical and socioeconomic needs and therefore could not turn their backs. Fifth, they saw the fruits of their labor in improved health conditions, thriving children, healed patients, and a robust spiritual community in Fort Yukon. And finally, as they allied themselves with the Gwich'in people, championing and defending their interests, they developed close, deeply cherished friendships.

St. Stephen's Mission complex formed a bulwark against the new social, political, and legal norms that disadvantaged Alaska Natives in their own homeland. At the same time, it fostered cleavages within the community and even within individuals, as allegiances to beliefs, people, institutions, and lifeways shifted. In the decades that followed Hap and Clara's tenure, much social turmoil, including alcohol abuse, domestic violence, and suicide, accompanied the economic opportunities and political movements that put Alaska Natives on more equal footing with other Alaskans and recognized their land rights. Many saw the social turmoil of the 1960s and 1970s, as well as the waves of epidemics that left survivors reeling, as products of the colonial forces and institutions of the late nineteenth and early twentieth centuries that disempowered Alaska Natives and devalued their belief systems and lifeways. The effects of colonial forces and multigenerational grief can still be felt in Alaska today.

Hap and Clara's presence at Fort Yukon unquestionably shifted power dynamics. Certain of their actions challenged traditional beliefs and practices, and these efforts may be perceived as having been culturally and psychologically harmful. Their personalities were so strong that children raised in the mission home may have experienced some confusion about their identities and allegiances.[38] Yet as myriad forces of change disrupted the lifeways of Alaska Native peoples, devalued their lives, and threatened their very survival, Hap and Clara Burke stood *with* the Native people, devoting their energies to their physical, social, and spiritual well-being. Their work enhanced health and longevity for generations. Rather than exhibiting the "sanctimonious snuffle" that Hudson Stuck so disdained among clergy or merely delivering high-sounding sermons, Hap and Clara cast their lot among the Gwich'in people and conducted *real* mission work—saving lives.[39]

GLOSSARY

break-up: Term referring to the springtime release of ice in the rivers. Alaskans hail the event, which can be associated with catastrophic flooding, as the definitive end of winter.

Dena'/Athabascan: Indigenous peoples of Alaska and Canada formerly referred to as Indians. The terms *Dene, Dena,* or *Dena'*, which mean "the people" in the Dena' language, are increasingly used to refer to this ethnolinguistic group.

grub: Food.

Gwichyaa Gwich'in: Subset of the Gwich'in (Dena' or Athabascan) language group whose homeland lies in eastern Alaska and western Canada. Gwichyaa Gwich'in live in or identify with the Fort Yukon area.

hind sack: A bag that hangs from the handlebars of a dogsled facing the driver and containing such essentials as snow goggles, extra gloves, and snacks.

Iñupiaq: The singular and adjectival form of the term for the Inuit people living along Alaska's northwest and north coasts, formerly referred to as Eskimo.

Iñupiat: The plural form of the term for the Inuit people living along Alaska's northwest and north coasts, formerly referred to as Eskimo.

Koyukon: Dena'/Athabascan language group who live along the Koyukuk, the Yukon, and the lower Tanana Rivers.

Niitsąįį Gwich'in: Subgroup of Gwich'in who live in the Venetie and Arctic Village area.

old-timer: A person who has been in the region for several years; not necessarily an aged person.

Outside: Term (capitalized) used by Alaskans to refer to the continental United States and beyond.

parka: An anorak-style outer winter garment, usually with fur around the hood.

pioneer: Someone who came into the Alaska-Yukon region during the gold rush era and remained. The term can also refer to someone who has been in the region for decades.

poke: A small bag used to contain gold.

ratting: Trapping muskrats.

Sourdough: Term referring to a migrant to the Alaska-Yukon region who has survived several seasons. Some said that one who survived through a break-up could call oneself a Sourdough.

specials: Term used by the Episcopal Mission Society for funds received as individual donations and set aside for specific mission fields or missionaries, sometimes for specific purposes. These are distinguished from regular allocations to the mission field and mission site by mission headquarters.

Tanana: Dena'/Athabascan language group who live along the middle Tanana River. Also a community at the confluence of the Tanana and the Yukon Rivers.

NOTES

1. U.S. Census Bureau figures from 1890 and 1900, https://www2.census.gov /prod2/decennial/documents/1890a_v8-01.pdf; and https://www2.census .gov/library/publications/decennial/1900/bulletins/demographic/103 -population-sex-nativity-color.pdf. Alaska's population nearly doubled in the last decade of the nineteenth century, from 32,000 in 1890 to 63,500 in 1900. We omitted numbers for mixed-race individuals because they were small and it was unclear what races these figures represented. Besides whites and Natives, Chinese were the other significant racial group.

2. Brady, *Report of the Governor* (1900), 35–36 (quotation on 36).

3. Brady, *Report of the Governor* (1901), 51.

4. Fortuine, *"Must We All Die?,"* 193, 198–99. The overwhelming majority of individuals exposed to the tubercle bacillus will not develop disease. The "virulence of the bacterial strain, the concentration of droplet nuclei in the environment, the proximity and length of exposure, and the genetic or immunological susceptibility of the person exposed" determine the likelihood of disease transmission (xxii).

5. Superintendent George Boulter wrote to Commissioner of Education Harlan Updegraff in November 1909 that "hundreds of times . . . people who ought to know better had expressed the sentiment that 'The sooner the natives are exterminated the better.'" Boulter to Updegraff, November 19, 1909, in Boulter and Grigor-Taylor, *The Teacher and the Superintendent*, 106.

6. *Unangan* is the term for the people in the eastern dialect. The term is *Unangas* in the western dialect. The language is Unangam Tunuu.

   The singular forms are *Sugpiaq* and *Alutiiq*. The term *Sugpiaq* is more traditional, whereas the term *Alutiiq* derives from the Russian term for the people, *Aleuty*, and thus acknowledges the Russian history in the region. "Alutiiq—What Is in a Name?," Alutiiq Museum, accessed April 16, 2021,

https://alutiiqmuseum.org/learn/the-alutiiq-sugpiaq-people/language/902
-alutiiq-what-is-in-a-name.

7. The term *Dena'* encompasses the many related peoples of northern Canada and Alaska shown in map 1.

8. We thank Dr. Hishinlai' Peter and professor emeritus Lawrence Kaplan of the Alaska Native Language Center for their assistance in identifying the correct terms for these Indigenous groups. In the early twentieth century, the missionaries at Allakaket, as well as Bishop Rowe and Hudson Stuck, referred to the two groups as Koyukuk Athabascans or Koyukuks and sometimes Indian, and Kobuk Eskimos, Kobuks, or Eskimos. Non-Natives tended to refer to the Iñupiat and Yupiit as Eskimos and to all the Dena' peoples as Indians or Athabascans.

9. At least some of the Gwichyaa Gwich'in likely originated in the Lower Ramparts, downriver from the Yukon Flats. Raboff, *Iñuksuk*, 103.

10. McKennan, "The Physical Anthropology of Two Alaskan Athapaskan Groups," 43–44. Historically, these Dena' groups were relatively isolated and generally endogamous, but by the 1870s, mobility had increased and much intermarriage had taken place among Dena' tribes and with whites.

11. Stuck, *Voyages on the Yukon*, 112–13.

12. Slobodin, "Kutchin," 515–17; Osgood, *The Han Indians*, 79.

13. C. Burke, *Doctor Hap*, 118–20.

14. VanStone, "Alaska Natives and the White Man's Religion," 175. The RAC built a fort at Nulato on the lower Yukon River in 1839, and the explorer Lavrenty Zagoskin traveled in the early 1840s into Dena' territory as far as just below Nuchalawoya where the Tanana and the Yukon Rivers meet, although Russian influence concentrated in the lower Yukon River and delta region. The Russian Orthodox Church first sent missionaries to Sitka, the Aleutian Islands, and Kodiak Island in 1823. It established a mission on Nushagak Bay in southwest Alaska in 1841, and in the coming years, the church built missions on Cook Inlet and on the Kuskokwim and the lower Yukon Rivers.

15. Naske and Slotnick, *Alaska, a History*, 3, 80, 84.

16. Stuck, *Voyages on the Yukon*, 109. HBC employees traveled downriver to purchase furs, and they encountered RAC traders at the mouth of the Tanana River, but the RAC never interfered with the HBC's presence on the upper Yukon. Note that we have used currently available river-mile distances between villages along Interior rivers rather than figures cited in our primary sources, which we have found to be inaccurate in many cases.

17. Raboff, *Iñuksuk*, 153.

18. The Anglicans actively missionized among Canada's Indigenous peoples, as did the Roman Catholics.

19. Sax and Linklater, *Gikhyi*, v–vi; Canham, "Old Fort Yukon," 53; Stuck, "A Loss to the Yukon," 611–13; Stuck, *The Alaskan Missions*, 2–3.

20. Yarborough, introduction to *Recollections of the Youkon*, xii.

21. Stuck, *The Alaskan Missions*, 2–3.

22. Canham, "Old Fort Yukon," 53–55.

23. Stuck, *The Alaskan Missions*, 9–11; Case, *Alaska Natives and American Laws*, 195, 198. Jackson had worked to establish Presbyterian missions in southeast Alaska and was considered an expert on conditions in Alaska. In 1900 Congress reaffirmed the Department of Interior's responsibility to provide education for Alaska's children, regardless of race.

24. Boulter and Grigor-Taylor, *The Teacher and the Superintendent*, 21. In 1819 the Civilization Fund Act had formalized its assimilation objective in Native American education in the continental United States. The government dispensed funds primarily to religious organizations, entrusting them with Native Americans' education.

25. Case, *Alaska Natives and American Laws*, 198–99.

26. Boulter and Grigor-Taylor, *The Teacher and the Superintendent*, 22–23.

27. Stuck, *The Alaskan Missions*, 12–13; Waggoner, *Missionaries in Alaska*, 63.

28. VanStone, "Alaska Natives and the White Man's Religion," 175.

29. Jenkins, *The Man of Alaska*, 50–51, 54. Two years later, the Episcopal Church's Woman's Auxiliary established a Missionary Episcopate Fund and dedicated its earnings to support the episcopate of Alaska. This fund paid the bulk of Bishop Rowe's salary throughout his more than four decades of service to Alaska. Franklin to Rowe, March 10, 1936, Rowe correspondence, PECUSA; "Our Alaskan Missions Concluded," 21. Rowe's was the only church official's salary paid solely by church women. The national Woman's Auxiliary of the Episcopal Church had been formed in 1871 to recognize women's role in supporting the church's mission work and to coordinate the work of the many local woman's auxiliaries throughout the nation. "The United Thank Offering (UTO)," The Episcopal Church of Delaware, accessed October 12, 2021, https://delaware.church/united-thank-offering/.

30. Boulter and Grigor-Taylor, *The Teacher and the Superintendent*, 22–23. Jackson had served as the superintendent of Presbyterian missions in Alaska from 1887 to 1903.

31. Case, *Alaska Natives and American Laws*, 199.
32. Case, *Alaska Natives and American Laws*, 195, 198–200. At the turn of the twentieth century, gold rushes in the Klondike and at Nome rapidly expanded Alaska's non-Native population, prompting Congress to allow the incorporation of towns in Alaska and the collection of taxes to fund schools. In 1908 the Alaska Federal District Court, in *Davis v. Sitka School Board*, upheld the dual school system and determined that being "civilized" meant adopting the "white man's" lifestyle and cutting ties with other Natives. Alaska became a territory in 1912, and in 1917 the territorial legislature assumed control over its schools and established a territorial department of education. Native education and the Native peoples' general welfare remained under the jurisdiction of the federal government. In 1931 responsibility for Alaska Native education transferred from the Bureau of Education to the Bureau of Indian Affairs (BIA). In 1962, three years after Alaska became a state, the BIA and the state entered into an agreement that called for the gradual consolidation of state and BIA schools into a single state system for all Alaskan children. For a variety of reasons, including local communities' desire to maintain control, the process of consolidation was not completed until the 1980s. Case, *Alaska Natives and American Laws*, 200–201, 203.
33. Leonides Wooden, "History of St. Stephen's Mission," Parish Record Book Fort Yukon 1900–1947, APRCA.
34. Cole, *Old Yukon*, 42.
35. Stuck, "New Beginnings at Fort Yukon," 597.
36. Carter, "Founding of St. Matthew's Hospital," 8–10; Dean, *Breaking Trail*, 71–72. The hospital operated until 1915, when declining population led the church to close it and shift the responsibility to the new Catholic St. Joseph's Hospital.
37. Dean, *Breaking Trail*, 72–74.
38. Stuck, *Voyages on the Yukon*, 31–32.
39. Stuck to John Wood, June 19, 1909, Stuck correspondence, PECUSA; Stuck, "The Boys at St. John's-in-the-Wilderness," 183.
40. Stuck to Wood, January 1, 1910, Stuck correspondence. Shortly before his death in 1920, having recently traveled the length of Alaska's Arctic coast and become familiar with the Iñupiat and their culture, Stuck expressed his thoughts on the limited role missionaries should play among these people: bringing "the blessings of Christianity," protecting them from the greed and depravity of "the white man," providing medical relief from diseases largely

introduced by outsiders, "and then I would let the Eskimo civilization develop itself, as it would develop itself." Stuck, *A Winter Circuit*, 254.

41. Stuck became a U.S. citizen during his time as dean of St. Matthew's Cathedral in Dallas. John Wood to Rowe, June 10, 1935.

42. Dean, *Breaking Trail*, 30.

43. Dean, *Breaking Trail*, 23.

44. Dean, *Breaking Trail*, 42–43.

45. Dean, *Breaking Trail*, 31–33; G. Burke, "Hudson Stuck from Texas to Alaska," 39–45. The initial structure housed forty children. By 1902 a new facility with playgrounds, a vegetable garden, and a milk cow accommodated seventy-five children. Later expanded and named the Episcopal Home for Children, the institution served Dallas children in need for decades.

46. The movement also advanced political reforms, including female suffrage and the curtailment of widespread government corruption.

47. Evans, *The Social Gospel in American Religion*, 2–5; Donovan, *A Different Call*, 1986.

48. Holm, *The Great Confusion in Indian Affairs*, 8–11 (quotation on 9).

49. Prucha, *The Great Father*, 609–10.

50. Young, *Hall Young of Alaska*, 259. Current spellings of these Indigenous groups are Haida and Tsimshian.

51. Young claimed that he and other Presbyterians believed that this decision, more than anything else, explained "the exceptional progress of the Southeastern Alaska natives in civilization." Young, *Hall Young of Alaska*, 260.

52. Rowe, "Annual Report" (1911–12), 54.

53. Rowe, "Annual Report" (1910–11), 68.

54. In 1919 Stuck wrote John Wood, the Episcopal Mission Society's foreign secretary, his closest friend outside Alaska, "I think the clash of diverse minds and diverse cultures (if indeed culture can be said to 'clash' at all) approaching problems from fundamentally diverse points of view, more likely to emit the electric sparks of *ideas* that set fire to the human mind." Stuck to Wood, Septuagesima (February 16), 1919, Stuck correspondence.

55. Geoffrey Burke, grandson of Grafton and Clara Burke, electronic communication with authors, September 4, 2018. Geoffrey Burke's father, Grafton Burke, related this story about his father, Dr. Grafton Burke, to Geoffrey, who never met his grandfather.

56. In the 1960s a woman who, along with her husband, had served as a VISTA volunteer for fifteen months in the village of Noorvik wrote a scathing letter

to Senator Robert Kennedy about the deficient and directly harmful teaching practices and materials in Bureau of Indian Affairs (BIA) schools for Alaska Native children on Alaska's Seward Peninsula. Kennedy chaired the Senate Subcommittee on Indian Education. The woman wrote of myriad ways in which BIA teachers implicitly and explicitly denigrated Alaska Native languages and cultures. "VISTA Takes Penetrating Look into Native Education System," *Tundra Times*, March 8, 1968.

57. See VanStone, "Alaska Natives and the White Man's Religion"; Burch, "The Inupiat and the Christianization of Arctic Alaska," 81–108; and Wallis, *Raising Ourselves*.

58. Dena' migratory patterns previously had kept them living in tents much of the year, which provided superior ventilation. Episcopal missions encouraged the building of well-ventilated cabins by supplying two windows and a door to any Native family that settled near the mission and built a cabin. When people began to settle near mission sites, new sanitation measures were needed, as the accumulation of human and animal waste became breeding grounds for disease when the snow melted each spring. Such sanitation concerns had been much less prevalent when the people moved about frequently and before many new diseases entered the region.

59. VanStone, "Alaska Natives and the White Man's Religion."

60. Fortuine, *Chills and Fever*, 192–93.

61. Burch, "The Inupiat and the Christianization of Arctic Alaska."

62. VanStone, "Alaska Natives and the White Man's Religion"; and Burch, "The Inupiat and the Christianization of Arctic Alaska."

63. Burch, "The Inupiat and the Christianization of Arctic Alaska."

64. Hosley, "Intercultural Relations and Cultural Change," 551–53.

65. VanStone, *Athapaskan Adaptations*, 73.

66. Laguna, *Tales from the Dena*, 47.

67. Stuck, *Ten Thousand Miles with a Dog Sled*, 267–69 (quotation on 269).

68. For instance, Bishop Rowe wrote John Wood at Mission Society headquarters in New York in summer 1910 of how the Natives at Tanana had begged him to assign them a minister and a doctor, if possible. Rowe to Wood, August 25, 1910, Rowe correspondence. Stuck noted in *The Alaskan Missions* that Natives at Stephen's Village repeatedly asked Rowe for a mission there (137).

69. Alaska's bishop William Gordon, who served from 1948 to 1974, initiated a broad shift in the Episcopal mission's orientation toward its congregants by turning away from paternalistic practices of the past and transferring more leadership roles to Alaska Natives. See Thomas, *An Angel on His Wing*.

70. Sax and Linklater, *Gikhyi*, 26–27.

71. Wallis, *Raising Ourselves*, 42–44.

72. G. Burke to Wood, February 14, 1922, Burke correspondence, PECUSA.

73. Dorsey, "Episcopal Women Missionaries," 253. *Iñupiaq* is the singular and adjective form, as well as the term for the language, whereas *Iñupiat* is the plural form.

74. Rowe, "Annual Report" (1908–9), 60.

75. Updegraff to Rowe, June 25, 1908, in Boulter and Grigor-Taylor, *The Teacher and the Superintendent*, 62.

76. Boulter and Grigor-Taylor, *The Teacher and the Superintendent*, 62.

77. Stuck admired the Jesuit missionary Jules Jetté, who labored for many years among the Dena' of the lower Yukon River, recording and committing their language to a writing system. Stuck diary, August 31, 1910, APRCA. On May 26, 1909, Stuck wrote in his diary, "And how fortunate that a man of Father Jette's scholarship & linguistic & philological attainments should have the leisure & opportunity & willingness to devote himself to it. I have great admiration & respect for this learned gentle Jesuit." In *Ten Thousand Miles with a Dog Sled*, Stuck's account of his travels throughout Interior Alaska in his role as Episcopal archdeacon, he derided ignorant and ethnocentric teachers who believed advancing civilization chiefly meant teaching Alaska Natives "to call themselves Mr. and Mrs." and teaching women to wear Western clothing while holding "a contemptuous attitude toward the native language and all native customs." He admitted that some missionaries fell into "the same easy rut." Stuck, *Ten Thousand Miles with a Dog Sled*, 23–24.

78. Stuck, *Ten Thousand Miles with a Dog Sled*, 23.

79. Boulter and Grigor-Taylor, *The Teacher and the Superintendent*, 39.

80. In May 1910 Stuck bemoaned the relationship between the school and mission at Fort Yukon, finding it "most unsatisfactory and provoking." Stuck diary, May 1, 1910. George Boulter, superintendent of the Upper Yukon School District, wrote his supervisor in 1913 that Episcopal missionaries showed such "antipathy toward the Bureau that it has been most difficult to always work in harmony with them." Boulter to Claxton (from "Annual Report to Claxton 1912–1913"), in Boulter and Grigor-Taylor, *The Teacher and the Superintendent*, 236–37.

81. Updegraff, "Report on Education in Alaska," 1297–98.

82. Rowe to Wood, January 25, 1918, Rowe correspondence.

83. Boulter to Wood, March 25, 1907, Boulter to Hoggatt, November 14, 1908, Boulter to Lopp, November 23, 1910, and Boulter to Brown, June 30, 1911,

"Annual Report of George E. Boulter, District Superintendent of Schools, Upper Yukon District of Alaska (1911)," in Boulter and Grigor-Taylor, *The Teacher and the Superintendent*, 59, 67–68, 129, and 176. When Boulter arrived in Alaska in 1906 after being hired by the Episcopal Mission Society as a teacher at Eagle, the government also hired him as a teacher at the city school. In 1908 he accepted the position of assistant superintendent of schools for the Northern District of Alaska. When this expansive district was divided in 1910, he became superintendent for the Upper Yukon District, which included Fort Yukon, where Hudson Stuck and the Burkes resided.

84. See Ehrlander, "The Paradox," 29–42.

85. Boulter to Hoggatt, November 14, 1908.

86. Stuck and Bishop Stringer of the Yukon Territory had observed stark differences between the conditions among the Peel River Indians, who practiced their traditional lifeways and maintained their vigorous physiques and independence, and the Natives at Moosehide, which lay close to Dawson, the heart of the Klondike gold rush. Conditions at Moosehide affirmed Stuck's belief that distancing themselves from non-Natives' degenerate and materialistic habits and values would enhance Indigenous peoples' quality of life and survival rates (Stuck, *Voyages on the Yukon*, 56–57).

87. Dorsey, *Episcopal Women Missionaries*, 253; Stuck diary, January 3, 1910.

1. EARLY LIFE AND ARRIVAL IN ALASKA

1. Dawson, the capital of the Yukon Territory, which lay nearly 500 miles upstream, and Fort Gibbon, which lay about 320 miles downstream near Tanana, had hospitals, but neither treated Alaska Natives. At Nulato, more than 500 miles downstream from Fort Yukon, Alaska Natives could find hospital care at a government-funded make-shift hospital.

2. G. Burke, application form for missionary service for the Missionary District of Alaska, Station Fort Yukon, completed July 5, 1912 (or received by the church then), RG 351, box 13, folder 5, Grafton Burke 1908–1937, Archives of the Protestant Episcopal Church of the United States of America (PECUSA). Clara's birth year is unclear. Her memoir (C. Burke, *Doctor Hap*, 10–11) implies that she was born later. For instance, she notes that she was underage when she became engaged in 1909. C. Burke, *Doctor Hap*, 120. Various articles and census records show conflicting birth years and ages. One obituary says she was born in 1882. Mrs. Ivol I. Curtis, "Burke Death Great Loss to Diocese," *Episcopal Review*, November 1962, 3. We use this date, submitted on a form that Hap completed for the church in 1912, as this is the earliest

document we have accessed that was written by Hap or Clara that identifies her birthdate.

3. C. Burke, *Doctor Hap*, 10–11; Curtis, "Burke Death Great Loss to Diocese," 3.

4. G. Burke, application form, July 5, 1912.

5. C. Burke, *Doctor Hap*, 10.

6. C. Burke, *Doctor Hap*, 11.

7. Stuck, "The Third Cruise of the Pelican," 398–99.

8. Dorsey, "Episcopal Women Missionaries as Cultural Intermediaries," 253; Stuck diary, January 3, 1910.

9. Stuck, "The Third Cruise of the Pelican," 399; "Appeals."

10. C. Burke, *Doctor Hap*, 11–12, 15. Clara wrote in 1932 that the bishop joined the women in Ketchikan. C. Burke, "Twenty-Five Years above the Arctic Circle," 349.

11. C. Burke, *Doctor Hap*, 33, 36; Carter, "Day by Day beyond the Arctic Circle," 546. Clara Heintz Burke wrote in *Doctor Hap*, published more than fifty years later, that they arrived in August, but Clara Carter wrote at the time that they arrived in July.

12. Rowe, "Annual Report" (1907–8), 47–48.

13. Stuck, *Ten Thousand Miles*, 158.

14. Stuck, *The Alaskan Missions*, 124–25; Stuck, *Voyages on the Yukon*, 329.

15. Stuck, *Ten Thousand Miles*, 158; C. Burke, *Doctor Hap*, 44.

16. C. Burke, *Doctor Hap*, 37. Clara had had some experience as a Sunday school teacher (57).

17. C. Burke, *Doctor Hap*, 36, 39; M. G. Heintz to John Wood (telegram), September 30, 1924, Burke correspondence. Clara's spelling of her nickname is an Anglicization of Nich'it Choo Tsingwąąch'yaa in Athabascan. We thank Hishinlai' Peter of the Alaska Native Language Center for her assistance in clarifying the Gwich'in orthography in this book.

18. C. Burke, *Doctor Hap*, 40–41. They burned grass to keep the swarms of mosquitos away (42).

19. Dean, *Breaking Trail*, 120; Stuck to Wood, October 6, 1917, Stuck correspondence.

20. C. Burke, *Doctor Hap*, 43–45.

21. Carter, "Day by Day," 546–48.

22. Stuck, "New Beginnings at Fort Yukon," 599.

23. C. Burke, *Doctor Hap*, 44–45.

24. C. Burke, *Doctor Hap*, 47–48.

25. C. Burke, *Doctor Hap*, 51–52.

26. C. Burke, *Doctor Hap*, 55–57.

27. Residents of the Yukon Territory also called the more connected regions of the United States and Canada "Outside."

28. C. Burke, *Doctor Hap*, 59, 60, 63. Alaska's Indigenous peoples have made use of the permafrost to preserve food for millennia.

29. Carter, "St. John's-in-the-Wilderness," 61.

30. Carter, "The Daily Round," 21; Carter, "Day by Day," 548.

31. C. Burke, *Doctor Hap*, 57; Carter, "Day by Day," 549.

32. Sabine, "From a Pioneer's Point," 26; Heintz, "Children of the North," 23.

33. Carter, "Day by Day," 550.

34. C. Burke, *Doctor Hap*, 64–65. Government teachers received $90 per month, while superintendents received $150 per month, with no provision for medical expenses incurred while working (Boulter and Grigor-Taylor, *The Teacher and the Superintendent*, 29). Both received pay for only the nine months from September 1 to May 31, with no certainty of having their contracts extended to the following year (27).

35. C. Burke, *Doctor Hap*, 57–58; Heintz, "Children of the North," 23–24; Stuck, "The Boys at St. John's-in-the-Wilderness," 181.

36. Carter, "Day by Day," 547–48.

37. C. Burke, *Doctor Hap*, 60, 68–70, 79, 88, 92–93.

38. Tommy the Wolf and Others, "Christmas Letters from the Koyukuk," 198–200.

39. Carter, "Is It Worth While?," 340.

40. C. Burke, *Doctor Hap*, 87–88. The Koyukuk mining district, which lay between Fort Yukon and Allakaket, to the north, enjoyed a mini-boom from 1907 to 1910 as miners in the region bore down to bedrock in search of gold in areas that had been surface mined during the first peak season from 1902 to 1904. Fewer than 250 miners lived and worked in the vast region. Hunt, "Gates of the Artic."

41. C. Burke, *Doctor Hap*, 88–90, 92–93; *Alaskan Churchman* 2 (May 1908): 37.

42. C. Burke, *Doctor Hap*, 95–96.

43. C. Burke, *Doctor Hap*, 100–101. Stuck's diary entry of September 12, 1909, notes that the shout "Steamboat!" ended a Sunday school class at Circle.

44. Carter, "Random Notes," 880–81 (quotations on 881).

45. Carter, "St. John's-in-the-Wilderness," 61.

46. Stuck, *Voyages on the Yukon*, 331.

47. G. Burke, application form, July 5, 1912.

48. "Men of Texas—Dr. William C. Burke."

49. Dean, *Breaking Trail*, 63.

50. Alex Blacklock to Benjamin Wiggins (n.d.), Grafton Burke bio file, Archives and Special Collections of the University of the South.

51. G. Burke, "Hudson Stuck from Texas to Alaska," 39.

52. "Men of Texas—Dr. William C. Burke"; Stuck to Wiggins, March 8 and March 15, 1904, Burke-Wiggins file, Archives and Special Collections of the University of the South.

53. Dean, *Breaking Trail*, 63.

54. G. Burke, "Hudson Stuck from Texas to Alaska," 39; C. Burke, *Doctor Hap*, 106; Dean, *Breaking Trail*, 28.

55. Dean, *Breaking Trail*, 50, 63; G. Burke to the secretary of the Board of Missions of the Protestant Episcopal Church in the United States of America, January 20, 1908, RG 351, box 13, folder 5, Grafton Burke 1908–1937, PECUSA.

56. G. Burke to the secretary of the Board of Missions.

57. Stuck to Wiggins, March 8 and March 15, 1904. Stuck had envisioned St. Matthews as a feeder school to Sewanee. Ten of the prep school's first fifteen graduates attended Sewanee (Dean, *Breaking Trail*, 50).

58. G. Burke to the secretary of the Board of Missions.

59. G. Burke to the secretary of the Board of Missions; Dean, *Breaking Trail*, 63–64. Burke did volunteer work at various missions in the Tennessee mountains throughout his years at Sewanee. G. Burke to secretary of the Board of Missions.

60. Stuck to Wiggins, March 15, 1904; G. Burke to the secretary of the Board of Missions.

61. Gordon D. Bratton, Information Blank for Domestic and Foreign Missionary Society of the Protestant Episcopal Church in the United States of America, February 14, 1908, RG 351, box 13, folder 5, Grafton Burke 1908–1937, PECUSA.

62. "Commencement Program," *Sewanee Purple*, June 14, 1905, 1; "Contest for Knight Medal Held," *Sewanee Purple*, May 24, 1907, 2; "Commence Week Begins," *Sewanee Purple* (commencement special), June 25, 1906, 1; "Preliminary for the Knight Medal," *Sewanee Purple*, May 24, 1907, 2.

63. Dean, *Breaking Trail*, 124–25; "Medical Department of the University of the South," 617 (final quotation herein).

64. G. Burke to the secretary of the Board of Missions.

65. "Some Recent Recruits for Distant Missions," 857.

66. Dean, *Breaking Trail*, 122; Rowe to Board of Missions, March 1, 1910, Rowe correspondence. Stuck, Bishop Rowe, and the Burkes regularly fundraised while on furlough Outside, either for special causes, such as St. Stephen's

Hospital, which opened in 1916, or to build the "specials" account that Rowe kept to supplement the meager salaries and expense allowances for the missionaries and missions. Dean, *Breaking Trail*, 122.

67. Requisition of the appropriations to the Missionary District of Alaska for the fiscal year beginning September 1, 1908, Rowe to Lloyd, January 3, 1908, Rowe correspondence.

68. G. Burke to the secretary of the Board of Missions.

69. John Bell Henneman, February 7, 1908, Information Blank for Domestic and Foreign Missionary Society of the Protestant Episcopal Church in the United States of America, February 14, 1908, RG 351, box 13, folder 5, Grafton Burke 1908–1937, PECUSA.

70. Notation on the unrestricted personnel folder of G. Burke, RG 351, box 13, folder 5, Grafton Burke 1908–1938, PECUSA; Rowe, "Annual Report" (1907–8).

71. The Mission Society allocated Stuck $500 per year for the *Pelican's* operational expenses, as requested by Bishop Rowe (Wood to Kimber, February 8, 1908, Rowe correspondence).

72. "With the Clubs," *Motorboat*, July 10, 1908, 34.

73. Wright earned $300 per year as Stuck's travel companion and interpreter, and Stuck received $300 for running the *Pelican*. Rowe, "Annual Report" (1907–8).

74. Stuck, *Voyages on the Yukon*, 77–79. The river carried immense quantities of debris, ranging from fully leafed and evergreen trees to rotten logs, that could hinder steamboats' passage, especially as they moved upriver. These logs served a purpose in the treeless region of the lower Yukon, where the Iñupiaq and Yup'ik peoples of the coastal region used them to build structures and for firewood. Dena' also harvested, and they continue to harvest, driftwood from the rivers.

75. Dean, *Breaking Trail*, 127, 129.

76. Stuck, "Along Alaska's Great River," 642.

77. Stuck diary, February 11, 1909.

78. Stuck diary, February 11, 1909.

79. Cole, "One Man's Purgatory," 86.

80. Stuck, *Voyages on the Yukon*, 121–22.

81. Stuck, *Ten Thousand Miles*, 158–59.

82. Stuck, *Ten Thousand Miles*, 159–61, 163.

83. Ice creepers, or crampons, were spiked soles worn outside normal winter footwear, to provide traction in walking or climbing on ice. They are still used today.

84. Stuck, *Ten Thousand Miles*, 164, 167, 171–72.

85. Stuck, *Ten Thousand Miles*, 172, 174, 178, 180–83, 186.

86. C. Burke, *Doctor Hap*, 104–5 (quotation on 105); Stuck, "Report of Official Acts," 59.

87. Stuck, "By Boat and Sled," 30; Carter, "Alaska Notes," 286.

88. "Midsummer and Midwinter at the Allachaket," 233.

89. Carter, "Alaska Notes," 286.

90. Stuck, "The Boys at St. John's-in-the-Wilderness," 182.

91. Stuck, "By Boat and Sled," 30; C. Burke, *Doctor Hap*, 106–7.

92. C. Burke, *Doctor Hap*, 105–6 (quotation on 106).

93. C. Burke, *Doctor Hap*, 109–11.

94. C. Burke, *Doctor Hap*, 106.

95. C. Burke, *Doctor Hap*, 108–9 (quotation on 108).

96. "Midsummer and Midwinter at the Allachaket," 233.

97. C. Burke, *Doctor Hap*, 108–9, 112. A dog musher would hang a hind sack from the handlebars of the sled, with any decorative beading facing backward. The sack could hold essentials such as goggles and extra gloves, for easy access.

2. FORT YUKON, COURTSHIP, AND MARRIAGE

1. Stuck diary, January 1, 1909; McGary, *Stories Told by John Fredson*, 23.

2. Stuck diary, January 1, 1909; McGary, *Stories Told by John Fredson*, 23. These stories were recorded in 1923. Fredson noted that if Christmas fell on a Sunday, then dancing would not take place that day.

3. McGary, *Stories Told by John Fredson*, 25. To Stuck's relief, no whiskey marred Hap's first New Year's celebration. Stuck diary, January 1, 1909.

4. Stuck diary January 5, 1909.

5. Stuck diary, February 8, 1909. Stuck did not state explicitly whether Hap traveled the full eighteen miles with them before turning back.

6. Drane diary, March 1921, APRCA.

7. Wallis, *Raising Ourselves*, 27, 30.

8. Dean, *Breaking Trail*, 133; Stuck, "New Beginnings at Fort Yukon," 593–600; C. Burke, *Doctor Hap*, 134. Clara spelled the name Sutcha. She explained that the name is pronounced with a strong accent on the second syllable, effecting the sound of a sneeze—*ah-choo*.

9. G. Burke, "Before and After," 45.

10. Raboff, *Iñuksuk*, 57.

11. Stuck, *Voyages on the Yukon*, 96, 108–9.

12. Stuck explained that the upper reaches of the Yukon River are too clear for the fish wheel's use, because the fish could easily see and avoid it. Streams fed by glaciers in the region of the upper Yukon filled the river farther downstream with silt that obscured the wheels from the fish's sight. Stuck, *Voyages on the Yukon*, 112–13.

13. Laguna, "The Dena Indians," 8.

14. McGary, *Stories Told by John Fredson*, 27; Stuck, *Voyages on the Yukon*, 112–13. Fredson explained that the people dried meat harvested while the weather was relatively warm, but during the cold months, they packed the fresh meat back to Fort Yukon and stored it in cellars dug into the permafrost.

15. Stuck, "The Yukon Salmon," 317.

16. Numerous oral and written sources attest to times of starvation and famine, including Wallis's recounting of the traditional Gwich'in story *Two Old Women* and Raboff, who in *Iñuksuk* noted the migration of Dena' groups in the nineteenth century owing to warfare and starvation.

17. Slobodin, "Kutchin," 515–17; Episcopal Diocese of Alaska, *A Century of Faith*, 124; Stuck, *Voyages on the Yukon*, 83–84, 96, 139–40; Osgood, *The Han Indians*, 79; Stuck, "The Yukon Salmon," 318; Landon, "Glimpses of Life in Arctic Alaska," 62; McGary, *Stories Told by John Fredson*, 29.

18. Stuck, "The Yukon Indians," 107–8; Stuck, "Fort Yukon," 59; Stuck, *Voyages on the Yukon*, 58; Stuck, *The Alaskan Missions*, 42–43; McKennan, "Tanana," 567; Dorsey, "Episcopal Women Missionaries," 253.

19. Stuck, "New Beginnings at Fort Yukon"; Rowe, "Report of the Bishop of the Missionary District," 60.

20. Burke, "A Boys' Club," 62; Stuck diary, February 6, 1909.

21. C. Burke, "Fort Yukon Rejoices," 339.

22. Rowe, "Annual Report" (1906–7), 44; Jacobs, *A Schoolteacher in Old Alaska*, 174. Loola earned $80 a year in this position. Another Native catechist at Tanana, Blind Moses, earned $200 per year, perhaps because he had no other means of supporting himself. Another Native catechist in southeast Alaska earned $100 per year. Rowe, "Annual Report" (1907–8).

23. L. J. Wood, "Fort Yukon's Activity," 23.

24. "Memorial Service at Fort Yukon"; Grete Bergman (great-granddaughter of William Loola), Zoom interview with authors, March 13, 2022. When Archdeacon McDonald died in fall 1913, Loola gave the eulogy at a well-attended memorial service at St. Stephen's Mission in which he told of his relationship with McDonald and recounted the tireless efforts of the beloved

archdeacon in serving the many scattered settlements of both Natives and white prospectors in the region.

25. G. Burke, "Alaska Hospital has Phenomenal Growth," 727–28.

26. G. Burke, "Missionary Medicine in the Arctic," 60; Sniffen and Carrington, *The Indians of the Yukon and Tanana Valleys*, 31.

27. Stuck, "Fort Yukon," 58. Schools superintendent George Boulter mentioned the issue of poorly ventilated cabins and better health when living out in the open in summer as well. "Annual Report of George E. Boulter, District Superintendent of Schools, Upper Yukon District of Alaska, for the Fiscal Year Ended June 30, 1911," in Boulter and Grigor-Taylor, *The Teacher and the Superintendent*, 176.

28. G. Burke to Rowe, "Annual Report," June 26, 1909, Rowe correspondence.

29. Waller, *The Discovery of the Germ*, 1–2, 25.

30. Stuck, *Ten Thousand Miles*, 28.

31. G. Burke, "Missionary Medicine in the Arctic," 61; Stuck, "Fort Yukon," 58–59 (quotation on 58).

32. Stuck diary, March 18 and 19, 1909; *Alaskan Churchman* 3 (May 1909): 44; G. Burke, "Annual Report," June 26, 1909.

33. G. Burke, "Annual Report," June 26, 1909; Stuck diary, March 18, 1909.

34. G. Burke, "Annual Report," June 26, 1909.

35. Langdon, "At Fort Yukon," 56.

36. Stuck diary, March 8, 1909.

37. "Notes" (May 1909), 36; Carter, "St. John's-in-the-Wilderness," 61; Stuck, *Voyages on the Yukon*, 331; Boulter to EE Brown, April 14, 1909, in Boulter and Grigor-Taylor, *The Teacher and the Superintendent*, 81–82. Through 1917 this was the only case of such a need for government aid at Allakaket. Stuck, *Voyages on the Yukon*, 331.

38. Stuck, "Winter and Spring at Allakaket," 795–98; Stuck, "Report of Official Acts," 59–60. Moon and starlight provided enough light to see after sunset. In springtime the days quickly grew longer, so that by the spring equinox, Allakaket and Fort Yukon experienced twelve hours of daylight, with the days quickly growing longer.

39. G. Burke, "Annual Report," June 26, 1909.

40. G. Burke, "Annual Report," June 26, 1909.

41. Rowe, "Annual Report" (1908–9), 53–62 (quotation on 61–62).

42. Stuck, "New Beginnings at Fort Yukon," 597–98. Ten propane lamps provided lighting at the mission. Wood to Rowe, July 3, 1909, Rowe correspondence.

43. "Fort Yukon Notes," 23; G. Burke, "Alaska Hospital has Phenomenal Growth," 727–28.

44. Stuck, "New Beginnings at Fort Yukon," 597–98; Stuck, "Alaska Notes," 284. George Boulter attributed the decline in alcohol abuse at Fort Yukon to the assignment of a more diligent and effective marshal upriver at Circle City, from where most of the alcohol that entered Fort Yukon originated. "The new marshal is carefully watching all small boats leaving Circle for Fort Yukon as great quantities of liquor have been carried down river in this manner." Boulter to Updegraff, June 23, 1909, in Boulter and Grigor-Taylor, *The Teacher and the Superintendent*, 88–89.

45. Cady, "School Work at Fort Yukon," 57.

46. Rowe to Lloyd, June 5, 1909, Rowe correspondence.

47. Clara and the peoples of the remote Koyukuk River region remained quite isolated from such negative influences. After marrying Hap and relocating to Fort Yukon, she witnessed such abuses regularly.

48. "Two Interesting Gatherings"; C. Burke, *Doctor Hap*, 114.

49. C. Burke, *Doctor Hap*, 115–16; "Two Interesting Gatherings"; Stuck diary, August 8, 1909. Stuck wrote in his diary, "I am pleased that the boy has done so well."

50. Stuck diary, August 8, 1909.

51. C. Burke, *Doctor Hap*, 116–17.

52. Stuck to Wood, January 1, 1910, Stuck correspondence.

53. Carter, "St. John's-in-the-Wilderness," 61.

54. Updegraff to Boulter, April 13, 1909, and Boulter to Updegraff, October 4, 1909, in Boulter and Grigor-Taylor, *The Teacher and the Superintendent*, 81, 99.

55. Cited in Boulter to W. T. Lopp, August 20, 1909, in Boulter and Grigor-Taylor, *The Teacher and the Superintendent*, 93.

56. Stuck diary, February 8, 1909.

57. U.S. Department of the Interior, "Report on Education in Alaska December 24, 1909."

58. Cady, "Fort Yukon," 47.

59. Stuck, "Report of Official Acts," 60.

60. Stuck to Wood, January 1, 1910.

61. Stuck, "Third Cruise of the Pelican," 400.

62. Stuck to Wood, April 5, 1909, Stuck correspondence. Stuck asked Wood to purchase the paper "fire balloons" well in advance. He wrote in great detail, seeking various colors, especially red and green, and various shapes and sizes.

"Send me a couple of dozen!" he wrote, clearly taking delight in planning the celebration. He told Wood that he wished he could purchase real fireworks, but he acknowledged that that was "out of the question."

63. Stuck to Wood, January 1, 1910.

64. Stuck to Wood, January 1, 1910. One of the reasons whites appreciated Stuck's visits to their remote mining camps was that as a notary public, he could witness legal documents, saving them long treks to population centers such as Fairbanks. Stuck diary, February 9, 1909.

65. Rowe to Howard (n.d., placed between correspondence of August 23 and September 25, 1910), Rowe correspondence.

66. *Alaskan Churchman* 4 (May 1910): 45; C. Burke, *Doctor Hap*, 118–19. Clara wrote that Hap arrived at Allakaket in January, but the cited note in the *Alaskan Churchman* and a diary entry by Stuck place Hap's arrival there in February. Stuck diary, February 3, 1910.

67. C. Burke, *Doctor Hap*, 120.

68. Stuck diary, February 3, 1910. During this encounter, Hap and Stuck wrote a joint letter to Hap's best friend, Edgar Loomis, another protégé of Stuck's who had also become a physician, urging him to come to Alaska the following summer to serve as Hap's best man at the wedding and to spend a year in the territory as a medical missionary. Both had written Loomis earlier, but he had so far declined the invitation. Stuck diary, October 7, 1909.

69. C. Burke, *Doctor Hap*, 120.

70. C. Burke, *Doctor Hap*, 120–22. The Koyukuk mining district was known for the size of its nuggets. Hunt, "Gates of the Artic."

71. Stuck diary, March 30, April 7, April 12, April 15, 1910. Wright City was renamed Nolan later that year.

72. Stuck diary, March 22, 1909, September 5, 1910. In the latter entry, Stuck noted that he was pleased to have arranged with the parents of four children— Daniel, Abraham, George, and Margaret—to attend St. Mark's mission school. On September 18, 1910, Stuck noted that he had spoken with another Native boy, Esaias, about enrolling at St. Mark's the next summer.

73. Stuck diary, February 11, 14, and July 14, 1910.

74. Stuck diary, February 15, 1910.

75. Stuck diary, May 1, 1910.

76. Boulter to Lopp, July 1, 1910, in Boulter and Grigor-Taylor, *The Teacher and the Superintendent*, 118.

77. Boulter to Updegraff, August 20, 1909, in Boulter and Grigor-Taylor, *The Teacher and the Superintendent*, 94; Boulter, "Report on the U.S. Public

School"; Harry to Boulter, March 19, 1912, in Boulter and Grigor-Taylor, *The Teacher and the Superintendent*, 203.

78. Stuck, *Ten Thousand Miles*, 293.

79. C. Burke, *Doctor Hap*, 122–23.

80. Stuck diary, June 1 and June 18, 1910. Stuck had invited the fourteen-year-old Johnny on the trip for the experience. He was not yet in Stuck's employ.

81. Stuck diary, June 21, 1910.

82. John Fredson's granddaughter, Diana Campbell, and Walter Harper's great niece, Johanna Harper, have remarked on the extraordinary experiences their relatives had in these roles and the invaluable mentoring they received from Archdeacon Stuck. Telephone conversation with Diana Campbell, March 19, 2021; email with Johanna Harper, April 1, 2021, and several times earlier.

83. Stuck diary, June 20, 1910.

84. Stuck diary June 27, 1911.

85. Rowe to Roberts, July 3, 1910, Rowe correspondence.

86. Anticipating that the man would follow through on threats to malign the Episcopal mission work in Alaska, both Rowe and Stuck informed mission authorities in New York of the incident. Rowe to Wood, July 26, 1910, Rowe correspondence; Stuck to Wood, July 28, 1910, Stuck correspondence.

87. Rowe to Kimber, August 4, 1910, Rowe correspondence.

88. Stuck diary, July 16, 1910.

89. Stuck diary, July 27, 1910.

90. Ehrlander's *Walter Harper, Alaska Native Son* relates the story of this remarkable young man's life.

91. Stuck diary, July 15, 1910; Rowe to Kimber, August 4, 1910.

92. C. Burke, *Doctor Hap*, 123–24.

93. C. Burke, *Doctor Hap*, 124–25.

94. C. Burke, *Doctor Hap*, 125–30.

95. Langdon, "Mission of Our Saviour," 59; Rowe to Wood, August 25, 1910, Rowe correspondence; Stuck diary, August 21, 1910.

96. Rowe to Wood, July 26, 1910, Rowe correspondence.

97. Carter, "St. John's-in-the-Wilderness," 61.

98. "The Woman's Auxiliary to the Board of Missions," 145.

3. SETTLING INTO MARRIED LIFE

1. C. Burke, *Doctor Hap*, 133. Clara translated the name as "Sutchah's young wife." The correct spelling for "my younger brother's woman" in Gwich'in is Shachaa vitr'injáa. The authors thank Hishinlai' Peter of the Alaska Native

Language Center for her assistance in clarifying the Gwich'in orthography in this book.

2. C. Burke, *Doctor Hap*, 134–36.
3. C. Burke, *Doctor Hap*, 136–37, 146.
4. Rowe, "Annual Report" (1907–8).
5. Rowe noted in early August that upon her marriage to Dr. Burke, Clara would "have to be dropped from our list of workers from and after Sept. 1st 1910." He wrote that he would marry the couple on August 6. Rowe to Kimber, August 4, 1910, Rowe correspondence.
6. Goddard, Alaska diary, 57, APRCA. In common terminology, Westerners distinguished between Indians and Eskimos in northern and western Alaska, just as they referred to Native Americans as Indians.
7. C. Burke, *Doctor Hap*, 148.
8. Stuck diary, November 17, 1910. This tradition of community members accompanying travelers for the first few miles of a journey continues in Alaska, although now people travel by snow machine, or snow scooter, in winter.
9. Jacobs, *A Schoolteacher in Old Alaska*, 174; Thomas, *An Angel on His Wing*, 202.
10. Stuck, *Voyages on the Yukon*, 40–41.
11. Jacobs, *A Schoolteacher in Old Alaska*, 172. The ethnologist Robert McKennan, who stayed two weeks in Fort Yukon in the summer of 1933, also noted this phenomenon (as have many others), including that the three stores in town opened, regardless of the hour, when the steamboat docked at Fort Yukon. Mischler, and Simeone. *Tanana and Chandalar*, 220.
12. Stuck, *Voyages on the Yukon*, 97–98. These passengers would have traveled north through the Inside Passage and taken the Yukon and White Pass Route railroad from Skagway to Whitehorse where they boarded a steamer.
13. Landon, "Glimpses of Life in Arctic Alaska," 262; McKennan, "Tanana," 567.
14. Stuck, *Voyages on the Yukon*, 96, 110–11; Stuck, "The Yukon Salmon," 317. During the summer, the dogs dug holes in the earth to escape the blistering heat and mosquitos.
15. Boulter to Brown, June 30, 1911, in Boulter and Grigor-Taylor, *The Teacher and the Superintendent*, 182. Natives resented incursions into their trapping territories by whites who used strychnine. A 1928 regulation strictly forbid the use of strychnine for trapping or even the possession of it by civilians. U.S. Department of Agriculture, "New Hunting and Trapping Regulations Issued for Alaska," press release, March 29, 1928, https://www.fws.gov/news/Historic/NewsReleases/1928/19280329.pdf.

16. Landon, "Glimpses of Life in Arctic Alaska," 62.

17. Boulter to Lopp, November 17, 1910, in Boulter and Grigor-Taylor, *The Teacher and the Superintendent*, 127.

18. C. Burke, *Doctor Hap*, 138–39, 145.

19. "Fort Yukon Notes" (May 1909), 23.

20. Rowe to Howard (n.d., placed between correspondence of August 23 and September 25, 1910), 15, and Rowe to Wood, July 26, 1910, Rowe correspondence; *Alaskan Churchman* 5 (November 1910): 16.

21. Jacobs, *A Schoolteacher in Old Alaska*, 176. When the infant Hannah Solomon arrived at Fort Yukon to be adopted by Mardow and Liza John, Clara supplied Liza with the items needed to care for her. St. Stephen's mission played a central role in Hannah's upbringing. Lee, "Hannah Solomon, Interior Alaska's Matriarch," Episcopal Diocese of Alaska website, September 20, 2011, http://www.episcopalak.org/dfc/newsdetail_2/2700007.

22. G. Burke to Stewart, Geoffrey Burke private collection; C. Burke, *Doctor Hap*, 167–69; G. Burke to Wood, December 2, 1921, Burke correspondence.

23. Burke to Rowe, February 28, 1921, Burke correspondence.

24. C. Burke, *Doctor Hap*, 147–48. Sadly, Hap could not save Lot from tuberculosis. He died a few years later.

25. Horace to Geoffrey Burke, Geoffrey Burke private collection; Douglas Fischer, "Remembrance of Things Past," *Fairbanks Daily News Miner*, October 17, 1999, 1.

26. C. Burke, *Doctor Hap*, 193, 259–60, 273–75.

27. C. Burke, *Doctor Hap*, 148 (quotation here), 167–69, 172, 226–27, 271–73; Thomas, *The Flying Bishop*, 202; Mackenzie, *Zhoh Gwatsan*, 97. Johnny's father, Old Fred, once took him away from Miss Wood's care when he was quite young to follow nearly a year of subsistence rounds with him. Johnny later described their experiences that year in detail, relating how very cold he was at times and how near starvation they were, subsisting on whatever ground squirrels they could find until Old Fred shot a large bull moose. McGary, *Stories Told by John Fredson*, 31–39. Johnny's father apparently only reluctantly left him at the mission the next fall.

28. We thank Grete Bergman of Fort Yukon and Fairbanks, a great-granddaughter of William and Julia Loola, whose grandmother Nina Loola was raised in St. Stephen's Mission Home, for her insight on the scope and depth of the mission's influence at Fort Yukon, both positive and negative.

29. Jacobs, *A Schoolteacher in Old Alaska*, 176. Woman's auxiliaries Outside sent boxes of used clothing and other useful items to St. Stephen's and other

missions, which Clara and other missionaries used to clothe children living in mission homes and to support community members in need.

30. Mackenzie, *Zhoh Gwatsan*, 18–19, 62.
31. Fortuine, *"Must We All Die?,"* 148–50.
32. Sniffen and Carrington, *The Indians of the Yukon and Tanana Valleys*, 31.
33. "Medical Nenana."
34. Langdon, "At the Mission of our Savior," 122.
35. C. Burke, *Doctor Hap*, 184.
36. Sniffen and Carrington, *The Indians of the Yukon and Tanana Valleys*, 11.
37. Fortuine, *"Must We All Die?,"* 198. See also Wallis, *Raising Ourselves*; and Napoleon, *Yuuyaraq*.
38. Boulter to Brown, June 30, 1911, in Boulter and Grigor-Taylor, *The Teacher and the Superintendent*, 184.
39. Sniffen and Carrington, *The Indians of the Yukon and Tanana Valleys*, 11; Fortuine, *"Must We All Die?,"* xxii.
40. C. Burke, *Doctor Hap*, 152, 157–60, 164; Mackenzie, *Zhoh Gwatsan*, 19–20.
41. Sniffen and Carrington, *The Indians of the Yukon and Tanana Valleys*, 31; C. Burke, *Doctor Hap*, 164.
42. Rowe, "Report of the Bishop of the Missionary District," 57.
43. Stuck, *Voyages on the Yukon*, 145; Stuck to Wood, December 28, 1910, Stuck correspondence.
44. Stuck diary, December 22, 1910.
45. Boulter to Lopp, "Report on the U.S. School at Tanana," in Boulter and Grigor-Taylor, *The Teacher and the Superintendent*, 149.
46. C. Burke, *Doctor Hap*, 150–52.
47. C. Burke, *Doctor Hap*, 152–55; Mackenzie, *Zhoh Gwatsan*, 16–18.
48. C. Burke, *Doctor Hap*, 155.
49. Stuck to Wood, July 28, 1910, Stuck correspondence; Wood to Rowe, July 6, 1918, Rowe correspondence. In March 1909, while at Hot Springs, Stuck had noted his annoyance at a piece in the "preposterous little sheet" the *Hot Springs Echo*, edited by a "drunken scamp" from Tanana. The article claimed that Stuck traded in furs and wanted the Natives "to have Rampart" so he could handle their furs, cutting out merchants (Stuck diary, March 10, 1909). Bishop Rowe forbade Episcopal mission workers from accepting furs as gifts from Natives, to avoid accusations of self-interest. Clara had been permitted an exception to the rule when Little Miss Heintz's mother gave her a beautiful white fox fur as a wedding gift. C. Burke, *Doctor Hap*, 130.
50. Dean, *Breaking Trail*, 171.

51. Dean, *Breaking Trail*, 184.

52. C. Burke, *Doctor Hap*, 169–70.

53. Boulter to Claxton, "Annual Report to Claxton 1912–1913," in Boulter and Grigor-Taylor, *The Teacher and the Superintendent*, 235–37 (quotation on 236).

54. C. Burke, *Doctor Hap*, 148.

55. C. Burke, *Doctor Hap*, 172.

56. C. Burke, *Doctor Hap*, 173–75.

57. C. Burke, *Doctor Hap*, 176. Clara spelled the nickname Ghee Hee Tsul. We thank Dr. Hishinlai' Peter for the correct spelling of Little Reverend.

58. Some family members believe that the boys' being sent away to school at such tender ages had lifelong negative consequences for Hudson and Grafton Burke.

59. G. Burke, "The Smallpox Situation," 99–101; Stuck, "Along Alaska's Great River," 642–44; Stuck diary, August 26, 1911; "Vaccinating the Indians"; Boulter to Lopp, October 26, 1912, in Boulter and Grigor-Taylor, *The Teacher and the Superintendent*, 210–15; "Notes from Anvik"; G. Burke, "Epidemic of Smallpox in Alaska," 803–4.

60. Stuck, *Ten Thousand Miles with a Dog Sled*, 23.

61. Jacobs, *A Schoolteacher in Old Alaska*, 174.

62. Stuck to Boulter, December 3, 1911, in Boulter and Grigor-Taylor, *The Teacher and the Superintendent*, 195–96.

63. Stuck to Boulter, December 3, 1911.

64. Boulter to Stuck, December 14, 1911, in Boulter and Grigor-Taylor, *The Teacher and the Superintendent*, 197.

65. Lopp to Boulter, February 6, 1912, in Boulter and Grigor-Taylor, *The Teacher and the Superintendent*, 197.

66. Lopp to Stuck, July 10, 1912, in Boulter and Grigor-Taylor, *The Teacher and the Superintendent*, 199.

67. Claxton to Stuck, August 9, 1912, in Boulter and Grigor-Taylor, *The Teacher and the Superintendent*, 199.

68. In 1913 Boulter reported to Claxton that the church aimed to build schools on their mission sites to avoid government oversight, and he therefore recommended that the bureau gradually close its schools along the Yukon River. Boulter, excerpt of 1912–13 annual report, in Boulter and Grigor-Taylor, *The Teacher and the Superintendent*, 237. Boulter's granddaughter, Barbara Grigor-Taylor, asserted that "it became Archdeacon Hudson Stuck's goal to build Episcopal missions and schools at remote, isolated locations on the Upper Yukon, where the church would educate and minister to the Alaska Natives

without government interference." Boulter and Grigor-Taylor, *The Teacher and the Superintendent*, 31. Stuck had often expressed his preference for building missions remote from the Yukon River, not to avoid the Bureau of Education's authority but to protect the people from diseases and to encourage them to reject harmful mainstream American norms and maintain their traditional lifeways. Stuck, "Along Alaska's Great River," 639; Stuck diary, January 3, 1910.

69. C. Burke, *Doctor Hap*, 166–67; Dean, *Breaking Trail*, 195.
70. C. Burke, *Doctor Hap*, 167.
71. Stuck, "The White Menace on the Yukon," 189.

4. HAP'S TERM AS COMMISSIONER

1. Stuck diary, June 6, 1911. Circle and Circle City were used interchangeably as names for the settlement.
2. Sniffen and Carrington, *The Indians of the Yukon and Tanana Valleys*, 10.
3. Stuck, "The White Menace on the Yukon," 189.
4. Rowe, "Annual Report" (1907–8), 49.
5. Boulter to Hoggatt, November 14, 1908, in Boulter Grigor-Taylor, *The Teacher and the Superintendent*, 67–68.
6. Hoggatt, *Report of the Governor* (1907), 12.
7. Hoggatt, *Report of the Governor* (1908), 15.
8. Strong, *Report of the Governor* (1914), 37.
9. Stuck, "The White Menace," 189.
10. Ehrlander, "The Paradox of Alaska's 1916 Alcohol Referendum," 29–42; Boulter to Hoggatt, November 14, 1908.
11. Dean, *Breaking Trail*, 192; Boulter to Hoggatt, November 14, 1908. Boulter wrote that he had known Natives who were "fully aware of the offences of certain men and yet, when in the witness box, they would swear to having no knowledge of them."
12. Dean, *Breaking Trail*, 194; Stuck, "The White Menace," 190.
13. Boulter to Hoggatt, November 14, 1908.
14. Stuck, "The White Menace," 190.
15. Stuck, "The White Menace," 191. In this article published in 1914, Stuck wrote that for the past five years, deaths among Alaska Natives had surpassed births at every Episcopal mission on the Yukon River.
16. Dean, *Breaking Trail*, 193; Davis, *We Are Alaskans*, 134, 152.
17. Stuck, "The White Menace," 188.
18. Sniffen and Carrington, *The Indians of the Yukon and Tanana Valleys*, 6.
19. Stuck, "The White Menace," 188.

20. Boulter to Lopp, April 29, 1913, in Boulter and Grigor-Taylor, *The Teacher and the Superintendent*, 227–29.

21. Dean, *Breaking Trail*, 193. Clara wrote that Bishop Rowe convinced Hap and the federal judge.

22. Folder 1: Justice Court in and for Ft. Yukon Precinct, 4th Division of Alaska, Grafton Burke, JP–1911–1929, Fort Yukon Precinct Justice Court Records, APRCA.

23. C. Burke, *Doctor Hap*, 192–93.

24. C. Burke, *Doctor Hap*, 182–83.

25. Jacobs, *A Schoolteacher in Old Alaska*, 171.

26. Jacobs, *A Schoolteacher in Old Alaska*, vi, x–xi. After leaving Alaska, Breece continued to teach for many years. In her retirement in the 1930s, she wrote the manuscript for her memoir based on letters to family members and friends. Breece, who died in 1940, had hoped to publish the manuscript during her lifetime. It was not until about fifty years later that her grandniece, Jane Jacobs, revisited the manuscript and conducted substantial research to contextualize Breece's experience and fill in the many gaps that her letters left in the narrative (xiv–xvi).

27. Jacobs, *A Schoolteacher in Old Alaska*, 177.

28. Boulter to Lopp, April 29, 1913, in Boulter and Grigor-Taylor, *The Teacher and the Superintendent*, 229.

29. Jacobs, *A Schoolteacher in Old Alaska*, 230.

30. Boulter to Lopp, April 29, 1913, and Boulter to Lopp, August 18, 1913, in Boulter and Grigor-Taylor, *The Teacher and the Superintendent*, 227 and 242, respectively.

31. Stuck to Lopp and Claxton, November 14, 1912, in Boulter and Grigor-Taylor, *The Teacher and the Superintendent*, 219.

32. Stuck to Lopp and Claxton, November 14, 1912, 220–21.

33. Claxton to Stuck, December 30, 1912, in Boulter and Grigor-Taylor, *The Teacher and the Superintendent*, 221.

34. Lopp to Breece, December 31, 1912, in Boulter and Grigor-Taylor, *The Teacher and the Superintendent*, 222.

35. Boulter to Lopp, April 29, 1913, in Boulter and Grigor-Taylor, *The Teacher and the Superintendent*, 227.

36. Dean, *Breaking Trail*, 196, 212; Stuck diary, January 15, 1913, American Geographic Society.

37. Stuck, "The White Menace," 191.

38. The previous fall, Karstens had cached one and a half tons of supplies at Diamond City at the headwaters of the Kantishna River, as close to the base of the mountain as possible. The team gathered those supplies and met with members of the Sourdough Expedition that had summited the lesser, north peak of Denali in 1910. These men provided invaluable advice to the 1913 Denali Expedition, including the location of a pass that allowed access to the higher reaches of the mountain.

39. The year before, an expedition that almost reached the summit had traversed the ridge in two days, shortly before a massive earthquake generated an avalanche that buried the route. The 1913 ascent team realized afterward that a massive earthquake the summer before had caused an avalanche that buried the ridge in snow and ice boulders.

40. Several books recount the 1913 pioneering ascent of Denali, including Stuck, *The Ascent of Denali*; Walker, *The Seventymile Kid*; Ehrlander, *Walter Harper*; and Dean, *A Window to Heaven*.

41. Carroll, *The First Ten Years in Alaska*, 57; "Communication," Stuck to *Fairbanks Sunday Times*, April 5, 1914; "Stuck's Slander," *Fairbanks Sunday Times*, April 5, 1914; "Stuck on Stuck," *Fairbanks Daily News Miner*, April 6, 1914.

42. C. Burke, *Doctor Hap*, 196; Boulter to Lopp, April 29, 1913, in Boulter and Grigor-Taylor, *The Teacher and the Superintendent*, 227. Clara later recalled this incident as having occurred in late winter or early spring of 1914, after the December 1913 trial in Fairbanks of several lawbreakers, but Boulter reported the incident in April 1913.

43. Stuck, "The White Menace," 190. Section 2001 of the criminal code for Alaska made cohabiting "with another in a state of adultery or fornication" illegal and prescribed a fine of "not more than five hundred dollars or imprison[ment] in the penitentiary not more than two years, or both." U.S. Congress, *The Compiled Laws of the Territory of Alaska 1913*.

44. Drane diary, Summer 1922.

45. Dean, *Breaking Trail*, 196.

46. Stuck, "The White Menace," 190; Dean, *Breaking Trail*, 196.

47. Jacobs, *A Schoolteacher in Old Alaska*, 178; Stuck, "The White Menace," 190; Dean, *Breaking Trail*, 196.

48. This was the council that the Gwich'in of Fort Yukon had established at Hudson Stuck's encouragement.

49. Boulter to Lopp, August 18, 1913.

50. Boulter to Lopp, September 27, 1913, in Boulter and Grigor-Taylor, *The Teacher and the Superintendent*, 245.

51. Carroll, *The First Ten Years in Alaska*, 58.

52. Rowe, "Annual Report" (1914–15), 34–35; Stuck, "Six Years at Fort Yukon," 192.

53. Stuck, "A Loss to the Yukon," 613.

54. Stuck, "Six Years at Fort Yukon," 192.

55. Drane, "Swinging the Circuit," 503.

56. Jacobs, *A Schoolteacher in Old Alaska*, 180–83 (quotation on 182); Boulter to Lopp, December 10, 1913, in Boulter and Grigor-Taylor, *The Teacher and the Superintendent*, 249.

57. Jacobs, *A Schoolteacher in Old Alaska*, 182–83.

58. Carroll, *The First Ten Years in Alaska*, 60; Jacobs, *A Schoolteacher in Old Alaska*, 183.

59. Dean, *Breaking Trail*, 196–97.

60. Jacobs, *A Schoolteacher in Old Alaska*, 183.

61. "Grand Jury Reports Again, Find Not a 'True Bill' in Two Cases for Selling Liquor," *Fairbanks Daily News Miner*, December 9, 1913.

62. Stuck, "The White Menace," 190.

63. "Deliberated Seven Minutes: Jury in Horton Case Brought Verdict for Defendant," *Fairbanks Daily News Miner*, December 22, 1913.

64. "Horton Case Is Now on Trial," *Fairbanks Daily News Miner*, December 18, 1913.

65. "Defendant on Stand Today," *Fairbanks Daily News Miner*, December 20, 1913.

66. "Defense Has Stand Today," *Fairbanks Daily News Miner*, December 19, 1913.

67. "Defendant on Stand Today," *Fairbanks Daily News Miner*, December 20, 1913.

68. Carroll, *The First Ten Years in Alaska*, 58; Boulter to Lopp, December 16, 1913, in Boulter and Grigor-Taylor, *The Teacher and the Superintendent*, 253–54.

69. "Defense Has Stand Today," *Fairbanks Daily News Miner*, December 19, 1913.

70. Boulter to Lopp, December 24, 1913, in Boulter and Grigor-Taylor, *The Teacher and the Superintendent*, 255.

71. "Deliberated Seven Minutes: Jury in Horton Case Brought Verdict for Defendant," *Fairbanks Daily News Miner*, December 22, 1913.

72. Jacobs, *A Schoolteacher in Old Alaska*, 232–33.

73. "Prosecution to Close Soon," *Fairbanks Daily News Miner*, December 22, 1913.

74. "Prosecution to Close Soon"; "Case Will Go to Jury Soon," *Fairbanks Daily News Miner*, December 24, 1913; "M'Cambridge Is Acquitted: Jury Brought Verdict of Not Guilty in Cohabitation Case," *Fairbanks Daily News Miner*, December 26, 1913.

75. Boulter to Lopp, December 24, 1913, in Boulter and Grigor-Taylor, *The Teacher and the Superintendent*, 255.

76. Sniffen and Carrington, *The Indians of the Yukon and Tanana Valleys*, 9.

77. Boulter to Lopp, December 16, 1913, in Boulter and Grigor-Taylor, *The Teacher and the Superintendent*, 256.

78. Sniffen and Carrington, *The Indians of the Yukon and Tanana Valleys*, 9.

79. Boulter to Updegraff, August 20, 1909, in Boulter and Grigor-Taylor, *The Teacher and the Superintendent*, 91–92.

80. Dean, *Breaking Trail*, 196–97. According to Dollar Times, $20,000 in 1914 would be worth $520,948 in December 2021. Accessed December 21, 2021, https://www.dollartimes.com/inflation/inflation.php?amount=20000&year=1914.

81. Boulter to Lopp, December 17, 1913, in Boulter and Grigor-Taylor, *The Teacher and the Superintendent*, 253–54.

82. Dean, *Breaking Trail*, 192, 196.

83. Dean, *Breaking Trail*, 196.

84. Carroll, *The First Ten Years in Alaska*, 45. Carroll wrote that Lizzie White died in 1916, but she died in 1920.

85. C. Burke, *Doctor Hap*, 189–190; Dean, *Breaking Trail*, 197.

86. Carroll, *The First Ten Years in Alaska*, 65.

87. Crossley to Lopp, July 17, 1914, in Jacobs, *A Schoolteacher in Old Alaska*, 234–35 (quotation on 235). Crossley noted that Wonecoff was a former pastor in both the Episcopal and Methodist churches.

88. Dean, *Breaking Trail*, 198.

89. U.S. v. Cadzow, 5 Ak. Rpts, 124 (D.C. Ak 1914).

90. Claxton to Lane, April 17, 1914, in Boulter and Grigor-Taylor, *The Teacher and the Superintendent*, 257.

91. "Communication," Stuck to *Fairbanks Sunday Times*; "Stuck's Slander"; "Stuck on Stuck."

92. Sniffen and Carrington, *The Indians of the Yukon and Tanana Valleys*, 7–8.

93. Dean, *Breaking Trail*, 198; Stuck, "Six Years at Fort Yukon," 192.

94. C. Burke, *Doctor Hap*, 201; Mackenzie, *Zhoh Gwatsan*, 59.

95. C. Burke, *Doctor Hap*, 202.

96. C. Burke, *Doctor Hap*, 202–4; Mackenzie, *Zhoh Gwatsan*, 62.

97. Stuck, "Six Years at Fort Yukon," 192.

98. C. Burke, *Doctor Hap*, 204.

99. Dean, *Breaking Trail*, 205.

100. Sniffen, and Carrington, *The Indians of the Yukon and Tanana Valleys*, 10. Stuck hoped that their report would convince mission friends of various denominations to support the construction and operation of hospitals and dispensaries in the region. Dean, *Breaking Trail*, 205.

101. Carrington wrote a separate, special report on medical conditions. Sniffen and Carrington, *The Indians of the Yukon and Tanana Valleys*, 24–25.

102. Sniffen and Carrington, *The Indians of the Yukon and Tanana Valleys*, 7.

103. Sniffen and Carrington, *The Indians of the Yukon and Tanana Valleys*, 9–10.

104. Sniffen and Carrington, *The Indians of the Yukon and Tanana Valleys*, 10.

105. Sniffen and Carrington, *The Indians of the Yukon and Tanana Valleys*, 9.

106. Sniffen and Carrington, *The Indians of the Yukon and Tanana Valleys*, 11. Sniffen and Carrington had assisted in the man's apprehension and detention prior to his trial in Fort Yukon. At the time, insanity was determined through trial, and if found guilty, the person was institutionalized.

107. Sniffen and Carrington, *The Indians of the Yukon and Tanana Valleys*, 8–9; Carroll, *The First Ten Years in Alaska*, 60–61.

108. "Long Memories of Good," *Fairbanks Daily News Miner*, October 17, 1999.

109. C. Burke, *Doctor Hap*, 206.

110. Stuck, "Six Years at Fort Yukon," 190.

111. C. Burke, *Doctor Hap*, 205.

112. Dean, *Breaking Trail*, 197; Stefansson to Ross, July 17, 1918 (from Fort Yukon), Burke correspondence.

113. Sniffen and Carrington noted that all the Protestant missions they visited in the Interior were understaffed and personnel were underpaid. *The Indians of the Yukon and Tanana Valleys*, 12.

114. Sniffen and Carrington, *The Indians of the Yukon and Tanana Valleys*, 9.

115. Rowe, "Annual Report" (1914–15), 34–35.

116. Sniffen and Carrington, *The Indians of the Yukon and Tanana Valleys*, 9.

117. Dean, *Breaking Trail*, 197. Note, the doctor was Edwin R. F. Murphy of Milwaukee. "Our New Recruits."

118. Rowe to White, October 3, 1921, Rowe correspondence.

119. Lloyd to G. Burke, September 15, 1917, Burke correspondence.

120. Carroll, *The First Ten Years in Alaska*, 61. James Carroll and his wife, Fanny, eventually had twelve children. James owned and operated a trading post for some years, but he continued to hunt and trap. Many of the Carrolls' progeny remained in the northern interior and continued the family tradition of trapping. The Alaska Trappers' Association website notes: "The Carroll family has played a prominent role in [Fort Yukon] for the past hundred years." Accessed September 3, 2022, https://www.alaskatrappers.org/bio _sketch_richard_carroll.html.
121. See Ehrlander, "The Paradox of Alaska's 1916 Alcohol Referendum," 29–42.
122. C. Burke, *Doctor Hap*, 168–69.

5. OPENING ST. STEPHEN'S HOSPITAL

1. C. Burke, *Doctor Hap*, 210; "Announcements Concerning the Missionaries, Alaska."
2. C. Burke, *Doctor Hap*, 208.
3. Bradner, *A 1916 Alaskan Diary*, 42.
4. At Nulato, just over five hundred miles downstream from Fort Yukon, Alaska Natives could find hospital care at a government-funded makeshift hospital.
5. Stuck, "The Arctic Hospital," 37–38. The Episcopal Mission Society had allocated funds and built a hospital at Tanana as well, but it was never able to staff the hospital with a doctor or full complement of nurses. It operated at a minimal level from 1916 to 1918 with one nurse and a matron and with the physician from Fort Gibbon performing an operation there from time to time. With no prospect of being able to staff the hospital with a doctor, the church closed the hospital. Drane diary, 1921.
6. Carter, "Founding of St. Matthew's Hospital," 8–10; C. Burke, *Doctor Hap*, 220.
7. Jenkins, *The Man of Alaska*, 108.
8. In 1917 Stuck wrote a long letter to his friend John Wood at mission head-quarters in New York, one of many in which he beseeched him for financial support for the essential, life-saving work being done at St. Stephen's. Stuck to Wood, April 13, 1917, Stuck correspondence.
9. C. Burke to Wood, April 4, 1918, Burke correspondence.
10. Stuck, "Our Hospitals in the Arctic Regions," 178–80.
11. Bradner, *A 1916 Alaskan Diary*, 49.
12. Bradner, *A 1916 Alaskan Diary*, 45, 47.
13. Stuck diary, August 6, 1916.
14. Biographical note in William A. Thomas Collection, APRCA.

15. Thomas diary, August 6–14, 1916 (quotation on August 9), APRCA.

16. Thomas diary, August 6–14, 1916 (quotation on August 7).

17. Thomas diary, September 10, 17, 1916; Drane, "From Cheechako to Archdeacon," 68–70.

18. Alton, *Alaska in the Progressive Age*, 202–3.

19. Alton, *Alaska in the Progressive Age*, 211–12; Bradner, *A 1916 Alaskan Diary*, 61; Drane, "From Cheechako to Archdeacon," 70.

20. They are called the Tanana River Chiefs, but they represented other rivers: the Yukon, the Tolovana, the Salcha, and indirectly the Nowitna.

21. Alton, *Alaska in the Progressive Age*, 214–15, 218 (quotation on 218).

22. Alton, *Alaska in the Progressive Age*, 218–19, citing proceedings of a council held in the library room at Fairbanks, Alaska, on July 5, 1915. Alaska Digital Archives, vilda.alaska.edu.

23. Rowe to Wood, September 19, 1919, and "Statement Touching St. Mark's Mission," September 17, 1920 (year not certain), Rowe correspondence, APRCA; Bradner, *A 1916 Alaskan Diary*, 61–62 (quotations on both pages).

24. Dean, *Breaking Trail*, 223–24; Mackenzie, *Zhoh Gwatsan*, 62, 81, 84; Henry to Stuck September 21, 1920, Stuck correspondence. Later, other family members adopted the name Fredson.

25. C. Burke, *Doctor Hap*, 224.

26. Stuck to Lloyd, January 16, 1919, Stuck correspondence.

27. Hartley, *A Woman Set Apart*, 121–22; C. Burke, *Doctor Hap*, 223–24.

28. Stuck diary, October 6, 10, 1916.

29. Stuck diary, October 31, 1916.

30. Stuck, "The Arctic Hospital," 41; G. Burke, Letter (December 31, 1916), "Our Letter Box," 281; Stuck, "St. Stephen's Hospital," 76.

31. Stuck to Wood, October 6, 1917, Stuck correspondence. Stuck and Burke had paid his salary for the previous months.

32. Wood to Burke, November 21, 1917, Burke correspondence.

33. Stuck diary, October 19, 1916; Boulter noted that Frank White owned a sawmill. Boulter to Lopp, August 18, 1913, in Boulter and Grigor-Taylor, *The Teacher and the Superintendent*, 242.

34. We found no record of how cold the ward was, but it could not have been extremely cold. Patients with other ailments and injuries were housed in warm wards.

35. Ultraviolet light, both natural sunlight and from lamps, destroys the tubercle bacillus. Fortuine, *"Must We All Die?,"* xiii.

36. G. Burke, Letter (December 31, 1916), "Our Letter Box," 281.

37. "Hudson Stuck Memorial Hospital, Fort Yukon, Alaska," October 1943, RG 351, box 13, folder 5, Grafton Burke 1908–1937, PECUSA.

38. Stuck diary, November 30 and December 1, 2, 4, 1916. The region experienced a prolonged cold siege early that winter, with weeks of −55°F to −60°F weather or colder. Stuck diary, December 10, 1916.

39. "Notes" (November 1916), 7.

40. Stuck to Drane, November 17, 1916, Drane correspondence, PECUSA; G. Burke to Wood, February 19, 1917, Burke correspondence.

41. G. Burke, Letter (December 31, 1916), "Our Letter Box," 281.

42. M. Wood to C. Burke, September 5, 1918, Burke correspondence.

43. Evans, *The Social Gospel in American Religion*, 135–36. Chapter 5 in the book addresses the transition from the classical Social Gospel movement to a more "radical" interwar movement that linked economic justice to racism, civil liberties, pacifism, and international cooperation (135–63).

44. Hitchings to Rowe, October 18, 1918, Rowe correspondence.

45. Rowe to Wood, January 21, 1920, Rowe correspondence.

46. C. Burke, *Doctor Hap*, 213; extract of letter written by G. Burke, sent to Bishop Rowe, October 27, 1920, Rowe correspondence; Wood, memo for Mr. Henry, December 29, 1920, and response by Henry, December 30, 1920, Rowe correspondence; Stuck to Wood, September 28, 1916, Stuck correspondence; Rowe to Wood, December 26, 1917, Rowe correspondence. Florence Langdon, who left Alaska in 1919 after serving Episcopal missions for fourteen years, reportedly "was ever on the verge of nervous prostration which had something to do with her inability to work well with others" (Rowe to Wood, January 18, 1920, Rowe correspondence).

47. G. Burke to Wood, February 19, 1917 (quotation herein), and G. Burke to Lloyd, February 19, 1917, Burke correspondence.

48. Stuck diary December 10, 12, 1916 (quotation on December 12).

49. Stuck to Wood, February 27, 1917, Stuck correspondence.

50. G. Burke to Wood, February 19, 1917, Burke correspondence; G. Burke, Letter (June 24, 1917), "Our Letter Box," 703; C. Burke to Miss Lindley, September 8, 1917, Burke correspondence.

51. C. Burke, "Children of the Arctic Circle," 109–10.

52. Douglas Fischer, "Remembrance of Things Past," *Fairbanks Daily News Miner*, October 17, 1999; Hudson Stuck Burke Jr., interview by Mary Ehrlander, October 25, 2021, Seattle; telephone interview with Fairbanks journalist Diana Campbell, who interviewed Hudson before his 1999 visit to Alaska, December 13, 2021.

53. Diana Campbell (journalist), telephone conversation with Mary Ehrlander, January 26, 2022.

54. C. Burke, *Doctor Hap*, 215–16. Donations of clothing and other items from woman's auxiliaries Outside and contributions of wild game from village hunters allowed her to manage the household with the modest funding the Episcopal Mission Board allocated.

55. Stuck to Wood, April 13, 1917, Stuck correspondence; C. Burke, *Doctor Hap*, 222.

56. Wood to Stuck, April 10, 1918, Stuck correspondence.

57. Dean, *Breaking Trail*, 18. In 1916 or 1917 the government school had to be torn down and moved to save it from the river (Rowe to Wood, August 20, 1923, RG 351, box 13, folder 5, Grafton Burke 1908–1937, PECUSA).

58. "In Memorium"; Stuck to Drane, September 29, 1917, Drane correspondence.

59. F. Wells to J. Wells, February 23, 1917, and May 11, 1917, Wells clan website, http://wellsclan.us/History/frances/Frances.htm.

60. F. Wells to All, July 15, 1917, Wells clan website.

61. Stuck to Lloyd, July 3, 1917, Stuck correspondence.

62. Wood to Stuck, July 10, 1918, Stuck correspondence.

63. Stuck, "With the Foreign Secretary in Alaska," 19; Stuck, "Along Alaska's Great River," 641.

64. Cruikshank, *The Life I've Been Living*, 26–27.

65. Stuck, "With the Foreign Secretary in Alaska," 21–22, 26–28; Wood to Stuck, March 26, 1917, Stuck correspondence. At a camp on the Koyukuk River, when the parents of three boys being baptized insisted that Stuck choose their Christian names, as was not uncommon, he baptized them John (after the foreign secretary), Benjamin (after Reverend Chambers), and Walter (after Harper).

66. Stuck to Drane, September 29, 1917 (a postscript containing the cited quotation is dated October 1), Drane correspondence. Hap and Clara saw Dr. Smith at Fort Gibbon near Tanana, not at Nenana.

67. Stuck to Wood, October 13, 1917, Stuck correspondence.

68. Stuck to Wood, October 13, 1917. Clara recounted in her memoir that she developed a fever, which led Hap to suspect that she had retained part of the placenta. He performed "minor surgery," likely to remove the placenta, but when her fever continued to rise, Hap suspected the "dread postpartum septicemia," or blood poisoning. In the end, it seems that mastitis, an infected milk duct, had caused her high fever. C. Burke, *Doctor Hap*, 224.

69. G. Burke to Wood, October 9, 1917, Burke correspondence; Stuck diary, October 15, 1917.

70. C. Burke, *Doctor Hap*, 224–25 (quotations on 225).

71. C. Burke, *Doctor Hap*, 225–26 (quotations on 225); Stuck diary, September 13, 1917.

72. G. Burke to Wood, October 30, 1917, and Wood to G. Burke, May 2, 1918, Burke correspondence. The emergency travel and care for Clara had cost $297, which the mission board paid, to Hap's great relief, as he was "hardly in the position to do [so]." Burke to Wood, October 30, 1917, Burke correspondence.

73. G. Burke to Wood, October 30, 1917.

74. Stuck, "St. Stephen's Hospital," 76; C. Burke to Lindley, September 8, 1917, Burke correspondence.

75. Many people died of typhoid fever in Alaska. Former superintendent of schools George Boulter (he was no longer superintendent but the teacher in charge at Tanana) contracted typhoid in April 1916. He relapsed in fall 1917 and died in October. Boulter to Lopp, April 16, 1916, and Sinclaire to Lopp, October 28, 1917, in Boulter and Grigor-Taylor, *The Teacher and the Superintendent*, 272, 280.

76. C. Burke, *Doctor Hap*, 226; Fortuine, *Chills and Fever*, 173; Waller, *The Discovery of the Germ*, chapter 16.

77. Stuck to Wood, November 24, 1917, Stuck correspondence.

78. On the trail, Stuck had been corresponding with associates on the East Coast about potential schools for Walter to take premedical courses in preparation for medical school. Rev. Benjamin Duvall Chambers, who had visited together with John Wood in summer 1917, found a premedical school that likely would offer a scholarship and that would prepare Walter well for acceptance into the University of Maryland's School of Medicine, where he also likely could attend on scholarship (Fell to Chambers, March 14, 1918, and Wood to Stuck, March 20, 1918, Stuck correspondence).

79. "News and Notes" (May 1918), 342.

80. Stefansson, *Discovery*, 210; Stuck to Wood, May 18, 1918, Stuck correspondence.

81. Stuck diary, April 24, 25, 1918.

82. Stefansson, *The Friendly Arctic*, 686–87.

83. Hrdlička apparently did studies on both living people and human remains during this visit. The spring flood had disturbed the Native graveyard, leaving numerous exposed skulls and other bones, which he examined "lovingly," to

compare with his data on Siberian peoples to confirm his theory that Alaska Native peoples had originated in Asia. C. Burke, *Doctor Hap*, 231. In 1929 Hap submitted to the Smithsonian a set of human remains that Hrdlička had removed from the village of Old Nulato. After passage of the Native American Graves Protection and Repatriation Act of 1990, this set of remains was returned in 2005 to the village of Nulato. Smithsonian Institution, National Museum of Natural History Repatriation Office Case Report Summaries Alaska Region, Revised 2020, https://naturalhistory.si.edu/sites/default /files/media/file/case-reports-alaska-region-rev2-2020.pdf. Hrdlička, who is deemed the father of physical anthropology in the United States, became a reviled figure in various regions of Alaska. In the 1930s he removed thousands of skulls and other remains from burial grounds in Alaska without the permission of community members and shipped them to the Smithsonian, where he was curator of physical anthropology. In particular, he did extensive work on Kodiak Island and in the Unangax̂ region. Hrdlička was brilliant and reportedly charming and likable, even with Alaska Natives but insensitive to their feelings and wishes when excavating burial sites. Veltre and May, *Diaries of Archaeological Expeditions*, 21.

84. Hartley, *A Woman Set Apart*, 159–61; C. Burke, *Doctor Hap*, 230–32.

85. Stuck to Wood, May 15, 1918, Stuck correspondence.

86. V. L. Stump, "Comments and Items of Interest: Too Much Time in Prayer," *Evangelical Visitor*, August 13, 1934, 1124, https://mosaic.messiah.edu /evanvisitor/1124. Stefansson later met with Bishop Rowe and reportedly repeated his criticism of missionaries and his firm belief that the Iñupiat would be much better off without any contact with missionaries, deeply offending Rowe. Rowe to Roper, October 28, 1918, Rowe correspondence.

87. C. Burke, *Doctor Hap*, 221.

88. C. Burke, *Doctor Hap*, 232.

89. C. Burke, *Doctor Hap*, 231.

90. C. Burke to Lindley, September 8, 1917, and Wood to C. Burke, November 7, 1917, Burke correspondence; Wood to Rowe, March 31, 1918, Rowe correspondence.

91. C. Burke, *Doctor Hap*, 233–34.

92. Wood to G. Burke, April 6, 1918, and Wood to G. Burke, April 16, 1918, Burke correspondence. Necessary on-site adaptations to building materials and the need to purchase some building materials locally increased the cost substantially. Stuck to Lloyd, November 16, 1918, Stuck correspondence.

93. Stuck to Lloyd, November 26, 1918, Stuck correspondence.

94. Wood to Rowe, December 29, 1917, August 12, 1918, and August 17, 1918, Rowe correspondence.
95. Stuck, "A Loss to the Yukon," 611–13 (quotation on all three pages).
96. Stuck, "A Loss to the Yukon," 613; Rowe to Wood, June 29, 1918, Rowe correspondence.
97. Wood to Rowe, July 19, 1918, and Wood to Rowe, August 5, 1918, Rowe correspondence; Grete Bergman, great-granddaughter of William and Julia Loola, email to Ehrlander, January 23, 2022. Rowe recommended that Loola's salary of $300 be divided among four Native catechists to support the mission work among the Natives. Rowe to Wood, June 29, 1918, Rowe correspondence.
98. C. Burke, *Doctor Hap*, 232.
99. Mackenzie, *Zhoh Gwatsan*, 92–93.
100. Drane diary, March 1921.
101. Stuck to Wood, May 18, 1918, Stuck correspondence.
102. Rowe to Wood, June 29, 1918, and Domestic Alaska, Subject: Additional appropriation requested for David Wallis, Indian interpreter, July 2, 1918, Rowe correspondence. In his budget request for 1921, Rowe requested $500 in salary for Wallis. Rowe to Wood, September 21, 1920, Rowe correspondence.
103. Lizzie White and other friends decorated the church. Stuck diary, September 4, 1918.
104. On August 10, 1918, the day Walter and Frances left Fort Yukon to travel Outside, a telegram arrived at Fort Yukon announcing an imminent armistice. Thus, the couple left Alaska lighthearted and looking forward to Walter's taking university courses in preparation for medical school. See Ehrlander, *Walter Harper, Alaska Native Son*, for the story of Harper's life; chapter 6 recounts Harper and Stuck's notable winter circuit of 1917–18. Walter and Frances were buried in Juneau, where the recovery operations centered. Stuck chose the words for their gravestone: "Here Lie the Bodies of Walter Harper and Frances Wells, His Wife, Drowned on the Princess Sophia, 25th October 1918. May Light Perpetually Shine on Them. They Were Lovely and Pleasant in Their Lives, and in Death They Were Not Divided."
105. Stuck diary, October 26, 1918.
106. Stuck to Drane, October 31, 1918, Drane correspondence.
107. Stuck to Lloyd, February 1, 1919, Stuck correspondence.
108. Drane, "The Death of Archdeacon Stuck," 3–5.
109. Stuck to Lloyd, December 30, 1918, with postscript dated December 31, Stuck correspondence; Stuck, *A Winter Circuit*.
110. Stuck to Lloyd, December 30, 1918.

111. Stuck to Lloyd, December 30, 1918.

112. G. Burke to Wood, March 25, 1931, Burke correspondence.

113. Hartley, *A Woman Set Apart*, 163–73. We could find no indication in Harriett Bedell's correspondence file of Ida's eventual fate. The 1920 census for the Circle-Yukon-Koyukuk census area shows an Indian girl of ten, Ida Behn, whose widowed father was Hans Behn, who was born in Germany. This may be the child in this story, in which case she was alive when the census was taken.

114. Rowe, "Second Joint Session of the Missionary Story," 763.

115. The Episcopal Church, through its missionaries, fought relentlessly to defend traditional Alaska Native lifeways and to save Alaska Native lives during these early decades of the twentieth century. In July 1912 Episcopal mission personnel had met in a five-day convocation at Anvik on the lower Yukon. In response to rumors of plans for the opening of a cannery on the lower Yukon, attendees unanimously passed a resolution expressing their "solemn protest against any such enterprise" and urging legislation to prohibit canneries. The resolution cited the people's dependence on salmon and the absence of a "superabundance" beyond residents' needs. The success of one cannery would surely lead to others, the resolution noted, creating a "menace to the whole Native population of Interior Alaska" ("Convocation of Alaskan Workers," 120). Despite this and other objections, canneries opened at the mouth of the Yukon, and harvests of salmon dwindled in subsequent years.

116. *Spirit of Missions* 84, no. 12 (December 1919): frontispiece; Stuck, "The Yukon Salmon," 317–22.

117. Rowe to Wood, September 5, 1919, Rowe correspondence.

118. Wood to Rowe, October 22, 1920, Rowe correspondence. That winter, amid his busy schedule, Stuck kept Hap and Clara in his mind and heart. He sent $250 to Hap's account, to be used for further postgraduate study when he next went out on furlough. Wood to G. Burke, February 25, 1920, Burke correspondence.

119. Drane, "From Cheechako to Archdeacon," 70.

120. The Iñupiaq settlement near St. John's-in-the-Wilderness was now called Alatna.

121. W. Thomas, Letter to Stuck (n.d.), "Our Letter Box," 397.

122. C. Burke, Letter to Woman's Auxiliary (n.d.), "Our Letter Box," 330.

123. Drane, "Winter, 1919–1920," referenced in 1921–22 diary.

124. Drane, "Winter, 1919–1920." As a pioneer of Alaska (he entered the territory by 1900), the man qualified for medical assistance from the Territorial Indigent

Fund for hospital expenses, which allowed him to travel Outside, "get new feet fitted," Drane wrote, "have a good time, and come back for more trouble."

125. Stuck to Wood, Septuagesima (February 16), 1919, and Stuck to Lloyd, January 16, 1919, Stuck correspondence.

126. Wood to Rosenow, May 17, 1920, and Wood to G. Burke, May 28, 1920, Burke correspondence.

127. "1945 Flu (Influenza): History of the Flu (Influenza): Outbreaks and Vaccine Timeline," Mayo Clinic website, accessed May 25, 2022, https://www.mayoclinic.org/coronavirus-covid-19/history-disease-outbreaks-vaccine-timeline/flu.

128. "The Influenza Pandemic," 67. This issue of the *Alaskan Churchman* was published two months late and thus included developments to midsummer. Untitled news item, *Spirit of Missions* 85, no. 7 (July 1920): 450.

129. C. Burke, *Doctor Hap*, 244.

130. As a delegate rather than a congressman, Grigsby could not introduce a bill, but he convinced an ally to do so.

131. "Progress of the Kingdom" (September 1920), 548–49.

132. Drane to Wood, December 14, 1920, Drane correspondence. That summer Stuck's beloved alma mater, the University of the South, offered him the position of chair of its history department. He declined the offer, steadfast in his resolve, even as his health was failing, to return to Alaska, where he felt he had been called in 1904. "Archdeacon Stuck, Minutes," 689.

133. Drane, "The Death of Archdeacon Stuck," 5.

134. Stuck, "The Yukon Salmon," 321–22 (quotations on both pages; emphasis in original); "Progress of the Kingdom" (June 1920), 351; "Progress of the Kingdom" (September 1920), 548.

135. Stuck, "Letter to the Editor," 450.

136. Dean, *Breaking Trail*, 296.

137. G. Burke to Wood, October 8, 1920, and October 27, 1920, Burke correspondence; C. Burke, *Doctor Hap*, 239.

138. G. Burke to Wood, October 27, 1920.

139. G. Burke to Wood, October 27, 1920.

140. Drane, "The Death of Archdeacon Stuck," 3–4 (quotations on both pages).

141. Drane, "The Death of Archdeacon Stuck," 5.

142. Edwin C. Ranck, "'Sky Pilot' of the North," *New York Times*, October 24, 1920.

143. "News and Notes" (December 1920), 793; W:H:K (likely John Wood) to Drane, November 10, 1920, Drane correspondence.

144. Stuck to Wood, February 27, 1917. Although Stuck angered many whites with his single-minded devotion to Alaska Natives' interests, Charles Christian Georgeson, founder of several agricultural stations in Alaska under the aegis of the U.S. Department of Agriculture, admired the archdeacon's humanitarianism. "He was a real missionary," Georgeson wrote, lamenting the loss of his services to Alaska. "He lived for the Natives. His work, his thoughts and his life were unquestionably devoted to their betterment, and they will miss him, and the work among them will miss him sorely, for it will be difficult to find a man to take his place. The Archdeacon was so devoted to the Natives in Alaska that he did not want to see the Territory developed. He deprecated the building of the railway, the development of agriculture and the influx of the white man. He was thinking in terms of the Natives only and he has accomplished notable work among them" (C. C. Georgeson to Charles Betticher, October 22, 1920, Rowe correspondence).
145. G. Burke to Wood, January 3, 1921, Burke correspondence.
146. Extract of letter written by Dr. Grafton Burke, October 27, 1920, and G. Burke to Rowe, February 28, 1921, Burke correspondence.

6. DEEPENING RESOLVE

1. Mason, *The Arctic Forests*, 68–69.
2. G. Burke to Rowe, February 28, 1921, Burke correspondence.
3. Drane diary, March 1921; Drane, "Swinging the Circuit," 502.
4. Drane, "Swinging the Circuit," 502. In his journal for March 1921, Drane said Wallis was "rated as one of the best if not the best interpreter in Alaska," along with Chief Jonas, who taught the Native adult Sunday school. The separate church services for Gwich'in and whites reflected the different languages they spoke. Native services were always in the Gwich'in language.
5. Drane, "Swinging the Circuit," 502–3 ("usefulness" on 502); G. Burke to Rowe, February 28, 1921 (quotation herein p. 4).
6. G. Burke to Rowe, February 28, 1921 ("old man" quotation here); Drane, "Swinging the Circuit," 502–3 (gratitude quotations here).
7. Drane, "Swinging the Circuit," 502–3; G. Burke to Rowe, February 28, 1921.
8. G. Burke to Rowe, February 28, 1921.
9. G. Burke to Rowe, February 28, 1921.
10. Diana Campbell, telephone interview with Mary Ehrlander, December 13, 2021. Campbell, a journalist, interviewed Hudson Burke before his visit to Alaska in 1999. He told her this story during that interview.

11. VanStone, *Athapaskan Adaptations*, 67. Frederica de Laguna related stories of Ingalik and Koyukon Dena' who could summon fish. Laguna, *Tales from the Dena*, 63–64.

12. Drane, "Swinging the Circuit," 497.

13. Drane, "Swinging the Circuit," 498.

14. Wood to G. Burke, December 27, 1920, Burke correspondence; Drane, "Swinging the Circuit," 502–3; "Meeting of the President and Council," 49; C. Burke, *Doctor Hap*, 214. Clara wrote that Mason donated $1,000. Hap reported $500 from Mason (G. Burke to Wood February 17, 1921, Burke correspondence).

15. "News and Notes" (February 1922), 47; "Fort Yukon" (April 1922), 72.

16. K. Hitchings to Rowe, November 22, 1918, Rowe correspondence. He and other Interior missionaries would also receive $100 freight allowance, owing to the higher shipping costs into the Interior.

17. Rowe to Wood, September 21, 1920, Rowe correspondence. It is unclear whether this lag in the pay raise for female missionaries reflected the common practice of gendered differences in pay. It may have resulted from the perceived greater need for ordained male missionaries.

18. Stowe, *The Episcopal Church*, 21. It also established the National Council as the executive body of the National Convention, to improve coordination of social service work and religious education.

19. In April the teacher at Point Hope, James MaGuire, had shot and killed Reverend Hoare, the missionary at Point Hope, reportedly because he had a Native woman living with him while Hoare was away at Barrow/Utqiaġvik, and he knew Hoare would disapprove. The woman assisted in the murder and tried to shoot two Native boys as well. MaGuire escaped but was apprehended by Natives and taken to Candle. Rowe to Wood, August 27, 1920, Rowe correspondence; "Statement of Facts in United States vs James MaGuire" (n.d., placed in Rowe correspondence for October 1920).

20. Rowe to Wood, August 27, 1920, Rowe correspondence.

21. Rowe to Wood, September 21, 1920, Rowe correspondence. The schedule included $500 for David Wallis and $600 for Esaias George—man-of-all-work.

22. Rowe to Wood, January 29, 1920, Rowe correspondence. Wood was now executive secretary of the Department of Missions and Church Extension.

23. Wood to Rowe, September 26, 1920, Rowe correspondence.

24. Wood to Rowe, August 16, 1921, Rowe correspondence.

25. "News and Notes" (September 1921); Rowe to Wood, October 3, 1921, Rowe correspondence.

26. Wood to G. Burke, February 1, 1921, Burke correspondence.

27. Wood to G. Burke, March 3, 1921, Burke correspondence.

28. C. Burke, *Doctor Hap*, 213; G. Burke to Wood, May 13, 1922, Burke correspondence.

29. Cleaver, Letter (n.d.), "Our Letter Box," 665.

30. Extract of letter written by Dr. Grafton Burke, sent to Bishop Rowe, October 27, 1920, Burke correspondence; Wood, Memo for Mr. Henry, December 29, 1920, and Henry to Wood, December 30, 1920, Rowe correspondence; G. Burke to Wood, February 17, 1921; Wood to Rowe, October 23, 1920, Rowe correspondence.

31. G. Burke to Wood, January 30, 1922, Burke correspondence; Wood to Rowe, January 20, 1922, Rowe correspondence.

32. G. Burke to Wood, November 2, 1921, and January 30, 1922, Burke correspondence; Cook to Rowe, December 11, 1922, Rowe correspondence; Dalziel to Wood, February 3, 1923, Dalziel correspondence, PECUSA.

33. Mackenzie, *Zhoh Gwatsan*, 88, 90.

34. Mackenzie, *Zhoh Gwatsan*, 104; "Fort Yukon" (February 1921), 38; Fredson to Wood, August 31, 1921 (quotations herein), Fredson correspondence, PECUSA.

35. Mackenzie, *Zhoh Gwatsan*, 110–11.

36. "Moccasin Telegraph" (February 1937), 14.

37. G. Burke, "The Frances Wells Harper Memorial Solarium," 465–66.

38. Fortuine, *"Must We All Die?,"* xxiii.

39. Stuck to Lloyd, December 12, 1918, Stuck correspondence; Resolution of the Episcopal Board of Missions Executive Committee, February 11, 1919, in Stuck correspondence. Heliotherapy remained the primary method of treatment for most forms of tuberculosis until antibiotic therapies were developed in the 1950s. Renowned physicians wrote enthusiastically about its benefits. Rollier, "The Therapeutic, Preventive and Social Value of Heliotherapy," 435–46; Alpert, "The Jeremiah Metzger Lecture," 219–26.

40. G. Burke to Wood, September 12, 1921, Burke correspondence.

41. G. Burke to Wood, November 2, 1921; Mackenzie, *Zhoh Gwatsan*, 110. Johnny received a salary of $600 per year, like hospital personnel, for his work. Esaias George received the same salary as a man-of-all-work. Wood to G. Burke, December 13, 1921, Burke correspondence.

42. G. Burke to Wood, December 2, 1921, Burke correspondence.

43. C. Burke, *Doctor Hap*, 215.

44. Wood to Rowe, September 2, 1921, Rowe correspondence. Hap typically sent telegrams "collect" to mission headquarters, which called attention to

the cost. The wireless rate from New York to London was twenty cents a word in 1921. Hall, "Historical statistics of the United States," 478.

45. Wood to Rowe, September 2, 1921. Irregular mail service often prompted Hap to use the wireless. For instance, from mid- to late April, when the trail was too soft for travel by dog team, until break-up, no mail went in or out. The same conditions occurred in the fall between the last steamer of the season and sometime in November or early December when the mail trail was passable. G. Burke to Wood, April 18, 1927, Burke correspondence.

46. Rowe to Wood, October 3, 1921, Rowe correspondence.

47. G. Burke to Wood, December 2, 1921, Burke correspondence. "Ratting" refers to trapping muskrats for their skins.

48. G. Burke to Wood (telegram), December 20, 1921, and Wood to G. Burke (telegram), December 30, 1921, Burke correspondence.

49. Rowe to Wood, September 5, 1921, Rowe correspondence; JWH/EDH to Burke, March 8, 1921, Burke correspondence.

50. From time to time, Bishop Rowe would receive an unanticipated deposit of a few thousand dollars in his specials account. In fall 1921 Wood informed him that $5,434.29 had been deposited into the account, to which Rowe responded that the letter brought him "wondrous comfort and relief." Rowe to Wood, October 3, 1921, Rowe correspondence.

51. Wood to Rowe, June 10, 1920, and "Alaska: Cancellation of sums advanced for the purchase of supplies" (n.d.), Rowe correspondence.

52. Rowe to Wood, September 5, 1921, Rowe correspondence. In his appropriations schedule for 1921, Rowe requested $5,000 for hospital operating costs, because the previous year, they had been $6,150. Rowe to Wood, September 21, 1920, Rowe correspondence. He increased the supply fund for the school at Nenana from $500 to $3,000.

53. Hap and Johnny's trip would be the first visit of a white missionary to the village. Robert McKennan noted that the mixed-blood brothers Robert and Kenneth McDonald had visited several Gwich'in camps in the 1870s and Native catechists had also proselytized among the Neets'aii Gwich'in, whom he referred to as Chandalar Kutchin because their territory generally included the drainage system of the East Fork of the Chandalar River. Hap's arrival, however, marked the first visit of a white missionary. McKennan, "Athapaskan Adaptations," 220–21.

54. G. Burke, "Northward the Course of the Kingdom," 172; C. Burke, *Doctor Hap*, 248.

55. Mackenzie, *Zhoh Gwatsan*, 112.

56. G. Burke, "Northward the Course of the Kingdom," 174; Mackenzie, *Zhoe Gwatsan*, 112. The name was variously spelled Drit, Ttrit, and Tritt. Today it is spelled Tritt.

57. G. Burke, "Northward the Course of the Kingdom," 173; C. Burke, *Doctor Hap*, 250–51; Mackenzie, *Zhoh Gwatsan*, 112, 114, 116.

58. Drane to G. Burke, January 2, 1922, Burke correspondence.

59. G. Burke to Wood, February 14, 1922, Burke correspondence

60. G. Burke to Wood, February 14, 1922. None of these individuals was ever ordained to the diaconate or priesthood, although they continued to support the church's work. In 1925 the mission board appointed Rev. G. H. Moody to serve at Fort Yukon.

61. "Progress of the Kingdom" (July 1922), 421.

62. G. Burke to Rowe, July 19, 1922, Burke correspondence; "Progress of the Kingdom" (July 1922), 421.

63. R. Tatum to Cutler, June 7, 1922, Moses John Cruikshank file no.10926, Mount Hermon Archives.

64. Cruikshank to Cutler, May 29, 1922, Cruikshank file no.10926.

65. Application for Admission to Mount Hermon School, Cruikshank file no. 10926.

66. Tatum to Cutler (to Mount Hermon School), January 1, 1922, Cruikshank file no. 10926.

67. Ethel R. Maddern to Whom It May Concern, December 16, 1970, Cruikshank file no. 10926.

68. Cited in Mackenzie, *Zhoh Gwatsan*, 117–18.

69. Mischler, "John Fredson: A Biographical Sketch," 14.

70. "Travel Account of Dr. Grafton Burke and family" (not dated but stamped "Received Dec 15, 1922," and signed by John Wood), Burke correspondence; G. Burke to Wood, May 13, 1922, Burke correspondence; Drane to G. Burke, January 2, 1922, Burke correspondence.

71. G. Burke to Wood, August 18, 1922, Burke correspondence.

72. Cook to Rowe, December 11, 1922, Rowe correspondence.

73. Rowe to Wood, January 11, 1923, and Wood to Rowe, January 20, 1923, Rowe correspondence.

74. "Travel Account of Dr. Grafton Burke and family." We found no indication of the condition that required surgery.

75. G. Burke to Wood (n.d., likely late October 1922), Burke correspondence.

76. Wood to Rowe, January 20, 1922, Rowe correspondence.

77. Wood to Rowe, February 15, 1923, Rowe correspondence. Their reception by church groups with whom they spoke while on furlough may have contributed to Hap's tendency to overspend on equipment and supplies for St. Stephen's. Rowe complained that Hap and other missionaries made purchases based on promises, rather than according to the balances in their expense accounts. Rowe to Wood, July 14, 1923, Rowe correspondence.

78. Wood (W:H:K.) to Rowe, May 28, 1923, Rowe correspondence.

79. Wood to Rowe, January 20, 1922, February 15, 1923, and March 23, 1923, Rowe correspondence; Wood to Cook, March 3, 1923, Cook correspondence, PECUSA.

80. C. Burke, *Doctor Hap*, 253–54.

81. C. Burke, *Doctor Hap*, 254–55.

82. On a short stopover in Washington DC, Hap arranged an exam for Hudson with an eye specialist. Dr. Wilmer told them that the surgery the previous fall had saved the boy's eyes; they were healing, and Hudson would need no further treatment. G. Burke to Wood, June 13, 1924, Burke correspondence. From Chicago, Clara and the boys broke away for a short detour to Los Angeles, where Clara had a speaking engagement, and they visited family. G. Burke to Wood, June 9 and July 10, 1923, Burke correspondence; Travel Clerk to G. Burke, June 1, 1923, Burke correspondence.

83. "Save Our Hospital!"; C. Burke, *Doctor Hap*, 254–56. A friend had already donated $5,000 to the cause. Mr. and Mrs. William T. Murphy of Germantown, Pennsylvania, later gave $500 in memory of Francis Wells Harper to move the hospital. Statement of specials received for Fort Yukon Hospital, Removal Fund, Alaska, October 14, 1924, Rowe correspondence.

84. G. Burke to Wood, August 13, 1923, Burke correspondence.

85. G. Burke, "Our 'Farthest North' Hospital," 823–24; Stewart, "Watch Your Rollers," 246–47; Rowe to Wood, August 21, 1923, Rowe correspondence. The Fordson proved to be a boon for the mission complex, saving the cost of a team of horses at $25 a day for the move. It filled many other needs in the coming years.

86. C. Burke, *Doctor Hap* 255–57; Wood to Rowe, March 23, 1923, Rowe correspondence. The water from the lake was safe for cleaning and washing but not for drinking. The nurse Mary Ryder's description the following summer of packing water from the river suggests that the water and sewage system was not completed until later. Mary wrote, "Imagine running a large hospital

and having to pack from the river every single drop of water. . . . Water is so scarce that we have to save the patients' bath water for washing out buckets etc." *A Yukon Romance: Claude and Mary Tidd*, accessed August 28, 2018, https://www.yukonromance.ca/en/romance/mountienurse/index8ef1.html ?topNav=rom&subNav=man.

87. Bergman, Zoom interview with authors, March 13, 2022.

88. G. Burke, Letter (n.d), "Our Letter Box," 49. These purchases cost $1,000, which drew a reprimand from John Wood, who wondered "where on earth the money is to come from." Wood to G. Burke, August 29, 1923, Burke correspondence.

89. "News and Notes" (March 1924), 194; "Brief Items of Interest" (May 1928), 332.

90. G. Burke, "Our 'Farthest North' Hospital," 824. Hap did not explain why he had to amputate the little boy's leg, nor did he say whether the boy with meningitis survived.

91. Fortuine, *"Must We All Die?,"* 134 and appendix B1, 222. In 1950 the mortality rate for Native children under fourteen years old was more than one hundred times the national rate for that age group (134).

92. Drane diary, page note, March 1923.

93. Drane married in September 1924, and he and his wife had a daughter in 1925. The baby's health was so delicate that mother and child left for Seattle where she could receive specialized care. Bishop Rowe assigned Drane to raise funds Outside for the mission work at Nenana. After six months of speaking engagements, while often being sidelined with a cough, Drane was diagnosed with tuberculosis. In late 1926 Drane, still under treatment for chronic tuberculosis, resigned from his position with the Episcopal missions in Alaska. Thus ended his ten-year sojourn in Alaska. Rowe, "Report by the Bishop (1926)," Rowe correspondence; Drane, "From Cheechako to Archdeacon," 72; Wood to Rowe, September 3, 1926, Rowe correspondence. In looking back through his journal, Drane believed that he may have contracted tuberculosis while on the trail in spring 1923. Drane diary, day note, May 1, 1923.

94. Burke to Wood, June 13, 1924, Burke correspondence. While Clara accompanied Hudson to Los Angeles, Winifred Dalziel cared for the mission children. The mission board paid $250 per academic year for the children of missionaries in the field to attend school in the continental United States.

95. Douglas Fischer, "Remembrance of Things Past," *Fairbanks Daily News Miner*, October 17, 1999; Hudson Stuck Burke Jr. (Hap and Clara's grand-

son), interview by Mary Ehrlander, October 25, 2021, Seattle; Diane Burke (Hap and Clara's great-granddaughter), telephone interview with Mary Ehrlander, October 15, 2021; and interview with Diana Campbell. All spoke of Hudson's unhappiness with being sent away. Hudson told Campbell that his grandmother pressured his parents to send him Outside to school. Campbell, a journalist, related the story of Hudson's sitting by the window, which he told her in an interview she conducted with him prior to his 1999 visit to Fairbanks and Fort Yukon. He did not explain to her what he meant by his remark that white people smelled like death. It may be that he thought the soaps and detergents they used smelled antiseptic.

96. Wood to G. Burke, October 1, 1924, Burke correspondence; G. Burke to Wood, January 30, 1922, and May 13, 1922, Burke correspondence.

97. G. Burke to Wood, August 27, 1924, Burke correspondence.

98. G. Burke to Wood, November 2, 1921, Burke correspondence. Scientists have recently documented the phenomenon of hair turning grey or white owing to stress and identified the physiological process. Rosenberg et al., "Quantitative Mapping of Human Hair Greying."

99. *A Yukon Romance.* The expressions "doctor, lawyer, Indian chief," as well as "rich man, poor man, beggar man, thief," were rhymes used in the children's counting game and nursery rhyme "Tinker, Tailor."

100. C. Burke, *Doctor Hap*, 261. There was no basis for Clara's statement about the Arctic's effect on her hair.

101. *A Yukon Romance.*

102. G. Burke to Wood, January 3, 1921, Burke correspondence. The conditions—a still wind and temperature of −40°F—helped limit the fire.

103. Chapman to Rowe, January 25, 1922, Rowe correspondence. Fortunately, insurance covered the building, and Rev. John Chapman and others saved several thousand dollars' worth of equipment and supplies.

104. C. Burke, *Doctor Hap*, 264–65; G. Burke to Wood, September 24, 1921, Burke correspondence.

105. G. Burke to Wood, September 24, 1921, and G. Burke to Wood (telegram), September 24, 1924, Burke correspondence.

106. Wood to G. Burke (telegram), September 26, 1924, Burke correspondence. Wood later advised Hap to "try to keep the cost within ten thousand." Wood to G. Burke (telegram), October 5, 1924, Burke correspondence.

107. Hitchings to G. Burke, October 1, 1924, Burke correspondence; Wood, "Fire Destroys Mission House at Fort Yukon," 636.

108. G. Burke to Wood, September 24, 1921, Burke correspondence; Wood, "Fire Destroys Mission House at Fort Yukon," 636.

109. G. Burke to Stewart, December 6, 1924, Geoffrey Burke private collection; C. Burke, *Doctor Hap*, 266.

110. "Good Words for Our Arctic Hospital"; C. Burke, *Doctor Hap*, 267–68; Drane, "Squeezing Through," 330; Rowe to Wood, July 25, 1925 (b), Rowe correspondence. Clara's position allayed any potential concerns about the Burkes and mission children staying in the government teachers' residence.

111. C. Burke to Wade, December 6, 1924, and G. Burke to Wood, October 28, 1924, Burke correspondence. Hap also secured bids for the logs at about half the cost of those for the hospital.

112. Statement of specials received for Fort Yukon Hospital, October 14, 1924, Rowe correspondence.

113. G. Burke to Wood (telegram), November 25, 1924, Burke correspondence.

114. C. Burke to Wade, December 6, 1924.

115. G. Burke to Wood (telegram), January 14, 1925, Burke correspondence.

116. G. Burke to Wood, January 23, 1925, Burke correspondence.

117. G. Burke to Wood, January 23, 1925.

118. Schedule for Fort Yukon, Alaska, for the year 1926, Burke correspondence.

119. Wallis, *Raising Ourselves*, 44–45.

120. G. Burke, "The Yukon Breaks Its Bounds," 466; G. Burke to Wood, June 1, 1925, Burke correspondence.

121. G. Burke, "Fire, Flood and Flue on the Yukon," 755.

122. G. Burke to Wood, June 1, 1925, Burke correspondence.

123. Mackenzie, *Zhoh Gwatsan*, 132.

124. Rowe, "Five Years on the Yukon," 297, 299. Nick used the *Pelican*'s engine in several subsequent building projects, including the new Betticher Memorial Hall at St. Mark's Mission in Nenana in 1926 and the new church and school there in 1927.

125. Rowe to Wood (telegram), July 14, 1925, Rowe correspondence; Missionary District of Alaska Annual Report (1925), Rowe correspondence. Traveling downriver, they found people stricken with influenza at Eagle and Circle.

126. Rowe to Wood, July 17, 1925, Rowe correspondence; G. Burke, "Fire, Flood and Flue on the Yukon," 755.

127. Rowe to Wood, July 17, 1925 (quotation herein), Rowe correspondence; Rowe, "Influenza Epidemic in Alaska," 540.

128. *Spirit of Missions* 90, no. 12 (December 1925): pictorial section, 758.

129. Rowe to Wood, July 25, 1925, Rowe correspondence.

130. Wallis, *Raising Ourselves*, 43–44. Rowe noted that one of David Wallis's daughters was "in a bad way" (Rowe to Wood, July 25, 1925 [b]), and court records noted an incident related to Ethel Wallis while she was being cared for in one of the tents (USA v. Andrew Brasfeldt, Complaint, July 21, 1925, folder 1: Justice Court in and for Ft. Yukon Precinct, 4th Division of Alaska, Grafton Burke, JP–1911–1929, Fort Yukon Precinct Justice Court Records, APRCA).

131. G. Burke, "Fire, Flood and Flue on the Yukon," 756.

132. Rowe to Wood, July 18, 1925, Rowe correspondence.

133. Payne to Wood, July 17, 1925, and Finney to Payne, July 17, 1925, Rowe correspondence.

134. Rowe to Wood, July 17, 1925, and July 25, 1925, and Missionary District of Alaska Annual Report (1925), Rowe correspondence; Payne to Wood, July 17, 1925, and Finney to Payne, July 17, 1925; Wood to G. Burke, July 24, 1925, Burke correspondence; G. Burke, "Fire, Flood and Flue on the Yukon," 756; Harkey, *Noel Wien*, 113. The nurse's name may have been Sleichter (a court record references a nurse in July 1925 named Dorothy Sleichter).

135. Rowe to Wood, July 25, 1925.

136. Rowe wrote that a generous friend who had donated this sum in the past was no longer doing so, because he or she had learned that the National Council had decreed that all such donations must go into general funds.

137. Rowe to Wood, August 1, 1925, Rowe correspondence.

138. Wood, "Flu Follows Flood along the Yukon," 463.

139. Wood to Rowe, November 13, 1925, Rowe correspondence.

140. Rowe to Wood, July 25, 1925, and Missionary District of Alaska Annual Report (1925); G. Burke, "Fire, Flood and Flue on the Yukon," 756.

141. G. Burke to Wood, January 18, 1926, Burke correspondence.

142. Rowe to Wood, August 1, 1925.

143. Rowe to Wood, July 25, 1925 (b).

144. Wood to Rowe, September 9, 1923, Rowe correspondence.

145. "Radical Retrenchment or Wise Economy"; "The Deficit Has Not Been Increased"; "The Progress of the Kingdom: Concerning the Debt," 727.

146. The church kept him on the payroll and would make a further settlement.

147. Missionary District of Alaska Annual Report (1925), and Rowe to Wood, August 1, 1925; C. Burke, *Doctor Hap*, 269; G. Burke to Wood, August 9, 1925, Burke correspondence; Mackenzie, *Zhoh Gwatsan*, 136.

148. Cited recollection of Grafton Burke, http://www.yukonromance.ca/en /romance/mountienurse/wedding.php?topNav=rom&subNav=man.

149. Rowe to Wood, August 7, 1923, Rowe correspondence. Nurse Theresa Sands had already married by this time. Rowe to Wood, July 25, 1925, Rowe correspondence.

150. G. Burke to Wood, January 16, 1926, Burke correspondence.

151. Wood to Rowe, November 15, 1925, Rowe correspondence.

152. Horton to G. Burke, October 29, 1925, Burke correspondence. The Alaska missions' fiscal officer was not related to the trader Harry Horton of Fort Yukon.

153. G. Burke to Horton, December 7, 1925, Burke correspondence.

154. Wood to Burke, July 23, 1923, Burke correspondence. This letter is just one of many that followed the pattern of Wood scolding Hap, then Hap pleading his case, and Wood saying yes, of course the expenses would be paid, but telling Hap not to assume things would always work out this easily.

155. Wood to Rowe, November 15, 1925.

7. ST. STEPHEN'S MISSION WORK EXPANDS

1. G. Burke, "Alaska Hospital Has Phenomenal Growth," 728.

2. C. Burke, *Doctor Hap*, 276–77.

3. G. Burke to Wood, June 11, 1927, Burke correspondence.

4. Harkey, *Noel Wien*, 113. The Norwegian Roald Amundsen would make his first Artic flight, from Spitzbergen, where his plane had been shipped, two weeks after Wien's first flight.

5. Parks, *Annual Report of the Governor* (1926), 34. By 1928 fifty-eight landing fields were built, and winter airmail service was expanding. Parks, *Annual Report of the Governor* (1928), 8–9.

6. Rowe to Wood, July 2_, 1927 (day illegible), and Rowe to Franklin, August 6, 1927, Rowe correspondence. The pilot waited for Rowe over Sunday and flew him back Monday.

7. Parks, *Annual Report of the Governor* (1928), 8–9. The fourth airline operated out of Anchorage.

8. "Hudson Stuck Memorial Hospital," October 1, 1943, RG 351, box 13, folder 5, Grafton Burke 1908–1937, PECUSA.

9. Parks, *Annual Report of the Governor* (1928), 17–18; Parks, *Annual Report of the Governor* (1929), 21.

10. C. Burke, *Doctor Hap*, 276–77. In summer 1935 the mission girls entered a hooked rug they had made in a contest at the Tanana Valley Fair, and it won a prize. They gave it to Suffragan Bishop and Mrs. Bentley for their home—the "Bishop's Lodge"—in Nenana. "The Newsletter, Missionary District

of Alaska" 23 (October 1935), RG 79-1, Alaska Miscellaneous Newsletters, 1934–1935, PECUSA.

11. Rowe, "Thirty-Fourth Annual Report," 61–64.

12. Moody, "Fort Yukon Notes," 75–76.

13. Bradley, "Pushing on to Health at Fort Yukon," 73–74.

14. Fortuine, *Must We All Die?*, 30–31, 35.

15. Rowe to Wood, March 25, 1926, Rowe correspondence.

16. Wood to G. Burke, March 10, 15 (telegram), and 19, 1926, and G. Burke to Wood (telegrams), March 16 and 17, 1926, Burke correspondence.

17. With an additional $2,000 budget line for fuel out of the question, Wood suggested starting a Fuel Club for Fort Yukon, with members pledging a sum each year to cover heating costs. Wood to Rowe, March 18 and March 29, 1926, Rowe correspondence.

18. Hap and Clara had considered going on furlough in 1926 but did not do so until September 1927.

19. Wood to G. Burke, March 10, 1926, Burke correspondence. It seems that Rowe's letter of January 7 to Burke never arrived. Wood to Rowe, April 29, 1926, Rowe correspondence.

20. G. Burke to Wood, March 17, 1926, Burke correspondence.

21. G. Buke to Wood (telegram), April 8, 1926, Burke correspondence.

22. G. Burke to Rowe, April 8, 1926, Burke correspondence.

23. C. Burke to Wood, April 4, 1926, Burke correspondence.

24. Wood to C. Burke, May 11, 1926, Burke correspondence.

25. Rowe to Wood, April 12, 1926, Rowe correspondence. In May he wired Wood his approval to fund the children's upkeep for the year. Rowe to Wood (telegram), May 6, 1926, Rowe correspondence.

26. Wood, "Must I Say," 547–50 (quotations on 549).

27. Wood to G. Burke, September 25, 1926 (night letter), Burke correspondence; Wood, "Note"; Wood to Rowe, May 19, 1927, Rowe correspondence.

28. C. Burke, *Doctor Hap*, 270–71; Vernon, "My Trip into the Interior of Alaska," 9–10 (quotation on 10).

29. C. Burke, *Doctor Hap*, 261.

30. C. Burke, *Doctor Hap*, 262–63. Clara misstated that Hudson had been away four years; he had been away two years. Bishop Rowe noted in a letter of June 23, 1926, meeting "Clara's mother or step-mother" and Hudson, either at Dawson or Fort Yukon.

31. Hudson Burke Jr., interview by Mary Ehrlander, October 25, 2021, Seattle.

32. "The Era of the Gambling Ships & the Battle of Santa Monica Bay," *Los Angeles Almanac*, October 28, 2021, http://www.laalmanac.com/history/hi06ee.php.

33. C. Burke, *Doctor Hap*, 275–76.

34. C. Burke, *Doctor Hap*, 262.

35. Vyvyan, *The Ladies, the Gwich'in, and the Rat*, 166.

36. MacLaren and LaFramboise, introduction to *The Ladies, the Gwich'in, and the Rat*, xxxix–xl (quotation on xl).

37. Vyvyan, *The Ladies, the Gwich'in, and the Rat*, 165–66 (quotation on 166).

38. Vyvyan, *The Ladies, the Gwich'in, and the Rat*, 166. The women's impressions offer insight into Hap's perception of Mrs. Heintz's initial objection to Hap and Clara's engagement and her subsequent insistent pleas to the couple to come to their senses and rejoin civilization in California.

39. Vyvyan, *The Ladies, the Gwich'in, and the Rat*, 167–68 (quotations on both pages).

40. Vyvyan, *The Ladies, the Gwich'in, and the Rat*, 171–72 (quotations on both pages).

41. Vyvyan, *The Ladies, the Gwich'in, and the Rat*, 170–71 (quotation on 171).

42. Vyvyan, *The Ladies, the Gwich'in, and the Rat*, 172.

43. Vyvyan, *The Ladies, the Gwich'in, and the Rat*, 167–68 (quotations on both pages).

44. Vyvyan, *The Ladies, the Gwich'in, and the Rat*, 172–73 (quotations on both pages).

45. Vyvyan, *The Ladies, the Gwich'in, and the Rat*, 173.

46. Story recounted by Geoffrey Burke (Grafton's son), email, November 10, 2021. Although we cannot corroborate the tale, Geoffrey reports that his father recounted the story so vividly that he believes it to be largely true.

47. Parks, *Annual Report of the Governor* (1925), 4, 6, 76, 77.

48. Parks, *Annual Report of the Governor* (1928), 76. In 1928 the craft carried a physician, two nurses, and a dentist.

49. Alaska Area Native Health Service, *Honoring Our Sacred Healing Place Tanana*, 8–9; Fortuine, *"Must We All Die?,"* 38–39.

50. Mischler and Simeone, *Tanana and Chandalar*, 217.

51. Wood to G. Burke, June 3, 1926 (night letter), Burke correspondence.

52. "Alaskans Value Hudson Stuck Memorial Hospital," 670; advertisement for completing the endowment, Burke correspondence (among May 1927 documents). The following year, the Bishop Rowe Endowment Fund

achieved its $100,000 goal. "The Bishop Rowe Foundation Fund Completed," 524.

53. G. Burke to Horton, January 18, 1927, Burke correspondence; G. Burke to Rowe (telegram), May 21, 1926, and Rowe to Wood, May 22, 1926, Rowe correspondence. Bergman signed a receipt-in-full for the promise of wages until July 1.

54. G. Burke to Wood (telegram), November 4, 1926, Burke correspondence; Rowe to Wood (telegram), November 6, 1926, and Wood to Rowe, November 18, 1926, Rowe correspondence.

55. Horton to G. Burke, November 8, 1926, G. Burke to Horton, January 18, 1927, and G. Burke to Wood, January 18, 1927, Burke correspondence.

56. C. Masten Beaver noted that Bergman walked with a pronounced limp in the 1940s owing to the sawmill accident (Beaver, *Fort Yukon Trader*, 53).

57. "Marriage Records Issued in Fort Yukon," Rootsweb, accessed December 9, 2021, http://freepages.rootsweb.com/~coleen/genealogy/fort_yukon_alaska.html; "Grafton L. Bergman, 1930–2016," *Fairbanks Daily News Miner*, July 8, 2016, https://www.legacy.com/us/obituaries/newsminer/name/grafton-bergman-obituary?id=20977444; Grete Bergman, Zoom interview with authors, March 13, 2022.

58. Dalziel to Wood, March 15, 1927, Dalziel correspondence, PECUSA. Dalziel wrote that Mrs. McCurdy, who worked as a matron and had no medical training, also tried to undermine patients' confidence in Hap's expertise.

59. G. Burke to Wood, June 28, 1927, Burke correspondence.

60. Duke accused Hap of, among other things, conducting an "illegal" operation and of admitting patients without just cause. She complained that Clara had taken in children who had not been hospital patients. Hap showed Duke's charges to be false through affidavits and records. G. Burke to Wood (telegram), May 12, 1927, Burke correspondence. Hap noted that five little boys who had not been patients were being supported by their fathers while Clara cared for them.

61. From Circle, Catherine Palm wrote Wood that having been asked, she felt compelled to write of the "terrible, I fear fatal failure of the work done—rather—not done by the Church in the Interior of Alaska." She provided no details but assured Wood that several pastors Outside, whom she named, could confirm whether her "statements are to be taken verbatim." Palm to Wood, May 18, 1927, Rowe correspondence and Burke correspondence. H. E. Carter, an NC Company employee whom Hap described as "unscrupulous and crooked" (G. Burke to Wood, June 28, 1927, Burke correspondence),

claimed to support the church but wrote that he avoided services because Burke's sermons exposed him to "a much greater evil than staying away from services." Carter to Franklin, March 2, 1927, Burke correspondence.

62. H. Horton to Rowe, March 16, 1927, Burke correspondence and Rowe correspondence.

63. Donald to Rowe, May 23, 1927, Rowe correspondence and Burke correspondence.

64. Foster to Rowe, March 10, 1927, Rowe correspondence.

65. Duke, January 23, 1927, note requesting Burke arrange for her early departure by airplane or trail at the expense of the Nation Council. "Also, I herewith accept $300 in full settlement of my claims." G. Burke to Duke, January 24, 1927, and G. Burke to Wood, February 3, 1927, Burke correspondence.

66. G. Burke to Wood, March 16, May 27 (telegram), and July 23 (telegram), 1927, Burke correspondence; Wood to Rowe, June 11, 1927, Rowe correspondence. McCurdy let Hap know that the NC Company was paying him twice the $1,200 salary the church paid him.

67. G. Burke to Wood, August 23, 1927, and Wood to G. Burke, June 8, 1928, Burke correspondence.

68. After Duke's charges had been dispelled, Rowe remarked to Wood, "All the same I want you to understand that I am not satisfied with Hap and the way he does things." Rowe to Wood, May 18, 1927, Rowe correspondence.

69. Rowe to Wood, June 13, 1927, Rowe correspondence.

70. Rowe to Wood, June 18, 1928, Rowe correspondence.

71. Rowe to Wood, August 23,1927, and "Schedule Beginning January 1928," Rowe correspondence. Rowe also urged the appointment of a priest at Fort Yukon, given its strategic significance. Rowe later wrote Wood that he felt Hap deserved "after his many years of loyal & faithful service, a salary of $3000 a year at least." Rowe to Wood, June 18, 1928, Rowe correspondence.

72. The board refused to raise Hap's salary over that of Dr. Chapman, even though Hap's responsibilities in operating the Hudson Stuck Memorial Hospital far exceeded Dr. Chapman's duties at Anvik. The schedule showed $350 for Hudson Burke and $200 for Grafton Burke for education. Considering the housing, food, and fuel benefits that Hap and Clara received, his "compensation package" well exceeded $2,000. Nevertheless, his compensation was far less than what he could have earned in the continental United States, for far less work.

73. Parson to Rowe, November 18, 1927, Rowe correspondence.

74. G. Burke to Wood, January 5 and August 23, 1927, Burke correspondence.

75. G. Burke to Wood, January 5 and August 23, 1927. From time to time, St. Stephen's received such bequests. In 1926 a woman gave $2,000 to purchase a bed for the hospital. The donor's mother had been a devotee of the Woman's Auxiliary. Wood to G. Burke, June 2, 1926, Burke correspondence.

76. Drane, "Three O'Clock in the Morning," 694. Three years later in spring 1927, an influenza epidemic killed twenty-nine adults at Anvik, leaving forty orphans. When Rowe visited Anvik in summer 1927, a "depression hung over the place." Many of the "best people" were gone. The mission and Chapman's home were filled to overflowing with children. A new dormitory could not be built until 1928. Rowe, "Annual Report" (1927), Rowe correspondence.

77. Rowe, "S.O.S. from Anvik, Alaska," 465.

78. Cruikshank, *The Life I've Been Living*, 62. After working during summer 1929 with Nicholson on Episcopal building projects, Cruikshank accepted a teaching position at St. Timothy's Mission at Minto, thirty-five miles down the Tanana River from Nenana, where Arthur Wright was now pastor. Rowe, "Thirty-Fourth Annual Report"; Wright, "The Minto Mission," 77–78.

79. Fredson to Rowe, November 18, 1926, Rowe correspondence; Mackenzie, *Zhoh Gwatsan*, 136–38. In summer 1927 he had worked at Mt. McKinley National Park under park superintendent Harry Karstens.

80. Wood to Fredson, July 26, 1927 (night letter), Rowe correspondence; Fredson to Wood, August 4, September 16, September 30, and October 10, 1927, and Wood to Fredson (telegram), August 22, 1927, Fredson correspondence. Mackenzie, *Zhoh Gwatsan*, 139. Completing a theology degree would have required seven years of study. Rowe to Wood, December 1, 1926, Rowe correspondence.

81. G. Burke to Wood, August 23, 1927, Burke correspondence; "Schedule Alaska for Fiscal Year beginning January 1, 1929," Rowe correspondence. Winifred Dalziel had taken several in her teacher quarters, and missionary Harriett Bedell had taken a few at Stephen's Village. Hap placed those needing constant oversight in the hospital and found the best homes possible for the others.

82. G. Burke to Wood, June 11, 1927, Burke correspondence. Hap felt confident that the hospital would run smoothly in his absence with the staff he had in place. G. Burke to Wood, August 23, 1927, Burke correspondence.

83. G. Burke to Parson, December 13, 1927, Burke correspondence.

84. Goddard, Alaska diary, 1934, 61.

85. C. Burke, *Doctor Hap*, 279. En route to New York, they made a detour to Dallas, where Hap visited his father, whom he had not seen in twenty years.

G. Burke to Parson, December 13, 1927, and Parson to G. Burke, December 20, 1927, Burke correspondence.

86. G. Burke to Wood, August 23, 1927, Burke correspondence; C. Burke, *Doctor Hap*, 279; Peter Hackett (grandson of Frank S. Hackett), telephone interview with Mary Ehrlander, September 7, 2021.

87. Hackett, *Quickened Spirit*, 140.

88. "Dr. Fred H. Albee," *Boston Globe*, February 15, 1945; C. Burke, *Doctor Hap*, 282.

89. C. Burke, *Doctor Hap*, 282.

90. C. Burke, *Doctor Hap*, 280–82.

91. Rowe to Wood, June 18 and July 31, 1928, and Wood to Rowe, July 7, 1928, Rowe correspondence.

92. Stefansson to Fitzgerald, July 20, 1928, Burke to Wood, March 25, 1931 ("old friend" quotation here), and Wood to G. Burke, July 16, 1935 (Wood quotation here), Burke correspondence; C. Burke, *Doctor Hap*, 280; American College of Surgeons website, accessed August 20, 2021, https://www.facs.org/about -acs/archives/acshistory.

93. In an April 1926 letter, Wood expressed concern about the cost of maintaining missions at far flung places that served so few people—for instance Tanana Crossing. He wondered if perhaps the work in the Interior of Alaska might be carried out at three stations—Fort Yukon, Tanana, and Anvik. He acknowledged that his questions might seem heretical, but might the Natives be persuaded to move closer to these three missions? Wood to Rowe, April 2, 1926, Rowe correspondence. Rowe also pondered closing his office in Seattle. Rowe to Wood, April 30, April 30b, May 4 (telegram), and May 5 (telegram), 1926, Rowe correspondence.

94. Bedell, "Stephen's Village Move to Tanana," 111–12; "Brief Items of Interest."

95. "Arrivals and Sailings" (December 1928), 830.

96. G. Burke to Wood, April 15, 1929, Burke correspondence. We found no explanation in the correspondence of the gap between O'Hara's departure and the Burkes' return.

97. G. Burke to Wood, April 15, 1929.

98. G. Burke to Wood, April 15, 1929.

99. G. Burke to Wood, April 15, 1929.

100. "Nurse Flies to Relieve Emergency at Fort Yukon"; "Arrivals and Sailings of Missionaries." In a stroke of luck, the perennially cash-strapped Mission Society received a gift of $150 from the youth group of the Indianapolis diocese, exactly the cost of the flight from Fairbanks to Fort Yukon.

101. Rowe, "Five Months in the Interior of Alaska," 731.

102. G. Burke to Wood, April 15, 1929 (quotations herein); C. Burke, *Doctor Hap*, 284–85.

103. Rowe, "Five Months in the Interior of Alaska," 731; G. Burke to Wood, October 20, 1929 (quotation herein), Burke correspondence.

104. G. Burke, *Kwunduk Nenlinatsidenja (Mixed Talk)*, St. Stephen's Hospital bulletin, no. 4 (1931): 1, Burke correspondence. Rowe had reassigned Rev. E. G. Moody to Eagle. Wood to Rowe, September 7, 1926, Rowe correspondence.

105. Rowe to Wood, August 2, 1929, Rowe correspondence; Rowe, "Thirty-Fourth Annual Report," 62.

106. "Alaskans Value Hudson Stuck Memorial Hospital," 671. Prospectors used sluice boxes in placer mining. The wooden trough with a riffled base would catch the heavier gold as silt and other rock materials washed through the box.

107. C. Burke, *Doctor Hap*, 285–86.

108. Geoffrey Burke (grandson of Grafton and Clara Burke and son of Grafton Edgar Burke), telephone communication with Mary Ehrlander, August 25, 2018.

109. G. Burke, *Kwunduk Nenlinatsidenja (Mixed Talk)*, 4, Burke correspondence.

110. Rowe, "Thirty-Fourth Annual Report," 64.

111. C. Burke, *Doctor Hap*, 286. Beattie Ky's story was recorded at the time by Hap and by Bishop Rowe. Moreover, two of Grafton's children spoke with Ehrlander of the striking scars on their father's forearms and of hearing the story of Beattie Ky many times during their childhood. Neither contemporary accounts nor Clara's account in *Doctor Hap* relate the need for subsequent autografts. However, this is the only plausible explanation for the grafts.

112. Rowe, "Five Months in the Interior of Alaska," 731, 733 (quotation on 733). A similar incident of a young boy falling backward into a cauldron of dog food occurred on the Tolovana River in 1918. Upon hearing of the accident, Archdeacon Stuck, with Walter Harper at the wheel of the *Pelican*, rushed the boy to the hospital at Fort Gibbon, but the child died soon after their arrival (see Ehrlander, *Walter Harper*, chapter 7).

113. Bishop Rowe had resigned himself to cutting missionary salaries by 5 percent, owing to his reduced allocation for 1930, but an article Wood published describing Rowe's despair at this unjust treatment of missionaries brought in sufficient donations to restore the cut that year. Wood, "Across the Secretary's

Desk" (September 1929), 603; "Three Percent Cut Schedule 1929"; and Wood to Rowe, September 11, 1929, Rowe correspondence.

114. "Fort Yukon Mission Needs Power Plant."

115. Wood, "Across the Secretary's Desk" (November 1929), 739.

116. G. Burke to Wood, October 20, 1929, Burke correspondence; G. Burke, "Alaska Hospital has Phenomenal Growth," 728; Rowe, "Thirty-Fourth Annual Report," 62.

117. Wood, "Across the Secretary's Desk" (July 1929), 469; G. Burke to Wood, April 15, 1929, Burke correspondence.

118. Rowe, "Five Months in the Interior of Alaska," 732.

119. Whittlesey to Spirit of Missions, February 26, 1932, Rowe correspondence.

120. "Excerpts from Letter from Dr. Grafton Burke" (n.d., "1930" is handwritten on the document), Burke correspondence. Hap hoped to adopt the wireless station's policy of keeping a two-year supply of fuel on hand to avoid another such crisis.

121. McIntosh, "The Fire at St. Mark's Mission," 181–82; Wood, "Nenana Alaskan Mission Visited by Fire," 84; Nicholson to Tompkins, March 4, 1930, Rowe correspondence.

122. Wood, "Jottings from Near and Far" (July 1930), 483.

123. Bentley, "Fire-Swept Alaskan Mission," 819–20. The new dormitory reverted to its original name, Tortella Hall, referencing the nearby mountain.

124. Rowe, "To the Editor," June 6, 1930, Rowe correspondence.

125. Tompkins to Rowe, March 14, 1930, Rowe correspondence.

126. Rowe, "Five Months in the Interior of Alaska," 731; Rowe, "Five Years on the Yukon," 302; G. Burke to Wood, March 25, 1931, Burke correspondence; G. Burke, Kwunduk Nenlinatsidenja (Mixed Talk), 2, Burke correspondence.

127. C. Burke, Doctor Hap, 275.

128. "Excerpts from Letter from Dr. Grafton Burke, Fort Yukon"; G. Burke, Kwunduk Nenlinatsidenja (Mixed Talk), 4, Burke correspondence.

129. "Excerpts from Letter from Dr. Grafton Burke, Fort Yukon."

130. "Excerpts from Letter from Dr. Grafton Burke, Fort Yukon."

131. Habersham, "Alaska Mission Is 'Stupendous Piece of Work,'" Church at Work (1930), 6, RG 351, box 13, folder 5, Grafton Burke 1908–1937, PECUSA.

132. Habersham, "Alaska Mission Is 'Stupendous Piece of Work.'"

133. Habersham, "Alaska Mission Is 'Stupendous Piece of Work.'"

134. C. Burke, Doctor Hap, 287; Peter Hackett, interview, September 7, 2021.

135. Hackett, "Character Education at Riverdale: Perspectives of the Founder," provided by Hackett to Ehrlander; Peter Hackett, interview, September 7, 2021.

136. C. Burke, *Doctor Hap*, 287.

137. D. Hackett, "An Undergraduate's Winter in Alaska," 808; C. Burke, *Doctor Hap*, 288–89.

138. G. Burke, *Kwunduk Nenlinatsidenja (Mixed Talk)*, 4, Burke correspondence; Fredson to Wood, August 31, 1930, and Wood to Fredson, September 18, 1930, Fredson correspondence; Mackenzie, *Zhoh Gwatsan*, 144, 148, 150. John Wood was delighted with the arrangement whereby John earned a good salary at the NC Company while he maintained his close ties with the mission and furthered the mission's work (Wood to Fredson, September 18, 1930).

139. Rowe to Wood, December 24, 1930, Rowe correspondence.

140. Wood to Williams, December 13, 1930, Williams correspondence, PECUSA.

141. Rowe, "Thirty-Fourth Annual Report."

142. Rowe, "Thirty-Fourth Annual Report."

8. EXPANDING DURING THE DEPRESSION YEARS

1. Fortuine, *"Must We All Die?,"* 222.

2. Williams, "Busy Times at Fort Yukon," 126–27; Wood, "Jottings from Near and Far" (December 1930), 849; D. Hackett, "An Undergraduate's Winter in Alaska," 808; G. Burke, "Alaska Hospital has Phenomenal Growth," 729. Hap consulted with several traveling physicians who visited the hospital during the epidemic, regarding the treatment regimen. It seems the matron, or cook, who left was Mrs. Stanford, although Williams did not name her. She returned, and Hap spoke highly of her.

3. G. Burke, "Alaska Hospital Has Phenomenal Growth," 729; G. Burke, "Excerpts from Letter from Dr. Grafton Burke" (n.d., "1930" is handwritten on the document; "sky high" quotation herein), Burke correspondence; G. Burke, *Kwunduk Nenlinatsidenja (Mixed Talk)*, 3–4, Burke correspondence; Wood, "Jottings from Near and Far" (December 1930), 849 ("septic throat" quotation); Wood, "Jottings from Near and Far" (February 1931), 112–13. In summer 1931 Maude Pratt transferred to St. Mark's Mission at Nenana. Bentley, "St. Mark's Mission," 65.

4. Williams to Wood, November 14, 1930, Williams correspondence.

5. Williams to Wood, November 14, 1930.

6. Wood to Williams, December 13, 1930, Williams correspondence.

7. Williams to Wood January 24, 1931, Williams correspondence.

8. Williams to Wood January 24, 1931.

9. G. Burke, "Alaska Hospital Has Phenomenal Growth," 728–29.

10. G. Burke, "Alaska Hospital Has Phenomenal Growth," 728–29.

11. G. Burke, "Alaska Hospital Has Phenomenal Growth," 729–30.

12. G. Burke, "Excerpts from Letter" (quotation herein); C. Burke, *Doctor Hap*, 259, 274–75.

13. G. Burke, "Excerpts from Letter" (Hap's quotation herein); C. Burke, *Doctor Hap*, 290.

14. C. Burke, *Doctor Hap*, 289–90; G. Burke, *Kwunduk Nenlinatsidenja (Mixed Talk)*, 4, Burke correspondence; D. Hackett, "An Undergraduate's Winter in Alaska," 808.

15. D. Hackett, "An Undergraduate's Winter in Alaska," 809.

16. "Alaskan Women Present Altar Cloth to Cathedral," 148; G. Burke, *Kwunduk Nenlinatsidenja (Mixed Talk)*, 2, Burke correspondence.

17. Address by Bishop Manning at the service in the Cathedral of St. John the Divine for the presentation of the gift from the Native women of Fort Yukon, Alaska on Sunday, February 8, at four o-clock, Archives of Cathedral of St. John the Divine.

18. G. Burke to Wood, March 25, 1931, Burke correspondence.

19. G. Burke, "Alaska Hospital Has Phenomenal Growth," 730.

20. Williams had reported in January 1931 that the mission home currently housed twenty-six children (Williams to Wood, January 24, 1931).

21. G. Burke, *Kwunduk Nenlinatsidenja (Mixed Talk)*, 1, Burke correspondence; G. Burke to Wood, March 25, 1931.

22. Wood, "Jottings from Near and Far" (February 1932), 113. We found no indication of whether the Yukon or Canadian government compensated the Episcopal Church for these medical services.

23. Lewis, "Scrofula"; Murray, Schraufnagel, and Hopewell, "Treatment of Tuberculosis."

24. "Hudson Stuck Memorial Hospital, Fort Yukon, Alaska," October 1, 1943, RG 351, box 13, folder 5, Grafton Burke 1908–1937, PECUSA.

25. "Marriage Records Issued in Fort Yukon," Rootsweb, http://freepages.rootsweb .com/~coleen/genealogy/fort_yukon_alaska.html; C. Burke, *Doctor Hap*, 294; Mackenzie, *Zhoh Gwatsan*, 148. Mackenzie placed the wedding in 1932, but the online list of marriage licenses shows 1931, and this timing accords with Clara's memory of having attended the wedding. She and Hap were on furlough in July 1932. Unangan were formerly referred to as Aleuts.

26. Wood, "Jottings from Near and Far" (February 1932), 113.

27. G. Burke to Rowe, February 8, 1933, Rowe correspondence.

28. "With Our Missionaries."

29. C. Burke, "Twenty-Five Years," 349–55; Dukes, "Surgeon Commends Stuck Hospital," 806.

30. Burke to Wood, March 25, 1931. Hudson was considering going into the ministry, despite his grandmother's opposition. Hap wanted him to attend Sewanee and asked Wood for financial advice, having "no [one] else in the world to turn to, but you." We found no further discussion of this potential career path for Hudson.

31. Peter Hackett, the grandson of Frank and Frances Hackett, told Ehrlander that it would have been very much like his grandparents to sponsor the Burkes' vacation. Telephone interview with Mary Ehrlander, September 7, 2021.

32. Goddard, Alaska diary, 61; "James Lindsay, 26th Earl of Crawford," Wikipedia, last modified January 18, 2023, https://en.wikipedia.org/wiki/James _Lindsay,_26th_Earl_of_Crawford.

33. C. Burke, *Doctor Hap*, 291; C. Burke, "Twenty-Five Years," 349.

34. C. Burke, *Doctor Hap*, 292–93.

35. Bentley, "Along the Yukon," 168; Wood, "Increase in Salary of Rev. Merritt Williams, September 8, 1932," Williams correspondence.

36. That fall the newlyweds went on the church speaker's circuit in the southeastern United States, giving perhaps forty talks to raise interest in Alaska's mission work. Williams to Wood (n.d., received November 14, 1932), Williams correspondence.

37. G. Burke to Wood November 14, 1932, and C. Burke to Wood, March 1, 1933, Burke correspondence; C. Burke, "Fort Yukon Rejoices," 339–40.

38. C. Burke, "Fort Yukon Rejoices," 339. The American Church Building Fund also contributed $1,000.

39. C. Burke to Wood, March 1, 1933, G. Burk to Wood, April 18, 1933, Burke correspondence.

40. G. Burke to Wood, April 18, 1933, Burke correspondence. The children had collected the fifteen cents from tourists and saved it for Lent, because at Fort Yukon, no denominations below a quarter were used. The following year, the children gave $205 for Lent, an average of $2.50 per child. G. Burke to Wood, April 3, 1934, Burke correspondence. Many Native children were out on their families' traplines longer than usual in 1934, because of low yields. Forty-nine Native and thirty-three white children contributed.

41. G. Burke to Rowe, February 8, 1933, Rowe correspondence.

42. G. Burke to Rowe, February 6, 1933; G. Burke to Wood (telegram), April 14, 1933; Rowe to Wood, July 12, 1933; Rowe, "Report of Rt. Rev. P.T. Rowe (1932)," 6, all in Rowe correspondence. Gertrude L. Hoffman had directed $20,000 of her estate to go to Hudson Stuck Memorial Hospital. Such bequests were especially helpful in maintaining mission operations during the Depression. Wood to G. Burke, June 11, 1935, Burke correspondence.

43. Alaska's allocation dropped from $86,970 in 1929 to $61,865 in 1935; the projected allocation for 1936 was $54,865. Rowe, "Report of the Bishop" (1929), and Franklin to Committee of Five, January 23, 1935 (appendix to this letter), Rowe correspondence. Rowe avoided cutting missionaries' salaries until 1933, when he reduced them by 10 percent. Wood to Rowe, October 16, 1933, Rowe correspondence. Salaries at mission headquarters had been cut 20 percent.

44. In the early 1930s, Fort Yukon, Allakaket, Nenana, and Point Hope all exceeded their meager budgets, which left Rowe to cover these costs from his allocation that he preferred to use for building projects. Rowe to Wood, July 18, 1931, and Rowe to Wood, June 25, 1934, Rowe correspondence.

45. Rowe to Wood, September 1, 1931, Rowe correspondence.

46. *Evening News* (Harrisburg, Dauphin, Pennsylvania), January 6, 1934, 10; Mackenzie, *Zhoh Gwatsan*, 148–50. The 1935 appropriations schedule shows Cruikshank as man-of-all-work at Fort Yukon.

47. Whittlesey to *Spirit of Missions*, February 26, 1932, Rowe correspondence.

48. C. Burke to Wood, March 1, 1933, Burke correspondence.

49. G. Burke to Rowe, February 8, 1933, Rowe correspondence. Old John recalled hunting game with bow and arrow when the first Hudson Bay traders arrived in 1846.

50. C. Burke, *Doctor Hap*, 219–20. Such fears had occasionally led to "kidnappings" of patients from the hospital, with fatal consequences, Clara wrote.

51. Harper, "New York Sculptor Visits Fort Yukon," 569; C. Burke, "Twenty-Five Years," 355.

52. Harper, "New York Sculptor Visits Fort Yukon," 571–72.

53. Rowe, "Report of the Bishop" (1933), Rowe correspondence.

54. Rowe, "Report of the Bishop" (1933), and John Bentley, "Annual Report" (1933), Rowe correspondence.

55. Mischler and Simeone, *Tanana and Chandalar*, 215.

56. Mischler and Simeone, *Tanana and Chandalar*, 216. Other guests stayed at the mission home that summer, including Bishop Rowe and the trader

Harry Anthony, who was prospecting on the Arctic slope now. Fort Yukon was quiet in mid-August, with most trappers and prospectors in the region having returned "to the hills" after earlier summer visits to trade their furs and purchase supplies (216, 217, 219).

57. Fredson had made a name for himself as a Neets'aii Gwich'in translator and information bearer by now. In July of the previous year, he interpreted for the ethnographer Cornelius Osgood and his wife, Harriet, who had been doing ethnographic work on several Gwich'in groups in the region (Mackenzie, *Zhoh Gwatsan*, 150). Fredson provided much valuable ethnographic information as well. Osgood wrote of his interpreting skills, "He could scarcely be excelled and his intelligent appreciation of the problem won from me my sincere admiration and esteem." Osgood, *Contributions to the Ethnography of the Kutchin*, 21.

58. Mischler and Simeone, *Tanana and Chandalar*, 216–17 (quotation on 216). A government dentist held a clinic at the hospital the following summer "pulling and filling teeth." Goddard, Alaska diary, 62.

59. McKennan, "The Physical Anthropology of Two Alaskan Athapaskan Groups," 45.

60. Mischler and Simeone, *Tanana and Chandalar*, 219.

61. Mischler and Simeone, *Tanana and Chandalar*, 220. McKennan did not mention whether John did any of the fiddling that evening.

62. Bergman, Zoom interview with authors, March 13, 2022.

63. Mary Beth Smetzer, "The Journey Ends: Fort Yukon Chief Is Finally Home," *Fairbanks Daily News Miner*, September 8, 2013.

64. #76—Alaska Game Law Violation of Reg. 19—August 23, 1933, folder 1: Justice Court in and for Ft. Yukon Precinct, 4th Division of Alaska, Grafton Burke, JP–1911–1929, Fort Yukon Precinct Justice Court Records, APRCA; Harper, "New York Sculptor Visits Fort Yukon," 572.

65. Mackenzie, *Zhoh Gwatsan*, 148, 152.

66. C. Burke, *Doctor Hap*, 294–95 (quotation on both pages).

67. G. Burke to mission headquarters (n.d., received March 26, 1934), Burke correspondence. Hap's account of the incident did not relate how they eventually returned to Fort Yukon.

68. G. Burke to Wood, April 16, 1934, Burke correspondence. At seventy-seven years old, Bishop Rowe could no longer travel as he once had to raise funds for the Alaska mission work.

69. G. Burke to Wood (Dear Friend), April 16, 1934, Burke correspondence; Wood, "Across the Secretary's Desk" (August 1934), 393. In 1908 the Austrian Clemens Von Pirquet had developed a skin test for tuberculosis.

70. Goddard, Alaska diary, 150. Hayes had worked hand in hand for several years with Dr. W. A. R. Goodwin, "the father of Colonial Williamsburg," in restoring the historical city, with the financial backing of John D. Rockefeller II. "Elizabeth Hayes Goddard," Colonial Williamsburg website, September 24, 2021, https://www.colonialwilliamsburg.org/learn/deep-dives/much -more-secretary/.

71. Goddard, Alaska diary, 52–54.

72. Goddard, Alaska diary, 54–55.

73. Goddard, Alaska diary, 55–57.

74. Goddard, Alaska diary, 57–58 (quotations on both pages).

75. Goddard, Alaska diary, 58–59 (quotation on both pages).

76. Goddard, Alaska diary, 60.

77. Goddard, Alaska diary, 62.

78. Goddard, Alaska diary, 64–65.

79. Goddard, Alaska diary, 66–67.

80. Hudson Burke Jr., interview by Mary Ehrlander, October 25, 2021, Seattle.

81. Goddard, Alaska diary, 67–69.

82. Goddard, Alaska diary, 69.

83. Goddard, Alaska diary, 70.

84. Wood, "The National Council," 549–50 (quotation on 550).

85. Rowe, "Report of Rt. Rev. P. T. Rowe (1932)," 6. A small hospital at Tikiġaq/ Point Hope was not staffed. The community of Wrangell now maintained the Wrangell General Hospital, which the church had established, but much responsibility continued to fall to Rowe.

86. In 1934 Rowe had suspended operations at Wrangell and Cordova that served non-Natives. Rowe to Wood, June 28, 1934, Rowe correspondence. He pressed the congregations in southern Alaska, at Ketchikan, Juneau, Sitka, and Anchorage, which were predominantly white, to transition toward self-support by paying half their pastors' salaries. Rowe to Wood, October 8, 1934, and Wood to Rowe, January 16, 1935, Rowe correspondence.

87. Rowe to Wood, September 13, 1934, Rowe correspondence.

88. G. Burke to Parson, November 23, 1934, Burke correspondence. Parson's letter is not in the file.

89. G. Burke to Wood, December 1, 1934, Burke correspondence.

90. G. Burke to Wood, February 12, 1935, Burke correspondence; Wood, "Foreign Missions: Across the Secretary's Desk" (July 1935), 327.

91. Wood to G. Burke, March 14, 1935, Burke correspondence.

92. G. Burke to Wood, May 15, 1935, Burke correspondence. Wood used Hap's letter as the basis for a *Spirit of Missions* article aimed at securing help with the fuel bill and reached out personally to individuals who had supported St. Stephen's in the past. Wood to G. Burke, July 16, 1935, Burke correspondence.

93. Nash, "The Generosity Cycle." Research on charitable giving typically uses itemized income tax deductions as a measure.

94. Gruber and Hungerman, "Faith-Based Charity." Government policies, including the Hoover administration's tax increase, led to a sharp decrease in philanthropy by the wealthy. In the late 1930s the federal government increased taxes on lower-income earners while providing tax deductions for charitable donations, thus incentivizing them to increase their giving. Phillip W. Magness, "Philanthropy and the Great Depression: What Historical Tax Records Tell Us about Charity," Phillipmagness.com, accessed September 26, 2021, https://philmagness.com/2017/05/philanthropy-and-the-great-depression-what-historical-tax-records-tell-us-about-charity/.

95. Wood, "Foreign Missions: Across the Secretary's Desk" (August 1935), 375; "Our Alaskan Missions, Concluded," 21. Additionally, the annual Woman's Thank Offering brought in $745.

96. C. Burke, "Doctor Burke Has Overwhelming Anxieties," 555; Rowe to Wood, June 27, 1935, Rowe correspondence.

97. C. Burke, "The Question Facing the Doctor."

98. Rowe to Wood, June 27, 1935, Rowe correspondence (emphasis in original). Sisters Dinah and Rachel Titus, students at St. Mark's in Nenana, joined the staff at St. Stephen's that summer, Dinah to assist Clara in the home and Rachel to assist in the hospital. "The Newsletter, Missionary District of Alaska" 23 (October 1935), RG 79-1, Alaska Miscellaneous Newsletters, 1934–1935, PECUSA.

99. G. Burke to Wood, November 5, 1935, Burke correspondence.

100. C. Burke to Wood (telegram), September 31, 1935 (strangely, the telegram is stamped "received 1935 SEP 31 AM 12 02"), Burke correspondence; C. Burke, "Doctor Burke Has Overwhelming Anxieties," 555; "The Newsletter, Missionary District of Alaska." John Wood asked Clara to write an account of Hap's collapse and hospitalization, including the local context. Wood to C. Burke, October 1, 1935, Burke correspondence.

101. C. Burke, "Doctor Burke Has Overwhelming Anxieties," 556.

102. Rowe to Wood, October 9, 1935, Rowe correspondence. We found no record of whether the BIA provided such relief that winter.

103. C. Burke, "Doctor Burke Has Overwhelming Anxieties," 556; Wood to C. Burke, November 5, 1935, Burke correspondence. Wood reported to Hap on September 28 the arrival of two gifts of $500 since midmonth. Wood to G. Burke, September 28, 1935, Burke correspondence.

104. Rowe, Revised Schedule of Appropriations for 1935, January 3, 1935, Rowe correspondence.

105. Wood to Rowe, October 14, 1935, Rowe correspondence.

106. "The Newsletter, Missionary District of Alaska" 23 (October 1935), RG 79-I, Alaska Miscellaneous Newsletters, 1934–1935, PECUSA; Bentley, "Missionary District of Alaska," 107.

107. "The Newsletter, Missionary District of Alaska" 23 (October 1935), RG 79-I, Alaska Miscellaneous Newsletters, 1934–1935, PECUSA; C. Burke to Wood, September 31, 1935; G. Burke to Wood, November 5, 1935, Burke correspondence.

108. Wood, "Foreign Missions: Across the Secretary's Desk" (December 1935), 564; Wood, "Foreign Missions: Across the Secretary's Desk" (April 1936), 182.

109. C. Burke to Wood, February 21, 1935, Burke correspondence.

9. THE END OF AN ERA

1. The population had dropped significantly, from 3,541 in 1910 to 1,555 in 1920, with the decline of the gold rush that founded the city in 1903. U.S. Census Bureau, accessed October 21, 2021, https://www2.census.gov/library /publications/decennial/1940/population-volume-1/33973538v1ch11.pdf.

2. "Our Alaskan Missions Concluded," 13, 22. In 1937 the Episcopal Missionary District of Alaska had six thousand baptized members, which represented 10 percent of Alaska's population of about sixty thousand. Church leadership in Alaska believed that this was by far the highest percentage of Episcopal congregants in any diocese or missionary district. "Moccasin Telegraph" (November 1937), 11.

3. Rowe, "Report of the Bishop" (1936), 102, Rowe correspondence.

4. Laguna, "The Dena Indians," 6.

5. "Moccasin Telegraph" (August 1938), 6–7. Previously, mail had traveled by ship from Juneau to Seward and then by rail to Fairbanks. Postage for a typical letter cost six cents.

6. "Alaska, St. Stephen's Mission and Hudson Stuck Hospital, Fort Yukon, Alaska" (n.d., perhaps 1939), RG 351, box 13, folder 5, Grafton Burke 1908–1937, PECUSA.

7. Wood, "Foreign Missions: Across the Secretary's Desk" (September 1935), 424.

8. Clara did not explain in *Doctor Hap* the timing of Hudson's arrival in Fort Yukon that fall, and no contemporary documents or publications note his arrival, but it seems likely that Hap's health crisis played a role in Hudson's extended visit to Fort Yukon.

9. Thomas R. Russell, "Remembering Oliver H. Beahrs," *Oncology Times*, April 10, 2006, 33–34, https://journals.lww.com/oncology-times/fulltext/2006/04100/remembering_oliver_h__beahrs.15.aspx. Clara wrote that the second person to assist Hap that year was a Harvard student, Jim Hubbard, but we suspect he came a different year. The tradition continued; in 1937 a Yale student volunteered at the hospital for a year. "Moccasin Telegraph" (November 1938), 10.

10. C. Burke, *Doctor Hap*, 297–98.

11. C. Burke to Wood, January 22, 1936, Burke correspondence.

12. "Alaska, St. Stephen's Mission and Hudson Stuck Hospital, Fort Yukon, Alaska."

13. G. Burke to Parson, April 14, 1936, Burke correspondence.

14. G. Burke to Parson, April 14, 1936. The children typically did tasks around town to earn money for their Lenten offerings each year.

15. Parson to G. Burke, May 13, 1936, Burke correspondence.

16. Rowe, "Report of the Bishop" (1936), 102, Rowe correspondence; Rowe to Franklin, March 5, 1936, Rowe correspondence. Franklin gently reminded Rowe that the Woman's Auxiliary underwrote $2,300 of his salary and that those funds could be used for no other purpose. Franklin to Rowe, March 10, 1936, Rowe correspondence.

17. C. Burke, *Doctor Hap*, 300–301. Tobacco's carcinogenic effects began to be recognized in the 1940s.

18. C. Burke, *Doctor Hap*, 301–2.

19. G. Burke to Parson, May 19, 1936, Burke correspondence. Hap often signed his letters to Wood and Parson with such affectionate words. "Believe Me" also appears to have been a conventional closing at the time. John Wood, executive secretary for foreign missions, had been hospitalized in December for ten weeks and had been close to death. He was out of the office for several months. Artley Parson, associate secretary of foreign and domestic missions,

assumed Wood's duties at mission headquarters during his absence. LMcG to C. Burke, March 11, 1936, Burke correspondence.

20. G. Burke to Parson, April 14, 1936. Burke correspondence.

21. Parson to G. Burke, May 13, 1936, Burke correspondence.

22. C. Burke, *Doctor Hap*, 297–98 (quotation on both pages); "Moccasin Telegraph" (August 1936), 9; G. Burke to Parson (telegram), May 27, 1936, Burke correspondence.

23. Hudson Stuck Burke Jr., interview by Mary Ehrlander, October 25, 2021, Seattle.

24. Parson to G. Burke, May 28, 1936 (night letter), Burke correspondence.

25. "Moccasin Telegraph" (November 1936), 9.

26. Parson to G. Burke, March 24, 1936, Burke correspondence.

27. Wood to Rowe, July 3, 1936, Rowe correspondence. Hap and Clara would have had no objection to Hume's Congregational Church membership. He had long made it clear that he wanted competent, compassionate, and congenial hospital personnel. Their religious affiliation was inconsequential in his view.

28. "Moccasin Telegraph" (November 1936), 11; "Moccasin Telegraph" (November 1937), 10, 12; "Missions and Staff," 21.

29. "Moccasin Telegraph" (February 1937), 14.

30. G. Burke to Wood, April 14, 1936, and October 28, 1936, Burke correspondence; "Moccasin Telegraph" (February 1937), 13; Fortuine, *"Must We All Die?,"* xxxiii; "Trudeau Sanitorium," Local Wiki, accessed September 21, 2021, https://localwiki.org/hsl/Trudeau_Sanatorium; "D. Ogden Mills Training School for Nurses," Local Wiki, accessed September 21, 2021, https://localwiki.org/hsl/D._Ogden_Mills_Training_School_for_Nurses. Founded in 1884 by Dr. Edward Livingston Trudeau, the tuberculosis treatment center in the Adirondacks emphasized patients' exposure to the open air. A $10,000 donation led to the establishment in 1912 of a nurses' training school on the site.

31. C. Burke, *Doctor Hap*, 302.

32. Hudson Burke Jr. and Diane Burke (his daughter), interview by Mary Ehrlander, October 25, 2021, Seattle. Hudson reported that his father had some experience flying a Ford trimotor, but he did not believe that Hudson Sr. was ever licensed to fly. He said that his father did not fly as part of his work at Boeing. Diane spent time with her grandfather when he lived in a west Seattle rest home in his final years. He shared many memories with her, including the day that he and Boeing went flying together, piloting separate planes.

33. C. Burke, *Doctor Hap*, 303; G. Burke to Wood, January 20, 1936, and G. Burke to Wood, June 28, 1936, Burke correspondence.

34. "Moccasin Telegraph" (November 1936), 10; C. Burke, *Doctor Hap*, 302–3.

35. C. Burke, *Doctor Hap*, 302–3; Wood, "Conference with Mrs. Burke," December 4, 1936, Burke correspondence. Hap wrote Wood regarding the Panama Canal cruise, "This trip, I am told is restful and cheap." G. Burke to Wood, January 20, 1936.

36. Wood, "Foreign Missions: Across the Secretary's Desk" (October 1936), 475.

37. Undated document that announces the Burkes' and Bishop Rowe's arrival in New York in September 1937, Burke correspondence; Hume to Wood, September 22, 1936, and G. Burke to Wood, October 28, 1936 (quotation herein), Burke correspondence.

38. G. Burke to Wood, October 28, 1936.

39. "Alaskan Bishop to Speak in City," *Baltimore Sun*, January 23, 1937, 4.

40. Summary of the Proceedings of the Forty-Eighth Annual Meeting, 150, 151, 154.

41. "Mission Hospital near Arctic Circle: Mrs. Grafton Burke Will Describe It," *Boston Globe*, May 1, 1937, 13. That summer she and Hap gave a joint presentation in Detroit at the Cranbrook Summer Conference. "Notable Religious Leaders Will Address Episcopalians," *Detroit Free Press*, October 19, 1940. This 1940 article noted Hap and Clara's 1937 presentation.

42. "New Spirit Prevails in Old Ceremony"; "Alaskans Honored."

43. C. Burke, *Doctor Hap*, 304. Clara mistakenly reported that Hap was inducted into the Omega Alpha Kappa fraternity, which never existed at Sewanee. Matthew Reynolds, archivist at Sewanee, informed us, "A hand-written notation in the copy of *Doctor Hap* that we hold suggests that it is actually the Sewanee chapter of the Omicron Delta Kappa honor fraternity. 'ODK' held an induction ceremony the afternoon of the day that Burke received his degree (though Burke is not explicitly mentioned). Though it cannot be confirmed, the most likely scenario is that he was actually inducted into the ranks of ODK while he was here in 1937" (email to Ehrlander, December 3, 2021).

44. Geoffrey Burke, interview by Mary Ehrlander, December 7, 2018, Montreal, Quebec. Geoffrey, who visited the cabin, said it was very sturdy, perhaps sixteen by twenty-eight feet, and it looked much like an Alaskan log cabin. Telephone conversation with Ehrlander, December 3, 2021.

45. "Moccasin Telegraph" (November 1937), 8; "55 Sewanee Alumni Meet in Cincinnati for Reunion Dinner," *Sewanee Purple*, October 28, 1937, 1. We

could find no information on how this European tour was financed; Clara
did not mention it in *Doctor Hap*.

46. G. Burke to Wood, November 11, 1937, Burke correspondence.

47. Wood, "Foreign Missions: Across the Secretary's Desk" (December 1937),
602; C. Burke, *Doctor Hap*, 304–5. Grafton Burke told his son Geoffrey of
the land Hap had purchased in Vermont with the thought of retiring there.
Geoffrey Burke, telephone conversation with Mary Ehrlander, December 3,
2021.

48. Rowe to Wood, August 22, 1938, Rowe correspondence (emphasis in original).

49. Rowe to Wood, July 2, 1938, Rowe correspondence; Hume to Wood, January
12, 1937 (Hume quotation here), Hume correspondence, PECUSA. While
the expenditures may have been justified, the burden they entailed compounded Hap's anxieties about the future. One can only speculate as to the
reasons for Dr. Hume's shocking behavior. It may have been sectarianism,
given Hume's Congregationalist background. He may have had difficulty
adjusting to hospital practices or may have found Addie Gavel's competence
and professionalism threatening. Mental health or marital problems may have
contributed. Neither the Rowe nor the Burke correspondence contains any
further explanation than Rowe's report of shockingly disrespectful, aggressive,
and unprofessional behavior.

50. Hume to Wood, January 12, 1937, Hume correspondence.

51. Mackenzie, *Zhoh Gwatsan*, 155–57.

52. Rowe to Wood, December 2, 1936, Rowe correspondence.

53. Wood to Rowe, October 16, 1933, Rowe correspondence. The letter is
unsigned, but given that Rowe wrote his request to Wood the day before
from New York and because the tone of the letter resembles Wood's typical
tone, we presume Wood authored the letter.

54. Mackenzie, *Zhoh Gwatsan*, 156–58.

55. Mackenzie, *Zhoh Gwatsan*, 158–60; Fredson, "Venetie," 7.

56. Mackenzie, *Zhoh Gwatsan*, 158–59; Fredson, "Venetie," 6.

57. Rowe, "Alaska," 97–99.

58. Fredson, "Venetie," 7.

59. Rowe, "Alaska," 97–99; Rowe to Wood, April 25, 1938, Rowe correspondence;
C. Burke, *Doctor Hap*, 282.

60. Rowe to Wood, April 25, 1938, Rowe correspondence.

61. "Moccasin Telegraph" (August 1938), 6.

62. C. Burke, *Doctor Hap*, 309–10 (quotation on 309).

63. Rowe, "An Alaska Ordination" (n.d.), Burke correspondence. Rowe referred to the biblical passage Acts 2:1 regarding the celebration of the Pentecost, which falls fifty days after Easter and marks the descent of the Holy Spirit upon a meeting of the Apostles in Jerusalem. The verse in the King James Bible reads, "When the Day of Pentecost had fully come, they were all with one accord in one place."
64. C. Burke, *Doctor Hap*, 309–10.
65. C. Burke, *Doctor Hap*, 310–11 (quotation on both pages).
66. C. Burke, *Doctor Hap*, 310–11.
67. Rowe to Wood, July 2, 1938, Rowe correspondence (emphasis in original).
68. Rowe, "An Alaska Ordination."
69. C. Burke, *Doctor Hap*, 311.
70. C. Burke, *Doctor Hap*, 311–12.
71. C. Burke to Wood, August 13, 1938, Burke correspondence; C. Burke, *Doctor Hap*, 313–14.
72. Wood to C. Burke, August 22, 1938, and Wood to C. Burke, August 22, 1938 (night letter), Burke correspondence. Hap paid a premium of $168.60 per year for his New York Life insurance policy. JWH/EDH to Burke, February 14, 1924, Burke correspondence. Wood wrote that Frank Hackett suggested sending Grafton to see Hap in Seattle, understanding him as offering to pay Grafton's expenses. Clara responded enthusiastically. C. Burke to Wood, August 30, 1938, Burke correspondence. Grafton later stopped by mission headquarters saying he wanted to go and explaining how he could pay the expense himself. Wood advised against his traveling to Seattle if he had to pay the expense himself, as it would likely be $250. Wood to C. Burke, September 7, 1938, Burke correspondence. At this time Hap's illness had yet to be diagnosed.
73. Rowe to Wood, August 22, 1938, Rowe correspondence. He sent Nicholson, who "would give his life for this work," to Fort Yukon to manage site operations and sent Gavel back to manage the medical care.
74. Clara spelled the name Freidlander. We have not been able to identify this institution further. It is possible that Hap was transferred to the Firland Sanitorium in Seattle, but this seems unlikely, because Firland Sanitorium treated tuberculosis patients.
75. Rowe to Wood, September 22, 1938, Rowe correspondence; C. Burke to Wood, October 5, 1938, Burke correspondence.
76. Rowe to Wood, October 6, 1938, Rowe correspondence.
77. "Grafton Burke: Arctic Physician."

78. "Grafton Burke: Arctic Physician."

79. Rowe to Wood, October 6, 1938, Rowe correspondence; C. Burke to Wood, October 5, 1938, Burke correspondence; "Moccasin Telegraph" (November 1938), 6–7.

80. Rowe to Wood, October 6, 1938, Rowe correspondence.

81. Bentley, Statement on Burke memorial service (n.d.), Burke correspondence; "Final Rites Are Held for Dr. G. Burke," *Fairbanks Daily News Miner*, November 1, 1938.

EPILOGUE

1. C. Burke, *Doctor Hap*, 317; Episcopal Diocese of Alaska, *A Century of Faith*, 200; Rowe to Wood, October 19, 1938, Rowe correspondence; "Moccasin Telegraph" (November 1938), 10; Wood, "Memorandum of a Conference with Mrs. Burke," November 29, 1938, Burke correspondence; "Moccasin Telegraph" (February 1940), 16.

2. In lobbying for the maximum pension for Clara, Bishop Rowe reminded the council that she had provided unsalaried service to the mission all the years of her marriage. "Provision for Mrs. Grafton Burke," resolution adopted by the National Council (of the Protestant Episcopal Church of the United States of America) on December 13 to 15, 1938, RG 351, box 13, folder 5, Grafton Burke 1908–1937, PECUSA.

3. C. Burke to Wood, October 18, 1938, Burke correspondence; Wood to Rowe, October 17, 1938, and Rowe to Wood, October 6 and 19, 1938, Rowe correspondence; "Moccasin Telegraph" (August 1940), 14.

4. C. Burke, *Doctor Hap*, 317–18.

5. C. Burke, *Doctor Hap*, 318–19; Phillips, "Unsung Heroines."

6. Beaver, *Fort Yukon Trader*, 33–35.

7. Jenkins, *The Man of Alaska*, 108.

8. Jenkins, *The Man of Alaska*, 270, 285, 286–88; "Bishop Bentley."

9. "David Wallis," 17.

10. Bentley, "Annual Report," 12.

11. Mackenzie, *Zhoh Gwatsan*, 160–70.

12. Cited in Mackenzie, *Zhoh Gwatsan*, 172. John currently headed the Selective Service in the region.

13. "John Fredson"; Mackenzie, *Zhoh Gwatsan*, 184. John was initially buried in the Native cemetery at Fort Yukon. In 1996 the family reburied him at Venetie, at his widow Jean's request. Diana Campbell (granddaughter of John Fredson), telephone conversation with Mary Ehrlander, January 26, 2022.

14. Parran, "Alaska's Health: A Survey Report," 96.

15. Parran, "Alaska's Health: A Survey Report," 14.

16. The *Parran Report* did lead to numerous improvements in health-care delivery in the 1950s and 1960s. Fortuine wrote, "For years the report became a kind of scripture used by many health professionals to justify increased budgets for tuberculosis and other disease problems." Fortuine, *"Must We All Die?,"* 136.

17. Fortuine, *"Must We All Die?,"* 120.

18. *The Living Church*, July 23, 1961, 7, Grafton Burke File, Archives and Special Collections of the University of the South, Sewanee, Tennessee. The Indian Health Service had operated a thirty-two-bed hospital at Tanana since 1941. Alaska Area Native Health Service, *Honoring Our Sacred Healing Place Tanana*, 8–9.

19. Thomas, *The Flying Bishop*, 208. Thirty years old when consecrated in 1948, Gordon was the youngest person to be so designated in the history of the Anglican Church (5).

20. Thomas, *The Flying Bishop*, 210–11. Tanana and Kotzebue also operated such training centers (213).

21. Thomas, *The Flying Bishop*, 212–13. Gordon, a pilot known as the Flying Bishop, often flew the students and their families to Arizona himself.

22. Thomas, *The Flying Bishop*, 223–24.

23. Guy Peters, Zoom interview with authors, January 1, 2022. On their first visit to Arizona, seven Peters children accompanied their parents. The following year, more of the older children remained in Alaska.

24. Curtis, "Burke Death Great Loss to Diocese," *Episcopal Review*, November 1962, 3, 7; *The Living Church*, July 23, 1961, 7. Albert Tritt had died in 1955. "The Rev. Albert Tritt."

25. The dream house with a 180-degree view of Puget Sound slid down the hill and was destroyed in 1970 when a city water main burst. Because the cause was not discovered until much later, the incident was deemed an act of God, allowing the insurance company to deny coverage. He and Lucy never fully recovered financially from the loss, but he eventually built another home on Alki.

26. Hudson Burke Jr. and Diane Burke, interview by Mary Ehrlander, October 25, 2021, Seattle.

27. Hudson Burke Jr. and Diane Burke, interview. Hudson Jr. does not recall Clara having visited his family in Seattle when he was a child.

28. Hudson Burke Jr. and Diane Burke, interview. As they flew into the village, Hudson Jr. marveled at the landscape, never having seen such topography as the Yukon Flats.

29. Douglas Fischer, "Remembrance of Things Past," *Fairbanks Daily News Miner*, October 17, 1999, 1.

30. "Chief David Salmon," Tanana Chiefs Conference website, accessed November 6, 2021, https://www.tananachiefs.org/about/our-leadership/traditional -chiefs/chief-david-salmon/.

31. Fischer, "Remembrance of Things Past," 12; Hudson Burke Jr., interview by Mary Ehrlander, October 25, 2021, Seattle.

32. "Dr. Grafton E. Burke, Healer, Teacher, Author," *Northeastern News*, October 27, 1982.

33. Marriage License, Grafton E. Burke and Mildred Kotek, August 25, 1941, Ingham County, Michigan, No. 41-1083.

34. Geoffrey Burke, telephone interview with Mary Ehrlander, September 21, 2021. The neighborhood had quick rail access to Manhattan, where Grafton continued to practice medicine.

35. Geoffrey Burke, interview, September 21, 2021

36. Geoffrey Burke, interview, September 21, 2021.

37. Geoffrey Burke, telephone interview with Mary Ehrlander, October 25, 2021.

38. Both David Wallis's granddaughter Velma Wallis and William Loola's great-granddaughter Grete Bergman have suggested that the mission may have contributed to negative self-perceptions among Gwich'in children that carried on to future generations.

39. Dean, *Breaking Trail*, 15.

BIBLIOGRAPHY

ARCHIVES AND MANUSCRIPT MATERIALS

American Geographic Society.

APRCA. Alaska and Polar Regions Collections and Archives. Rasmuson Library, University of Alaska Fairbanks.

Archives and Special Collections of the University of the South, Sewanee, Tennessee.

Archives of Cathedral of St. John the Divine.

Archives of the Protestant Episcopal Church of the United States of America.

Mount Hermon School Archives.

PECUSA. Protestant Episcopal Church in the USA, National Council (Domestic and Foreign Missionary Society). Alaska Records. 1884–1952 (MF142). Originals in Domestic and Foreign Society Alaska Papers 1889–1939, Archives of the Episcopal Church, Austin, Texas.

Private collection of Geoffrey Burke.

Private collection of Hudson Burke.

Wells clan website, http://wellsclan.us/History/frances/Frances.htm.

A Yukon Romance: Claude and Mary Tidd, https://www.yukonromance.ca/.

PUBLISHED WORKS

Alaska Area Native Health Service. *Honoring Our Sacred Healing Place Tanana, Alaska: Development, History, Community & Cultural Significance of the Tanana Hospital Complex.* Anchorage: Alaska Area Native Health Service, 2012. Prescription for Adventure, accessed December 17, 2021, http://www .prescriptionforadventure.com/assets/docs/TananaBooklet.pdf.

"Alaskans Honored." *Alaskan Churchman* 32 (November 1937): 3.

"Alaskans Value Hudson Stuck Memorial Hospital: 'Old Timer' Who Found Help in Sore Need Tells Thrilling Story." *Spirit of Missions* 92, no. 11 (November 1927): 670–71.

"Alaskan Women Present Altar Cloth to Cathedral." *Spirit of Missions* 96, no. 3 (March 1931): 148.

Alton, Thomas. *Alaska in the Progressive Age: A Political History 1896–1916.* Fairbanks: University of Alaska Press, 2019.

"Announcements Concerning the Missionaries, Alaska." *Spirit of Missions* 81, no. 7 (July 1916): 505.

"Appeals." *Alaskan Churchman* 2, no. 1 (November 1907): 15.

"Appreciation of an Alaska Sourdough." *Spirit of Missions* 97, no. 6 (June 1932): 350.

"Archdeacon Stuck, Minutes Adopted by the Council, October 13, 1920." *Spirit of Missions* 85, no. 11 (November 1920): 689.

"Arrivals and Sailings." *Spirit of Missions* 93, no. 12 (December 1928): 830.

"Arrivals and Sailings of Missionaries." *Spirit of Missions* 94, no. 6 (June 1929): 408.

Beaver, C. Masten. *Fort Yukon Trader: Three Years in an Alaskan Wilderness.* New York: Exposition Press, 1955.

Bedell, Harriet. "Stephen's Village Move to Tanana: Deaconess, Lay-Reader, Children and Buildings Are Rafted down the Yukon to Find an Enlarged Sphere of Usefulness among Alaska Indians." *Spirit of Missions* 94, no. 2 (February 1929): 111–12.

Bentley, John. "Along the Yukon with the Pelican IV, Part Two: Conclusion." *Spirit of Missions* 98, no. 3 (March 1933): 165–68.

———. "Annual Report of the Rt. Rev. Jno. B. Bentley, D. D., Bishop-in-Charge of Alaska for the Year 1942." *Alaskan Churchman* 38, no. 1 (February 1943): 4–21.

———. "Fire-Swept Alaskan Mission Is Rebuilt: Our New Archdeacon of the Yukon Whose Headquarters Are at Nenana Describes New Tortella Hall, the Finest Building in Interior Alaska." *Spirit of Missions* 95, no. 12 (December 1930): 819–20.

———. "Missionary District of Alaska, Report of the Bishop for the Year 1935." In *The Annual Report of the National Council for the Year 1935*, 98–109.

———. "St. Mark's Mission, Nenana." *Alaskan Churchman* 22, no. 3 (July 1931): 65–66.

"Bishop Bentley." *Alaskan Churchman* 38, no. 4 (November 1943): 2–3.

"The Bishop Rowe Foundation Fund Completed Amount Aimed at, $100,000." *Spirit of Missions* 93, no. 8 (August 1928): 524.

Boulter, George E. "Report on the U.S. Public School at Stevens Village (1910–1911)." In Boulter and Grigor Taylor, *The Teacher and the Superintendent*, 167.

Boulter, George E., and Barbara Grigor-Taylor, eds. *The Teacher and the Super-intendent: Native Schooling in the Alaskan Interior, 1904–1918*. Edmonton: Athabasca University Press, 2015.

Bradley, Agnes. "Pushing on to Health at Fort Yukon." *Alaskan Churchman* 20 (July 1926): 73–74.

Bradner, Lester. *A 1916 Alaskan Diary*. Saunderstown RI: Robert Bradner, 2008.

Brady, John. *Report of the Governor of Alaska to the Secretary of the Interior 1900*. Washington DC: Government Printing Office, 1900.

———. *Report of the Governor of Alaska to the Secretary of the Interior 1901*. Washington DC: Government Printing Office, 1901.

"Brief Items of Interest." *Spirit of Missions* 93, no. 5 (May 1928): 332.

"Brief Items of Interest." *Spirit of Missions* 93, no. 10 (October 1928): 685.

Burch, Ernest. "The Inupiat and the Christianization of Arctic Alaska." *Etudes/Inuit/Studies* 18, no. 1–2 (1994): 81–108.

Burke, Clara Heintz. "Doctor Burke Has Overwhelming Anxieties." *Spirit of Missions* 100, no. 12 (December 1935): 555–56.

———. "Fort Yukon Rejoices in New Parish House." *Spirit of Missions* 98, no. 6 (June 1933): 339–40.

———. Letter to Woman's Auxiliary of St. Luke's Church, Prescott, Arizona, n.d. "Our Letter Box." *Spirit of Missions* 85, no. 5 (May 1920): 330.

———. "Twenty-Five Years above the Arctic Circle." *Spirit of Missions* 97, no. 6 (June 1932): 349–55.

Burke, Clara Heintz, as told to Adele Comandini. *Doctor Hap*. New York: Coward-McCann, 1961.

Burke, Clara M. "Children of the Arctic Circle." *Spirit of Missions* 80, no. 2 (February 1915): 109–10.

Burke, Grafton. "Alaska Hospital Has Phenomenal Growth: Every Native in Vicinity of Fort Yukon Is Baptized While Last Decade Has Seen Work of Hudson Stuck Memorial Hospital Increased Sevenfold." *Spirit of Missions* 96, no. 11 (November 1931): 727–28.

———. "Before and After." *Alaskan Churchman* 3 (May 1909): 45–46.

———. "A Boys' Club." *Alaskan Churchman* 3 (August 1909): 62.

———. "Epidemic of Smallpox in Alaska." *Journal of the American Medical Association* 58 (January–June 1912): 803–4.

———. "Fire, Flood and Flue on the Yukon: The Calamity a Thing of the Past—Kindness Received Cannot Be Forgotten." *Spirit of Missions* 90, no. 12 (December 1925): 754–56.

———. "The Frances Wells Harper Memorial Solarium." *Spirit of Missions* 88, no. 7 (July 1923): 465–66.

———. "Hudson Stuck from Texas to Alaska." *Alaskan Churchman* 15 (February 1921): 39–46.

———. Letter, n.d. "Our Letter Box: Intimate and Informal Messages from the Field." *Spirit of Missions* 89, no. 1 (January 1924): 49.

———. Letter, December 31, 1916. "Our Letter Box: Intimate and Informal Messages from the Field." *Spirit of Missions* 82, no. 3 (March 1917): 281.

———. Letter, June 24, 1917. "Our Letter Box: Intimate and Informal Messages." *Spirit of Missions* 82, no. 10 (October 1917): 703.

———. "Missionary Medicine in the Arctic." *Alaskan Churchman* 3 (August 1909): 60.

———. "Northward the Course of the Kingdom: The Church at the Foot of the Arctic Range." *Spirit of Missions* 88, no. 3 (March 1923): 171–74.

———. "Our 'Farthest North' Hospital Moves Still Farther North." *Spirit of Missions* 88, no. 12 (December 1923): 823–24.

———. "The Smallpox Situation." *Alaskan Churchman* 6 (May 1912): 99–101.

———. "The Yukon Breaks Its Bounds: From Dawson to Fort Yukon the Mighty River Sweeps over Its Banks—The Hudson Stuck Memorial Hospital Loses Its Supplies." *Spirit of Missions* 90, no. 8 (August 1925): 466.

Cady, Anne E. "Fort Yukon." *Alaskan Churchman* 4, no. 3 (May 1910): 47.

———. "School Work at Fort Yukon." *Alaskan Churchman* 3 (August 1909): 57.

Canham, T. H. "Old Fort Yukon." *Alaskan Churchman* 3 (August 1909): 53–55.

Carroll, James. *The First Ten Years in Alaska: Memoirs of a Fort Yukon Trapper 1911–1922.* New York: Exposition Press, 1957.

Carter, Clara M. "Alaska Notes." *Spirit of Missions* 74, no. 4 (April 1909): 286.

———. "The Daily Round and Common Task." *Alaskan Churchman* 2 (February 1908): 20–22.

———. "Day by Day beyond the Arctic Circle." *Spirit of Missions* 73, no. 7 (July 1908): 546–50.

———. "Founding of St. Matthew's Hospital." *Alaskan Churchman* 1 (November 1906): 8–10.

———. "From St. John's-in-the-Wilderness." *Alaskan Churchman* 7 (November 1912): 22–23.

———. "Is It Worth While? A Christmas Message Five Months Later." *Spirit of Missions* 73, no. 5 (July 1908): 340.

———. "Random Notes from Allachaket." *Spirit of Missions* 73, no. 11 (November 1908): 880–81.

———. "St. John's-in-the-Wilderness." *Alaskan Churchman* 4 (August 1910): 61.

Case, David S. *Alaska Natives and American Laws*. Fairbanks: University of Alaska Press, 1984.

"The Church's Mission Faces Crisis." *Spirit of Missions* 97, no. 3 (March 1932): 141–45.

Cleaver, Fannie E. Letter, n.d. "Our Letter Box: Intimate and Informal Messages from the Field." *Spirit of Missions* 87, no. 10 (October 1922): 665–66.

Cole, Terrence, ed. *Old Yukon: Tales, Trails, and Trials: Memoirs of Judge James Wickersham*. Fairbanks: University of Alaska Press, 2009.

———. "One Man's Purgatory." *Alaska Journal* 9, no. 3 (Summer 1979): 85–90.

"Convocation of Alaskan Workers, Anvik, July 5–10, 1912." *Alaskan Churchman* 6, no. 4 (August 1912): 115–21.

Cruikshank, Moses. *The Life I've Been Living*. Recorded and compiled by William Schneider. Fairbanks: Alaska and Polar Regions Department, Elmer Rasmuson Library, University of Alaska Fairbanks, 1986.

"David Wallis." *Alaskan Churchman* 37, no. 4 (November 1942): 17.

Davis, Mary Lee. *We Are Alaskans*. Boston: W. A. Wilde, 1931.

Dean, David M. *Breaking Trail: Hudson Stuck of Texas and Alaska*. Athens: University of Ohio Press, 1988.

Dean, Patrick. *A Window to Heaven: The Daring First Ascent of Denali, America's Wildest Peak*. New York: Pegasus, 2021.

"The Deficit Has Not Been Increased by the National Council." *Spirit of Missions* 89, no. 11 (November 1924): 688.

Donovan, Mary Sudman. *A Different Call: Women's Ministries in the Episcopal Church, 1850–1920*. Peabody MA: Morehouse, 1986.

Dorsey, Janine. "Episcopal Women Missionaries as Cultural Intermediaries in Interior Alaska Native Villages, 1894–1932." PhD diss., University of New Mexico, 2008.

Drane, Frederick. "The Death of Archdeacon Stuck." *Alaskan Churchman* 15, no. 1 (November 1920): 3–5.

———. "From Cheechako to Archdeacon." *Alaskan Churchman* 21, no. 3 (April 1930): 67–72.

———. "New Experiences on the Yukon and Koyukuk." *Alaskan Churchman* 20 (January 1926): 13–18.

———. "Squeezing Through, or Sub-Arctic Circuit Riding in Alaska: Fifteen Hundred Miles with a Dog Team—Intense Cold Makes Traveling Difficult but the Archdeacon 'Squeezes Through.'" *Spirit of Missions* 90, no. 6 (June 1925): 329–33.

————. "Swinging the Circuit behind Archdeacon Stuck." *Spirit of Missions* 86, no. 8 (August 1921): 497–504.

————. "Three O'clock in the Morning." *Spirit of Missions* 89, no. 11 (November 1924): 689–94.

"Dr. Grafton Burke Ordained—Collapses." *Spirit of Missions* 103, no. 10 (October 1938): 422.

Dukes, Charles A. "Surgeon Commends Stuck Hospital." *Spirit of Missions* 96, no. 12 (December 1931): 805–7.

Ehrlander, Mary F. "The Paradox of Alaska's 1916 Alcohol Referendum: A Dry Vote within a Frontier Alcohol Culture." *Pacific Northwest Quarterly* 102, no. 1 (2010): 29–42.

————. *Walter Harper, Alaska Native Son*. Lincoln: University of Nebraska Press, 2017.

Episcopal Diocese of Alaska. *A Century of Faith: Centennial Commemorative, 1895–1995*. Fairbanks: Centennial Press and Episcopal Diocese of Alaska, 1995.

Evans, Christopher H. *The Social Gospel in American Religion: A History*. New York: New York University Press, 2017.

Fortuine, Robert. *Chills and Fever: Health and Disease in Early Alaska*. Fairbanks: University of Alaska Press, 1989.

————. *"Must We All Die?" Alaska's Enduring Struggle with Tuberculosis*. Fairbanks: University of Alaska Press, 2005.

"Fort Yukon." *Alaskan Churchman* 15 (February 1921): 37–38.

"Fort Yukon." *Alaskan Churchman* 16 (April 1922): 72.

"Fort Yukon." *Alaskan Churchman* 38, no. 1 (February 1943): 11–12.

"Fort Yukon Mission Needs Power Plant: Breakdown of Only Power Plan within Hundreds of Miles Causes Serious Situation in Alaskan Mission. Immediate Replacement Is Urgent." *Spirit of Missions* 94, no. 6 (June 1929): 374.

"Fort Yukon Notes." *Alaskan Churchman* 3 (February 1909): 23.

Fredson, John. "Venetie." *Alaskan Churchman* 35, no. 1 (February 1940): 6–8.

"Good Words for Our Arctic Hospital: Tributes to the Good Work Done at St. Stephen's Mission, Fort Yukon, Alaska." *Spirit of Missions* 90, no. 3 (March 1925): 169.

"Grafton Burke: Arctic Physician." *Spirit of Missions* 103, no. 11 (November 1938): 450.

Gruber, Jonathan, and Daniel M. Hungerman. "Faith-Based Charity and Crowd-Out during the Great Depression." *Journal of Public Economics* 91, no. 5–6 (2007): 1043–69.

Hackett, Allen. *Quickened Spirit: A Biography of Frank Sutliff Hackett*. New York: Riverdale Country School, 1957.

Hackett, Daniel. "An Undergraduate's Winter in Alaska." *Spirit of Missions* 96, no. 12 (December 1931): 808–9.

Harkey, Ira. *Noel Wien, Alaska Pioneer Bush Pilot*. Fairbanks: University of Alaska Press, 1999.

Harper, Lillie H. "New York Sculptor Visits Fort Yukon." *Spirit of Missions* 99, no. 12 (December 1934): 569–72.

Hartley, William. *A Woman Set Apart: The Remarkable Life of Harriet Bedell*. New York: Dodd, Mead, 1963.

Heintz, Clara. "Children of the North." *Alaskan Churchman* 2 (February 1908): 23–24.

Hoggatt, Wilford. *Report of the Governor of Alaska to the Secretary of the Interior*. Washington DC: Government Printing Office, 1907.

———. *Report of the Governor of Alaska to the Secretary of the Interior*. Washington DC: Government Printing Office, 1908.

Holm, Tom. *The Great Confusion in Indian Affairs: Native Americans and Whites in the Progressive Era*. Austin: University of Texas Press, 2005.

Hosley, Edward H. "Intercultural Relations and Cultural Change in the Alaska Plateau." In *Subarctic*, edited by June Helm, 549–55. Vol. 6 of *Handbook of North American Indians*, edited by William C. Sturtevant. Washington DC: Smithsonian Institution, 1981.

Hunt, William R. "Gates of the Artic." In *Golden Places: The History of Alaska-Yukon Mining*. Anchorage: National Park Service, 1990. Available online at the National Park Service website, https://www.nps.gov/parkhistory/online_books /yuch/golden_places/chap11.htm.

"The Influenza Pandemic." *Alaskan Churchman* 14 (May 1920): 67.

"In Memorium." *Spirit of Missions* 83, no. 12 (December 1918): 18.

Jacobs, Jane, ed. *A Schoolteacher in Old Alaska: The Story of Hannah Breece*. New York: Vintage, 1997.

Jenkins, Thomas. *The Man of Alaska, Peter Trimble Rowe*. New York: Morehouse-Gorham, 1943.

"John Fredson." *Alaskan Churchman* 40, no. 4 (November 1945): 9.

Laguna, Frederica de, ed. *Tales from the Dena: Indian Stories from the Tanana, Koyukuk, & Yukon Rivers*. Seattle: University of Washington Press, 1995.

Landon, Nellie. "Glimpses of Life in Arctic Alaska." *Spirit of Missions* 87, no. 4 (April 1922): 260–62.

Langdon, Florence. "At Fort Yukon." *Alaskan Churchman* 3, no. 4 (August 1909): 56.

———. "At the Mission of our Savior, Tanana." *Alaskan Churchman* 8, no. 1 (November 1913): 122.

———. "Mission of Our Saviour, Tanana." *Alaskan Churchman* 6 (February 1912): 57–61.

Lewis, Michael R. "Scrofula." Medscape, February 18, 2021. https://refp.cohlife .org/_tuberculosis_scrofula/scrofula.pdf.

Mackenzie, Clara Childs. *Zhoh Gwatsan: Wolf Smeller: A Biography of John Fredson, Native Alaskan.* Anchorage: Alaska Pacific University Press, 1985.

MacLaren, I. S., and Lisa N. LaFramboise, eds. Introduction to *The Ladies, the Gwich'in, and the Rat: Travels on the Athabasca, Mackenzie, Rat, Porcupine and Yukon Rivers in 1926,* by Clara Vyvyan, xv–xlix. Edmonton: University of Alberta Press 1998.

Mason, Michael H. *The Arctic Forests.* 1924. London: Hodder and Stoughton, 1934.

McGary, Jane, ed. and trans. *Stories Told by John Fredson to Edward Sapir.* Fairbanks: Alaska Native Language Center, University of Alaska, 1982.

McIntosh, E. A. "The Fire at St. Mark's Mission, Nenana." *Spirit of Missions* 95, no. 3 (March 1930): 181–82.

McKennan, Robert A. "Athapaskan Adaptations: Hunters and Fishermen of the Subarctic Forests, by James W. VanStone." *Arctic* 28, no. 3 (1975): 220–21.

———. "The Physical Anthropology of Two Alaskan Athapaskan Groups." *American Journal of Physical Anthropology* 22, no. 1 (1964): 43–52.

———. "Tanana." In *Subarctic,* edited by June Helm, 562–76. Vol. 6 of *Handbook of North American Indians,* edited by William C. Sturtevant. Washington DC: Smithsonian Institution, 1981.

"Medical Department of the University of the South—Annual Commencement Exercises." *Southern Practitioner* 29 (1907): 617.

"Medical Nenana." *Alaskan Churchman* 6, no. 2 (February 1912): 45.

"Meeting of the President and Council." *Spirit of Missions* 86, no. 1 (January 1921): 47–51.

"Memorial Service at Fort Yukon." *Alaskan Churchman* 8, no. 1 (November 1913): 14–18.

"Men of Texas—Dr. William C. Burke." In *The Encyclopedia of Texas,* vol. 2, edited by Ellis A. Davis and Edwin H. Grobe, 777. Dallas: Texas Development Bureau, 1922. https://texashistory.unt.edu/ark:/67531/metapth39129 /m1/501/.

"Midsummer and Midwinter at the Allachaket." *Spirit of Missions* 74, no. 3 (March 1909): 231–34.

Mischler, Craig. "John Fredson: A Biographical Sketch." In *Stories Told by John Fredson to Edward Sapir*, edited and translated by Jane McGary, 11–20. Fairbanks: Alaska Native Language Center, University of Alaska, 1982.

Mischler, Craig, and William E. Simeone. *Tanana and Chandalar: The Alaskan Field Journals of Robert A. McKennan*. Fairbanks: University of Alaska Press, 2006.

"Missions and Staff." *Alaskan Churchman* 32 (February 1937): 21.

"The Moccasin Telegraph." *Alaskan Churchman* 31 (August 1936): 9–12.

"The Moccasin Telegraph." *Alaskan Churchman* 31 (November 1936): 9–11.

"The Moccasin Telegraph." *Alaskan Churchman* 32 (February 1937): 13–20.

"The Moccasin Telegraph." *Alaskan Churchman* 32 (May 1937): 7–14.

"The Moccasin Telegraph." *Alaskan Churchman* 32 (November 1937): 5–12.

"The Moccasin Telegraph." *Alaskan Churchman* 33 (August 1938): 6–12.

"The Moccasin Telegraph." *Alaskan Churchman* 33 (November 1938): 6–17.

"The Moccasin Telegraph." *Alaskan Churchman* 35, no. 1 (February 1940): 11–17.

"The Moccasin Telegraph." *Alaskan Churchman* 35, no. 3 (August 1940): 14–18.

Moody, G. H. "Fort Yukon Notes." *Alaskan Churchman* 20 (July 1926): 75–76.

Murray, John F., Dean E. Schraufnagel, and Philip C. Hopewell. "Treatment of Tuberculosis. A Historical Perspective." *Annals of the American Thoracic Society* 12, no. 12 (2015): 1749–59.

"Name Dr. Burke Successor." *Spirit of Missions* 104, no. 4 (April 1939): 30.

Napoleon, Harold. *Yuuyaraq: The Way of the Human Being*. Fairbanks: University of Alaska Fairbanks Center for Cross-Cultural Studies, 1991.

Nash, Betty Joyce. "The Generosity Cycle: Charitable Giving during Downturns." *Region Focus* (second quarter 2010). Accessed September 26, 2021. https://www.richmondfed.org/-/media/richmondfedorg/publications/research/econ_focus/2010/q2/pdf/feature3.pdf.

Naske, Claus-M, and Herman E. Slotnick. *Alaska, a History*. 3rd ed. Norman: University of Oklahoma Press, 2011.

"News and Notes." *Spirit of Missions* 83, no. 5 (May 1918): 342.

"News and Notes." *Spirit of Missions* 85, no. 7 (July 1920): 449.

"News and Notes," *Spirit of Missions* 85, no. 12 (December 1920): 793.

"News and Notes." *Spirit of Missions* 86, no. 9 (September 1921): 607.

"News and Notes." *Spirit of Missions* 87, no. 2 (February 1922): 47.

"News and Notes." *Spirit of Missions* 89, no. 3 (March 1924): 194.

"New Spirit Prevails in Old Ceremony." *Sewanee Alumni News* 4, no. 1 (August 1937): 6.

"Notes." *Alaskan Churchman* 2 (May 1909): 36.

"Notes." *Alaskan Churchman* 7 (February 1913): 41.

"Notes." *Alaskan Churchman* 11, no. 11 (November 1916): 7.

"Notes from Anvik." *Alaskan Churchman* 6, no. 1 (November 1911): 20.

"Nurse Flies to Relieve Emergency at Fort Yukon." *Spirit of Missions* 94, no. 7 (July 1929): 463.

Osgood, Cornelius. *Contributions to the Ethnography of the Kutchin.* Yale University Publication in Anthropology 14. New Haven CT, 1936.

——. *The Han Indians: A Compilation of Ethnographic and Historical Data on the Alaska-Yukon Boundary Area.* New Haven CT: Yale University Department of Anthropology, 1971.

"Our Alaskan Missions Concluded." *Alaskan Churchman* (November 1936): 13–23.

"Our Letter Box: Intimate and Informal Messages from the Field." *Spirit of Missions* 76, no. 12 (December 1911): 1024–26.

"Our New Recruits." *Spirit of Missions* 79, no. 11 (November 1914): 778.

Parks, George. *Annual Report of the Governor of Alaska to the Secretary of the Interior for Fiscal Year Ended June 30, 1925.* Washington DC: Government Printing Office, 1925.

——. *Annual Report of the Governor of Alaska to the Secretary of the Interior for Fiscal Year Ended June 30, 1926.* Washington DC: Government Printing Office, 1926.

——. *Annual Report of the Governor of Alaska to the Secretary of the Interior for Fiscal Year Ended June 30, 1928.* Washington DC: Government Printing Office, 1928.

——. *Annual Report of the Governor of Alaska to the Secretary of the Interior for Fiscal Year Ended June 30, 1929.* Washington DC: Government Printing Office, 1929.

Parran, Thomas. "Alaska's Health: A Survey Report to the United States Department of the Interior." Pittsburgh: Graduate School of Public Health, University of Pittsburg, 1954. Accessed December 17, 2021. https://dhss.alaska.gov /Commissioner/Documents/PDF/Parran_Report.pdf.

Phillips, Carol. "Unsung Heroines." *Alaskan Epiphany* 17, no. 2 (Spring 1996): 2–3.

"The Progress of the Kingdom." *Spirit of Missions* 85, no. 6 (June 1920): 351.

"The Progress of the Kingdom." *Spirit of Missions* 85, no. 9 (September 1920): 548–49.

"The Progress of the Kingdom." *Spirit of Missions* 87, no. 7 (July 1922): 419–22.

"The Progress of the Kingdom." *Spirit of Missions* 88, no. 1 (January 1923): 4–7.

"The Progress of the Kingdom: Concerning the Debt." *Spirit of Missions* 89, no. 11 (November 1924): 727–28.

Prucha, Francis Paul. *The Great Father: The United States Government and the American Indians*. Vol. 2. Lincoln: University of Nebraska Press, 1984.

Raboff, Adeline Peter. *Iñuksuk: Northern Koyukon, Gwich'in & Lower Tanana 1800–1901*. Fairbanks: Alaska Native Knowledge Network, 2001.

"Radical Retrenchment or Wise Economy: Council Adopts Budget for 1925." *Spirit of Missions* 89, no. 11 (November 1924): 687–88.

"The Rev. Albert Tritt—In Memoriam." *Alaskan Churchman* 50 (August 1955): 12.

Rollier, August. "The Therapeutic, Preventive and Social Value of Heliotherapy in Surgical Tuberculosis." *Journal of State Medicine* (1912–1937) 36, no. 8 (1928): 435–46.

Rosenberg, Ayelet M., Shannon Rausser, Junting Ren, Eugene V. Mosharov, Gabriel Sturm, R. Todd Ogden, Purvi Patel, Rajesh Kumar Soni, et al. "Quantitative Mapping of Human Hair Greying and Reversal in Relation to Life Stress." *eLife* 10 (2021): e67437. https://elifesciences.org/articles/67437.pdf.

Rowe, Peter Trimble. "Alaska: Airplane Carries Bishop on Visitations." In *Looking Forward: The Annual Report of the National Council of the Protestant Episcopal Church for 1938*, 95–100.

———. "Annual Report of the Bishop of the Missionary District of Alaska 1906–1907." In *The Seventy-Second Annual Report of the Board of Missions of the Protestant Episcopal Church in the United States of America, 1906–1907*, 43–48.

———. "Annual Report of the Bishop of the Missionary District of Alaska 1907–1908." In *The Seventy-Third Annual Report of the Board of Missions of the Protestant Episcopal Church in the United States of America, 1907–1908*, 47–50.

———. "Annual Report of the Bishop of the Missionary District of Alaska 1908–1909." In *The Annual Report of the Board of Missions of the Protestant Episcopal Church in the United States of America 1908–1909*, 53–62.

———. "Annual Report of the Bishop of the Missionary District of Alaska 1910–1911." In *The Annual Report of the Board of Missions of the Protestant Episcopal Church in the United States of America 1910–1911*, 61–72.

———. "Annual Report of the Bishop of the Missionary District of Alaska 1911–1912." In *The Annual Report of the Board of Missions of the Protestant Episcopal Church in the United States of America 1911–1912*, 49–56.

———. "Annual Report of the Bishop of the Missionary District of Alaska 1914–1915." In *The Annual Report of the Board of Missions of the Protestant Episcopal Church in the United States of America 1914–1915*, 30–38.

———. "Five Months in the Interior of Alaska." *Spirit of Missions* 94, no. 11 (November 1929): 731–32.

———. "Five Years on the Yukon with the *Pelican*: Carrying Passengers, Towing Logs, Running a Sawmill Are All in the Day's Work of the *Pelican*, the Church's Most Useful Bit of Machinery in Alaska." *Spirit of Missions* 95, no. 5 (May 1930): 297–302.

———. "Influenza Epidemic in Alaska: Heroic Work Done at the Hudson Stuck Memorial Hospital, Fort Yukon—The Canadian Church Lends a Helping Hand." *Spirit of Missions* 90, no. 9 (September 1925): 540.

———. "Missionary District of Alaska, Report of the Bishop for the Year 1936." In *The Annual Report of the National Council for the Year 1936*, 101–9.

———. "Missionary District of Alaska, Report of the Bishop for the Year 1937." In *The Annual Report of the National Council for the Year 1937*, 99–109.

———. "Report of the Bishop of the Missionary District of Alaska, 1909–1910." *Alaskan Churchman* 4, no. 4 (August 1910): 56–60.

———. "Second Joint Session of the Missionary Story of the General Convention." *Spirit of Missions* 84, no. 11 (November 1919): 763–64.

———. "S.O.S. from Anvik, Alaska: Forty Helpless Children Orphaned by Epidemic Find Their Shelter in Mission." *Spirit of Missions* 92, no. 8 (August 1927): 465.

———. "Thirty-Fourth Annual Report: Missionary District of Alaska for the Year Ending Dec. 20, 1929." *Alaskan Churchman* 21, no. 3 (1930): 61–64.

Sabine, Bertha W. "From a Pioneer's Point." *Alaskan Churchman* 2 (February 1908): 26.

"Save Our Hospital!" *Spirit of Missions* 88, no. 7 (July 1923): 473–74.

Simeone, William E. "The Northern Athabaskan Potlatch in East-Central Alaska, 1900–1930." *Arctic Anthropology* (1998): 113–25.

———. *Rifles, Blankets, and Beads: Identity, History, and the Northern Athapaskan Potlatch*. Norman: University of Oklahoma Press, 1995.

Slobodin, Richard. "Kutchin." In *Subarctic*, edited by June Helm, 514–32. Vol. 6 of *Handbook of North American Indians*, edited by William C. Sturtevant. Washington DC: Smithsonian Institution, 1981.

Sniffen, Matthew K., and Thomas Spees Carrington. *The Indians of the Yukon and Tanana Valleys, Alaska*. No. 98. Washington DC: Indian Rights Association, 1914.

"Some Recent Recruits for Distant Missions." *Spirit of Missions* 73, no. 11 (November 1908): 856–65.

Stefansson, Vilhjalmur. *Discovery: The Autobiography of Vilhjalmur Stefansson.* New York: McGraw-Hill, 1964.

———. *The Friendly Arctic: The Story of Five Years in Polar Regions.* New York: MacMillan, 1921.

Stewart, R. N. "Watch Your Rollers." *Spirit of Missions* 89, no. 4 (April 1924): 246–47.

Stowe, Walter Herbert. *The Episcopal Church: A Miniature History.* Philadelphia: Church Historical Society, 1944.

Strong, J. F. A. *Report of the Governor of Alaska to the Secretary of the Interior.* Washington DC: Government Printing Office, 1914.

Stuck, Hudson. *The Alaskan Missions of the Episcopal Church.* New York: Domestic and Foreign Missionary Society, 1920.

———. "Alaska Notes." *Spirit of Missions* 74, no. 4 (April 1909): 284–85.

———. "Along Alaska's Great River." *Spirit of Missions* 77, no. 9 (September 1912): 641–42.

———. "The Arctic Hospital." *Scribner's Magazine* 76, no. 1 (July 1919): 37–44.

———. *The Ascent of Denali (Mount McKinley): First Complete Ascent of Highest Peak in North America, Containing the Original Diary of Walter Harper, First Man to Achieve Denali's True Summit.* New York: Charles Scriber's Sons, 1914. Reprint, Seattle: Mountaineers, 1977.

———. "August Reginald Hoare." *Spirit of Missions* 85, no. 6 (June 1920): 378.

———. "The Boys at St. John's-in-the-Wilderness." *Spirit of Missions* 75, no. 3 (March 1910): 178–83.

———. "By Boat and Sled to the Koyukuk Country." *Spirit of Missions* 74, no. 1 (January 1909): 25–30.

———. "Fort Yukon." *Alaskan Churchman* 3, no. 4 (August 1909): 58–59.

———. "Letter to the Editor: The Cannery at the Mouth of the Yukon." *Spirit of Missions* 85, no. 7 (July 1920): 450.

———. "A Loss to the Yukon." *Spirit of Missions* 83, no. 9 (September 1918): 611–13.

———. "New Beginnings at Fort Yukon." *Spirit of Missions* 74, no. 7 (July 1909): 593–600.

———. "Our Hospitals in the Arctic Regions." *Spirit of Missions* 83, no. 3 (March 1917): 177–80.

———. "Report of Official Acts from Easter, 1907, to Easter, 1910, by Archdeacon Stuck, to the Rt. Rev. Peter Trimble Rowe, D. D., the Bishop of Alaska." *Alaskan Churchman* 4, no. 4 (August 1910): 59.

———. "Six Years at Fort Yukon." *Spirit of Missions* 80, no. 3 (March 1915): 189–92.

———. "St. Stephen's Hospital, Fort Yukon, Alaska." *Alaskan Churchman* 8 (May 1919): 73–77.

———. *Ten Thousand Miles with a Dog Sled: A Narrative of Winter Travel in Interior Alaska.* New York: Charles Scribner's Sons, 1914. Reprint, Lincoln: University of Nebraska Press, 1988.

———. "The Third Cruise of the Pelican." *Spirit of Missions* 76, no. 5 (May 1911): 397–404.

———. *Voyages on the Yukon and Its Tributaries: A Narrative of Summer Travel in the Interior of Alaska.* New York: Charles Scribner's Sons, 1917.

———. "The White Menace on the Yukon." *Spirit of Missions* 79, no. 3 (March 1914): 188–91.

———. "Winter and Spring at Allakaket." *Spirit of Missions* 74, no. 9 (September 1909): 794–98.

———. *A Winter Circuit of Our Arctic Coast: A Narrative of a Journey with Dog Sleds around the Entire Arctic Coast of Alaska.* New York: Charles Scribner's Sons, 1920.

———. "With the Foreign Secretary in Alaska: A Narrative of the Tenth Cruise of the Pelican." *Spirit of Missions* 83, no. 1 (January 1918): 17–44.

———. "The Yukon Indians." *Spirit of Missions* (February 1906): 105–14.

———. "The Yukon Salmon." *Spirit of Missions* 85, no. 5 (May 1920): 317–22.

Summary of the Proceedings of the Forty-Eighth Annual Meeting of the Florida Branch of the Woman's Auxiliary of the National Council, Jacksonville. In *Journal of the Ninety-Second Annual Council of the Diocese of Florida, Together with the Forty-Fifth Annual Report of the Florida Branch of the Woman's Auxiliary to the National Council and the Twenty-Seventh Diocesan Assembly of the Daughters of the King, Pensacola, 1935–1938.*

Thomas, Tay. *An Angel on His Wing: The Story of Bill Gordon, Alaska's Flying Bishop.* Wilton CT: Morehouse, 1989.

Thomas, William. Letter to Stuck, n.d. "Our Letter Box: Intimate and Informal Messages from the Field." *Spirit of Missions* 85, no. 6 (June 2020): 397–98.

Tommy the Wolf and Others. "Christmas Letters from the Koyukuk." *Spirit of Missions* 73, no. 3 (March 1909): 198–200.

"Two Interesting Gatherings." *Alaskan Churchman* 3, no. 4 (August 1909): 59.

Updegraff, Harlan. "Report on Education in Alaska December 24, 1909." In *Report of the Commissioner of Education for the Year Ended June 30, 1909*, vol. 2, 1296–326. Washington DC: Government Printing Office, 1910.

U.S. Congress. Senate. *The Compiled Laws of the Territory of Alaska 1913.* 62nd Congress, 3rd session, Senate Document 1093, 673.

U.S. Department of the Interior. "Report on Education in Alaska December 24, 1909." In *Report of the Commissioner of Education for the Year Ended June 30, 1909*, 1298–99, 1302. Washington DC: Government Printing Office, 1910.

"Vaccinating the Indians." *Alaskan Churchman* 6, no. 1 (November 1911): 21.

VanStone, James W. "Alaska Natives and the White Man's Religion: A Cultural Interface in Historical Perspective." In *Exploration in Alaska: Captain Cook Commemorative Lectures*, edited by Antoinette Shalkop and Robert L. Shalkop, 175–79. Anchorage: Cook Inlet Historical Society, 1980.

———. *Athapaskan Adaptations: Hunters and Fishermen of the Subarctic Forests.* Chicago: Aldine Publishing Company, 1974.

Veltre, Douglas W., and Alan G. May. *Diaries of Archaeological Expeditions to Alaska with the Smithsonian's Aleš Hrdlička in 1936, 1937, and 1938.* Anchorage: Archives and Special Collections University of Alaska Anchorage, 2021.

Vernon, Mildred H. "My Trip into the Interior of Alaska." *Alaskan Churchman* 20 (January 1926): 6–13.

Vyvyan, Clara. *The Ladies, the Gwich'in, and the Rat: Travels on the Athabasca, Mackenzie, Rat, Porcupine and Yukon Rivers in 1926.* Edited by I. S. MacLaren and Lisa N. LaFramboise. Edmonton: University of Alberta Press, 1998.

Waggoner, Michael. *Missionaries in Alaska: A Historical Survey to 1930.* Anchorage: Alaska Historical Commission, 1980.

Walker, Tom. *The Seventymile Kid: The Lost Legacy of Harry Karstens and the First Ascent of Mount McKinley.* Seattle: Mountaineers, 2013.

Waller, John. *The Discovery of the Germ: Twenty Years that Transformed the Way We Think about Disease.* New York: Columbia University Press, 2003.

Wallis, Velma. *Raising Ourselves: A Gwich'in Coming of Age Story from the Yukon River.* Seattle: Epicenter, 2002.

———. *Two Old Women: An Alaska Legend of Betrayal, Courage and Survival.* Seattle: Epicenter, 1994.

Wilbur, Ray Lyman. "The Romance of Government Schools in Alaska" (reprint of a telegram from Wilbur). *Alaskan Churchman* 21, no. 3 (April 1930): 34–36.

Williams, Merritt. "Busy Times at Fort Yukon." *Alaskan Churchman* 21, no. 5 (October 1930): 126–27.

"With Our Missionaries." *Spirit of Missions* 96, no. 11 (November 1931): 780.

"The Woman's Auxiliary to the Board of Missions: A First Year within the Arctic Circle." *Spirit of Missions* 81, no. 2 (February 1916): 145–48.

Wood, John. "Across the Secretary's Desk." *Spirit of Missions* 94, no. 7 (July 1929): 469.

———. "Across the Secretary's Desk." *Spirit of Missions* 94, no. 9 (September 1929): 602.

———. "Across the Secretary's Desk." *Spirit of Missions* 94, no. 11 (November 1929): 739.

———. "Across the Secretary's Desk: Foreign Missions." *Spirit of Missions* 99, no. 8 (August 1934): 393.

———. "Fire Destroys Mission House at Fort Yukon: Missionary and Family and Indian Children Escape in Scant Attire—Work Adjoins Stuck Memorial—Loss $16,000—Look to Friends for Prompt Assistance." *Spirit of Missions* 89, no. 10 (October 1924): 636.

———. "Flu Follows Flood along the Yukon in Alaska: Bishop Rowe Rushing Relief by Boat to Fort Yukon Sends Earnest Plea for Aid." *Spirit of Missions* 90, no. 8 (August 1925): 463.

———. "Foreign Missions: Across the Secretary's Desk." *Spirit of Missions* 95, no. 10 (October 1930): 690.

———. "Foreign Missions: Across the Secretary's Desk." *Spirit of Missions* 98, no. 11 (November 1933): 613.

———. "Foreign Missions: Across the Secretary's Desk." *Spirit of Missions* 100, no. 7 (July 1935): 327.

———. "Foreign Missions: Across the Secretary's Desk." *Spirit of Missions* 100, no. 8 (August 1935): 375.

———. "Foreign Missions: Across the Secretary's Desk." *Spirit of Missions* 100, no. 9 (September 1935): 424.

———. "Foreign Missions: Across the Secretary's Desk." *Spirit of Missions* 100, no. 12 (December 1935): 564.

———. "Foreign Missions: Across the Secretary's Desk." *Spirit of Missions* 101, no. 4 (April 1936): 181–82.

———. "Foreign Missions: Across the Secretary's Desk." *Spirit of Missions* 101, no. 10 (October 1936): 475.

———. "Foreign Missions: Across the Secretary's Desk." *Spirit of Missions* 102, no. 5 (May 1937): 247.

———. "Foreign Missions: Across the Secretary's Desk." *Spirit of Missions* 102, no. 12 (December 1937): 602.

———. "Jottings from Near and Far." *Spirit of Missions* 95, no. 7 (July 1930): 483.

———. "Jottings from Near and Far." *Spirit of Missions* 95, no. 12 (December 1930): 849.

———. "Jottings from Near and Far." *Spirit of Missions* 96, no. 2 (February 1931): 112–13.

————. "Jottings from Near and Far." *Spirit of Missions* 97, no. 2 (February 1932): 113.

————. "Must I Say: 'Let Them Die'? A Doctor's Question to Which the Whole Church Must Give an Answer." *Spirit of Missions* 91, no. 9 (September 1926): 547–50.

————. "The National Council: Foreign Missions." *Spirit of Missions* 99, no. 11 (November 1934): 549–50.

————. "Nenana Alaskan Mission Visited by Fire." *Spirit of Missions* 95, no. 2 (February 1930): 84.

————. "Note." *Spirit of Missions* 92, no. 1 (January 1927): 54.

Woods, L. J. "Fort Yukon's Activity Depicted by Notes." *Alaskan Churchman* 2 (May 1909): 23.

Wright, Arthur. "The Minto Mission." *Alaskan Churchman* 21, no. 3 (April 1930): 77–78.

Wrobbel, Karen A., and James E. Pleuddemann. "Psychosocial Development in Adult Missionary Kids." *Journal of Psychology and Theology* 18, no. 4 (1990): 363–74.

Yarborough, Linda Finn. Introduction to *Recollections of the Youkon: Memoires from the Years 1868–1888*, by Francois Zavier Mercier, ix–xii. Anchorage: Alaska Historical Society, 1986.

Young, S. Hall. *Hall Young of Alaska: The Mushing Parson*. New York: Fleming H. Revel, 1927.

INDEX

Page numbers in italics refer to illustrations.

air travel: and airlines, 164; and air-
    mail, 215, 306n5; and expansion of
    aviation and runways, 164, 181, 215,
    290n5, 290n7; Fairbanks as hub
    for, 164, 215; and first flight into
    Fort Yukon, 159
Alaska: demographics of, 2, 215,
    243n1, 306n1; frontier culture of,
    50–51, 84–87, 98, 100–101, 104;
    general conditions and impressions
    of, 1, 2; pre-twentieth-century
    history of, 1–2, 3, 5–9, 244n14;
    territorial status of, 246n32
Alaska Native Claims Settlement Act
    (ANCSA), 233
Alaska's Health: A Survey Report. See
    Parran Report
alcohol: consumption and abuse of,
    19, 50–51, 69, 75, 82–83, 84–86,
    98–99, 240; culture, 83, 84, 100–
    101; policies, 18–19, 84, 85, 103–4
Alexander (chief of Tolovana), 110
Allakaket: community growth of, 63;
    famine in, 48, 257n37; setting of,
    3, 23, 257n38, 258n47. *See also* St.
    John's-in-the-Wilderness

American College of Surgeons, 180, 197
Anglican Church, 7, 245n18
Anvik: establishment of Episcopal
    mission at, 8, 17, 44; and fire at
    Episcopal mission, 151, 287n103;
    influenza epidemic at, 295n76
Arctic Village, 9, 143–44, 208, 225, 232
Athabascans. *See* Dena'
aviation. *See* air travel

Beatrice (Beattie Ky), 181, 182–83,
    297n111
Bedell, Harriet, 124, 128
Bentley, Elvira, 205–6
Bentley, John, 202–3, 205–6, 207,
    208, 213, 230, 290n10
Bergman, Emil: compensation of,
    after accident, 174, 289n146,
    292n53; injuries of, 161, 174,
    293n56; remarriage of, 174–75;
    support of, for mission, 175
Bergman, Grete, 262n28, 314n38
Bergman, Nina, 174–75
Bishop Peter Trimble Rowe Chapel,
    143–44
Black River, Sara, 193

Bohmer, Fred, 180–81
Bohmer, Theresa Sands, 155, 157, 175, 181, 289n149
Boulter, George: activities of, with Hudson Stuck, 41, 53, 60; against alcohol abuse, 18, 59, 85, 86, 258n44, 265n11; attitude of, toward Gwich'in language, 82; collaboration of, with Hudson Stuck, 48; death of, 275n75; and Fairbanks trials, 89, 94–96; promoting Alaska Natives' well-being, 18, 19, 48, 78; and teacher position controversy at Fort Yukon, 92, 96; and tension with Hudson Stuck and Episcopal Church, 52–53, 81–82, 249n80, 264n68
Bradner, Lester, 108, 110
Breece, Hannah: and alcohol conflicts, 88, 93–95; background of, 88, engagement of, in Fort Yukon community, 88; and Hap and Clara Burke, 87–88; life of, after Fort Yukon, 266n26; publication of memoirs of, 266n26; teaching at Fort Yukon by, 82, 88–89, 92
Brown, Wyatt, Jr., 201
Burke, Clara, 147, 220, 238; arrival of, at Allakaket, 21, 24–25; arrival of, at Fort Yukon, 64; assisting with medical work, 73, 74, 99, 113, 142, 155, 191; births of sons of, 66, 120; childcare work of, 22, 65, 71–73, 135, 141–42, 160, 166–67, 177, 186, 189, 196; childhood and adolescence of, 22, 250n2; commitment of, to mission work and people, 22, 65–66, 135, 148, 190, 239–40; courtship and marriage of, 21, 36–39,

51–52, 57, 59, 62; depictions of, 108, 109, 135, 160, 167, 171–72, 175–76, 186, 194, 203, 206; exposure of, to alcohol abuse, 69–71, 76–77, 258n47; fundraising of, 107, 148, 222, 253n66; furloughs of, 146, 147–48, 178–79, 197, 198, 219, 221–22, 285n82; hospitality of, 106, 124, 128, 135, 142, 171, 172, 203, 206–7, 209, 302n56; illnesses of, 120–21, 217, 274n68; Indigenous names of, 25, 64, 160n1; legal cases and conflicts and, 92, 94–95; life of, after Hap's death, 231, 235, 312n2; mission work of, 20, 28, 52, 65–66, 157, 160, 189; salary of, 24, 27, 64–65, 138, 143, 155; teaching duties of, 27, 52, 154–55; and training of boys' choir at Allakaket, 27, 52
Burke, Grafton (Hap), 80, 147, 220; appointment of, to Alaska, 34; childhood and early life of, 31, 32–33, 33, 253n59; as commissioner, 83, 87, 91–92, 93–94, 96, 97, 102, 103–4; commitment of, to St. Stephen's and Native people, 22, 41, 52, 65–66, 135, 148, 179, 190, 239–40; community activities of, 207–8, 208; community conflict surrounding, 87, 89, 91, 93, 97, 102; court and legal work of, 87, 91–92, 93–94, 192, 204; courtship and marriage of, 21, 36–39, 51–52, 57, 62; dependence of, on Clara, 106–7, 120–21; depictions of, 31–32, 33, 34, 83, 103, 108, 135, 151, 171, 172, 175, 180, 194, 203, 206, 209; economic woes of, 142, 161–62,

166, 188, 209, 210–11, 212–13, 214, 222–23, 230, 233; fundraising of, 107–8, 148, 166, 174, 178, 190, 213, 222, 253n66, 285n77, 309n41; furloughs and medical training of, 102, 145, 146–48, 178, 179, 189, 197, 198, 219, 221, 222, 301n31, 309n35; health crises and death of, 102, 106, 113–14, 181, 191, 192, 212–13, 217, 229–30; honors and recognition of, 180, 196–97, 222, 309n43; and Hudson Stuck, 31, 33, 106, 132, 134; Indigenous names and honors of, 41, 144, 255n8; medical work of, 34–36, 37–38, 44, 45–46, 47–48, 56–57, 73–74, 99, 112–13, 115, 123, 127–29, 136, 143–44, 149–50, 181, 182, 183, 192–93, 195–96, 201–2, 205, 216, 217–18, 286n90; memorial services and interment of, 230, 231; nickname of, 31; ordination of, as deacon, 138; ordination of, as priest, 226–27, 283n53, 310n63; pastoral duties of, 22, 45, 47, 48, 49, 144, 182, 202, 208–9, 228–29; personnel problems of, 114, 139–40, 147, 163–64, 175–76, 181, 273n46, 293n58, 293nn60–61, 294n65, 294n68; physical threats and attacks against, 77–78, 82; promoting Alaska Natives' well-being, 18, 74, 87, 189, 194; and removal of human remains from Alaska, 276n83; salary of, 64, 180, 281n16, 294nn71–72; speaking Gwich'in, 41; views of, on Native cultures, 13; work environment of, 114, 190–91, 194, 195–96, 308n27

Burke, Grafton Edgar: adult life of, 236–37, 239; birth of, 120; and boarding school, 79, 178–79, 188, 198, 210, 221, 264n58; childhood of, at Fort Yukon, 136, 147, 150, 152, 169, 172–73, 182; medical training and career of, 236–37; and presentation of altar cloth, 194, 195

Burke, Hudson Stuck: birth and baptism of, 79, 80; boarding school experiences of, 79, 146, 151, 169, 198, 264n58, 287n95; childhood of, at Fort Yukon, 116, 120, 122, 136–37, 147, 151, 168–69; flying experience of, 219, 221, 308n32; fostering children, 236; Gwich'in name of, 79, 264n57; and ham radio, 218; and return to Alaska as adult, 208, 216, 218, 236, 237, 307n8; visits to, by Hap and Clara, 219, 223

Burke, Hudson Stuck, Jr., 223, 236, 237, 313n28

Burke, Judy, 236

Burke, Lisa, 236

Burke, Lucy Test, 216, 218, 219, 223, 235, 236, 313n25

Burke, Michael, 236, 237

Burke, Millie Kotek, 237, 239

burn injuries, 26, 47, 73, 119, 183, 297n112

Cady, Anne, 50, 63

Canham, Thomas, 7

caribou: meaning of, in Gwich'in culture, 5, 42–43; migrations, 43, 212, 216, 219; people's dependence on, 212, 216; St. Stephen's Mission's dependence on, 140, 188, 193, 212

Carlisle Packing Company, 128, 129, 130–31
Carrington, Thomas, 99–101
Carroll, James, 92, 97, *101*, 103, 271n120
Carter, Clara: at Allakaket, 24, 25, 26, 27, 28, 29–30, 39, 55, 61, 62, 63; at Episcopal Church Training School and Deaconess House, 63, 117; and recruitment of Clara Heintz, 22–23
Cathedral of St. John the Divine, 132, 166, 194, 195, *195*
Catholic Church, 13
Chandalar Village. *See* Venetie
Christian, Chief (Venetie), 143–44
Circle City, 9, 17, 44, 50, 265n1
Claxton, Philander, 82, 88–89, 97–98
Cleaver, Fannie, 139
cohabitation, Alaska law regarding, 267n43
colonialism: and arrival of colonizers, 1, 5–10; and Civilization Fund Act, 245n24; in education, 245n24, 247n56, 249n77; and effects of migrants on Native peoples, 2, 9, 12, 14, 17, 73, 74, 78, 84–87, 104, 239–40. *See also* Alaska; missionaries; Native education
Comity Agreement, 8
contract era. *See* Native education
Cook, Ernest, 146–47
Cook Christian Training School (Arizona), 234
Cornell, Lucy. *See* Williams, Lucy Cornell
Crossley, James, 86, 95, 96, 97, 98
Crow, Stephen, 82–83

Cruikshank, Moses, 119, 137, 145, 146, 295n78, 302n46
Curtis, Mrs.. *See* Nielsen, Miss (Fort Yukon teacher)

Dalziel, Winifred: arrival of, at Fort Yukon, 111; assisting with medical work, 113, 131, 157, 181, 193; support of, for mission, 154, 176, 286n94, 295n81
Dawes Act, 11
Dawson YT, 107, 250n1
Dena', 3, 244n7, 254n74, 256n16, 257n27, 262n27, 265n15. *See also* Gwich'in; Koyukon Dena' lifeways; Tanana Dena' lifeways; Yoonegge hʉt'aane Dena'
Denali, 1913 ascent of, 89–90, 267n38
Depression, Great, 190, 192, 201, 205, 209, 210–11, 217, 302n43, 304n86, 305n94
diathermy, 193
diphtheria, 2, 47
dogs: and dog mushing culture, 66, 261n8; and mail service, 46, 56, 67, 75, 91, 115, 152, 283n45; and maulings, 128, 181, 205; and salmon, 5, 42, 67, 159, 212; and starvation, 48, 129, 142
Donald, J. A., 174, 175–76
Drane, Frederick: as archdeacon, 144; and family, 286n93; on Hudson Stuck, 132; rounds of, for Hudson Stuck, 127, 130, 136, 137; at St. Mark's Mission, 109; tuberculosis of, 150, 286n93
Duke, Adelaide, 175, 293n60, 294n65
Dukes, Charles, 196–97

English-only policy. *See* Native education

epidemics. *See specific diseases*

Episcopal Church: advocating for Native lives, lifeways, and subsistence rights, 278n115; Alaska district as diocese of, 234; Alaska district giving to, 211; Alaska mission sites of, 68; allocations of, for Alaska missions, 189, 201, 217, 302n43; antagonism toward, 260n86, 264n49; and Bureau of Education, 18, 48, 264n68; and challenges in recruiting and retaining missionaries, 55–56, 114, 270n113; and demand for missions and boarding schools, 55, 177, 248n68; door and window policy of, 23; Great Depression's effect on, 190, 192, 201, 205, 209, 210–11, 217, 302n43, 304n86; history of, in Alaska, 8–9; membership of, 306n2; and missionary salaries, 137–38, 217, 270n113, 281n16, 297n113, 302n43; National Council of, 160, 281n18; and Native catechist salaries, 256n22; Native Deanery program of, 234, 313n20; and provision of reading materials, 9–10, 35, 50, 55, 172; views of, on Native culture and languages, 13; Woman's Auxiliary of, 121, 245n29, 263n29, 274n54, 307n16. *See also* Anglican Church

Esaias, Chief (Venetie), 143–44

eye disease and complaints, 33–34, 46, 73, 157, 178, 202

Fairbanks, 9–10, 93–96, 215. *See also* St. Matthew's Church (Fairbanks); St. Matthew's Hospital (Fairbanks)

Farthing, Annie, 51, 58

fishwheels, 42, 43, 256n12

Forbes, Olive, 219, 231

Fort Gibbon, 19, 44, 107, 174, 250n1

Fort Yukon, 91; and alcohol abuse, 58–59, 69, 75–76, 98–99, 100, 101, 102, 115; break-up and flooding at, 124, 145, 148, 156–57, 168, 217–18, 274n57; Christmas and New Year traditions at, 40–41, 54, 255nn2–3; and dancing, 204, 207; and dogs, 67; "Fort Yukon Bunch" at, 101; Fourth of July festivities at, 118, 206–7; health conditions at, 101–2; history of, 6–7, 42; late 1930s traits of, 215; race relations at, 185, 204; setting of, 3, 5, 6, 66–67, 257n38; socio-economic conditions at, 50, 67, 69, 100–101, 102, 165. *See also* St. Stephen's Mission

Foster, Frank, 171, 175

Foster, Margaret, 181, 182, 185–86, 191

Frank, Johnnie (chief of Venetie), 224

Fred (Old Fred), 154, *154*, 262n27

Fredson (Fred), John, *141*; adoption of Fredson surname by, 111, 272n24; assisting Hap at hospital, 73, 106, 111; benefits of, from association with Episcopal Church, 232, 260n82; as child at St. Stephen's Mission, 6, 45, 60, 71, 260n80; death and burial of, 232, 312n13; on Denali, 90; at Hap's memorial service, 231; at Hap's ordination as priest, 226–27; interpreting and documenting Gwich'in, 146, 203, 204, 256n14, 303n57; and John Fredson High School, 232; marriage

Fredson (Fred), John (*cont.*)
and children of, 197, 204, 300n25;
at Mount Hermon School, 111, 126,
140; potential ordination of, 223;
salary of, 282n41; service of, to St.
Stephen's Mission, 76–77, 140–41,
141, 189, 194, 299n138; travel of, as
child with father, 262n27; and trek
to Arctic Village with Hap, 143–44,
283n53; and trek to Chandalar Vil-
lage/Venetie with Hap and Clara,
74; at University of the South,
146, 178, 188, 295n80; at Venetie,
16, 223–25, 226, 232, 312n12; and
Venetie Reservation, 232; work of, at
NC Company, 188–89, 203, 299n138
Fredson, Jean: at Fort Yukon, 204,
231; marriage and children of, 197,
204, 224, 225, 300n25; at Venetie,
224, 226
Fredson, Virginia Louise, 224, 225
Fredson, William Burke (Billy Burke),
204, 225
Friends of Indians, 11–12
Fuller, Frederick, 94–95, 98

Gavel, Adelaide: baptism of, 226;
medical training of, 219; medical
work of, 185, 193, 219, 231, 310n49,
311n73; teaching of health classes
by, 194; teaching of Sunday School
by, 186; travel of, with Hap in final
illness, 229
George, Esaias, 90, 112, 193, 281n21,
282n41
Georgeson, Charles Christian,
280n144

Goddard, Elizabeth Hayes. *See*
Hayes, Elizabeth
Gordon, William, 234, 248n69,
313n19, 313n21
Great Society programs, 233, 234
Gwich'in: and beadwork of Gwichyaa
Gwich'in, 42, 69, 70, 88, 194; fatalism of, as perceived by Hap Burke
and Hudson Stuck, 46–47, 84, 217;
history of, 244n9; lifeways and
subsistence practices of, 5, 42–44,
78, 199, 256n14, 261n15, 283n47,
301n40, 303n56; and Neets'aii
Gwich'in, 203, 204
Gwich'in Council, 59, 92, 93, 102–3,
115, 118, 125, 127, 267n48

Hackett, Dan, 188, 191, 193, 194, 198, 222
Hackett, Frances, 179, 198
Hackett, Frank, 179, 188, 198
Hanson, Alice, 209, 217
Harper, Lillian, 202
Harper, Walter: on Denali, 90; depiction of, by Hudson Stuck, 127; final
journey Outside and death of, 126,
132, 277n104; at Mount Hermon,
90, 108; relationship of, with Frances Wells, 122, 123, 126; typhoid
fever of, 121–22; and winter circuit
of Arctic coast, 121, 122–23; work
of, with Hudson Stuck, 58, 60, 61,
66, 79, 81, 89–90, 113, 119
Hayes, Elizabeth, 205–9, 304n70
Heintz, Carl, 22
Heintz, Clara. *See* Burke, Clara
Heintz, Maude, 22–23, 57, 59, 168,
170, 171, 172, 292n38

Helenius, John, 175, 176, 191
heliotherapy, 140, 282n39
Horton, A. H., 162, 174
Horton, Harry: as ally with mission, 99, 174, 175; and cohabitation case, 91, 94–95, 267n43; in "Fort Yukon Bunch," *101*; interaction of, with Clara and drunk man, 77; marriage of, *101*
Hrdlička, Ales, 123–24, 275n83
Hudson Bay Company, 6, 7, 244n16
Hudson Stuck Memorial Hospital (St. Stephen's Hospital), *112, 170*; construction and opening of, 98, 106, 107, 108–9, 111; expansions of, 140–41, 182, 185, 200–201; health classes of, 165–66, 185, 194, 199, 229; and Hoffman Legacy, 200, 210, 302n42; impacts of, 20, 136, 182, 213, 233, 240, 262n28; institutional operations of, 111–12, 121, 139, 149, 180–81, 183–84, 185, 285n86; memorial fund of, 137, 174; relocation of, 148–49, 285n83; renaming of, 137; staffing challenges of, 114, 147, 163–64, 218–19, 270n113; support of, from community, 163, 174, 182, 185; and transfer of Native heath care to U.S. government, 233; visitors' assessments of, 165, 177, 183, 196–97. *See also* Burke, Grafton (Hap); St. Stephen's Mission
Hume, Robert, Jr., 219, 308n27, 310n49
Hume, Robert, Sr., and wife, 221–22
hygiene and sanitation, 46, 47, 74, 248n58

Ida (polio victim at Steven's Village), 128, 278n113
Indian Rights Association (IRA), 99
Indigenous peoples and languages of Alaska, 4
influenza: in general, 2, 47; 1920 epidemic of, 130; 1925 epidemic of, in Fort Yukon, 157–60, 288n125; 1927 epidemic of, in Anvik, 295n76; 1936 epidemic of, in Fort Yukon, 217–18
Iñupiat, 3, 244n8, 249n73, 254n74. *See also* Kuuvaŋmiut Iñupiat

Jackson, Sheldon, 7, 8, 245n23, 245n30
Jetté, Jules, 249n77
Jonas (chief of Fort Yukon), 280n4

Kaplan, Lawrence, 244n8
Karstens, Harry, 90, 267n38
Koyukon Dena' lifeways, 5
Kuuvaŋmiut Iñupiat, 3, 21

Landon, Nellie, 139–40, 147
Langdon, Florence, 48, 50, 273n46
lawlessness, 50–51, 84–87, 98, 100–101, 104
Lindsay, Margaret, 198
Loola, Esaias, 204, 230
Loola, Julia, 72, 126
Loola, Katherine, 204
Loola, Mary, 72, 126, 193
Loola, Nina. *See* Bergman, Nina
Loola, William: and Bible study with children, 81, 83; and birth of daughter Mary, 72; character and standing of, 108, 125, 136; death of,

Loola, William (*cont.*)
125–26; and eulogy of Robert
McDonald, 256n24; memorial
plaque of, 126; pastoral work of,
16, 45, 48, 125; salary of, 277n97;
translation work of, 7, 16, 45
Loomis, Edgar, 60–61, 63, 75, 81
Lopp, W. T. (Thomas), 82, 88–89
Lot (boy at St. Stephen's Mission), 45,
56–57, 71, 262n24
Lucy, Old (Fort Yukon Elder), 204
Luke, Old (patient at Hudson Stuck
Memorial Hospital), 217

Maggie, Old (Fort Yukon Elder), 204,
207
Manning, William, 195, *195*
Martha Angeline (riverboat), 173,
292n48
Mason, Michael, 131, 135, 137, 198,
281n14
Matthews, Joe, 212
McCambridge, Merle, 95–96
McCurdy, Mrs., 175, 293n58
McCurdy, William, 175, 294n66
McDonald, Robert, 7, 16, 45, 136,
256n24, 283n53
McGowan, Thomas, 94
McKennan, Robert, 203–4, 283n53
measles, 2, 47, 74, 211–12, 216
missionaries: aims of, 1, 104; attitudes
of, toward Native cultures and
languages, 104; and community
tensions, 14, 17, 77–78; impacts
of, on Native well-being, 12–14,
17, 20, 23, 314n38; understaffing
and underpay of, 113, 270. *See also*
colonialism

Moody, G. H., 157, 284n60, 297n104
Moore, Billy, 98–99, 101
Moravian Church, 7, 13
mosquitos, 140, 168, 169, 251n18, 261n14
Mulroney, Nellie, 151, 155

National Council. *See* Episcopal Church
Native Council. *See* Gwich'in Council
Native Deanery Program, 234, 313n20
Native education: allocations for, 7,
54; assimilation aims of, 7, 245n24;
and Bureau of Education, 17–18,
52–54, 104; and Bureau of Indian
Affairs, 246n32; contract era of,
7; and *Davis v. Sitka School Board*
(1908), 246n32; English-only
policy of, 8, 12, 18, 247n51; and
Fort Yukon school, 18; history of,
246n32; and Nelson Act, 8, 14; and
teacher salaries, 252n34; U.S. government responsibility for, 245n23
Natives: discrimination against, 73,
86–87, 185, 240, 243n5; effects of
migrants on, 2, 9, 12, 14, 17, 73, 74,
78, 84–87, 104, 239–40; health disparities of, 232–33; and justice system, 265n11; multi-generational grief
and trauma of, 74; responses of, to
Christianity, 15–16, 20, 22, 105, 118,
136, 137, 186. *See also* Indigenous
peoples and languages of Alaska
Nelson Act. *See* Native education
Nenana, 17, 109–10. *See also* St.
Mark's Mission (Nenana)
Nicholson, Neil: confirmation and
baptism of, 226; construction projects of, 148–49, 157, 161, 177, 184,
199, 200–201, 311n73; and Hap's

memorial service, 230; and management of St. Stephen's, 311n73
Nielsen, Miss (Fort Yukon teacher), 81, 88, 92, 96
Northern Commercial Company, 86
Nulato, 250n1, 271n4, 276n83
Nuneviller, Beatrice, 117, 118

O'Hara, Floyd, 178, 180
Organic Act, Alaska, 7, 8
Osgood, Cornelius, 303n57

Parran Report, 232–33, 312n16
Parson, Artley, *195*, 210, 216, 218, 307n19
Pelican (riverboat), 34–35, 116, 157, 254n71, 254n73, 288n124
permafrost, 27, 117, 252n28, 256n14
Peter (prizefighter at Fort Yukon), 173, 292n46
Peter, Hishinlai', 244n8, 251n17, 260n1, 264n57
Peters, Guy, 234, 313n23
Peters, Hardy, 234
Peters, Helen, 234–35
pneumonia, 2, 47, 113, 217
Point Hope. *See* Tikiġaq (Point Hope)
Pratt, Maude, 180–81, 186, 191, 299n3
Presbyterian Church, 7, 12–13

Rampart, 17, 44
Red Cross, 153–54, 159
Ribaloff, Jean. *See* Fredson, Jean
Riverdale Country School, 179
Roman Catholic Church, 13, 109, 245n18
Rowe, Peter T.: altar cloth honoring, 194–95, *195*; and Bishop Rowe Endowment, 292n52; concerns of,

regarding alcohol abuse, 50–51, 75, 85, 102–3; consecration and arrival of, in Alaska, 8; death and burial of, 232; financial concerns of, 114, 159, 161–62, 163, 201, 209, 217, 289n136, 297n113; fundraising of, 107–8, 253n66, 303n68; on government neglect of Natives, 50–51, 75; specials of, 143, 283n50, 302n44; and St. Stephen's after Hap's death, 311n73; views of, on value of work at St. Stephen's Mission, 49, 142, 159, 160, 165, 166, 168, 176, 189, 202, 211–12, 226, 227–28, 230, 231–32; visits of, to Fort Yukon, *119*, 157, 158, 159–60, 161, 182, 202, 211–12, 226–29, 310n63
Russian American Company, 6, 244n14, 244n16
Russian Orthodox Church, 6, 244n14
Ryder, Mary, 151–52, 155, 157, 161

salmon: dogs and, 5, 42, 67, 159, 212; legislation on, 130–31; shortages of, 128–29, 130–31; as subsistence food, 212
Salmon, David, 235, 236, 237
Sands, Theresa. *See* Bohmer, Theresa Sands
Sapir, Edward, 146
Schleester (possibly Sleichter), Dorothy, 159, 289n134
segregation, racial, 73, 86–87, 185, 240, 243n5
Sewanee. *See* University of the South (Sewanee)
shamans and shamanistic beliefs, 136–37, 281n11, 302n50

Shirley, J. A., 157

Simon, James, 235

smallpox, 2, 74, 79–81

Smith, Deaconess, 136, 139

Smith, Gwendolyn, 170–72

Sniffen, Matthew, 99–101, 102, 103

social gospel, 11, 114, 273n43

specials, 117, 142, 160, 161, 162, 213, 222, 253n66. *See also* Rowe, Peter T.

Stanford, Ma (matron at Stuck Memorial Hospital), 186, *187*, 191, 299n2

steamboats, 67, 164, 215, 252n43, 261n11. *See also* tourism and travel

Stefansson, Vilhjalmur, 123–24, 180, 276n86

Stevens, Johanna, 94–95, 101

St. John's-in-the-Wilderness: children's bath time at, 53; church at, 30; dual languages at, 24; effects of, on Native health and well-being, 54; establishment of, 3, 17, 23; fiscal matters of, 302n44; growth of congregation at, 30, 63; responses of Native and other peoples to, 24–26, 27, 55; services at, 52, 55

St. John the Divine, Cathedral of (New York), 166, 194, *195*

St. Mark's Mission (Nenana), 44, 57–58, 109–10, 177, 184, 298n123, 302n44

St. Matthew's Church (Fairbanks), 9–10, 17, 44

St. Matthew's Hospital (Fairbanks), 9, 246n36

streptococcus, 191, 299n2

strychnine, illegal use of, 261n15

St. Stephen's Hospital. *See* Hudson Stuck Memorial Hospital (St. Stephen's Hospital)

St. Stephen's Mission: Boys Club of, 44–45, 141, 163, 194, 199, 202; church attendance and membership at, 118, 136, 186, 213; church structure of, 145–46; establishment of, 8, 17, 44; expanding scope of, 189, 196, 197, 213, 291n25; flooding and erosion at, 111, 116–17, 168, 218; food needs of, 126, 131, 140; fuel and other expenses of, 120, 142–43, 161–62, 166, 183, 184, 212–13, 291n17, 298n120, 305n92; funding of, including hospital, 100, 107–8, 121, 142, 159, 160, 162, 163, 166–68, 176, 177, 190, 205, 212–13, 217, 227–28, 283n52, 289n136, 294n75, 306n103; Hudson Stuck Men's Club of, 142, 199, 202; impacts of, on community and region, 164, 177, 197, 213, 239–40, 262n21, 262n28; Native people's engagement in work of, 22, 136, 142–43, 153–54, 194–95, 197–98, 207; Northern Lights Club of, 163, 165, 194–95, 290n10. *See also* Fort Yukon; St. Stephen's Mission Home

St. Stephen's Mission Home, 200; children giving for Lent at, 167, 199–200, 216, 301n40, 307n14; children's chores at, 202, 203, 206; community activities of, 54, 142, 199, 207, 208, *208*, 209; community support of, 20, 136, 163, 177, 274n54; fire at, 152–55, *153*; impacts of, on children, 20, 72–73, 213, 314n38; playground equipment of, 176–77; rebuilding and expanding of, 155, 157, 160–61, 162, 196, 199, 276n92, 287n106, 288n111; structure of, 50, 125, 199, 200; uses of, 127. *See also* Burke, Clara

St. Thomas's Mission (Point Hope/ Tikiġaq), 8, 17, 137–38, 302n44, 304n85

Stuck, Hudson, *133*; advocacy of, for Native rights and well-being, 10, 19, 97–98, 99, 124, 128–29, 130–31, 132, 134, 137, 270n100, 271n8, 280n144; at Allakaket, 23, 24, 25, 27–28, 36, 37, 38, 39, 48–49, 54–55, 258n62; arrival of, in Fairbanks, 9–10; and ascent of Denali, 89–90; combatting alcohol abuse, 9, 44, 84, 103–4, 115; as dean of St. Matthew's Cathedral, 10, 247n45, 253n57; eulogies, memorial service, and altar cloth honoring, 132, 134, 195, *195*; final illness and death of, 131–32, 134; fundraising of, 90, 98, 103, 107–8, 129, 253n66, 271n8; and Hap and Clara Burke, 33, 132, 258n49, 278n118; humanitarianism of, 10, 11, 48, 280n144; motto *Haereo* of, 117; negative press attention on, 264n49; summer travel of, on *Pelican*, 10, 34–35, 60–62, 78–79, 98, 119, 129; tension of, with Bureau of Education, 18, 52–53, 81–82, 88–89, 249n80, 264n68; views of, on Native cultures, languages, and lifeways, 13, 122, 124, 246n40, 247n54, 249n77, 250n86; winter

travels of, among missions, 10, 36, 41, 48, 89, 121, 122–23

Tanana: alcohol abuse in, 19, 44, 75; Episcopal hospital in, 271n5; Indian Health Service hospital in, 313n18; and Mission of Our Savior, 17, 44; Old Fort Hospital in, 173–74; social conditions in, 75

Tanana Chiefs, 110, 272n20

Tanana Dena' lifeways, 5

Tatum, Robert, 90, 146

Test, Lucy. *See* Burke, Lucy Test

Thomas, Ruth, 137–38

Thomas, William, 108–9, 121, 122, 129, 137–38

Thompson, W. F., 86, 98

Tidd, Mary. *See* Ryder, Mary

Tikiġaq (Point Hope), 8, 17, 304n85. *See also* St. Thomas's Mission (Point Hope/Tikiġaq)

Tobuk (Inupiaq chief at Allakaket), 38

tourism and travel, 29, 67, 88, 124, 164–65, 215, 261n12

Tritt, Albert, 16, 144, 178, 208, 209, 231, 284n56, 313n24

Tritt, Isaac, 235

Trudeau Sanitorium, 219, 308n30

tuberculosis: incidence and mortality rates of, 2, 47, 74, 136, 150, 190, 193, 205, 231, 233, 286n91; prevention of, 23, 74, 166; spread of, 243n4; treatment of, 113, 196, 233, 272n35, 282n39, 300n22, 303n69. *See also* Trudeau Sanitorium

typhoid fever, 120, 121–22, 123, 275n75

Unangax̂, 3, 6, 243n6, 276n83,
300n25
University of the South (Sewanee), 31,
146, 222, 279n132
Updegraff, Harlan, 17–18
U.S. v. Cadzow, 97

Vendesquísí, John, 201–2, 203, 302n49
Venetie, 74, 143–44, 232
Veniaminov, Ioann (John), 6
Vyvyan, Clara Rogers, 170–72

Wallis, David, 158; background of,
41; compensation of, 126, 155–56,
277n102, 281n21; court work of,
204; death of, 232; and Gwich'in
names for Hap and Clara, 41, 64;
and Hap's memorial services, 230,
231; interpreting skills of, 126,
155–56, 186, 204, 207, 280n4; and
service to St. Stephen's Mission,
16, 17, 41, 66, 69, 108, 126, 136,
144–45, 155–56, 178, 202, 227, 231,
232; stature of, in community, 145;
teaching Gwich'in to Hap, 41
Wallis, Ethel, 158, 288n130
Wallis, Grafton, 115, 150
Wallis, Martha, 17, 41, 156
Wallis, Nina, 156, 158
Wallis, Peter Trimble, 17
Wallis, Velma, 17, 313n38
Ward, Ruth. See Thomas, Ruth
Wells, Frances: arrival of, at St. Stephen's, 117–18, final journey Outside and death of, 126, 277n104; and
Frances Wells Memorial Solarium,
140–41, 285n83; relationship of,
with Walter Harper, 122, 123, 126

White, Frank, 89, 132
White, Lizzie. See Wood, Lizzie
Whittlesey, George, 201
whooping cough, 115
Wickersham, James, 109, 110
Wien, Noel, 159, 164
William, Esau, 230
Williams, Lucy Cornell, 198, 301n36
Williams, Merritt: arrival of, at St.
Stephen's, 181–82; assisting in med-
ical work, 191, 194; concern of, for
Hap, 192; marriage and departure
of, 198; pastoral work of, 186; on
speakers' circuit, 301n36
Williams, Paul, 110
Wilson, Woodrow, 97, 98, 109
Wonecoff, Thomas, 97, 269n87
Wood, John: on consolidation of
Alaska mission work, 296n93;
on costs at St. Stephen's Mission,
142, 160, 162, 166–67, 174, 227,
290n154; fundraising of, 142, 153,
159, 162, 163, 167–68, 183, 190,
209, 210, 213, 305n92; on missionary salaries, 138; at presentation of
altar cloth, 195; visit of, to Alaska,
118–19
Wood, Lizzie, 71, 89, 92, 96–97, 99,
112–13, 131, 132
Wooden, Leonides, 8
Wright, Arthur, 34, 35–36, 41, 48, 57,
254n73, 295n78
Wright, Celia, 52

Yanert, Herman, 35, 207–8
Yanert, William, 35, 207–8
Yoonegge hʉt'aane Dena', 3, 21
Young, S. Hall, 12–13, 247n51